I0042496

THE GREATER INDIA EXPERIMENT

SOUTH ASIA IN MOTION

EDITOR
Thomas Blom Hansen

EDITORIAL BOARD
Sanjib Baruah
Anne Blackburn
Satish Deshpande
Faisal Devji
Christophe Jaffrelot
Naveeda Khan
Stacey Leigh Pigg
Mrinalini Sinha
Ravi Vasudevan

ARKOTONG LONGKUMER

THE GREATER INDIA EXPERIMENT

Hindutva and the Northeast

STANFORD UNIVERSITY PRESS

STANFORD, CALIFORNIA

Stanford University Press
Stanford, California

© 2021 by the Board of Trustees of the Leland Stanford Junior University. All rights reserved.

No part of this book may be reproduced or transmitted in any form or by any means, electronic or mechanical, including photocopying and recording, or in any information storage or retrieval system without the prior written permission of Stanford University Press.

Printed in the United States of America on acid-free, archival-quality paper

Library of Congress Cataloging-in-Publication Data

Names: Longkumer, Arkotong, author.
Title: The greater India experiment : Hindutva and the northeast / Arkotong Longkumer.
Other titles: South Asia in motion.
Description: Stanford, California : Stanford University Press, 2021. | Series: South Asia in motion | Includes bibliographical references and index.
Identifiers: LCCN 2020019950 (print) | LCCN 2020019951 (ebook) | ISBN 9781503613461 (cloth) | ISBN 9781503614222 (paperback) | ISBN 9781503614239 (epub)
Subjects: LCSH: Sangh Parivar. | Hindutva—India, Northeastern. | Hinduism and politics—India, Northeastern. | Nationalism—India, Northeastern. | Hinduism—India, Northeastern—Relations. | India, Northeastern—Politics and government.
Classification: LCC DS482.8 .L66 2021 (print) | LCC DS482.8 (ebook) | DDC 320.55—dc23
LC record available at https://lccn.loc.gov/2020019950
LC ebook record available at https://lccn.loc.gov/2020019951

Cover photo: Mural commissioned for the Tribal Heritage Museum, Rajiv Gandhi University, removed and relocated to the balcony of the Museum due to criticism that it resembled a Hindu deity. Arunachal Institute of Tribal Studies and the Tribal Heritage Museum.

Typeset by Westchester Publishing Services in 10.75/15 Adobe Caslon

CONTENTS

ACKNOWLEDGMENTS

Working as an anthropologist in Northeast India for over a decade has been an exciting and challenging journey of discovery. Returning regularly to the region brings to mind the many people I have encountered along the way and the depth of gratitude I owe them.

Never did I imagine myself working on the Hindu right, let alone their activities in the Northeast. Many thought I was barking up the wrong tree, others were mildly amused, while some wondered if the presence of the Hindu right (with its singular drive to make India "Hindu") signaled the gradual demise of the kind of independence and stubbornness that characterized a region with a rich history. This book will hopefully assuage some of the critics, generate debate, and raise questions about the future of the Hindu right and the Northeast.

My first encounter with the Hindu right was during the period of my PhD fieldwork (2004–05) in Haflong and Laisong in the Dima Hasao District of Assam. I was intrigued by their commitment to teach in village schools run by the Vishwa Hindu Parishad. Interacting with them made me realize their ambition to extend their activities all over the region. Over time, I could see their ambition gradually spreading and gaining momentum. This book is an attempt to capture their metamorphosis, which has made them into the most important force in contemporary India.

I was fortunate to receive a British Academy Mid-Career Fellowship (2017–18; grant no. MD170012), which truly kick-started parts of the research and the writing. I am grateful to the fellowship committee for recognizing the importance of this project and for allowing me the freedom to think and write when so much of our time in academia is curtailed by other tasks. I am also grateful to the Arctic University of Norway, Tromsø, for inviting me as a visiting fellow for three months in 2019. The warm and friendly environment allowed me the time to finish the manuscript.

I am especially grateful to Siv Ellen Kraft and Bjørn Ola Tafjord for making the visit possible. I am also grateful to the School of Divinity at the University of Edinburgh for their support, particularly colleagues in religious studies who had to shoulder much of the burden when I was away. My thanks to Naomi Appleton, Hannah Holtschneider, and Steven Sutcliffe. Shruti Chaudhry was appointed as teaching fellow, and my thanks to her for taking on the teaching responsibilities during my absence.

Thomas Blom Hansen first invited a book proposal for the Stanford University Press series South Asia in Motion. My thanks to him and the acquisitions editor Marcela Cristina Maxfield, the editorial assistant Sunna Juhn, and the production team for shepherding this process and for their professionalism. Where would academic publishing be without anonymous referees? My deepest gratitude to the reviewers for their time and engagement with the manuscript and for providing insightful suggestions that have hopefully made the book better. As I was finalizing the manuscript for publication, the Citizenship Amendment Bill (2016) became the Citizenship Amendment Act (2019). The analysis in the book is based on the bill and not the act (though they are the same in principle). A version of chapter 3 appeared in *Handbook of Indigenous Religion(s)* (Leiden, Netherlands: Brill, 2017) entitled "Is Hinduism the World's Largest Indigenous Religion?" and an earlier version of chapter 5 was published as "The Power of Persuasion: Hindutva, Christianity, and the Discourse of Religion and Culture in Northeast India," *Religion* 47, no. 2 (2017): 203–27. My thanks to the publishers for their permission in allowing me to reproduce revised versions for the book.

Without the participation of the many Sangh Parivar activists, this book would not have been possible. I thank them and the number of allies and sympathizers to their cause who opened doors for me when sometimes I had to knock at least a few times. I know you won't want me to divulge your names but am grateful to you and for showing me respect amid the tumultuous political climate. I disagreed with the Sangh Parivar activists when we discussed their work or when they sought opinions or questions about their work, and we debated (sometimes heatedly!) about their ideology.

Aheli Moitra joined me on the last leg of my research to understand the aftermath of the state elections in Assam, Meghalaya, Nagaland, and Tripura when the Bharatiya Janata Party (BJP) entered the electoral map in a large way. Her work as an independent journalist (and now a PhD student) and her understanding of the political landscape have been invaluable. The work and support she provided in interviews, transcription, and analysis have been second to none, and I want to express my indebtedness to her. Many people all over the region welcomed me, and I am particularly grateful to Zilpha Modi (in Itanagar), who provided a home in Arunachal and introduced me to her vast network of friends and colleagues, and for taking me all the way to her hometown of Pashigat. Many thanks to Wanglit Mongchan in whose car we listened to Hindi music (surprised that I hadn't heard of any of them) all the way to Pashigat; to Jumyir Basar, who invited me to give a talk at Rajiv Gandhi University; and to Lisa Lomdak and Tarun Mene for answering many questions about Hindutva politics. Their work in the Arunachal Institute of Tribal Studies is a source of inspiration. In Guwahati, Xonzoi Barbora provided intellectual curiosity and company over plenty a dram, and my thanks go to R. K. Debbarma, who introduced me to his friends and networks in Agartala (Tripura). In Shillong, Margaret Lyngdoh went out of her way to help, and I must thank Tarun Bhartiya and the Raiot collective for challenging the consensus. In Agartala, Upen Debbarma's knowledge of indigenous politics and his network as a student activist showed me the intricacies of Tripura politics that would have been otherwise impossible to discern. He and his family organized lunch with other Indigenous People's Front of Tripura (IPFT) activists at his home, and I was humbled by their involvement in creating a better future for their movement. B. K. Hrangkhawl hosted me, and I remain indebted to him for sharing his time and his long-term commitment to the cause of indigenous people's issues in Tripura. In Nagaland, I am thankful to the Sumi Alakishi Kighinimi for welcoming me with such open arms and for sharing the prophecy files with me. Your vision of what is possible has pushed me to think seriously about indigenous futures. My gratitude too to V. K. Nuh, Zelhou Keyho, Aküm Longchari, Monalisa Chankija,

Rosemary Dzuvichu, and Wati Aier for entertaining my difficult questions and for always providing encouragement.

Many people from all over the world read drafts of chapters, and for their time, encouragement, and criticism I am immensely grateful; I am certain that their comments have greatly improved the book. My thanks to Dolly Kikon, Xonzoi Barbora, R. K. Debbarma, Beppe Karlsson, Duncan McDuie-Ra, Shruti Chaudhry, Greg Johnson, Bjørn Ola Tafjord, Siv Ellen Kraft, Jeanne Openshaw, Greg Alles, Elspeth Graham, and Jim Cox. Early conversations with Steven Sutcliffe helped me see the problems with indigeneity (chapter 3), and Aya Ikegame and Gwilym Beckerlegge provided comments on parts of chapter 5. I have given presentations on parts of chapters in different locations, and I thank the audiences for asking provoking questions in Guwahati, Itanagar, Lancaster, Edinburgh, Göttingen, Tromsø, Bern, and Nottingham. Over the past five years, I have been involved in a large international project funded by the Norwegian Research Council on indigenous religions, and I am grateful to my comrades-in-arms for supporting this work. My thanks to my colleagues at the Kohima Institute for their support and in particular Michael Heneise. Jacob Copeman has been the most supportive friend and fellow South Asianist. He has read the entire manuscript and offered insightful comments always with an eye toward the bigger picture. The sharpness and careful way in which he explored my material have been invaluable.

My family in Nagaland, Delhi, Edinburgh, Wormit, and London have been the most ardent supporters of my work. Without their care and love, this book would not have been possible. My father passed away before he could see the book, but his curiosity and his own interest in my work since my PhD have been a constant presence in my writing. Ayimna and Razelé have been the most loving, curious, funny, inventive, and patient children through this writing process. I owe them my love and lots and lots of playtime! Lindsay has been the rock upon which this book has been built. She has read every word (many times over). Her critical voice and endless conversations have been a constant source of encouragement, especially when the tumult of life found ways to disrupt my sanity. She always reminded me about the important things and kept me anchored. I dedicate this book to her, as ever.

THE GREATER INDIA EXPERIMENT

CHAPTER 1

ARBOREAL NATION

The demography of Assam is changing. You have Christian missionaries active all over Assam (in Majuli for example) and in Arunachal Pradesh, and Bangladeshi Muslim illegal immigrants are threatening those who are indigenous to the Northeast. We have to stop this menace!

JAGDISH'S VOICE WAS RISING as we discussed his work for the Rashtriya Swayamsevak Sangh (RSS) a right-wing Hindu volunteer organization, in a café in Guwahati, the capital of Assam. Out of the corner of my eye, I could see two young Assamese men getting agitated. Suddenly, they moved toward Jagdish, hurling abuse and threatening to beat him up. Angry and inebriated, the two men turned to me and said: "What is an educated man like you doing with this sister fucker [*behn chod*]?" "Come out," they shouted at Jagdish, "or we will drag you out." One of them continued addressing Jagdish. "It is because of people like you, who have stirred up communal hatred, that the peaceful atmosphere here has been disturbed. We should call the police and have you arrested for inciting violence." Jagdish protested and claimed his innocence: "What's wrong with having a conversation about current issues?" I joined in too and argued for peace and calm, not wanting to see violence erupt. I felt a responsibility toward Jagdish, to keep him safe. Luckily, a friend was in the café a few tables away and recognized me amid this commotion. He came over and calmed the situation down.

Jagdish was visibly shaken but insisted on resuming our conversation. The tense atmosphere continued unabated through prying eyes and hushed voices from the tables around us, making me feel uneasy. It was now out in the open that he was an RSS man and unwelcome, and me a willing interlocutor in entertaining his views without objecting. I could sense that the work of the RSS was emotional terrain in many parts of Guwahati, and Jagdish's combative manner of talking only heightened the uneasiness.

Jagdish, for his part, reassured me that he was fine and that these kinds of occurrences were not unusual for him. He told me he had experienced many slaps and "boxings," a colloquial way of expressing physical assault, and that to work as an RSS man in a largely Christian Indian state such as Nagaland (where he was usually based) was like being a cow tied to a butcher's post. He provided evidence by mentioning that some RSS workers had been kidnapped and killed, particularly in Tripura, in "cold blood" by militants associated with the "Baptist church," while the Communist state government remained silent. Although I was unsure of Jagdish's exact story at that time, I learned later of the killing of four RSS workers in Tripura in 1999, with the National Liberation Front of Tripura as the prime suspect.[1]

I start with this episode to provide a backdrop to the kind of interactions and activities I have been engaged in for the past five years, during which I conducted the research for this book. While the RSS and the larger Sangh Parivar (a family of organizations comprising the Hindu right; henceforth Sangh) are viewed as objectionable by many, this makes it all the more important that their lived realities are dispassionately understood. Rather than simply dismissing them or arguing against them, I take both what they have to say and their modes of operation seriously. Based on long-term ethnographic and archival research, I examine the nuances of Hindutva knowledge production across the region, the relational work, the adjustments, the compromises, in some cases the remarkable creativity and generation of new possibilities: *Hindutva becoming*. Some of the data may surprise, disrupting what we think we know about Hindutva. Sangh activists are often known for their violence, but in this region, they become the target of violence and virulent rhetoric. Rather than focusing simply on their programmatic ideological stance, we must unearth the lives of individuals, their relationships, and their stories.

A parallel can be found in Hilary Pilkington's (2016) sensitive study of the English Defence League, where she argues that there is much hesitancy in dealing seriously with right-wing populist movements, establishing an academic *cordon sanitaire*. She instead argues that recoiling in our academic shells and refusing to acknowledge the political realities "out there" in the world, however uncomfortable, have political implications too. Such a view comes with real political costs, Pilkington reminds us. By ridiculing, ignoring, and undermining these formative political voices, we are in effect exercising our own (biased) political motivations, ignoring the fact that the commitment to reclaiming politics spans different social, economic, and religious spectrums; challenges ethnic and racial prejudices; and illuminates majoritarian and marginalized positions. Warning us not to shun those who have different, and at times challenging, perspectives, Susan Harding (1991, 374) argues that to call someone a "repugnant cultural other" is to assume a "homogenous" subject that can be explained in opposition to those who are "modern." However, she suggests that both "fundamentalist" and the "modern" subjects are produced by "modern discursive practices" that have certain "categories, assumptions, and trajectories implicit in [their] narrative representations" (375). Like Harding, who struggles with how to represent Christian fundamentalists in the American imaginary, I try here to comprehend the different facets of the Sangh, even as I grapple with my own inclination not to ally with them, while to a certain degree collaborating with them "in disrupting modern representations of them" (375).

One way to negotiate the impasse of problematic categories—fundamentalist/populist/militant/modern/liberal—is to examine how the political is entangled in human relations. The political theorist Chantal Mouffe (1993) argues for an approach that focuses on the relational aspect of identity. She points out that human society is made up of relations—how "we" see ourselves in relation to "them." In this sense, both we and they are limited by establishing the boundaries of these identities. Placing restrictions of this sort, Mouffe suggests, often leads to difference. The challenge arises when the Other starts infringing on "our" identity and negates it (and vice versa). Mouffe argues:

> From that moment onwards any type of we/them relation, be it religious, ethnic, national, economic or other, becomes the site of a political antago-nism. . . . As a consequence, the political cannot be restricted to a certain type of institution, or envisaged as constituting a specific sphere or level of society. It must be conceived as a dimension that is inherent to every human soci-ety and that determines our very ontological condition. Such a view of the political is profoundly at odds with liberal thought, which is precisely the reason for the bewilderment of this thought when confronted with the phe-nomenon of hostility in its multiple forms. This is particularly evident in its incomprehension of political movements, which are seen as the expression of the so-called "masses". Since they cannot be apprehended in individualistic terms, these movements are usually relegated to the pathological or deemed to be the expression of irrational forces. (1993, 2–3)

If we are to take Pilkington, Harding, and Mouffe's guidance seriously in how we understand the commitment to the political in whatever form, we must not only recognize differences in opinion but be open to engage critically with those that threaten to negate identities for some perceived greater good. One could easily view the Sangh as the hegemon with its carefully choreographed political blueprint in place to strike at the heart of every region. But at the same time, if we are to recognize how politics function at the level of relations, we must make some distinction, however uncomfortable and difficult, between the individual and the institution, and between precedence and context. Although the reputation of the Sangh and their involvement in violence, hatred, and vituperative politics in many parts of India point—in broad strokes—toward their "militancy" or "fascism," in the Northeast their activities are largely sanguine, mallea-ble, idealistic, and under the radar. They may not appear to be in your face, abrasive, or combative, but at the same time, they find unequal spaces to exploit and to ally with like-minded persons, organizations, institu-tions, and ideas to pursue their long-term strategy of winning over hearts and minds. This book therefore is not simply about institutions and their ideas and practices; it is a book about people, people who make up the Sangh and people who are small in number in a place where they execute decisions, a place that, to a large extent, is hostile to their ideas.

ARBOREAL NATION

Over the five years of this research, I have spoken to and interacted with numerous Sangh activists ranging from those involved in the Rashtriya Swayamsevak Sangh (RSS), Janajati Vikas Samiti (JVS; also known as the Kalyan Ashram and Akhil Bharatiya Vanvasi Kalyan Ashram [tribal welfare association]), the Vishwa Hindu Parishad (VHP; World Hindu Council), Vidya Bharati (VB; educational network), Sewa Bharati (SB; service network), the Vivekananda Kendra Vidyalaya (VKV; schools and research), Akhil Bharatiya Vidyarthi Parishad (ABVP; all-India student organization), and the Bharatiya Janata Party (BJP; political party). Central to their idea of nationalism is that of Hindutva and establishing a Hindu nation (Hindu Rashtra).

The idea of Hindutva comes largely from V. D. Savarkar's 1923 book *Hindutva: Who Is Hindu?* (Since its original publication there have been five editions.) It articulates a monumental vision of articulating the essence of Hindu nationalism. It is a book that has inspired the work of the RSS and affiliates (known as *parivar*, or family) as it has entered into new and uncharted territories, culminating in the BJP's sweeping electoral victory in 2014. It is also a challenging book, an interpretation of which has propagated violence and hatred against religious minorities— particularly Muslims and Christians—in the name of Hindutva, which continues unabated to make India a majoritarian Hindu state (Chatterji, Hansen, and Jaffrelot 2019; Jaffrelot 2017). So what is Hindutva? How are we to understand an ideology that has polarized the subcontinent in unprecedented ways?

On the title page of Savarkar's book it says, "A Hindu means a person who regards this land of BHARATVARSHA, from the Indus to the Seas as his Father-Land as well as his Holy-Land that is the cradle land of his religion" (1969). This way of being Hindu is Hindutva, or Hinduness. In the preface to the second edition of the book, the publisher explains that Savarkar wanted to expand the idea of Hindu and Hinduism beyond its religious sphere to that of a "totality of the cultural, historical, and above all the national aspects along with the religious ones, which mark out the Hindu People as a whole" (1969, iv). Thus, the concepts of Hindutva, Hinduness, and Hindudom were invented to capture this totality. Savarkar says Hindu is comprised of nation (*rashtra*), race (*jati*), and civilization (*sanskriti*) (Savarkar 1969, 101). While this may appear to be a wholly secular and cultural enterprise (after all Savarkar was an atheist—a point that is made persistently by Sangh workers), the problem arises when Savarkar introduces the idea of *pitrubhoomi* (holy land). The religious element therefore cannot be ignored in this conception of Hindutva. According to the historian Tanika Sarkar, Hindutva paradoxically conjoins "nation with faith, and, in the same move, makes the land of India the property, in a literal sense, of Hindus alone" (2012, 279). While these criteria enable the inclusion of the Hindus, Sikhs, Jains, and Buddhists, other "non-Hindu" religions like Christianity, Islam, Judaism, and Zoroastrianism can only meet the first two because India is not their "holy land" (Varshney 1993, 231).

The rise of Hindu nationalism and the studies that have accompanied it have grown exponentially in the last few decades (Basu et al. 1993; Bénéï 2008; Doniger and Nussbaum 2015; Froerer 2007; Ghassem-Fachandi 2012; Gopal 1991; Hansen 1999; Hasan 1994; Jaffrelot 1998; Ludden 1996; McKean 1996b; Rajagopal 2001; Sarkar and Butalia 1995; van der Veer 1994). While the concept of Hindutva has become common parlance in most of these studies and used in everyday conversations, we must remember that many of these ideas and concepts have a longer historical development that goes back to the nineteenth-century reform movements in India during colonial times (Gould 2004; Hansen 1999; S. Sarkar 1996; Zavos 2000). William Gould's work on late colonial India makes precisely this point, showing that Hindu nationalism and its symbolisms also pervaded the political language among the Indian National Congress, who wavered between the majoritarian language of being Hindu and their commitment to secular nationalism. They often ended up playing the "communal" (or religious) game regardless of party ideology (Gould 2004, 1–34). This point demonstrates that we must acknowledge the often diffuse and heterodox nature of Hindutva as it has developed over the decades. Christophe Jaffrelot has argued that one must be attuned to their many forms, particularly the affective "division of labour" (1996, 123) that comprise the many organizations of the Sangh, to its move beyond the strong hold of the "Maharashtrian crucible" (2007, 14) into, say, the Northeast of India and even into diaspora (E. Anderson 2015; Anderson and Longkumer 2019; Kanungo 2011, 2012; Longkumer 2015b; Therwath 2012; Zavos 2008). Indeed, this book is about how they have entered new spaces that are beyond their traditional stronghold, and particularly into the "Mongolian fringe" (Baruah 2013), where the ideology and discourse of Hindutva is largely unfamiliar.

One of the key strands of Hindutva that has permeated the thinking of many Sangh activists in the Northeast derives from M. S. Golwalkar, or Guruji (1877–1958), the second RSS *sarsanghchalak* (supreme leader). Guruji's more philosophical and service-oriented approach toward changing the political, social, and cultural aspect of society over the long term surfaces in many of my conversations with Sangh activists. Golwalkar was keen to reorder the country according to the basic conviction of Hindu Rashtra. He says, "Some may feel that all people are not likely to agree to our concept of Hindu Rashtra. But it is immaterial whether some people accept or reject the truth we propound. Our ideas should be clear and our faith in them unswerving. Then alone will the people be persuaded to accept the truth. I am confident that, ultimately, people will be convinced" (Golwalkar 2000, 358). Convincing the people of the region of these national ideals is at the heart of the Sangh project. Their numerous activities all over the region attest to these principles of patient zeal, in the hope that one day the region will come to realize their place within the great Hindu Rashtra.

Speaking about Hindutva at length with me, a Janajati Vikas Samiti (JVS) worker, Anand, was puzzled about the negativity surrounding Hindutva's association with the Sangh. He had read the early ideologues like Hedgewar, Savarkar, and Golwalkar, coming to the conclusion that Hindutva is a "wonderful concept." They do not envisage a Hindu state based on religion; Anand in fact categorically stated that Savarkar's Hindutva was never about that. (It also demonstrates the way various Sangh workers read these works and apply them.) Strip away all these categories and assumptions, and what you see is that Hindutva is about "relations," he told me. It is how we relate to one another, to animals, nature, deities, and the universe. The image and metaphor used to capture this is nature and, more specifically, trees.

For the Sangh, the tree symbolizes life, strength, stability, and vitality (see Rival 1998). Trees are also the living links between the past and the future, with roots associated with land, culture, identity, and people. In asking the question "Why are trees important in Indian society?" David Haberman (2013, 188) recounts that the answer he regularly received was that Indians' ancestors venerated trees. He suggests further that, in part because of the link with ancestry, an intimate connection develops between the tree and the person caring for it. Thus the person becomes profoundly attached to the tree, feels greater emotional affection, and becomes committed to honoring the tree (2013, 188). This arboreal description finds a reflection in Anand's conception of Hindutva as relations (see Chapter 2).

Golwalkar (2000) too uses arborescent imagery to explain national identity in his *Bunch of Thoughts*, ideas that are recycled in images and words in the Northeast. He uses the tree as a spatial metaphor to argue for a single way of life (Hindu) despite India's evident heterogeneity (language, customs, habits, etc.). These variations, he says, are of the same tree, the "same sap running through and nourishing all those parts. They are no more a source of dissension and disruption than a leaf or a flower is in the case of a tree. This kind of natural evolution has been a unique feature of our social life" (2000, 92). He calls on the national workers to nourish and strengthen the roots, without which the fruit will be sour and dry, so that "we can stand free and erect amidst all tempests in the world" (176). Question those "separatists" (in the Northeast), he says, who argue that tribals are animists and not Hindus. Isn't worshipping trees, stones, and snakes the common principle that links both the tribal and the Hindu? In fact, anima, or animus, is the principle of all life that is immanent in creation. "Do not the Hindus all over the country worship the tree? Tulasi, Bilva, Ashwattha are all sacred to the Hindu" (274). This arboreal metaphor of the tree is an apt blueprint for the nation. Take away the place-names, the artificial state boundaries, the towns and cities, and

Figure 1.1. Local publications emphasizing the idea of indigenous roots. Courtesy of the author.

all you have is a nation of trees and roots: it plots a certain order, fixes a point—one nation, one people, and one culture.

GREATER INDIA EXPERIMENT

The aim of this book is to analyze the activities of the Sangh and their impact in the sensitive region of the Northeast of India. This book is first of all about what I call *Hindutva becoming*, an experiment of how the Sangh ideology of Hindi, Hindu, and Hindustan allows us to think

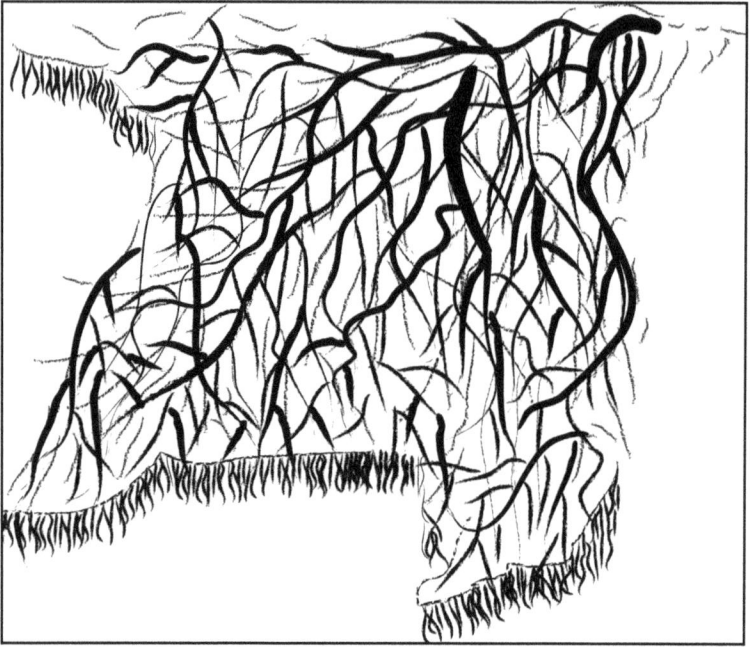

Figure 1.2. Adapted from Joshi (2000), who uses this image as both Bharat and Ashwattha (the peepul tree). Made by the author.

productively about their encounters and activities in the "Mongolian fringe." Connected closely with Hindutva becoming is the Greater India experiment. This book reflects—explicitly and implicitly—on ideas of Greater India through various modalities. Sangh activists and ideologues evoke the idea of Bharatvarsh, an idea found in the Sanskrit epic the Mahabharata covering an area from the "Indus to the seas" and below the Himalayas (Golwalkar 2000; Savarkar 1969, 31–32). The natural features (mountains and rivers), places of pilgrimage, and ritual spaces act as material evidence, grounded in the "earth" (*bhumi*), that connects the Northeast to Bharatvarsh, which is explored in detail in Chapters 2 and 3 as place-making and about land and belonging. Here, the "Sanskrit cosmopolis" (Pollock 1998) and places of ritual precede administrative maps.

The Sangh also use the irredentist notion of Akhand Bharat (undivided India) drawing on the similar idea of Bharatvarsh, but with more precision to include Afghanistan, Pakistan, India, Bangladesh, Sri Lanka,

Map 1.1. Map of India and the Northeast (map not to scale). Made by the author.

Nepal, Bhutan, Tibet, Myanmar, and in some cases Cambodia, Thailand, and Indonesia.[2] To some extent, Akhand Bharat is an idea that the RSS inherited from Savarkar's ruminations, but it was also asserted by Golwalkar (2000), based on religious, cultural, and now visual evocations:

> Our epics and our puranas also present us with the same expansive image of our motherland. Afghanistan was our ancient Upaganasthan. Shalya of the Mahabharata came from there. . . . Even Iran was originally Aryan. Its previous king Reza Shah Pehlavi was guided more by Aryan values than by Islam. Zend Avesta, the holy scripture of Parsis, is mostly Atharva Veda. Coming to the east, Burma is our ancient Brahmadesha. The Mahabharata refers to Iraavat, the modern Irrawady valley, as being involved in that great war. It also refers to Assam as Pragjyotisha since the sun first rises there. In the South, Lanka has had the closest links and was never considered as anything different from the mainland.
>
> It was this picture of our motherland with the Himalayas dipping its arms in the two seas, at Aryan (Iran) in the West and at Sringapur (Singapore) in the East, with Sri Lanka (Ceylon) as a lotus petal offered at her sacred feet by the Southern Ocean, that was constantly kept radiant in people's mind for so many thousands of years. (2000, 83)

Akhand Bharat and notions of Greater India manifest too in electoral politics (Chapter 7), particularly as the Sangh promulgate the Citizenship Amendment Act with its reverberations both in terms of ethnic and religious effects. Therefore, I use the term *Greater India* in a number of ways. As a cultural idea, it articulates the larger cosmopolis of Indic civilization spreading all across Central, South, and Southeast Asia and the Himalayan regions. Questioning widespread assumptions and assertions regarding the Northeast's separation from this cosmopolis, Sangh ideologues and activists ask how can it be alienated and isolated when the center of influence emanates from there? As a territorial idea, I show the ambiguity generated by Greater India. Many in the Northeast question their "Indian" identity, some even taking up arms to fight for independence from the Indian state. Therefore, Greater India is both a rhetorical device and geocultural method of territorial incorporation. As a visual idea, I want to emphasize the way maps of Greater India allow viewers

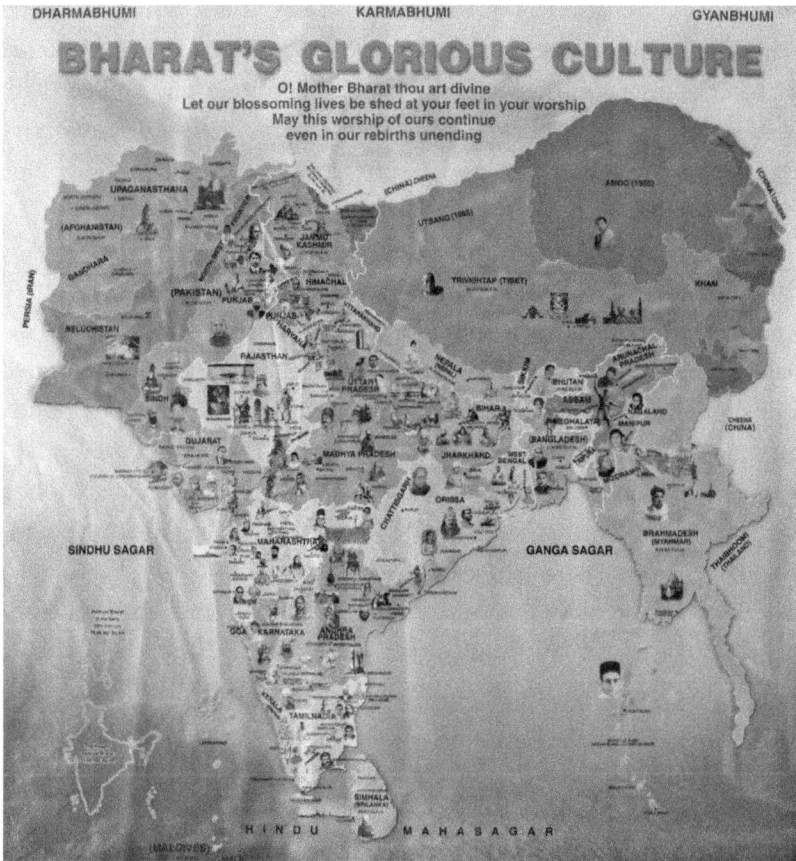

Figure 1.3. Map of Glorious Bharat (Greater India), a poster in an RSS hostel in Arunachal Pradesh. Courtesy of the author.

to imagine the grandeur of what once was, while always inviting them to realize that they are part of a larger geosphere of influence—it is not simply about nation building but about expressing and imagining the fundamental aspects of Hindutva as universal. As a concept of potentiality and becoming, Greater India centers on the greatness of Indian civilization, a consideration made too by Susan Bayly (2004) when she recognizes the far-reaching impact of "imaginings" that are both translocal and supranational. Sangh members, as foot soldiers of the idea of Hindutva, carry forth its message and forge new paths, with transnational designs in mind. Hindutva in the Northeast is a multipronged process of worlding.

Greater India also confounds in its excesses. It is a revival of Hindu civilization expressed in Hindutva, a cultural greatness that is projected as universal in scope. In this process, it also confronts and collides with other national projects in the Northeast that are similarly about expansive territorial futures—for instance, Greater Nagaland, Greater Mizoram, and independent Assam.

Based on movement, questions, and involutions, this book is thus about a Hindutva experiment. Highlighting the difficulty of conducting experiments amid the becomings that are so characteristic of their work, Deleuze and Guattari remind us that "although there is no preformed logical order to becomings and multiplicities, there are *criteria*, and the important thing is that they not be used after the fact, that they be applied in the course of events, that they be sufficient to guide us through the dangers" (2000, 293; italics in original). This book is a forensic examination of a Hindutva laboratory that is attempting to promote a singular identity amid the blustering and fractal nature of belonging in this vast region known as the Northeast of India, comprising Arunachal Pradesh, Assam, Nagaland, Manipur, Meghalaya, Mizoram, and Tripura.[3] In this process, they seek to redefine what it means to be "Indian" (or Bharatiya) by deconstructing, remaking, and reassembling the very nature of Hindutva. Inasmuch as Hindutva in these frontier spaces is strategically forged, it also reveals the nature of Hindutva as dynamic, malleable, and a creative force of becoming as it confronts new spaces. The quotidian lives of individuals as they commit themselves to serving the nation and their encounters in the face of recalcitrance are where the real process of becoming unfolds.

Thirdly, this book is about the Northeast of India as much as it is about Hindutva. The Northeast is engulfed in numerous voices and variations of ethnic, national, religious, and cultural activities that a book like this cannot fully capture. What this book can do is try to make sense of this rich but scarred and fractured landscape that has existed as an anomaly within the Indian state, as it has historically challenged the idea of India, in all its magnitude and incongruity. I look at how this Indic movement, or this gaze, this Hindutva gaze—with its ideology, its *criteria*, firmly rooted in Hindi, Hindu, and Hindustan—confronts the Mongolian fringe with its own orbit of historical, cultural, and political constellations. This study is centered around how the complex algorithms of "homeland" politics engineered by ethnopolitical movements, with their own culture of nationalism, negotiate with Hindutva forces. It illuminates the salience and tenacity of indigenous nationalisms, and how they confront long-standing questions of land, blood, and belonging. If the cultural politics of belonging has been the cradle upon which the region has found a safe enclosure, the ideology of Hindutva asks challenging questions about how this land is constituted using the arboreal image of roots that share the same ground.

Fourthly, grounded in anthropology, this book is an ethnography of passion and politics, in the sense that I have observed the intensity of human actions in the first person, face-to-face. My task here in presenting the voices of individuals involved in the Sangh is to convey a sense of "meaningful striving" (Mahmood 1996, 21), enabling their words to animate their purpose. Cynthia Keppley Mahmood, in working with Sikh militants, argues that her ethnography is an effort "to bring to the reader a sense of the immediacy of the Sikh militant world. It is less distant and more accessible than most people think" (1996, 21). Throughout the book, I have similarly allowed different voices to resonate through their words to evoke a sense of immediacy, emotion, and passion as they are caught up in the events of their own, and sometimes not of their own, making. Most of my conversations and interviews were with male Sangh workers. Other people that I interacted with were allies sympathetic to their cause, while some were critics opposed to this saffron wave. Due to the nature of the Sangh and its strong male presence in the Northeast, it is their view that dominates.

The spaces where these interactions happened were varied; I was invited to some events, but mostly our conversations took place in offices and homes. Many of their activities were not openly advertised nor their presence obviously visible in the public sphere. This secrecy is because Hindutva activities are treated with suspicion. For example, despite receiving initial invitations to visit RSS *shakhas* (lit. branches, but regular RSS group meetings) in Dimapur (Nagaland), Guwahati (Assam), and Shillong (Meghalaya), these meetings never materialized, perhaps because local Sangh members anticipated the uneasiness of my presence in their intimate affairs, where the disclosure of allies and sympathizers might lead to awkward conversations, possible reproach, and unwitting consequences.

Finally, the book contributes to wider debates on Hindutva and the Sangh. While much of the contemporary scholarship on Hindutva has focused on pogroms and their involvement in excluding Muslims and minorities, Hindutva violence is quieter in the Northeast. In fact, I suggest that the marked persecution of proponents of Hindutva in the region requires its ideologies to take a more unconventional shape when compared to their counterparts in other parts of India. This means that they engage primarily in social service (*seva*) and countering the hegemony of the "Christian other" in the sphere of ideas and polemics, and in allying with non-Christian movements to pursue their agenda of Hindutva through cultural appropriation and assimilation with challenging consequences for intercommunity relations in the region. Hindutva actions may foment violence, but, importantly, they do so indirectly.

There are currently no substantive works on Sangh activities and the ideology of Hindutva in Northeast India. Only limited studies have been done focusing on Arunachal Pradesh (Kanungo 2012, 2011) and Assam and Nagaland (Bhattarcharjee 2016; Longkumer 2010, 2015b). If Hindutva is one of the most important facets of modern Indian history, comprehending its transformation in the Northeast of India, a region that has been largely ignored, has vital implications for our understanding of not only the work of the Hindu right but also the very concept of India, and indeed Greater India. This book will draw on and contribute to the vast literature on the Sangh and their philosophy, while providing comparative theoretical value from a region where their activities have remained largely unexplored.

ACCESS: ANIMATING POLITICS

I met two Vishwa Hindu Parishad (VHP) schoolteachers in 2004 on a cold February morning in Hejaichak, a Zeme Naga village in the Dima Hasao District, where the VHP have established a school and a hostel. One of the teachers, from Orissa, spoke to me at length about his work. "The villagers eat everything—from insects, to jungle rats—and therefore it is the job of the VHP to bring civilization to them," he said. His task, like the task of many other Sangh workers, is to uplift the tribals of the region, because the *vanvasi* (jungle dweller, often used for tribal) are vulnerable, particularly against Christian conversions. I left the meeting with more questions than answers, unsettled by his paternalism and this new evidence of a "civilizing mission."

In the summer of 2014, I visited the village again to meet some old friends, and we were sitting on the VHP school office veranda taking shelter from the monsoon rain. Outside six young boys between the ages of six and sixteen were playing football. One of the local caretakers of the school and a young head teacher in his early twenties (a Zeme Naga from Manipur) talked about their work with the VHP and the RSS. The head teacher went inside his office, took out the RSS saffron flag (Bhagwa Dhwaj), and showed it to us. He called the boys and announced that it was time for a shakha. I wondered aloud whether the rain would allow them to do the shakha, and the teacher replied that it must go on whatever the conditions.

In order of height, the youngest stood in the front with his arm ninety degrees across his chest saluting the flag. Dirty from the football, with disheveled clothes, ruffled hair, and rain falling down his face, I could see his blank expression as he looked toward the flag. Ashish, a RSS/VHP worker in Guwahati, explained what the saffron flag, Bhajwai Dhwaj, meant for

Figure 1.4. Shakha, Hejaichak Village, Assam. Photo taken by the author.

Figure 1.5. RSS procession, Haflong, Assam. Photo taken by the author.

them: "Our guru is that flag, not any person. A person may get spoiled, like through nepotism. But our guru is the flag. The saffron flag is called *bhagwa*. If you see the chariots of Mahabharata, they have this same flag on them. The color stands for sacrifice, power. It is the color of fire."

I was disconcerted upon leaving the shakha and seeing the young boys run for shelter, as if playtime was over. Are they aware of the history of these Hindu organizations? Many people that I interacted with in the village felt that these schools and organizations are a good thing because they provide service, allowing their children to progress through life, something otherwise difficult to come by. As we drove toward the capital of Dima Hasao, Haflong, we came across an RSS procession. Most participants were "tribal children," some of whom I had met in the Kalyan Ashram hostel a few days earlier in Haflong. We stopped to witness the procession, led by senior *pracharaks* (full time RSS workers). My friends waved and smiled at some of the young boys who were acquaintances from their villages. I wondered if these children were ideologically motivated to serve the nation, like so many of the RSS workers. Or was it simply a part of their school routine? In my time in Dima Hasao over the previous decade, these public processions had been unheard of. To see it twice in the span of two days indicates the impact of the Sangh writ large in the area.[4]

CROSS-STITCH, 3G, ANIME

When I visited many of these Vishwa Hindu Parishad / Vidya Bharati / Janjati Vikas Samiti (VHP/VB/JVS) schools all over the Northeast, providing sanctuary to tribal children, I was unprepared for the scale of their involvement, and I often wondered at what price. Looking at the visual material in these schools—ranging from quotes from eminent figures, maps, painted images of deities to pictures of the goddess Lakshmi (goddess of wealth), Bharat Mata (Mother India), or even a cross-stitch decoration of the Sanskrit syllable *Om*—reminded me of a quote in one of the classrooms of the Zeliangrong Heraka School in Tening, Nagaland, run with the help of Janjati Vikas Samiti. The quote by Ramakrishna reads: "Knowledge leads to unity; ignorance to diversity." In this quote, these Sanskritized forms of messages make a presence and form *mental maps* in an attempt to organize, to forge a certain route through which knowledge is gained, and to simplify diverse and rich narratives to a story of oneness, a gradual but seemingly inevitable process of creating a totalizing force.

These ideas of oneness also manifest in practical matters like food, musical instruments, and connectivity. I met an older woman who had come from Mumbai as part of My Home Is India, a program run by Akhil Bharatiya Vidyarthi Parishad (ABVP). She volunteered to come to Tening for six months and participate in teaching and helping the young girls in the Heraka school hostel. Perhaps she wanted to talk to someone outside of the community, so she confided in me about her problems of living in isolation with no internet or 3G phone connections. She confessed that being a vegetarian was challenging in Tening: the local community accommodated her diet restrictions, but the choice of food was limited. She also said that she was exhausted because she could not get the girls to learn the sitar, a musical instrument popular in many parts of India but not in Nagaland. I suggested the guitar as a more appropriate choice among the Naga youth. But she insisted that the sitar has a history as a classical Indian instrument, so surely, she exclaimed, the students should be interested due to its established pedigree. She also felt isolated, in part, because she could not make friends with the local women; she was glad that the Indian army officers' wives were there for company. I wondered about the My Home Is India project's success—whose goal is to bring emotional integration among people of different regions, and in particular to "bridge the gap between the people of north east India and the rest of India."[5] Of course, it is unfair to judge the successes of My Home Is India through anecdotal evidence, but it does highlight some of the issues when idealism and day-to-day practicalities collide.

Sangh workers are, however, cognizant of popular cultural trends and are willing to accommodate practices (even foreign ones) that might seem unconventional, according to their own standards. I was particularly struck by a major event in Vivekananda Kendra Vidyalaya (VKV) in Nirjuli, Arunachal Pradesh. It was the birth centenary celebration of Eknath Ranade, an RSS worker who established the Vivekananda Kendra in Kanyakumari and the VKV. My main guide, Sanjeev, was the organizing secretary of the VKV in Arunachal and an RSS pracharak. Unbe-

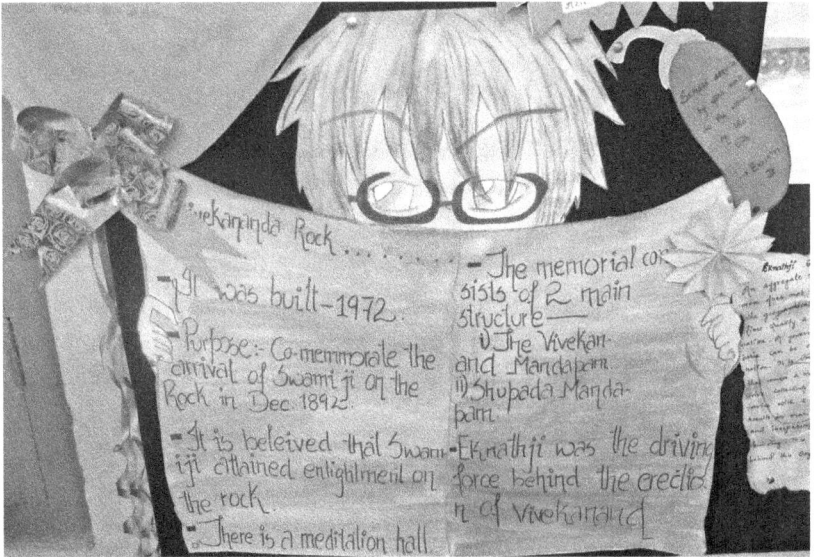

Figure 1.6. Anime character displaying the story of Eknath Ranade, Vivekananda Kendra Vidyalaya, Nirjuli, Arunachal Pradesh. Photo taken by the author.

knownst to me, I was invited as one of the chief guests for the event on 19 November 2014. I was shown the posters that the children had made, about Eknath's life, the beginnings of the Vivekananda Kendra, and the Rock Memorial he helped build in Kanyakumari. I was intrigued by the stories of Eknath Ranade told through Japanese anime characters (popular in the region), written mostly in English, and in attractive and colorful designs.

Anime had made Ranade more endearing—now an icon of youth culture—with his RSS background and the militant organization that he subscribed to fading into the background. I wondered about the function of these schools, harboring children from largely poor families, providing free education, but so much more besides—not least forms of Hindutva ideology. A disgruntled university teacher, and a former pupil in Itanagar, revealed what they do in these schools.

> I was in VKV from LKG to class 12 [the whole of primary and secondary school]. Classes are regular; teachings are up to date, and they focus on serving the nation et cetera. All that is OK. But morning [to] evening, they keep chanting Ram-Sita-Hanuman songs. They are all Hindu activities. They teach you Ramayana and Mahabharata. In the cities they give holidays for Christmas, but in the interior they don't give holidays for Christmas. They maintain the Unity in Diversity theory in general on the outside. But they pressure children in their schools and ask, "Why are you Christian? Why have you left your ancestral religions?" I was traumatized as a child—Om chanting during food, and Om, Om all day long.

The way these schools work in tribal areas and their influence over tribal minds are disconcerting for many. In Chapter 3, I discuss the tensions inherent in the way Hindutva ideas are disseminated by arguing for similarity between Hinduism and ancestral religions.

ETHNOGRAPHY: PASSION AND POLITICS
Central to the book is its ethnography, which brings to the fore intense human actions, conversations, and engagement. How do lives invested with such vigor for the nation meet with those that defy or are unconcerned for it? Suspending the association in my mind between Sangh activism's myriad acts of violence, my aim was to establish a courteous

and polite dialogue across chairs and tables. This willingness to listen to their stories opened up numerous doors.

I was viewed favorably because I was an academic and not a journalist. Journalists for them exaggerate events for headlines through a fleeting "helicopter visit." Most of their stories focus on the Sangh's successes and the way they managed to change the electoral landscape of a region strongly opposed to them only a few years ago; but others, they say, are extremely negative and sensational accounts of how the Sangh are involved in "child trafficking" or how they have been involved in instigating violence.[6] I am specific about these cases because these are examples the Sangh use to illustrate the nature of the news coverage that, for them, is factually incorrect. In fact, an important RSS worker in Arunachal, Jommi, an emerging leader of the state BJP, told me about his apprehension of journalists. He said that he himself was unsure about me. He Googled my profile, skimmed through my publications, and then attended a talk I gave (on religion and politics in Northeast India) at the Rajiv Gandhi University (RGU) in Itanagar. He wanted to "investigate" me properly before he spoke to me. Although he was critical about my lecture, he nevertheless acknowledged that I was making "academic" points.

> We have always said that we are not a religious institution; nor are we running a dietician company. Anybody can come and attend *shakha* and be a part of it. If you think we are talking about any other subject but motherland, then I am sorry. Other than trying to invoke the pride and dignity of motherland or self-respect, we don't do anything other than that. They are physical activities, of course. We do cite examples of opposition like Pakistan and China, but we invoke those names to ensure that as an Indian we are prepared when Pakistan or China attacks us. All role plays revolve around that. We never say Islam or Christian; we don't play those role plays. It's always China or Pakistan.

It is clear that Jommi wants to present the RSS and the BJP as cultural and political institutions, concerned only with the protection of the motherland and maintaining territorial integrity. The media, he said, want to reduce the Sangh to a religiously motivated Hindu nationalist movement—based on the 1992 Ram Janmabhoomi issue (the destruc-

tion of a mosque in Ayodhya to build a Hindu temple for Lord Ram)—
and ignoring the spectrum of positions and perspectives. The question
of whether Jommi's portrayal of the BJP/RSS is political, cultural, or
religious is vexed, for they are slippery concepts, a point I return to in
later chapters. When I suggested that the RSS are secretive about their
activities, he grudgingly accepted that this is due to the "bad press" they
receive. To show his willingness to be open and that the RSS are a social
institution with "nothing to hide," he invited me to an RSS shakha in
Pashigat the next day.

Part of the reason I was granted access was because I was seen as a
sympathetic observer. Different Sangh networks introduced me as the
scholar who wrote on Ranima (Rani Gaidinliu) and the Heraka movement (Longkumer 2010). In fact, in Chapter 6, I address specifically the
importance of Ranima for the Sangh, with even Narendra Modi said to
have worked with her as a young pracharak in Gujarat. Having written
the only in-depth academic book about the movement, a movement that
is largely ignored (and marginalized), many of the Heraka who were educated in the VHP and RSS schools now vouched for my legitimacy and
sensitivity to their cause. In fact, in Assam and Nagaland, it was primarily
former students of these schools who introduced me to Sangh workers
and organized interviews. In Arunachal Pradesh, Meghalaya, and Tripura, too, these networks proved useful and facilitated access.

The final aspect of my acceptance was to do with my status as both
an "insider" and a "local" from the region. They saw me as someone with
strong family connections and roots in the region, a sentiment they expressed in various ways. I would receive texts asking when I would return
to Bharatvarsh or sending me best wishes on indigenous Ao (my tribe)
festivals like Moatsü (harvest festival) and Tsüngremong (thanksgiving
festival), linking these, of course, to "mother nature" and always to roots.
That they made the effort to find out my clan name, the village I was from,
and the festivals of my tribe told me plenty about their own research and
knowledge of my identity, as much as it did about theirs. To accord me
honor, I was sometimes introduced to their acquaintances as a "son of the
soil," a term widely used to identify someone as "indigenous" but also marking an explicit political difference from an "illegal immigrant" (most often

the "Muslim other" from Bangladesh). As Hindus, they are also "sons of the soil," and therefore the immediate connection we shared was assured. In Chapter 7, I explore in more detail the way in which these identifiers are contentious in terms of how the Sangh understand citizenship and what it means to be Hindu, even if one is an illegal immigrant from Bangladesh. Sometimes the power of these identity markers is revealed in spontaneous moments, particularly when these were things I was not meant to see.

On one occasion, I was sitting with an RSS pracharak outside his Dimapur office on the veranda drinking tea. Three young Naga students staying in an RSS hostel approached us and touched our feet and greeted us in Hindi. I was taken aback to see young Nagas behaving this way. My host was clearly embarrassed by the situation and playfully chided the students, saying, "This is Nagaland—no touching feet. Please shake sir's hand, and speak in English." In many of my interviews with RSS activists, they were aware of the cultural sensitivities around acts like touching feet or speaking in Hindi, neither of which are Naga cultural practices. Clearly, despite their loudly proclaimed respect for cultural diversity, these students had been educated in a manner that contradicted this rhetoric. It was a slippage that I was not meant to see. It was an ethnographic moment of disclosure, of contradictions that confirmed the coming together of the performance of identity and the inner lives of their ideologies set on a public stage. Moments like this highlight the vitality of ethnographic research, the ability to peer behind the scenes, however fleeting and unintended, which brings to the surface the complex and contradictory nature of Sangh activities in the Northeast.

COMMITMENT AS NATIONAL WORKERS:
FOOD AND ITS BOUNDARIES

While this highlights the paradoxical nature of their local involvement, it is also necessary to observe how they participate in the tribal way of life. One example, contrary to their traditional upper caste practices, is that workers will publically consume meat and alcohol. This public act engages in the evidence of the senses, which places the "activist" as the "enunciator and public performer of ideals of selfhood, interiority and conviction across the world" (Hansen 2009, 20). What better way to illustrate this conviction than through a story.

There is a story of a young pracharak from Gujarat. During his first visit to a village in Arunachal Pradesh, he is introduced as a young social worker who has come to teach Hindi in a school. The villagers prepare a small feast in his honor in the evening. Famished and tired from a long day's journey, they sit down to eat, and he is served a dish that resembles a large piece of meat. Upon asking his friend next to him the nature of this dish, his friend replies that the dish is jungle rat, a delicacy in the region. Unable to say no as it will undermine the RSS's entire mission of cultural adaptability, he squeamishly consumes the meat to please his village hosts. That night he sneaks out of his hut and is sick. (A tribal RSS worker telling the story bursts out in laughter.) He cannot sleep that night, the story goes. He recalls with anguish the sight of his mother and grandmother upon finding out that he broke the cardinal rule, the ultimate taboo of his caste—eating meat. He remembers his strict vegetarian upbringing and imagines with disgust the texture of the meat that he had just consumed. But he remains steadfast in his commitment to serve the community come what may. The next evening, he is served the same dish and eats with the same piquancy as the night before. Thinking that he is enjoying the jungle rat so much, the villagers decide that it is only right to serve jungle rat every day for the whole week. The price one pays for commitment!

The story is urban legend, in some sense, among Sangh workers, as a way to bring humor and entertainment around the campfire. It is also told as a story of commitment, of keeping one's eye toward the ultimate goal—of winning hearts and minds. Eating meat and drinking rice beer are often accepted among Sangh workers in the region, whose vegetarianism is sacrificed for the nation. This is how Nikesh, an RSS volunteer for Sewa Bharati, described it when I met him in Guwahati in 2018.

> When I went to Tripura, I went to a Reang home. I had just started nonveg then. They thought I don't eat nonveg, so they made food for me first. Only after I had eaten, they made food for themselves. I thought, "This is wrong. If my body is not harmed by nonveg, then there is no problem in consuming it. Why should someone make for me first and eat later?" So I started eating nonveg little bit at a time. If my workstation is shifted there, then I will eat whatever is found there. What to eat, what not to eat, how much of it to eat

is my decision to make. So we have given our time to the Sangathan [organization], and they have sent us there, so we have to do the work. If the path is good, we will go, but we will go even if the path is rugged. This society is ours and we are from this society. When I say this it means I have to go to everyone.

The choice of food, as basic sustenance, is part and parcel of their sacrifice for working for the nation, where these categories—meat eater and vegetarian—fade into the background. A journalist in Shillong told me recently how she confronted the then governor of Nagaland, Padmanabha Balakrishna Acharya, an RSS worker in Meghalaya at that time, when he told her that he ate beef to assimilate with the tribals in Meghalaya. She then retorted by questioning how he could be sacrificing for the nation when he now eats the very thing he deemed sacred, the cow as mother (*gau mata*). He remained silent, she told me. The larger point that the journalist was making is that if the RSS are willing to go to any lengths to demonstrate assimilation, even willing to eat their "sacred mother," how can anybody trust them?

THE INVISIBILITY OF THE NORTHEAST
AND CHRISTIANITY AS RESISTANCE

Negotiating these challenging moments in fieldwork must also be contextualized in a place where militarization, conflict, and nationalism have marked the lives of the people in unprecedented ways. The Sangh are quick to highlight the root of these problems; the "blame" falls squarely on "insurgency" and "Christianity." In the Northeast, in particular, Indian independence was not a celebrated event like in some parts of India.

In 1948, the ex-governor of the Northeast provinces, Robert Reid, travels to the Naga hills. While there, he hears that M. K. Gandhi has been shot. In his shock and grief, he tells his Naga host, the Konyak chief, Changrai, that Gandhi is dead. Changrai is baffled and explains he does not know who Gandhi is. Reid explains that it was Gandhi who brought about Indian independence and is the reason the British are leaving India. Changrai replies: "I see, it is he who has caused all this trouble for the Nagas" (quoted in Saikia 2004, 52).

Even before 1947, the Naga National Council (NNC) were demanding a Naga state. When they were denied their sovereignty, they declared independence a day before India. The NNC's activities stirred the political cauldron in the region, with the Mizo National Front (MNF), the United Liberation Front of Assam (ULFA), the People's Liberation Army (PLA) in Manipur, and many others following. They demanded sovereignty and autonomy and sought legitimacy amid state and military sanction, on the one hand, and the armed resistance wrought by such indigenous movements, on the other. But these movements were also proliferating under what they saw as the ignorant and patronizing attitude of the Indian government toward the region, the "problem of untranslatable cultural norms" (Saikia 2004, 52). There is no honorable place for the people of the region, these groups believed, who are "compelled to concede to an imposed Indian identity, which they feel can neither accommodate their peculiarities nor let them be different" (Saikia 2004, 52). This sense of alienation was sharply felt during the 1962 Indo-China War and its aftermath.

The historian Yasmin Saikia recounts how those in Assam were asked to vacate their homes by state officials when the Chinese invaded. The Indian military and the bureaucratic institutions abandoned their posts and fled, leaving the Assamese to fend for themselves. The Indian government only exacerbated the alienation and neglect for a region when Prime Minister Nehru's historic speech on November 22, 1962, drove the final wedge into the heart of the region: "My heart goes out to the people of Assam, but I cannot do anything" (Saikia 2004, 166). Those who were told of the "Chinese aggression" found out that actually it was the Chinese, not the Indians, who were the friends of the Assamese. The founding chairman of the ULFA, Buddheshwar Gogoi, described his impression of the 1962 war to Saikia. He tells her that when they abandoned their villages, the farms and rice paddies were left unattended. They could have died of starvation that year, but upon returning to their fields, they saw that the Chinese soldiers had harvested the grain, organized them into bundles, and stored them in their paddy barns. Gogoi remarks: "Our enemies had saved our paddy.... Rice is our only wealth, and the Chinese gave it back to us" (Saikia 2004, 167). The other factor associated with the region's alienation is its Christianity. Its adoption and proliferation was started by the British when they began administering this region from the nineteenth century onward.

Although I have not discussed the issue around the Muslim presence substantially in this book (a limitation that I am mindful of), and mention it only in rhetoric or when it is used to express otherness, the issues surrounding Christianity are vital to the Sangh discourse about belonging, not least because five out of the seven Northeast states have a sizeable Christian population. I refer to a poem published by the Vivekananda Institute of Culture (VKIC) to open up the debate. Christianity's problem, it says, is its extraterritorial allegiance:

He is "Son of the soil"
This is his ancestor's land
He may not do anything
Doesn't mean you can try
His gods are outside the land
So are his heroes and bosses
Accidentally he was born here
But for them he must die. (Joshi 2000, 46)

To reflect on this poem, let me highlight a number of factors, drawing on James C. Scott's book *The Art of Not Being Governed* (2009) and Frederick Downs's (1980, 1992) work on tribal resistance. James C. Scott (2009, 13–14) argues that Zomia—that is, the highland communities of South and Southeast Asia—remains one of the largest nonstate spaces in the world, spreading over China, India, mainland Southeast Asia, and Bangladesh, essentially an area the size of Europe. Because of the difficult terrain and overlapping ethnic and tribal boundaries, alongside poorly managed (and understood) state and international boundaries, such gray areas infuriate modern regimes, who see hill peoples as potential sources of separatism.

Scott explains some of the way in which Christianity influenced the region. First, Christianity brought a modern identity and with it education, literacy, and medical and material prosperity (Downs 2010; Eaton 1984; May 2009; Pachuau 2014; Thomas 2016). The new written script established in an effort to translate the Bible into local languages brought about a literate public that initiated monumental changes, not least the rise of nationalisms that saw in the biblical stories a blueprint for their own struggles and also the ability to articulate their concerns to a larger audience (Longkumer 2019; May 2016; Thomas 2016). Chapter 4 in particular looks at the idea of emancipation and prophetic messages drawn largely from the Exodus narrative of the Bible.

Second, the adoption of Christianity provides an additional resource of group identity that allows them to reposition themselves in the ethnic and national mosaic. Such positioning strengthens social mobilization through institutional access and power, which in turn acts as a "proxy for hill nationalism" (Scott 2009, 320). The historian Frederick Downs (1992, 92) similarly argues that Christianity provided a pan-tribal identity that would become the basis of modern political movements. Even without overtly professing a kind of Christian nationalism, many people see Christianity, and here in the example of the Garos, as a means of "moral defense against the plains people" (Downs 1980, 410). This point in particular has turned out to be contentious within the Indian nation-state, with many Hindutva actors accusing Christianity of fomenting secessionism, something I elaborate on in Chapter 5. One of the arguments is that because of the British patronage of Christian missions, a process of Sanskritization (in which tribal Hindu customs are absorbed into a dominant Hindu one) had been halted and replaced by Christianity in the hill areas. "The implication is that if it had not been for this external interference all the tribals would have become Hindus, and an integration of the hills and plains people would have occurred, instead of the present uneasy and sometimes adversary relationship. Such an assumption presumably explains why Christian activity is prohibited or discouraged in Arunachal Pradesh while the Ramakrishna Mission is allow to function there" (Downs 1980, 411).

Downs is however more circumspect and makes the case that "isolation" as a physical reality separating the hills and plains is not the only factor in the lack of Sanskritization. He gives the example of the Jaintia kings of present-day Meghalaya, who became Hindu and even built several Hindu temples in their hill villages. But once they shifted their capital to the plains of Jaintiapur, the king's hill subjects under his jurisdiction maintained their tribal customs, suggesting that Hinduism was not embraced in the first place. Downs's assessment of Hinduism as buffered from tribal customs is rather simplistic, however, and one that will be challenged by numerous indigenous actors in Chapter 3.

Mere physical proximity could not be the only explanation for Hinduism or Christianity being embraced or rejected. It could simply be the case that the "tribals" were not interested in seeking assimilation (Downs 1980, 411–12). Even if tribal society was assimilated within Hinduism, argues Downs, they would be classed at the lowest of social levels. Furthermore, the tribes would be assimilated within a dominant neighboring Hindu society. Christianity was attractive, in contrast, because "there was no dominant neighbouring Christian society into which they could be assimilated at a disadvantage" (1980, 414). This allowed the Christians in the hills to dabble with indigenous cosmologies, blend material and social conventions, and shape an identity that suited them on their own terms, or what Andrew May calls "Asia-normative" (2016, 16). This is why, argues Scott, Zomians adopted movements (Christian, traditional religions, and a blend of the two) that were prophetic: it provided both a distance from neighboring states and allowed a flexible alternative to the orthodoxies of dominant ideologies. I take up this issue in Chapter 4 and evaluate Downs's and Scott's claims when marginalized people are confronted by the ominous, encroaching state power through the language of prophecy and hope.

PEOPLING HINDUTVA: PORTRAITS OF MEN
AND WOMEN IN ACTION

While this book is about the Northeast of India, it is also a story about the evolution of Hindutva. As I have been suggesting, it is vital that we go beyond these institutions and focus on individuals and their stories. I have met electrical engineers, business management professionals, schoolteachers, and people who arrived in Nagaland to escape the Emergency (1975–77) (imposed by Indira Gandhi when the RSS was banned, civil liberties curbed, and the press was censored). I interviewed a former Indian navy officer from Nagpur in Arunachal who left the navy in 2001 after the attack on the Indian parliament. Disillusioned with the armed forces, he joined the RSS in 2002 and is now a pracharak. The army, navy, and air force cannot work for nation building, he said. Only voluntary and selfless service (seva) can bring the nation together: "It has to be out of love for the country." I also met scientists, mathematicians, physicists, linguists, and chemists from all walks of life who serve the nation primarily as members of the RSS, a fact that came to light during a meeting of scholars at North East Hill University (NEHU) in Shillong.

I was invited by the RSS pracharak of Meghalaya, Sunil, to attend a "knowledge seminar," Gyan Sangam, at NEHU with J. Nandkumar, the convener of Pragya Pravah, an RSS-sponsored think tank.[7] There were around twenty-five academics and activists associated with the RSS (mostly nontribals) who introduced themselves to Nandkumar. Nandkumar started the seminar by talking about decolonizing the Indian mind. The academic Left in India, he argued, are influenced by Aristotle and Foucault, but Indian scientists and thinkers like Shankaracharya and Abhinav Gupta are mere footnotes in Indian textbooks. He continued: "Martin Luther King Jr. said, 'History will have to record that the greatest tragedy of this period of social transition was not the strident clamor of the bad people, but the appalling silence of the good people.' Antinationals are few, but good people need to speak out. It is high time for the decolonization of Indian minds." What followed was a discussion that felt more like a Sangh meeting, and I slowly moved away from the table, frantically taking notes as these exchanges occurred.

Linguistics professor: Tukde Brigade [break India] has been creating problems. We should be the alternative voice to the Western world. We should discard the word *decolonization* as it still holds the word *colonization* in it. We should be the alternative.

We know Noam Chomsky is part of the Tukde Brigade. We need to create knowledge, not synthesize what exists. In the process of nation making, we have to use our own scholars like Chanakya. The nation is the biggest institution in itself. Nation is not a myth.

There are three stages to the Sangam concept: knowledge creation, production, and dissemination.

Chemistry professor: We need heads of departments to push this forward. We need the vice-chancellor of NEHU to be at these meetings (he is one of us) if we want to make it more inclusive. We have to stop remaining hidden when doing such programs. We need to come overground from underground at some point.

I have asked local RSS people to contest [in university boards] but they refuse, as there may be problems in the future if they are exposed.

Nandkumar: We must do these Sangams at universities, not just any place, like Pinewood Hotel. There will be *hungama* [chaos] in JNU [Jawaharlal Nehru University, a premier Indian institute based in New Delhi] only if the program is political but not if it is academic.

RSS pracharak (Sandeep): We need to have local faces with us and forward the agenda through them so that there is no media hungama. We need to call it an "academic session." We could discuss things like the sociocultural ethos, indigenous knowledge, matrilineal society, et cetera. Let us talk about these so that no binaries [no controversial topics] are discussed. We know that crores of people here are followers of British [Christians].

Linguistics professor: We could discuss indigenous knowledge and diversity. There is a new idea doing the rounds called Traditional Ecological Knowledge (TEK) so our seminar could be called TEK in Northeast.

Nandkumar: Yes, and that sounds overtly secular. But Bharatiyata [Indianness] should be at the crux of the seminar format and content. We should remember that it is not a university meeting; it is a Sangh meeting.

I caught up with a few of the seminar attendees after the event. I was interested to hear why people are drawn to the RSS in a place like NEHU or even Shillong. Some like the Chemistry professor, himself an RSS man, are skeptical of the current group of RSS workers both locally and nationally. One must not assume, he said, that because one is a nontribal (he is from Bihar), one is immediately sympathetic to the RSS. That is how the RSS recruit—they target nontribals, primarily due to grievances that they have against tribal populations. A professor (from West Bengal) explained this sentiment, which I paraphrase here in brief. If you are a nontribal, you cannot own land in Shillong or in tribal states like Nagaland and Mizoram, even if you have invested all your life there. You do not have rights, because tribal "customary laws" prevail. A nontribal is a second-class citizen. What happens, he says, is that the RSS play on these sentiments and argue for the abolition of customary law, scheduled tribe status, inner line permit—all the mechanisms introduced by the British and the postcolonial governments to appease and protect tribal interests against "outsiders." The RSS promise that these laws will be abolished eventually: "With a promise like that, which nontribal wouldn't join?" asks the professor. These conversations provide insight into how the RSS recruit nontribals in the region, playing on nontribal insecurities and offering a sense of identity and purpose. But not all are seduced by the work of the RSS.

I met Aakash, a Bihari living in Shillong. From a staunch socialist family from Bihar (his father taught at NEHU), Aakash was exposed to the RSS shakha through a Bengali friend, whose father, another academic in a local college, used to run. He distinctly remembers the RSS whistle, which sounded like playtime. What attracted him were the games and the camaraderie they built with other boys from the neighborhood. His father eventually found out and dissuaded him from attending the shakha due to his ideological opposition to the RSS. But Aakash also realized that the RSS were willing to bend certain truths for their ideological ends, despite advocating openness and honesty:

> At one of the *boudhik varg* [intellectual classes], they [RSS] started discussing the Indian flag, and they said, you know, "If Muslims had their way or Congress had their way, the tricolor [referring to the Indian flag] would have had green on top. It is only because Guru Golwalkar ji argued for it that saffron is on top." Thanks to growing up in a socialist family, I knew that the flag has a different history. I found it stupid, and I said to them, "This is not true because saffron is not only the color of Hinduism" et cetera. I stopped going to the RSS shakha after that, but if you are a nontribal growing up in a place like Shillong, there are certain cultural associations that are unavoidable, like the attraction of a Hindu community.

The power of these shakhas to provide a sense of community for nontribals are the buildings blocks for inheriting a sense of belonging in a region that may seem hostile to their way of life. Institutions and governments, particularly during the Congress governments since 1947, have supported the RSS and other like-minded organizations to counter anybody challenging the fragmentation of India. Take the example of the nontribal bureaucrat, Aakash continues, "who comes here like a king and doesn't get treated nicely by the local nationalists. He says, 'I will show you!'" Aakash vividly recalls how these bureaucrats in Shillong—now disgruntled—would celebrate the second RSS chief, Golwalkar's, birthday without mentioning either the RSS or Golwalkar, using just the latter's initials, M. S. The upper caste Hindu bureaucrat also played a role in the way Hindutva has entered the institutional spaces of government and state infrastructure in the region. Aakash perceptively notes, "When you try to make India one, one of the projects that will always gain an upper hand is the Hindutva project. Sadly, the stronger strain of Indian nationalism is the Hindu Indian nationalism. Plural Indian nationalism is an imagination, which may not necessarily have a support base." Aakash's point is especially interesting when we consider those who come to the Northeast expecting the tribals to accede to their diktats, only to recoil with bruised egos waiting to fight another day. When an ideology comes to revive the glory of Hindu culture, nontribals become potential conscripts, especially when tribal hegemony mixed with indigenous nationalisms prevails in large parts of the Northeast. Here we must acknowledge the violence that takes place against Hindus, both physically and symbolically. It is important to recognize the sentiments it gives rise to, because it is a feature of Hindu experience in strong Christian states that can lead to feelings of insecurity, feelings that the Sangh can exploit.

Jagdish—the fiery, combative RSS pracharak we met earlier—tells me about an event in Dimapur that was organized by the Catholic Church. This was after the murder of the Australian missionary Graham Staines in 1999 in the Indian state of Orissa. Staines and two of his young children were burned to death while sleeping in their car. The deaths, which were linked to the Hindu Bajrang Dal, a group associated with the VHP, and a member of the Sangh, ignited debate all over the country regarding the freedom of religion. An event was organized in Dimapur to discuss its aftermath and particularly to advocate for peace in a multicultural city such as Dimapur. Jagdish was invited along with twenty civil, national, and church leaders.

One of the well-known editors of a Nagaland daily newspaper told the audience, "Nagaland is such an ideal place; there are no communal clashes, and we are maintaining peace here because of Christianity. But see what happened in Orissa—the Hindus killed Graham Staines." All the religions in Dimapur coexist and share the city space with complete harmony, the editor emphasized. Jagdish knew that this was not true and became increasingly agitated. Among the audience—comprising different factions of the National Socialist Council of Nagaland (NSCN)—Jagdish stood up, in his dhoti and kurta, and offered his riposte:

> Peace is maintained because we [Hindus] receive a slap and we keep quiet. Peace is maintained because Muslims kidnap our sisters and we are silent. When we report to the police station, they shout at me and say, "*Chutia* [idiot], why have you come here? Get out." We don't react; we remain silent. The moment we react, we are killed by NSCN-IM [Isak-Muivah faction] and by the church. . . . And, we [Hindus] are such a suppressed community in Dimapur and Nagaland that if we get one slap, if we react, we get another slap. Delhi does not hear us, and Kohima and Dimapur administrators do not hear us, and they are absolutely biased . . . So they say that Hindus are intolerant. But if we are intolerant, where would the Christians be—you are 2 percent. You think we can't tear down a church? We are capable of that. Because it is not in our blood and not in the RSS philosophy. We are opposed only to those who are antinational. Church and those antinational forces don't represent us in the true light and thus show us to be heinous forces.

Jagdish is a man forged through his steely determination to stand for what he believes in, however questionable the organization he represents may be. Jagdish's emotive response highlights the Hindu hurt in a place like Nagaland and also Hindutva victimization: the RSS are branded as heinous; Jagdish himself was interrogated, threatened by the NSCN factions, and assaulted by the Naga Student Federation (NSF), he tells me. I wondered whether this is the fragile emotional space that allows many to join the RSS ranks or support their activities. I met a young entrepreneur whose grandparents fled Burma after ethnic riots against Indians broke out in 1962. They settled in "Burma Camp" in Dimapur; soon after, his father joined the RSS, and he followed him a few years later. He is not a pracharak but a *grhastha karyakarta* (householder activist). After three generations in Nagaland, he says the vegetable *lypata* (mustard greens) are more "local" than he is, a constant outsider. He told me he receives countless slaps from the Nagas when he does his Sangh work but is steadfast in his commitment to serving in Nagaland because he does not want "my Naga sisters to wear hijab and burkas." For him, the Nagas are ignorant of the threat of Islamization coming from Bangladesh at pace, which needs to be addressed. He sees the RSS as their protectors, seeking to tackle their ignorance with education and seva.

The reason I highlight these stories is to illustrate what James C. Scott (1990) calls "infrapolitics." Scott argues that when studying political and social movements, the concept of infrapolitics allows us to question established norms of political action. Applying the term primarily to subaltern groups, Scott argues that because subaltern people lack legitimate channels to express their grievances, the forms of their anger and frustrations take on subtler and more hidden forms that are unconventional. Scott says, "So long as we confine our conception of *the political* to activity that is openly declared, we are driven to conclude that subordinate groups essentially lack a political life or that what political life they do have is restricted to those exceptional moments of popular explosion" (1990: 199). I want to suggest that Hindutva actions in the Northeast are unconventional in this sense, despite the conventions that are strongly established in many parts of India where they have strength in numbers. Although the Sangh have numerous networks and workers in the Northeast, the numbers are comparatively few compared to, for example, Gujarat or Uttar Pradesh. But it is through forging emotional connections with ordinary nontribal householders, teachers, bureaucrats, armed forces personnel, and professionals that their networks take on a more distributed (but not fragmented) character that makes them "hidden" and infrapolitical. It is precisely this hiddenness that allows them to be amorphous, blending according to the nature of the host.

Let me pause to give a flavor of how one may come upon ordinary people whose lives are invested in building the nation. It is important to view the spectrum of Sangh activists as ranging from committed individuals to people who are undecided to those who support their work of nation building regardless of their religious and political colors. By drawing attention to the diversity of individuals involved, I want to bring to light the people and the stories narrated to me as they tackle the long and messy process of nation building.

NEIL

I met Neil, in his midtwenties, during the Gyan Sangam at NEHU in 2018. We were traveling to a neighboring town, Jowai, and I asked if he would like to join us, primarily to facilitate introductions, to talk about the situation in Meghalaya, and to learn more about the work of the Sangh.

Neil is a Seng Khasi (traditional Khasi religion), many of whom have an ambivalent relationship with the RSS: some want closer association as a bulwark against the dominant Christians; others reject them altogether as brash nationalists. Before that he was a Presbyterian, and his family, poor farmers, were unceremoniously alienated from the church for failing to pay a regular tithe. He found refuge in the RSS, because they supported him through his schooling and cared for him as a family member.

He went to Swami Vivekananda Saraswati Vidya Mandir, an RSS-run school in Shahidabad, Uttar Pradesh (UP). There he met many tribal children from Nagaland, Mizoram, Kashmir, Bihar, Rajasthan, Arunachal Pradesh, Assam, and Uttarakhand and Chakmas from Mizoram and Tripura. It was a melting pot of tribals comprising 70 percent of the population and 30 percent nontribals. The schoolteachers would always support them and punish other students when they used words like *chinky* or *Nepali*. Once they went on an excursion nearby, and a Muslim boy called one of them "eh Nepali." His Naga friend immediately went up to this Muslim boy and slapped him. There were no reprisals since the RSS students who were hosting them in UP protected them.

After school Neil came back to Shillong, the capital of Meghalaya. He now works for a blacksmith in his village, a few kilometers outside the capital, and is involved in local Seng Khasi issues. He supports the RSS but will not tolerate them imposing their religion on the Khasis; if they did, he said, the local Khasis would expel them. He is currently completing a master's degree in Hindi at NEHU and hopes to earn a PhD. In fact, the local pracharak, Sunil, told me that they are trying to raise funds from nontribal businesspeople to sponsor Neil for a PhD in Hindi. Throughout his time with us, Neil received texts and phone calls from his RSS friend Sandeep. When we asked him what the messages were about, Neil nonchalantly replied, "Sandeep was inquisitive about the kinds of questions you were asking." He is close to Sandeep, Neil says, and they constantly keep in touch through texts and phone calls. He tells us that he encourages his Christian friends to come back to the Seng Khasi fold, and one of them is seriously considering this. When I asked if this is actively encouraged by the RSS, he replied that they are supportive but, of course, never directly involved. His ultimate aim, Neil tells us, is to finish his PhD in Hindi and become a RSS pracharak. He recognizes that pracharaks have difficult lives—and he would have to learn a different language and adapt to the local environment. He thinks he might have to learn Malayalam, as he will most likely be sent to Kerala. I asked him if this choice of location was predetermined. He replied that one Khasi pracharak he knows is currently in Kerala, and his having established links there might help Neil as he too begins the journey.

ASHISH

I meet Ashish in the VHP office in Guwahati, Assam. Ashish is in his late forties and is from the Nalbari district of Assam. He was exposed to a shakha at an early age, when he was around four, without knowing what it was. The sonic resonance of the shakha whistle first caught his attention, as it reminded the children from the neighborhood of playtime. He went to the shakha because he was interested in the games and exercises it offered, but latterly the prayers and *shlokas* (Sanskrit poetry) attracted him. When he left his town for the National Institute of Technology (NIT, in Nagpur), the shakha eventually closed down due to the killing of a RSS pracharak from Kerala by the ULFA in the 1980s. One day he was milling around a temple in Nagpur when he saw what looked like a shakha, with people performing the RSS salute. The memory of his childhood shakha came flooding back, and the nostalgia made him eager to know more about the RSS. He eventually learned that the shakha of his childhood was associated with the RSS. He read up on Hindutva literature and confided in close confidants like Rajju Bhaiya. He also met others who inspired him like K. S. Sudarshan and Mohan Bhagwat, who all served as sarsanghchalak (1993–2003, 2000–2009, 2009–present, respectively).

After finishing his education at NIT as a civil engineer, he worked as a government engineer in Chhattisgarh for nine years and completed the

Initial Training Camp (ITC) for new RSS members in Kurukshetra, in the Indian state of Haryana. In his spare time, he worked as a RSS organizer in villages in Raigarh, helping them by hiring teachers for their schools from nearby Orissa and guiding them to make practical decisions about education and jobs. He left the government service and joined the corporate sector, working for Jindal Steel & Power. Even there he continued his work in the RSS, until he left the corporate sector and was asked to join the VHP as organizing secretary for Northeast India.

He is not sure if he wants to be a pracharak; there are lots of expectations among the local RSS that the rank and file from the region be bulked up, but he remains undecided. He talks about his work of cow seva and protecting gau mata and is certain that the Ram temple in Ayodhya will be built, along with the reclamation of the Taj Mahal as a Shiva temple. He discusses the foreign hand in supplying arms to Christian nationalists, the slaughter of cows taken from Assam and Meghalaya into Bangladesh, and the theory that various nationalist movements are out to rid the Northeast of the RSS, which he says will allow Christian conversion to happen unopposed. I ask him about the draconian Armed Forces Special Powers Act (AFSPA): "Isn't that one of the laws that alienate people in the region, because the AFSPA is used to keep the region as a colony of the Indian state?" His tone changes, appearing unsettled by my question. He raises his voice and says that as a fellow Northeasterner, he is aware of the sense of alienation that AFSPA causes, and the VHP are working to bridge those gaps. "But who is saying that the military are our enemies? It is the Christian missionaries and the Muslim *mawlawi* and maulana [religious scholars]." These nationalists live in the jungles and have no education and do not know India: How can they judge the actions of other people? They are fed these lies, he replies. The VHP are changing these perceptions by helping those who are branded "our enemies."

When the National Register of Citizens (NRC) process was going on in 2018, he helped a friend find the legacy data (or electoral rolls) as evidence of his residence in Assam.[8] His friend is a Muslim. Both share the last surname. When his friend noticed that his ancestors (who were Hindu) had the same surname as Ashish, the friend cried and confessed,

"I never knew I was Hindu." Ashish then told him, "You were converted by force." With a smile Ashish says that his friend gradually accepted this historical injustice. Ashish is hopeful that his friend will consider changing his religious identity. This process is slow and gradual, Ashish confessed, but it will happen, even if it takes a hundred years!

ANAND

Anand is from Mumbai and is the organizing secretary of Janjati Vikas Samiti (JVS) Nagaland. After finishing his PhD, he was a junior research fellow at Pune University in International relations and politics. He left academia and joined JVS in 2007. He cannot pinpoint how and who inspired him, but it was the passion for seva that motivated him. When one gets a good night's sleep, then it shows that one is satisfied. Once he joined JVS, he felt like that, satisfied. Seva for him is like doing a household chore for your mother. "You do it and ask nothing in return. You help."

His joining JVS, he kept insisting, was nothing momentous; it was natural. He read Marx, Golwalkar, Savarkar, Faulkner, Eugene O'Neill, Mark Twain, and Bertrand Russell. He mixed and matched; he read freely. But something was not right. He thought about having a family, children, and a house that he could call home. But when he thought about his life at that moment the "emotional grip" associated with ambition and success left him. Emptiness crept in, and he thought his life was meaningless. He found solace in seva. Like a Zen philosopher contemplating the nature of change and emptiness, Anand's philosophy of seva is about doing nothing. The more one tries to perform seva, the more one is attempting to leave a mark, to talk oneself up. And that is not seva. Selfless action cannot be explained; it can only be done. Anand's philosophical reflections are intriguing, and I felt that he wanted to explain these concepts to someone who probably appreciated his ruminations more than the average Sangh worker.

Anand came to Nagaland in the early 2000s; he traveled, stayed in villages, and experienced Naga hospitality. He went to Assam and Arunachal Pradesh too. He chose Nagaland because of Atul Jog (who was based in Nagaland), now the national organizing secretary of Kalyan

Ashram, who encouraged him to explore and travel the rich region that is so misunderstood in mainland India. He knows how people from outside this region might find places like Nagaland difficult to visualize because of what they have heard—it is full of "insurgents," and the people are backward. But what he has experienced is the opposite. He now organizes visits for people from all over Mumbai and annually takes Naga students to the big city too.

JVS's work is primarily in the interior regions of Nagaland. They organize educational camps and invite volunteers primarily from Maharashtra to help in tutoring students in science, math, economics, and history and also help organize medical camps for the poor. He believes that knowledge is power and exposing children from rural areas to science and engineering is crucial to their sense of wonder and amazement at what humans can achieve. He took thirteen Naga students to Mumbai recently and showed them the Bandra-Worli Sea Link, a cable-stayed bridge. They were mesmerized by how the bridge was built. He even took them to meet the engineers so that they could explain to the students how it worked. These experiences are all about the integration of this region with different parts of India. When I suggested that this might be a little too simplistic, Anand became annoyed, appearing a little impatient with my line of questioning.

He believes that Naga society is great enough to accommodate even a Hindu person like him. He knows this from evidence, from his travels, and from his free conversations without any political inhibitions. It is scholars like me, he said, that complicate the picture. For example, some of the Naga students were in tears because they thought they would face racial discrimination in Mumbai, but all they experienced was love, care, and understanding. Cultural nuances—between Mumbai and Dimapur—are present but these are few, and if someone constantly searches for difference, that is what one gets. Look for oneness, and that is what one finds. That is what he is trying to accomplish as a full time *karyakarta* (he does not like the term *pracharak*). There is no equivalent translation of the word *karyakarta* in English. Karyakarta means devoting and investing your time until ultimately you see yourself in society and society sees itself in you. You merge yourself with the people, and your identity merges with the person, multiplying until society itself becomes an organic, natural flow based on seva. That is the work of a karyakarta, and seva is the rudder that guides the ship to open waters.

JAMMUNA

The RSS pracharak working for VKV in Arunachal insisted that I meet Jammuna madam, a Hindi professor at one of the local universities. She invites me for dinner the following evening in her house in Nirjuli and discusses the work she does. As a member of the Nyishi tribe in Arunachal, she tells me, her father wanted none of the girls to have any religion. It is only men who have religion. Once they get married, they will follow their husband's religion. She was born into an indigenous household, a non-Christian/non-Hindu, and was ill when young. Due to the influence of her uncle, her parents became Baptists. Her grandmother refused to follow the "new religion" and instead chose to remain with Jammuna, feeding her *oppo* (rice beer) to strengthen her. Christian prayers were said for healing but nothing happened and Jammuna remained ill. It was the gradual feeding of oppo alongside traditional herbs that healed her sickness. Seeing her health reinvigorated, the parents decided to revert to their previous religion.

Over the years, her mother and brother unfortunately too became unwell. During that time, a blind Christian preacher from Nagaland came and visited them. He said that only Jesus could cure them and said, "There is a clear path ahead." They soon understood what that meant—money came at the right time for hospital treatments, doctors and nurses provided them with care, and the prayers of the neighbors gave succor. Her parents decided to revert to being Baptists again, and the whole family followed. Later Jammuna married a Catholic, and she is now Catholic. One of her sisters is in the Kalyan Ashram in Mirzapur, another is in VKV Joram, another is in Don Bosco Yachuli, and the last is in a St. Francis of Assisi School. The women are associated with a panoply of religious institutions, which may appear odd, but for her family it is unproblematic. Likewise, Jammuna is puzzled when I ask her about working with the Sangh as a Christian. Unlike Nagas, she says, Arunachalis are proud Indians; they are highly patriotic. In fact their patriotism comes from two factors. First, she says, is the fact that they speak Hindi. Hindi helps to link them with other parts of India and brings awareness of Indian culture. Second, the influence of the military in these border areas is significant. Through the military, their Hindi improved, but it also brought the population into the national limelight, especially after the 1962 Indo-China War.

Jammuna did her schooling in a Sangathan Hindu school in Rajasthan and grew up speaking Hindi and chanting Ram-Ram (associated with a Hindu deity), so although she was a Baptist and is now a Catholic, she knows more about Hindu practices than Christian ones. So when the Sangh tells her that Christianity is bad, she pauses and reads the Bible without jumping to conclusions. Similarly, when Christians make negative remarks about the RSS, she refers to the various Hindu texts, such as Mahabharata and the Bhagavad Gita. She is actively involved with the ABVP, particularly with their My Home Is India project, and attends and supports the work of the Sangh if it is about patriotism and integration with Bharat (India). When I try to push a little about the violence of the RSS against Christians, she chides me by noting that even Christians committed various atrocities and asserts, "We are all one, and let us live together—that is the reality of Bharat *desh* [India]." She reflects on the growth of Christianity in Arunachal and suggests that the RSS cannot compete, because during "prayer festivals" all over the state, each event draws five thousand people, giving people psychological comfort through healing and prayer. The RSS cannot do that; nor can they mobilize that many people. But what they can do is provide service for nation building, and even if Arunachalis become Christian, they will remain patriotic.

HINDUTVA BECOMING

The four portraits presented here illustrate, in varying ways, the motivation, influences, and biopower of working for the Sangh. Both Ashish and Anand are committed karyakartas working for the nation, having left privileged professional positions. Being from Assam, Ashish understands the problems facing the region, such as the questions that remain about AFSPA and human rights abuses. But his commitment is steadfast and more definite than Anand's, who retreats into the space of philosophy to untie some of the knotted questions and problems facing the region. One can perceive Golwalkar's (2000) ruminations about service and national being in Anand's ideas.

Neil is on the cusp of Hindutva becoming. Living in a climate dominated by Christians, Neil and his beliefs are marginalized to the extent that he has to depend on the Sangh for resources and institutional support. This is an unpopular move no doubt but, amid the existential choices, probably the only one available. While he might go on to complete a PhD in Hindi and become an RSS pracharak working in Kerala, aided by Sangh supporters in Shillong, he could also return to Christianity. Is Neil's process of Hindutva becoming due to an ideological pull? Or is it disgruntlement with his Christian neighbors for disenfranchising him and his family? These are questions that are difficult to answer but questions that could be asked about many RSS sympathizers in the region.

Jammuna's story sidesteps these questions in part because of her upbringing, her experience of multiple religious identities, and her ability to reflect without judgment. Her fluid allegiances mean she can both work for the Sangh and remain a committed Christian, a contradiction that might confound many. Jammuna represents the quintessential or ideal Christian for the Sangh, and that is why the RSS pracharak was keen I meet her. More than anyone, Jammuna understands the ability to be Christian and Hindu, in the Hindutva sense of keeping her civilizational identity intact no matter where the wind blows.

Her story also highlights the issue of the Hindi language that permeates Arunachal, making patriotic subjects unlike other parts of the region. It also suggests that not all are opposed to the "idea of India" in the region. To juxtapose two voices in this debate, it would be interesting for Jammuna to meet Ampareen Lyngdoh, a member of the legislative assembly (MLA) in Meghalaya and an opponent of nationalizing Hindi (a project of the BJP) as a way of expressing one's patriotism but yet a committed citizen of India. Lyngdoh explained to me that the governor, Ganga Prasad, a senior BJP/RSS man appointed by the president of India, insists on speaking in Hindi. Lyngdoh went on to explain that the fact that Meghalaya is a state where English is the language of adminis-

tration and where Hindi is not widely spoken should have been acknowledged by the governor, particularly when the governor is the "emissary"
of the president. She says, "The saddest part is that the governor in office
not only speaks Hindi; he speaks Bhojpuri Hindi, with a Bihari swag. We
don't know what he is saying most of the time, and it is very insulting."
In protest at the governor's opening speech in the Meghalaya Legislative Assembly in 2018, Lyngdoh used a regional language, Khasi, to address the assembly; many of the legislators did not understand Khasi.
"The point was made," she exclaimed, when we met to discuss this in her
house:

> Hindi means nothing. Don't speak Hindi when you come officially. Fine, we
> can watch a Hindi movie together, and I'll try and laugh at a Hindi joke in
> a movie.... But you cannot parade around me and say that from tomorrow,
> it's only Hindi. You can't do that. We also have our own regional languages,
> which are all important in the fabric of the Indian community at large. That's
> the beauty of India.

The issue of language is obviously important for legislators like Lyngdoh.
Her speech went viral on social media, gaining considerable support
within the state as well as from other regions in the Northeast. There is a
growing sense that the national agenda of "one country, one language, and
one culture," as Lyngdoh explained, is making people apprehensive about
the BJP and the Hindutva forces trying to undermine regional voices. For
Lyngdoh, the imposition of Hindi, which for Jammuna brings patriotism,
might lead to the disintegration of India if its hegemony continues.

For Ashish and Anand, however, there is no doubt that their motivations are ideological, and they are in the Northeast for the long run. The
main motivating factor for them both is the idea of seva, which is built
into the RSS ideology of selfless service to society—RSS translates as
"national volunteer corps." And this service is always "secular" and "social"
in the sense that the RSS is keen to distance itself from the religious side
of things by not involving themselves in mandirs or churches. Anand in
particular is keen to stress that Hindutva is like breathing, a natural concept that is like air. It is an inheritance that comes from land itself, and
therefore there are no sectarian labels that one can attach to it. Once one

tries to take this inheritance away, the idea of exclusivity enters, Anand explains. Hindu, as a secular identity, is never exclusive in this way; it wants to share this inheritance. Once people start demanding political rights on the basis of religion, the whole idea of inheritance fragments, leading to the dissolution of the body of Bharat Mata. Protecting against this dissolution is part and parcel of their commitment as workers for the nation.

BOOK OVERVIEW

This book is deeply ethnographic. It is interdisciplinary in the sense that it keeps a keen eye on the broader scholarship on Hindu nationalism. It is mindful, however, that the principles of Hindutva, with its genesis and development in colonial times, do not take into account what we now call Northeast India. My attempt, throughout the book, is to be aware of the broader precedence of Hindutva without letting it overwhelm the striking local interpretations and innovations that we find in the Northeast. I do not want to give the impression that I represent the richness of this region in a single book. Instead I operate on the microscale using the Hindutva gaze as an analog, where I home in on certain issues, while keeping in mind the macroscale through an ethnographic and historically grounded narrative.

Chapter 2 examines how the Hindutva gaze operates through a reconstructed spatial history that argues for relations with the Indic center since time immemorial. Based on the idea of Greater India ("One India, Great India," a slogan used by the BJP), it examines the implications of the Sangh use of imaginative geography. If geography is a crucial component of how the Northeast fits within the larger Indic imagination of Akhand Bharat (undivided India), the landscape shaped by a people, their institutions, and customs must also be understood. Chapter 3 continues this thread and asks searching questions about the nature of Hindutva, especially if its root meaning has to do with land. It enters the age-old debate of the synergy between Hindu and tribal practices as a way to assimilate non-Christian religions or indigenous religions into a composite Hindu nation. Making links with other indigenous movements and arguing for Hindu practices as the base for all civilizations, Hindutva makes a compelling case for including, by extension, all indigenous traditions through the discourse of indigeneity.

Chapters 4 and 5 focus on Hindutva interactions with Christianity. While Christianity dominates the conversation in the Northeast as the Other of Hindutva, these two chapters examine first how the Naga Christians view the Sangh and the Indian state as an extension of the Hindu other. This reverse gaze is helpful in order to understand the longstanding demand for sovereignty by the Nagas, but at the same time, it asks crucial questions about belonging through the language of hope. Prophecy, both in the way Christians see the Indian state and in the way it guides the Naga people, helps us understand what Isabelle Stengers (2005) calls "cosmopolitics." Second, the Christian hegemon, for the Sangh, must be deconstructed and reassembled to accord with the larger Hindutva project of forming benevolent and patriotic subjects by separating belief—an inner, private matter between God and human—from practice, a public declaration of acts that are consistent with being Hindu in a civilizational space. This is a debate that has a longer history in India, which takes on surprising new facets when considered in the light of Christianity in the Northeast.

Chapter 6 builds on some of these religious anxieties by focusing on icons. It concerns how the Sangh seek to imbue the icon of Rani Gaidinliu with "raw semiotic power" (Ghosh 2011) through new technologies of veneration and public visuality and thereby incorporate it into the social and political space of Mother India (Bharat Mata). Focusing on the iconicity of Rani Gaidinliu, a non-Christian Naga leader, I address issues around the power of icons and how their distinct encounter with iconoclastic Christians can bring about intriguing questions of what the icon actually indexes. If the body of Bharat Mata ought to include or align with such tribal leaders, to what extent can this be utilized to forge unity with Hindutva ideals through pragmatic change?

Finally, Chapter 7 examines the way the BJP have managed to make an electoral mark in a region that has historically been hostile to it. Electoral politics helps the Sangh translate their visions and goals into a coherent and pragmatic set of practices, compromises, and promises. Making alliances and partnerships with regional parties across the Northeast states represents another phase in Hindutva's path toward influence in a region that for them just a few decades ago was an anomaly, a nonentity. Indeed, the journalist Pradip Phanjoubam's phrase regarding the most recent election in Nagaland—"How the BJP won without winning"—portrays the paradoxical nature of Sangh politics. It highlights unanswered questions as they struggle to consolidate their forces. This book is an attempt to document and interpret Hindutva activists' struggles, dilemmas, and indeed their innovations and creativity as Hindutva takes powerful and in some ways surprising new strides in contemporary India.

CHAPTER 2

THE NORTHEAST AND TIME'S RELENTLESS MELT

ON 28 MARCH 2018, the chief ministers of Manipur, Arunachal Pradesh, and Gujarat came together to celebrate the marriage of Lord Krishna and Rukmini during the four-day Madhavpur Mela (fair) in Gujarat, a state in western India. Thousands gathered at this *mela* from all over India, with around 150 cultural troupes from the Northeast as the bride's representatives to celebrate the "immortal journey" that Rukmini undertook from Arunachal Pradesh to Gujarat to marry Lord Krishna. The coverage, which was broadcast on television and social media sites, demonstrated color, diversity, and "unity," with the latter achieved through bringing together the East and West under the Union Ministry of Culture's slogan "Ek Bharat Shreshtha Bharat" (One India, Great India).

Many versions of this ancient story abound though it is most popularly told in the ninth-century *Bhagavata Purana*, a classical source for Krishna devotees. It is a story of Rukmini's defiance against arranged marriage, "self-invited abduction," and how Krishna and Rukmini elope together against the wishes of her family (Pauwels 2007, 407). In another earlier version, the *Harivamsa Purana*, Rukmini is instead a victim of Krishna's raid (Pauwels 2007, 408). Two sixteenth-century texts about Rukmini, the *Rukmini Mangala* and *Kisan Rukmini ri Veli*, provide competing explanations concerning whether it was "abduction" or "elopement" and the role of Rukmini in deciding her own fate (Austin 2018; Coleman 2003; Pauwels 2007).

During the mela in Gujarat in 2018, a new version of the Rukmini story came to light that involved Arunachal Pradesh. The most popular version of the Krishna-Rukmini story is portrayed as being from Maharashtra, in the western part of the country (Austin 2018). Therefore, the reactions to connecting Krishna and Rukmini to Arunachal were particularly poignant. Some were incandescent that such a story—that Rukmini was allegedly from the Idu Mishmi community—had found its way into the national headlines. They accused the Sangh of engineering this connection and of "cultural appropriation."[1] Questions were raised regarding the veracity of the Arunachal version of Krishna and Rukmini as ancient lore and instead point to its recent invention. This is how "a worried citizen" reported it to the *Arunachal Times*:

> Around the 70s, Christian missionaries started making inroads into Arunachal. To counter it, the Hindu rightwing groups, with the patronage of the then central government, started this theory of Rukmini being Idu. The presence of Parsuram Kund and Bismaknagar, which has a connection with Hindu mythology, near the Idu belt gave further fillip to this story. But there is no historical or scientific evidence to support it. The union government is distorting tribal history by promoting this kind of imaginary story.[2]

Rasto Mena, public relations secretary of the Idu Mishmi Cultural and Literary Society (IMCLS), was more circumspect and argued for rapprochement, primarily as a way to foster national integration. Moji Riba, a notable filmmaker and cultural activist from Arunachal Pradesh, argues that whether the story's historicity is accurate or not is not the point. Rather, what we are witnessing, he suggests, is the larger process of the "appropriation of folklore" in the service of national integration.[3] One must be alert to the various ways in which folklore and the "objectification of culture" (Handler 1988; Longkumer 2015a) have been pressed into political service. To bring the past to life and to argue for national oneness comprise an old story, which reinvents itself, over and over again (see Comaroffs 2009).

Whatever the true nature of the story—myth, fabrication, or invention—it brings into focus a larger geopolitical dimension, especially the existential threat of China to the borders of the Indian nation-state. The Arunachal chief minister, Pema Khandu, explicitly addressed this issue during the

Figure 2.1. Arunachal version of Krishna and Rukmini. Photo courtesy of Prem Mikhu. Reprinted with permission.

mela: "We watch in news channels today that some other country is claiming some part of Northeast. But nobody can change the history and the ancient history says that Arunachal was not a separate state but entire Northeast was one. For centuries, we have been with India, mainland India. This is our strength."[4] The governor of Arunachal Pradesh, B. D. Mishra, echoed Khandu's refrain.

> You are here on the western border of India and we are from the eastern border, 3,500 kilometres away. But this distance has always remained connected.

If somebody from the other side of our border claims that Arunachal belongs to them, they are grossly wrong because if our princess could come here 5,000 years ago and you could make her the queen, it clearly means Arunachal has always been with India and will continue to be so.[5]

There was much riding on this mela, with even the prime minister backing it through his tweets and retweets. So what can we take away from this Madhavpur Mela? How can we read the various comments from variegated sources that challenge our conventional understandings of time, space, myth, and history? How is the Northeast imagined through this mela, and what intriguing questions does this raise regarding place and indeed place-making? This chapter examines these questions by placing them at the heart of the analysis of how the Sangh are utilizing what historians such as Pierre Nora (1989) and Michel de Certeau (1988) call the *problématique* of history—that of reconstructing the past and how "a lacuna of history makes the production of a *culture* both possible and necessary: a collective epos, a legend, a tradition" (de Certeau 1988, 324–25; italics in original).

In recent years, a growing number of studies of the Northeast of India have emerged (Barbora 2015; Baruah 1999, 2007; Karlsson 2011; Kikon 2019; McDuie-Ra 2016, 2012; S. Misra 2011; Thomas 2016; Wouters 2018a) that challenge the conventional understanding of the region and are either dominated by security perspectives and national developmental projects or viewed through an orientalist lens of primitivism. James C. Scott's (1998) phrase "seeing like the state" is certainly applicable to this postindependence gaze toward the region. These new studies show nuance and sensitivity toward distinct and various indigenous voices. My aim, however, is to view the region mostly through the eyes of the Sangh protagonists. Inasmuch as there are local variations to how the Sangh approach different states, their ideological sights are programmed largely toward a uniform and singular vision of the Northeast as one. This chapter suggests that there are no accurate versions of a Northeast map that provide a bird's-eye view of where places lie, where monuments are erected, or where cosmic shards reverberate. Maps are visual text, stories, cultural artefact, sonic waves, and political guides, plotted along paths by generations, either to leave traces, to act as mnemonic devices, or to commandeer empires. Like the uprooted tree that no longer guides the traveler along a familiar path, maps are ever changing. By looking at the ways Hindutva engages in the spatial history of the region, this chapter complements the overall theme of the book and the politics of becoming.

The key questions the chapter asks are as follows: What kinds of practices and techniques are used to inscribe an Indic presence in the region? What sorts of names, places, stories, artefacts, and natural features of a landscape bring to focus the art of governing a region that has historically questioned its links with India? Arguing for a more nuanced way of understanding modern cartography as a complex system of knowledge making and place experiencing, crafted under certain cultural habits and practices, Tim Ingold reminds us that the "world of our experience is a world suspended in movement, that is continually coming into being as we—through our own movement—contribute to its formation" (2000, 242). I will show how the Sangh make two points concerning this "formation." First, one must not be preoccupied with the fine-grained details about places. Rather, establishing a direction by plotting "a course from one *location* to another in *space*" (Ingold 2000, 219; italics in original) establishes a map. One of the Sangh workers, Vijay, suggests that once certain geographical reference points are established—like Pragjyotishpura (represented as Guwahati in Assam) and Lohit River (in Arunachal Pradesh) mentioned in the Mahabharata—then it is easy to encompass the region spatially. Vijay continues, "Behind Pragjyotishpura are the eastern mountains [Himalayas], and in the eastern mountain there is a river. Location and roots we get, but the place we don't know. We cannot say exactly this is the place. But the roots we get." With the starting point located, now you plot the order. Vijay's reasoning is consistent with the way spatial imagination is understood in the Mahabharata. The noted Indologist Sheldon Pollock reminds us how space is marked not by a precision but by its indeterminacy, perplexity, and exoticism, "where the culture of Sanskrit, and its message, a kind of political power, have application" (1998, 16). It is this geospheric power that leads us in search for more precision.

Finer details are also important, especially when it comes to mapping certain place-names and place-worlds, indexed with Sanskrit. Much of this naming process is then tied in with conjuring a presence from the silences and absences of history. Acts of naming and place-making are intimately tied to how the Sangh relate to and thus possess the region. Similarly, one can imagine these descriptions as a "universe of objects and events," as place-worlds, where a particular historical or mythical absence is brought into being (Basso 1996, 6). Using a dominant model of routes—from monastic journeys to the expanding cultural map of India realized through Akhand Bharat (undivided India), Greater India, and "One India, Great India"—the Sangh in effect create roots, in the sense of both rooted in land and rooted in history, especially if we are to acknowledge, along with Ingold, that "places do not have locations but histories" (2000, 219). I will show how specific pathways and journeys, marked by Sanskrit inscriptions all over the region and extending eastward toward Southeast Asia, act as traces of Indian civilization. As Michel de Certeau notes, "The map . . . [is] a totalising stage on which elements of diverse origins are brought together to form a tableau of a 'state' of geographical knowledge" (1984, 121). For the Sangh, this method of using cartography transforms the region as India, a continuous, integral, and totalizing force.

THE SANGH AND THE NORTHEAST

In the larger Indian imagination, the Northeast represents, both visually and culturally, the margins of the Indian state. The region is situated at the crossroads of South and Southeast Asia, having shared cultural affinities, and largely removed from the political capitals of Delhi, Dhaka, and Rangoon. It is this affinity—based on ethnic coalition, common oral traditions, and racial anthropological kinship—that has led to the fight for separation from "non Mongolian communities that dominate the Indian subcontinent" (Hazarika 1995, xvi). Hazarika (1995, xvi) argues that their looks, dances, and shawls are more like their counterparts in Thailand, Laos, and Vietnam, rather than men and women in Bihar, Bengal, and Uttar Pradesh. Stories that point to the difference in the region's Mongoloid phenotype in contrast to a non-Mongoloid other are

common. Drawing on Sumathi Ramaswamy's (2001) visualization of India as bodyscape imbued with nationalist passion through Bharat Mata
(Mother India) that imagines the map as alive and not a desocialized
space, Jelle Wouters and Tanka Subba similarly extend this metaphor
into "face-scape," or a "physiognomic map" where the idea of India and
what an Indian may look like is the "somatic embodiment that represents
the Indian nation" (2013, 127). They argue that the Mongoloid phenotypes
have not found a place in this "Indian face" and by extension the "idea of
India," although these are highly diverse and inclusive concepts. In a way,
this kind of mapping technique that visualizes the nation as an imagined
community relies, they argue, on the conventional assumptions of what a
cocitizen might look like (2013, 127).

Most of the Hindutva activists that I have met are aware of this historical hurt and the bewildering diversity of this "Mongoloid region" yet
are absolutely certain that the fundamental unity, the age-old concept of
Bharat as one, is there to be discovered. According to the Sangh, if we
rely on the post-1947 map to form our geopolitical reality, the Northeast is forever separate from mainland India. Remembering the idea of
Akhand Bharat (undivided India), a Vivekananda Kendra worker, Narendra Joshi, says:[6]

> When Tibet, Brahmadesh [Burma], Bangladesh, Nepal, Bhutan, Pakistan,
> Afghanistan, Sri Lanka, Indonesia, Malaysia, Java, Sumatra, etc., are all no
> more with us; then naturally North-east looks as one extreme corner....
> Therefore the first and foremost step in thinking about any problem of
> Northeast . . . will be keeping the map of real India, immortal India, Akhand
> Bharata in our dreams, in our brains, in our hearts, in our words and eventu-
> ally in the reality. (2000, 8)

Joshi highlights the problem that Hazarika (1995) and Wouters and Subba
(2013) pose on the basis of ethnicity, cultural distinctiveness, and national
allegiance. The Sangh in general agree that many in the Northeast feel
un-Indian, and a sense of alienation has come about due to mismanage-
ment and heavy-handed state diktats, like militarization, in the region.
For example, the Sangh acknowledge that ethnic identity in the region is

connected with the Mongoloids, the Chinese, Tibetan, or Burmese, but never with mainland India. Joshi says that many in the Northeast will say, "'We are Mongoloids'—this will be told by even those who may not be knowing where Mongolia is" (2000, iii). The second factor is the call for cultural distinctiveness with phrases like "we were never a part of India" or "we were never ruled by anyone" (Joshi 2000, iii). This is especially true, the Sangh argue, with the different ethnonational movements that have emerged, in part, to resist the hegemony of the Indian state. Third is the question of allegiance and patriotism, often siding with China, the United States, and Pakistan but not with India. Joshi represents this sentiment thus, spoken by a "Naga representative" to a Chinese premier in the 1960s: "If China attacks India, we will help China" (2000, iii). One of the boldest and sharpest articulations of these differences, alluded to by the Sangh, comes from A. Z. Phizo, the leader of the Naga National Council (NNC), who expresses the incongruity of the "Mongoloid race" with that of the "Indian race" in his 1951 plebiscite speech in Kohima:

> The Nagas have nothing to do with India. And the Indians have nothing to do with Nagaland. This is the exact position. Historically, Nagas and the Indians did not have a common tradition. Racially, Nagas belong to the Mongolian family while the Indians belong to entirely a different race of their own. Politically, neither the Nagas nor the Indians know each other. . . .
>
> As it is, there is nothing in common between the Nagas and the Indians. The difference is too varied, the feeling is too deep, and the attitude is too wide and too malignant for the two nations ever to think to live together in peace much less to become "Indian citizens".[7]

Now, much of Phizo's rhetoric may appear antediluvian particularly when the changing face of India and the rise of the educated middle-class with their concerns for jobs and access to better livelihoods may mean a shift in perspective from these earlier claims to nationalism on the basis of difference (Longkumer 2018a; McDuie-Ra 2012). But the point for the Sangh is that the scale of misrepresentation of the region, whether intentional or unintentional, is accepted blindly, Joshi argues, because "we [mainland Indians] are really very ignorant . . . to this part of Punyabhumi [holy land] Bharat" (2000, iii). There are two aspects here noteworthy for examination that are nourished by ideas of place-making and through acts of naming that are, as Paul Carter observes, paradigmatically an act of possession and making it one's own: "By the act of place-naming, space is transformed symbolically into a place, that is, a space with a history" (1987, xxiv). To make sense of Carter's observations and how these relations are made intelligible and habitable in the language and story of belonging, I return to the case of Krishna and Rukmini.

RUKMINI, HISTORY, AND MYTH

"For the first time ever," the BJP culture minister Mahesh Sharma said, "the festival will celebrate the immortal journey which Rukmini undertook from Arunachal Pradesh to Gujarat with Lord Krishna."[8] This Madhavpur Mela was organized under the larger idea of "One India, Great India," said the culture minister, arguing, "The purpose of this integration is to bring various parts of the country especially the Northeast, close to each other . . . announced by Prime Minister Narendra Modi."[9]

In this case, the Northeast represents Rukmini, the bride's family. N. Biren Singh, the chief minister of Manipur, greets the audience in Madhavpur with this in mind, though from a male gaze:

> I have come from the Northeast, China border. I will speak in Northeast Hindi; please bear with me. . . . I want to say that we are from the girl's side. Give us respect today. Keep us on a pedestal because Lord Krishna abducted our girl [*loud cheers from the audience*]. We have not come to fight, but a wedding has to happen. Without a wedding, we will not go back.[10]

Biren Singh then goes on to give a geohistorical lesson to the audience. During Krishna's time, he says, Arunachal Pradesh, Assam, and Manipur were not geopolitical entities, as we know them, but one large landmass that comprises the current Northeast. In fact, he says the westward Gujarat near Pakistan and eastward Northeast near China were traversed by Lord Krishna, creating "Bharat into one Bharat." This is how he ends his speech:

> In between, we didn't have the chance to meet politically and socially. Today, a godsent person born on the soil of Gujarat, like Prime Minister Narendra Modi, has brought Bharat together and made it into one Bharat. He is showing

to the world now that the Northeast is part of Bharat. He is working. This kind of opportunity that he is giving to us in the Northeast—we will not let it slip away. We will give our life for one Bharat. We will sacrifice for one Bharat.

These emotional and patriotic remarks by Biren Singh highlight two important aspects of how the Northeast has been viewed. The region has seen numerous nationalist movements that have, to a large extent, questioned the historical and contemporary spatial continuity of what Sunil Khilnani (2016) has called "the idea of India." The fact that the two geographical nodal points—the East and the West—have been united under the leadership of Narendra Modi is celebrated by Singh, however febrile and contested the idea.[11] While Singh's speech develops the idea of oneness through mythological time, Kiren Rijiju, the state home minister in the BJP government, evokes the temporality of the daily rhythm of eating, sleeping, and waking to juxtapose the vastness, and yet oneness, of India. He says,

> We [in Gujarat] have just progressed into the evening while in Arunachal Pradesh people have already had their food and slept. Our sun sets there by five to five thirty P.M. In the villages, people eat, drink, and do whatever they have to do and sleep off by six thirty P.M. Our country is so huge. We can understand this by the fact that a difference of two hours means so many different things in one country. Arunachal Pradesh is in the eastern corner, and we are standing here on the western shores of Gujarat—there is such a huge space between the two places, but today our gathering and coming together here at Madhavpur Ghed Fair shows that we may be geographically distant, but we are one.

Rijiju reminds the audience to think about the geographical spread of India. While the natural rhythms of day and night mark one region from another, it is worth ruminating about, he says, how Lord Krishna traveled from Arunachal Pradesh, married Rukmini, and finally reached Gujarat. Rijiju confesses, "I don't get sleep thinking about this!" Lord Krishna's activities, argues Rijiju, question the idea that India as "one country" was created only during colonial times. Instead, "India [has] existed [for] epochs," marked by this conjugal union. This Krishna-Rukmini connection, suggests Naba Kumar Doley (Assam's culture minister and another of the attendees at this mela), is a way to counter the isolationism of the region. Even though several political movements have argued for separation, this marriage demonstrates a divine link, according to Doley.

In the Madhavpur Mela, it is interesting how relations are explored through marriage. Marriage, at least in the South Asian context, has a rich history that establishes relations of affinity where concepts such as elopement, abduction, and kinship, including what is considered legitimate or illegitimate, have contextual meanings (Mody 2008; Uberoi 1994). How does one make relations through marriage that cement a geohistorical connectedness from time immemorial? In thinking about relations, Marilyn Strathern (1995) argues that the idea of "relations" as a category is familiar but largely understudied and taken for granted in social theory. She argues that relations are not only pregiven (through blood) but may also be forged and made. Concerning relations, one can minimize or magnify "the kinds of connections" (Strathern 1995, 10) in various ways—such as familial/conceptual, ideas/persons, and concrete/abstract. Once scale is introduced into this mix, relations can be broken down into two further phenomena. First, the "holographic effect" is when "the concept of relation can be applied to any order of connection" (17). The scope of the "holographic effect" is pluralized to include manifold factors not affected by scale: "The demonstration of a relationship, whether through resemblance, cause and effect or contiguity, reinforces the fact that through relational practices—classification, analysis, comparison—relations can be demonstrated" (18). The second property of relations requires other elements to complete it, making the connecting functions "complex" (18). It can be relations between two entities (relation between things) or relations that exist "within" it (things as relations) (18–19). The key for Strathern in these relational modes is the facility of the relation to skip between scales and also maintain its distinctiveness. What does this reading of relations tell us about the Krishna-Rukmini episode?

First, the attempt at connecting noncontiguous—indeed distantly separated—geographical locales via the story of Krishna and Rukmini's conjugal union concerns establishing kinship between two families; the analogy used here is between East and West. It is holographic and complex in the sense that the relation is made regardless of scale: Did Gujarat and Arunachal actually exist in the time of Krishna and Rukmini? Was there such a thing as India? And was the Arunachali Rukmini actually Rukmini? Second, regardless, these relations are made due to the promiscuity of relations. There may not be an actual connection, but once an idea of a relation has been conjured up, one is already trapped in that relation, despite even opposition to it. Third, ideas and persons (national unity, Krishna and Rukmini) are fused in innovative ways that show how (the forming of) relations may be coercive. (After all Rukmini was abducted.) This not only creates relations, but relations give rise to refusal and failure too, such as when Christianity enters the conversation regarding indigenous nationalisms, where a different order of relations is imagined without the Indic provenance (see the introduction and Chapter 4). The NNC President too rejected this relation in his plebiscite speech in 1951 when he asks, "What connection is there between the two people?"[12]

Finally, although a key theme of Strathern's work is the way scale operates to maintain the distinctiveness of the relation, relations might also suggest a way in which differences are effaced and even erased in order to achieve "sameness." A "political" reading of Strathern's discussion when applied to the Krishna-Rukmini episode elevates our understanding of relations and how they function as myth and history.

Some contrast myth as manufactured stories for instrumental reasons with history as recorded facts, while others argue that this entire Rukmini story is an imposition by the Sangh to make connections with Arunachal. One immediate connection that readers may make is with the historical and mythic reading of the Ramjanmabhumi controversy in Ayodhya that saw the destruction of a mosque in 1992 to build a Hindu temple, supposedly in the spot where the god Ram was born (Bhattacharya 1993; Gopal 1993; Ludden 1996; van der Veer 1994). This is not the place to rehash these arguments but simply to point out, along with Neeladri Bhattacharya, that

> we cannot counterpoise history to myth as truth to falsehood. There are different modes of knowledge, varying ways of understanding the world, or-

dering one's life and defining one's actions. If myths convince people, we must understand why they do so. If fabulous stories circulate and light up the popular imagination, we cannot merely demonstrate the fabulous character of such stories; we must know why they circulate, why they play on popular imagination. (1993, 122)

Similarly, my aim in the next few paragraphs is not to exclude or override the legitimacy of one over the other but simply to show how myth and history overlap and move along time and space, affecting both societal and political mechanisms.

During my lengthy conversations with different people and groups in Arunachal over this issue, the general feeling was expressed under three main themes. First, the process through which the Rukmini story unfolds—whether fact, fabrication, or rumor—has the potential to become accepted as history within the Idu Mishmi tradition. Anil, an Idu Mishmi academic at the local Rajiv Gandhi University in Itanagar, told me that he was skeptical of this story because it is absent in their oral tradition. He only remembers hearing these stories in the 1970s in a school run by Bharat Vikas Parishad in his local area of Roing. He even recalls that there were efforts made by the RSS to link an Idu character, Ano-Taju, with Krishna. When local shamans started studying Ano, they told the RSS that Ano could not be Krishna. Atege, another Idu Mishmi activist working for the IMCLS, said that although some people object to the story, most in the grassroots have gradually accepted that Rukmini is an Idu princess and that she married Krishna. Although Atege dismisses his village people unfairly as gullible, falling prey to any whiff of authority, these Indic connections that I have already discussed go on to take shape and become established as fact, accepted even by scholars. The key though—which Vijay, a Vivekananda Kendra activist, thinks is central to these stories—is a sense of ownership. It is helpful to recall how Michael Jackson elaborates on this theme: "To reconstitute events in a story is no longer to live those events in passivity, but to actively rework them, both in dialogue with others and within one's own imagination" (2002, 15).

Without simply joining the bandwagon, Vijay was more wary. He pointed out that there are many versions of this story—in Vidarbha

(Maharashtra), in Gujarat, and in Arunachal. There is also a mismatch, he tells me, in the archaeological evidence that places the Rukmini story (though largely undetermined and around the tenth century) in Bhismaknagar in Arunachal Pradesh. The Rukmini story, he tells me, is over five thousand years old. But the significance of the power of these stories exceeds these contradictions. Focus on the stories, and "this is how myth becomes history," Vijay tells me. Second, the larger geopolitical dimension of this story plays a part in giving small communities like the Idu Mishmi social capital, while becoming part of the larger Hindu universe. It may be Hindu absorption of tribal practices, Atege told me, but the important distinction he makes is that it is not "us who are trying to assimilate with the Hindus; it is the Hindus who are trying to assimilate with us." Unlike Anil, who is doubtful, Atege is more open and accepting of this Hindutva influence. He says:

> Thing is that this is a Hindu mythology that Rukmini is an Idu. This is not an Idu story. It is a Hindu/RSS story. Idus are accepting it but they are not imposing it. It is the mainstream Hindus who are imposing it. If this is the case, then there is no problem. Then we can say that after all we are all Indians, and if they are accepting us as a part of them, it is good for nationalism and for the nation.

Although I am unsure about Atege's exact political leanings, he has attended schools run by Vivekananda Kendra Vidyalaya (VKV) and is therefore conversant in the language of nationalism. Not many agree with Atege, however, but rather see in these views the larger process of Hindu hegemony that I discuss in the next chapter. When Rukmini becomes accepted as part of the larger Hindu cosmology, both Anil and Atege imagine how this process might bring about social and political capital. "When I say, 'Rukmini [from Arunachal] is my sister,' I gain much more," emphasizes Atege. The power of relation and the way names inherit linguistic capital are evident in Rukmini's instant recognition. Finally, in order to strengthen national borders (especially against China), these stories are told to establish kin relations with other parts of India. "There is one Arunachali version of the story," Atege tells me, "that is trending on Facebook." Rukmini goes to Dwarka in Gujarat to attend a wedding, where she meets Krishna and falls in love. But because Rukmini is already betrothed to Shishupala by her father, Bhismak, and brother, Rukmo (also Rukmi), the situation is complicated. Krishna ignores these cultural interdicts and defeats both the father and the brother for Rukmini's hand in marriage. This version, though edited down and simplified, is the commonly accepted traditional narrative. However, in the Arunachali version, the story takes a turn. Atege continues:

> At Malinithan [an archaeological site with ruins of Hindu temples] there was a marriage certification authority. So Krishna had to go to Malinithan and get a marriage certificate; otherwise, he couldn't pass. So Krishna goes to Malinithan and comes across the Modi people. Rukmini starts crying, "None of my family is there to do my Kanyadan [gift of a virgin from father to husband] so how can I go to Mathura [in Uttar Pradesh—believed to be the birthplace of Krishna]." Then, Modi people came and said, "We Modi and Idu are like brothers, so don't worry. We will go to Gujarat for your Kanyadan!" And that is how they went to Gujarat and those Modi people never came back to Arunachal. Those who stayed there eventually became the Modi people of Gujarat, and hence Narendra Modi! So Narendra Modi has lineage from Milan village [in Arunachal]. This is how things can be created.

The kind of relations envisaged in this narrative suggests kinship between the Modi people of the East and the West. This holographic and complex aspect of relations makes any connection possible, which then slowly becomes "fact." An internet search about Malinithan or Arunachal Pradesh will turn up stories in Trip Advisor or Wikipedia of Rukmini and Krishna, replicating connections until it becomes naturalized.

The Sangh are aware of the power stories have, especially in societies that privilege orality. No wonder the Krishna-Rukmini story took hold of the national imagination, making vital relations along the way. If we are to view this episode variously as a story and a myth, it is instructive to recall Roland Barthes's striking remark about how myth economizes our language to a level of simplicity: "It abolishes the complexity of human acts, it gives them the *simplicity of essences*. . . . It organises a world which is without contradictions because it is without depth, a world wide open and wallowing in the evident, it establishes a blissful clarity: things appear to mean something by themselves" (1993, 143; italics added). Perhaps

Roland Barthes and Razzeko Dele's views align when Dele thoughtfully reflects on this controversy in the local newspaper in Arunachal Pradesh:

> The ongoing phenomenon itself manifests how myths are created and rela-
> tion forged. This is the way myths spread and new bonding begins. Every-
> thing can be related to myth as it appeals to the people in general and makes
> them feel connected. For instance, the Bnei Menashe (group comprising of
> Mizo, Kuki and Chin people) believe that they are lost tribe of Israel and
> many of them have migrated to Israel. Apart from the cultural aspect, the
> Indian government it seems is building the narrative to counter the Chinese
> claim over the region. China asserts that most part of Arunachal is Southern
> Tibet, which again is a crystal clear lie. The concept of "Akhand Bharat", a
> united India is to show the world that the whole India is one culturally, inte-
> grated since the earliest time.[13]

The act of claiming stories as myths allows the Sangh to connect the region with mythopolitical certainty. Slowly but inevitably these connections are naturalized. The Rukmini story and the way relations are forged is one instance of how the region, brimming with mythology, is reconceived. In the next few sections, I discuss how the Sangh envisage the landscape through the process of place-naming that creates familiar patterns of relations.

PROVINC(E)IALIZING THE NORTHEAST

I first met and interviewed a senior member of the RSS, Sanjay, in Guwa-hati in 2015. He had been working in Assam since 1976. He emphasized that for the "Sangh the entire Northeast is one *prant* [province]. . . . "Be-fore, we used the term *Bor Axom* [undivided Assam], which consisted of the seven sisters, a colorful culture. We started work keeping that in mind: that all the people and communities who live here live without conflict, live together and live as Hindus, that we become Bor Axom once again and culture is revived. This is the vision we kept in mind while starting Sangh work." Undivided Assam is now separated into five (not seven) states—Assam, Nagaland, Mizoram, Arunachal Pradesh, and Meghalaya. Tripura and Manipur were not a part of Assam but were independent princely provinces that later merged with India. But it is not a surprise, however, that the Sangh would see the entirety of the Northeast within the frame of Assam, as Assam is the largest of the states and the region that has had many recorded confluences with Indic, Tibeto-Burman, Mon-Khmer, and trans-Himalayan cultures (I. Chatterjee 2013; Saikia 2004; Saikia and Baishya 2017; Zou and Kumar 2011).

Indeed, Assam is often seen as "predominantly Hindu," where the *Kalika Purana* (a text in the Shakti tradition) was composed in the tenth century and where local versions of the Ramayana were written in the fourteenth century by a Kachari King (Goswami 1967, 20–24). Assam is also home to Sankardev, a religious icon, popular with the Sangh, who lived in the fifteenth and sixteenth centuries. He led a neo-Vaishnavite movement and established *sattras* (or monasteries) all over Assam that were largely anti-Brahmanical (the Sangh rhetoric does not mention this fact, simply that he celebrated being born in Bharatvarsh) and sought to attract people from different caste, religious, and tribal backgrounds (Bhattacharjee 2016; also Deka 2005; U. Misra 1999). The mention of Pragjyotispura and Kamarupa, represented by the Sangh as the ancient and medieval names of Assam, which are drawn from the Ramayana and Mahabharata and in the Puranas, is intended to demonstrate that Assam was "essentially a Hindu-province and was well-connected to the rest of 'Hindustan'" (Bhattarcharjee 2016, 81). A Vivekananda Kendra worker, Vijay, further suggested that one could link the Kirata people of the Mahabharata with the region. Offering physiognomic traits, such as "they are short, color is pale, their muscles are strong," he is certain of this mythogeographic link.

Narendra Joshi (2000) similarly mentions the Northeast as a land of Tantra. Tracing this genealogy primarily from India via Tibet and toward the foothills of the Himalayas (Nepal, Arunachal Pradesh, and Assam [read: undivided Assam]), he notes their prevailing influence through the material artefacts that preserve its Indic provenance (and not its Chinese one!):

> All over the Buddhist area of Arunachal, there are prayer flags, chortens, prayer wheels, stone walls, etc. Same mantra is repeated all over the Himalayan border, "OM MANI PADME HUM": Hail! The jewel (grand Lama?) in the lotus. And this mantra is written in Assamese script (very close to Devanagari) *not in the Chinese script*. Om is considered as the essence of the Vedas. It is the beginning of all the mantras. From Om this world was created. (It is interesting

to note that Adis [of Arunachal Pradesh] believe that the world was created from a word: Keyum.) (Joshi 2000, 17; emphasis added)

It is hard to track how these eclectic ideas were developed, synthesized, and deployed to provide a focus on a series of events with definite Indic articulations. One can only speculate as to their strong nationalist tinge and the overt geopolitical ring to the observations: Arunachal is a part of India, not China. The way the religious aspects have been influential in how the history of the region connects with Hindu-Buddhist practices, and thus the unity of Bharat, is evident in the way various scholars also illustrate these links, establishing a paradigm. For example, the noted Tantric scholar Hugh Urban situates Assam as both the "motherland of Sakta Hinduism" and "widely regarded as the heartland and perhaps original homeland of Hindu Tantra, which spread throughout South Asia from roughly the 4th or 5th century onwards" (2009, 17). This often gives the impression that Assam is intimately connected with practices largely consistent with Indic civilization and is a connection that the Sangh will emphasize with assurance.

NAMING AND SPATIALIZING HISTORY

At the crux of history as possible and necessary, how does one create an understanding of the region's geohistory in relation to that of the rest of India? It is in these "geographical imaginations," the geographer Derek Gregory argues, that naming becomes "a way of bringing the landscape into textual presence" and where these "practices created a network of places within which events could unfold in time, in which history could begin to take place once it had *taken* place" (1994, 172; italics in original). This toponymic labor, argues the historian Boddhisattva Kar (2004, 2), was widespread in colonial India, where "names of persons and places functioned as stable signposts in an otherwise opaque and slippery network of shared narratives." Empty space had to be reinscribed with the valor of events, associated with laudable persons, ritualized through auspicious landscapes, and narrated through epic plots that provide a mappable spatial history. What Kar suggests is that this process—of plotting places with precolonial textual traditions—benefitted three primary audiences. First, it provided the colonial regime with a sense of security, underwritten with ideological motivation, knowing that their governance of India illustrated a seamless composite narrative (Hamilton 1820). Second, it allowed regional elites and intellectuals from all over India to promulgate their stories and customs and give them a place in "the great Indian tradition." And finally, it provided a space for Indology (both textual and material [for example, archaeological] studies) to flourish so that in the end it produced a highly Sanskritized version—because it required textual specialists who were highly educated, but inadvertently also Brahmins—of Indian history based on an idea of "Brahmanical geography" (Kar 2004, 3). The reconstitution of history, Bharatiya history, deployed by the Sangh speaks to some of these issues that relegate the region not simply as an appendage to the great Indic civilization but in some sense at its very core.

In tracing the genealogy of place-names in Assam through a fine-grained textual analysis of epic-puranic and other sources produced by administrative officials, scholars, and local intelligentsia, Kar (2004) argues that the whole idea of how the Indian past is imagined through the system of chronology is itself questionable. Scholars in other contexts also acknowledge this point. Examining the rich data on how chronology benefits those in power, Paul Carter's work *The Road of Botany Bay* reminds us of the precarity of these interplays when spatial history merges into a "new nationalism" that remains as insular as the one it replaced (here from British power to Australia, where the Aboriginal past, especially, is absent).

> The new chronology remains a form of legitimation. *It continues to confuse routes with roots.* When archaeologists "push back" the date of the first aboriginal settlement, who gains? To be sure, our legal preoccupation with issues of priority ensures each new date some political leverage. More profoundly, though, the increase of knowledge increases our control. For it is we Europeans who associate antiquity with "a rich cultural heritage". In discovering the Aboriginal past, we demonstrate our piety towards the household gods of our own history. . . . The very elusiveness of any convincing cause-and-effect pattern becomes, paradoxically, evidence of a special destiny. (Carter 1987, xviii; italics added)

This eloquent rendering by Paul Carter in the context of imperialism and Australia suggests three vital connections with this chapter. First, the idea of establishing a historical chronology of events consonant with Indian traditions is about control and legitimation. Unlike Carter, Joshi (2000) argues that routes and roots are not confusing. Rather, he says, "route to the roots is always through darkness" (2000, i). The other side of discovery is illuminated with light. Second, the indigenous past of the region must be rendered into knowledge, knowable to those veritable compilers of scholarship, forming an archive that can be compared and made intelligible by drawing on established textual traditions. Sorting through the haze that preceded clear outlines, this search for stability of names to render the past coherent "continued to govern the new historical imagination even when it claimed to break free from the absurd elasticity of etymology" (Kar 2004, 41). Finally, the cause-and-effect pattern is highly unstable in the Indological discussions, which could only suggest a revival that is synthesized and syndicated, a concern that is not only confined to this chapter but discussed in the next one as well. Although the people in the Northeast are not physically invisible in these narratives, they are culturally so; this leaves open the question of cause and effect that departs from the conventional workings of history and how the frontier region's "map-made emptiness" is "written over" and inhabited by a network of names and places that gradually colonize their provinces (Carter 1987, xx–xxi).

Similarly, the local Assamese intelligentsia were also preoccupied with honoring Assam as a respectable place within the aegis of history, and indeed within the geohistorical Indic imagination. For example, nineteenth-century scholars like Anundram Borooah argued that Guwahati, the capital of Assam, was the site of the ancient Pragjyotisapura (City of Eastern Light) and that the district of Kamrup was the ancient Kamarupa (Form of Desire), where Krishna fought Naraka in the Mahabharata, though many scholars were uncertain of these genealogical and etymological claims. This epic-puranic connection is also pursued by other twentieth-century scholars, such as A. C. Agarwala, who not only placed the acme of Aryan civilization in Assam, having arrived from Tibet, but also maintained it was from Assam that the Aryans "migrated to other places in Burma and Northern India" (quoted in Kar 2004, 29).

What we see in these examples is the remarkable use of sources and influences, sometimes haphazardly drawn from epic-puranic texts to argue for an intimate history of the region within the larger Indological imagination. This is due in part to the expanding British Empire and the questions that remained about its eastern flanks—Assam and eastward—which were frontier spaces that tended to lean toward the fabulous. This area's Mongoloid character had to be reimagined and sanitized to fit the narrative of the larger Indological center.

What are some of these place-names, and how are they envisioned? The case of Assam has been alluded to earlier, and this invariably dominates the discussion, but "it is not true that the whole history of Northeast is only that of plain areas, or only of Assam. During those centuries the whole area was considered as Assam and the adjoining hills were converted into independent states in the recent decades" (Joshi 2000, 37). Joshi's view is consistent with the Sangh idea of the region as one province revealed through relations and place-names:

Nagaland: First, of course—"Vyasotchhishtam jagatsarvam": Mahabharata: Arjuna married Nagkanya Ulupi [allegedly a Naga princess].

Manipur: Arjuna [a character in the Mahabharata] married a Manipuri princess Chitrangada; their son Babhruvahan was a great hero and defeated his own father. He also established a kingdom of Assam.

Meghalaya: This area particularly Jayantiya hills was known as Narirajya, or Pranavijaya Rajya. Markendeya Purana and other Puranas also use the same name. Griva Kamakhya is the famous temple; the shoulder of the Mother fell here.[14] Hatakeshwara is the huge Shiva temple built by Hataka. His son Guhaka installed the image of Krishna, Balarama killing Kamsa: Kamsanisudana.

Tipperah (Now part of Tripura): In Barak valley, (Cachar hills, Lushai hills, Karimganj, South Sylhet and Tipperah Hills) had mixed worship of 14 Gods: Shiva, Durga, Vishnu, Lakshmi, Saraswati, Kartikeya, Ganesha, Brahma, Sea, Ganges, Fire, Cupid, Himalayas, all these were represented by small earthen symbols.

Arunachal Pradesh: The land of the rising Sun? Parashuramkunda, Rukmininagar, Bhishmakanager, the whole Kundil valley civilisation,

Malinithan, Mayapur and Ita fort, Naksha parvat, Menga Mandir and other innumerable Shivalingas all over the land, forests, mountains, and valleys which till now are seen in dreams and excavated in the days. Famous Tawang monastery, other Gompas, Stupas of Buddhists spread all over the borders. (2000, 37–45; italics added)[15]

Like a priest enunciating spells, these incantations give birth to sacred geography, releasing sonic resonances onto the landscape. It names and occupies it. One may or may not know all these place-names and descriptions, requiring considerable verbal gymnastics to plough through them, but the Sanskrit tone has a particular ring to those for whom "naming words were forms of spatial punctuation, transforming space into an object of knowledge, something that could be explored and read" (Carter 1987, 67). The Sangh are not alone in imagining place-worlds; Christians too engage in naming (places such as Billy Graham Road, Hebron Camp, Don Bosco Road in Nagaland for instance), so marking them against the grammar of Hindu conquest. This discussion is reminiscent of Walter Benjamin's idea of a "linguistic cosmos," (2002, 522) whereby names take on an allegorical dimension. They are not simply arbitrary meanings but have a destiny and fate. One could even read this as an instance of what Mikhail Bakhtin has called "chronotopes," which are

> points in the geography of a community where time and space intersect and fuse. Time takes on flesh and becomes visible for human contemplation; likewise, space becomes charged and responsive to the movements of time and history and the enduring character of a people. . . . Chronotopes thus stand as monuments to the community itself, as symbols of it, as forces operating to shape its members' images of themselves. (1981, 7)

Bakhtin's observations on the cultural importance of geographical landmarks and the way their authority shapes discourse apply nicely to the ruminations of history that Joshi narrates. Here the spatial conceptions of history bear witness to the anchoring of these places to a time when things that brought fragmentation and forgetting happened, as if to say that these names have been revived against time's relentless fission. One must, however, keep in mind the rich tapestry of place-naming among indigenous communities themselves in the region. Nor must we marginalize orality over writing, which according to Gilles Deleuze and Felix Guattari is akin to "a dance on the earth, a drawing on a wall, a mark on the body [that] are a graphic system, a geo-graphism, a geography" (2000, 188). As I travel across the region, I am reminded of how place-worlds describe events and provide certain descriptions, such as those of a hill, a cliff's edge, a fallen tree, a living stone, as mnemonic devices that help revive memories and represent them.

However, throughout these writings, indigenous peoples have been excluded from this kind of mapping experience. Much of the mapping occurs over empty ground or blank space—and indigenous place-names are not rendered, their routes difficult to recover. In naming these places, not only is the country willed to its unity by drawing on established textual Sanskrit traditions, but also, in effect, there appears to be an erasure, a reconstitution of the modern place called Northeast India.

OF MOUNTAINS AND RIVERS

To explore some of these themes further, I return to the seminal text on Hindutva by V. D. Savarkar written in 1923. I show Hindutva's reach in the region both through Savarkar's geographical conception of it and how modern-day Sangh read them into the landscape, reinterpreting and giving flesh to Savarkar's ideas. The ideas of Hindutva were written a few decades before the Sangh started work in the Northeast. In fact, Savarkar did not write about the modern geopolitical entity called the Northeast of India. However, in Savarkar's work, the Himalayas feature as an eternal presence that gives Bharat its territorial shape and also its enduring unity. That is the indelible topographic reference point. He envisioned the breadth and length of the country through his use of the term *Sindhusthan* (or Hindustan), based on the idea of Saptasindhu (the seven rivers of the Indus River system). This designation, he argues, is even older than Bharatvarsha and the Emperor Bharat, who is gone, but the "Sindhu goes on forever," he says.

> Forever inspiring and fertilizing our sense of gratitude, vivifying our sense
> of pride, renovating the ancient memories of our race—a sentinel keeping

watch over the destinies of our people. It is the vital spinal cord that connects the remotest past to the remotest future. The name that associates and identifies our nation with a river like that, enlists nature on our side and bases our national life on a foundation, that is, so far as human calculation are concerned [*sic*], as lasting as eternity. (1969, 31)

He continues:

The word Sindhu in Sanskrit does not only mean the Indus but also the Sea which girdles the southern peninsula—so that this one word Sindhu points out almost all frontiers of the land at a single stroke. Even if we do not accept the tradition that the river Brahmaputra is only a branch of the Sindhu which falls into flowing streams on the eastern and western slopes of the Himalayas and thus constitutes both our eastern as well as western frontiers. Still it is indisputably true that it circumscribes our northern and western extremities in its sweep and so the epithet Sindhusthan calls up the image of our whole Motherland: the land that lies between Sindhu and Sindhu—from the Indus to the Seas. (1969, 31–32)

What is interesting in Savarkar's description is how natural symbols such as the dizzying heights of mountains and the rushing rapids of rivers carry the weight of geographical evidence; nature stays true to its course and does not change according to human whims. Sindhu's presence also implies the timelessness of the nation. Savarkar was not the only one extolling the natural features of the geographical remit of Bharat; other Indologists with a strong nationalistic bent were more precise in locating the region by appealing to topographical and nomological characteristics. Sindhusthan and Sapta Sindhu, whose location Savarkar associates with Bharat, are swiftly connected to the region with historical certainty. Paraphrasing the Indologist A. C. Agarwala's text *Notes on the Ancient History of Assam, Part 1: Vedic Period*, written in 1921, Kar says: "The famous Sapta Sindhu region was identified with Sadiya [in Assam], Ākāsa with the Aka Hills [Arunachal Pradesh], Bhūtasthāna with Bhutan and Dyouh with the Daphla Hills [Arunachal Pradesh]; the Bodos [tribe in Assam] were given to carry the name of Varuna and Dukku in the Abor Hills [Arunachal Pradesh]" (2004, 30).

One can pin down these idiosyncratic descriptions to the bracing immediacy of a familiar geography. The place-names (though largely around Assam and Arunachal Pradesh) evoke relation—peering into the time-space unknown to an emerging geopolitical reality, unravelling its future. Evidence is not hard to come by for those in the vanguard of preserving and protecting these frontier flanks. It is interesting that the act of naming itself, according to Savarkar, is determined by what others like to signify. "In fact," he says, "a name is called into existence for this very purpose" (1969, 15). Here it is helpful to recall the discussion between Paul Carter and David Malouf (1989) regarding frontiers and naming. They argue that frontiers are spaces where communication heightens because the "unknown" or "wilderness" (or wildness) needs to be domesticated as a cultural space that can be loved and described. In a sense, frontiers fructify in the meeting points, in the encounters, that produce "communication," and where all that is outside is obliterated and rendered same (Carter and Malouf 1989, 182). Names, Savarkar argues, are like the survival of the fittest, redolent memes that stand the test of time, enduring forever. "Hindu," he suggests, is one such meme that asserts itself "once more and so vigorously as to push into the background even the well beloved name of Bharatakhanda itself" (1969, 16). Bharatakhanda, for Savarkar, includes all that lay between the Himalayas and the seas; it has now given way to a Hindu universe that provides a familiar enclosure.

Repudiating those who say the Northeast is "isolated, unknown, cornered," and giving flesh to Savarkar's ideas and agency to "mother nature," Joshi offers his support like this:

> After all we can hide or destroy papers, stones, paintings or pothis, but we cannot hide the Himalayas, we cannot destroy Kailasa, Manasarovar and mighty rivers originating from there. Those divine mothers are originating from the same place, innocent of the political boundaries and the associated heinous divisions they have to witness as they come down to the ground realities. But even now, with all our great "achievements", *we may perhaps negate the history [but] we cannot negate the geography of this region.* (2000, 7; italics added)

The confluence of Savarkar's ideas and Joshi's rearticulation of them in contemporary times allows us to think about Savarkar's phrase—connecting the "remotest past to the remotest future." The past/present inhabit a time frame informed by certain textual traditions that are jostling for semiotic space amid the language of signification. The Northeast, viewed largely as a "Mongolian fringe," is now remade through the toponymic renderings that I have discussed. Now the region's future is being established, and like the names that resurface due to their power, ancient appellations like the epithet Hindu reassert themselves, fashioning new futures.

The "future as cultural fact," to borrow a phrase from Arjun Appadurai (2013), is then about possibilities as the human imagination expands territorial horizons into uncharted territories. The Sangh preoccupation with the Northeast, one could argue, is primarily shaped by the past. This does not mean that they are beholden to its unchanging character, but they augment and enhance the past's capacity—however flexible, inaccurate, or innovative their energies may be—to conceive new geopolitical horizons. The semantic immensity through which the Sangh have deployed the language of place-worlds suggests a way of anticipating the future as cultural fact in both its verdant imagination and actuality. In Chapter 4, I discuss the future's potential for those resisting this Hindutva force through prophecy and how Christian futures, too, imagine new horizons in uncharted territories through a politics of hope. Whether it is through Christian missionaries (Longkumer 2018b), through cross-cultural engagement in transnational spaces (May 2016; Pachuau and van Schendel 2015), or through ideas of "homelands" (see Chapter 7), the region remains a puzzle to those wanting to govern or stamp their authority on it. Textual and historical observations therefore must be tempered by various interpretations and local contestations that provide different hues.

FRAMING RESISTANCE

These Indic links are not always definite; others have questioned them in various ways. Scholars from Assam like Romesh Buragohain (1989), Girin Phukan (1996), and Udayon Misra (2000) have variously argued that Hinduism was primarily an imposition, an invasion, that led to the erasure of Tai-Ahom religious systems and the Tai-Ahom language and that Hinduism ostensibly eradicated tribal practices through the process of Hinduization, even though informants like Atege are open to its influ-

ence for national integration. The category Tai-Ahom is primarily an ethnic and linguistic one and relatively recent, argues the historian Yasmin
Saikia (2004). It connects with other Tai-speaking people of Southeast
Asia in Myanmar, Thailand, Vietnam, and Southern China, as a way of
distinguishing them from the Assamese ethnic identity, which they claim
is largely Hindu (Saikia 2004, 68). The Tai-Ahoms are mainly in Assam
and can trace their ancestry to the Ahoms, an invading force from the
Mong Mao region (around Upper Myanmar and Yunnan Province of
China) that occupied Assam in the thirteenth century. The Tai-Ahoms
thus represent the nationalist color of Assam's political diversity.

In attempting to uncover some of these "fragmented memories," Yasmin Saikia (2004) recounts a meeting with a well-known leader of the
Tai-Ahoms, Domboru Deodhai, in Upper Assam. He is an important
scholar of the "Ahom language" and the ritual specialist in evoking the
Ahom *swargadeos* (kings, or literally "spirit of heaven") (Saikia 2004, xiii).
He not only articulates what may seem labyrinthine and archaic rituals,
but Deodhai brings to focus the contemporary and nationalist Tai-Ahom
identity struggles. He tells Saikia, "We have a long and arduous struggle
ahead. The Hindus have totally crushed us. But we have to fight for our
rights. This is the country of our forefathers, our *swargadeos*. We have to
regain our lost glory and might. I will continue the struggle till my last
breath" (2004, xiv). Udayon Misra too recounts how scholars in Assam,
unlike the earlier Indological enthusiasts, have "re-read, re-interpret(ed)
and even re-create(d) history" to argue that Assam has always been independent of India (Baruah 2004, v; U. Misra 2000, 62).

Framing these positions as mere academic debates is shortsighted—
they spill beyond books and onto the streets. What history is and how
one interprets it are crucial questions that are asked by both revivalist
groups like the Tai-Ahoms and the armed nationalist group United Liberation Front of Assam (ULFA), whose ideologies of past Ahom glory
are welded together through the confluence of time and space. The Swed-
ish journalist Bertil Lintner's 1980s account of Kesan Chanlam Camp in
Burma gives insight into some of the early interactions among the ULFA,
the National Socialist Council of Nagaland (NSCN), and the Manipuri
People's Liberation Army (PLA), who were receiving training from the

Kachin Independence Army's (KIA). Their connections were based on the idea of strong regionalism that would lead to cooperation among marginal groups, pressuring the fragile Indian republic to dismantle and fragment. This would lead to Naga independence, a belief shared by the NSCN leader Muivah, who claimed to have contacts with Sikh militants in Punjab, as well as Kashimiri separatists. He hoped that the Tamils of the South would also rebel against India, leading to her dissolution (Lintner 1990, 84). The camaraderie and shared ideals is evident in the camp when Lintner has a conversation with Mr. Gogoi of the ULFA, who says: "We're also Mongol people and we must unite with our Naga brothers against the Indians who are encroaching upon our country, Sir" (84). When they realize that Lintner's wife is Shan, they sing a song in "ancient Assamese," drawing on their Tai-Ahom connection with the Shan people of Burma. She is able to understand it, which leads them to exclaim, "See! We're the same people" (84). In a lighter moment, when the KIA arrive in Kesan Chanlam, the ULFA cadres invite some of the Shans in the KIA ranks for tea. The Shans are slightly taken aback by the ULFA's enthusiasm for this newfound solidarity. One of them turns to Lintner and says: "Aren't they Indians? . . . They keep saying they are Shans!" (96).

Nevertheless, these collective identities were a weapon against the Indian state, as well as against Hindus in Assam. This is a familiar story of nationalisms—the question of "us" and "them"—which magnifies social boundaries and exclusive identities to serve ideas of cultural distinctiveness and superiority. Sanjib Baruah (2004), a noted political scientist of the Northeast, argues that the use of ancient history to understand modern political communities is questionable. Responding to Kar's work on the labors of Assamese history that I alluded to earlier, Baruah notes, "It is best to take political community as a contingent historical possibility rather than assert continuity with some pre-political primordial given" (2004, v–vi). Viewing politics as largely performative, Baruah puts the question of the contingent political agent in the act of becoming, not in the recognition of its inevitability. For the Sangh, history cannot be a specter of the past, the present, or the future but must be given flesh to understand the reality on which a nation exists and sustains itself. And here ancient history continues to play its role.

One must realize, however, that for some we are standing on shaky historical ground when it comes to producing precise evidence that the Northeast was linked with the rest of Bharat since time immemorial, and even through *yugs*, or ages, according to Vedic ideas of time. Even the phrase *time immemorial* evokes the image of "time so long past as to be indefinite in history or tradition," while concurrently suggesting that because of its long associations and continuations, practices have become so deeply engrained and naturalized that one need not question their authenticity.[16] But why is this region so important for the unity of India and for the Sangh? To answer this question, one must explore the idea of Akhand Bharat (undivided India) and the discourse of Greater India. If the cultural map of India extends all the way to Southeast and Southwest Asia, the Northeast of India is central to bridging these geographical regions eastward.

MAPPING EMPTY SPACES AND RELINKING ROUTES

Narendra Joshi argues that Akhand Bharat was realized through monastic voyages—Buddhist and Hindu sages, traders, and scholars—expanding the cultural map of Bharat. Once British colonialism happened, these connections were severed, and the map of India was reduced after 1947. He writes, "The map of partitioned, broken, Khandita Bharata cannot be allowed as the basis of any argument forwarded to break our Motherland again" (Joshi 2000, 8). These cultural connections concerning Northeast India and the larger region have been framed by the historian Indrani Chatterjee as "monastic governmentality" (2013; Saikia 2004). Chatterjee traces many of the ideas of kinship and friendship through these monastic networks across the trans-Himalayan world, particularly from Tibet to present-day India's Northeast. Chatterjee, admonishing postcolonial scholars of Northeast India to "relocate the region in a broader trans-regional space that included Ladakh, Kashmir, Inner Asia and beyond" (2013, 18), makes a bold case of connecting these regions through monastic legacies—such as cosmology, ethnonyms, travel, and trade, even if sometimes the "animist-textual tensions have been elided" (Zou 2016, 118).

Chatterjee's book is an example of how these precolonial connections need to be analyzed. As I have illustrated earlier, arguing for disjuncture from the Indian state paralyzes these discussions; each ethnic group is an

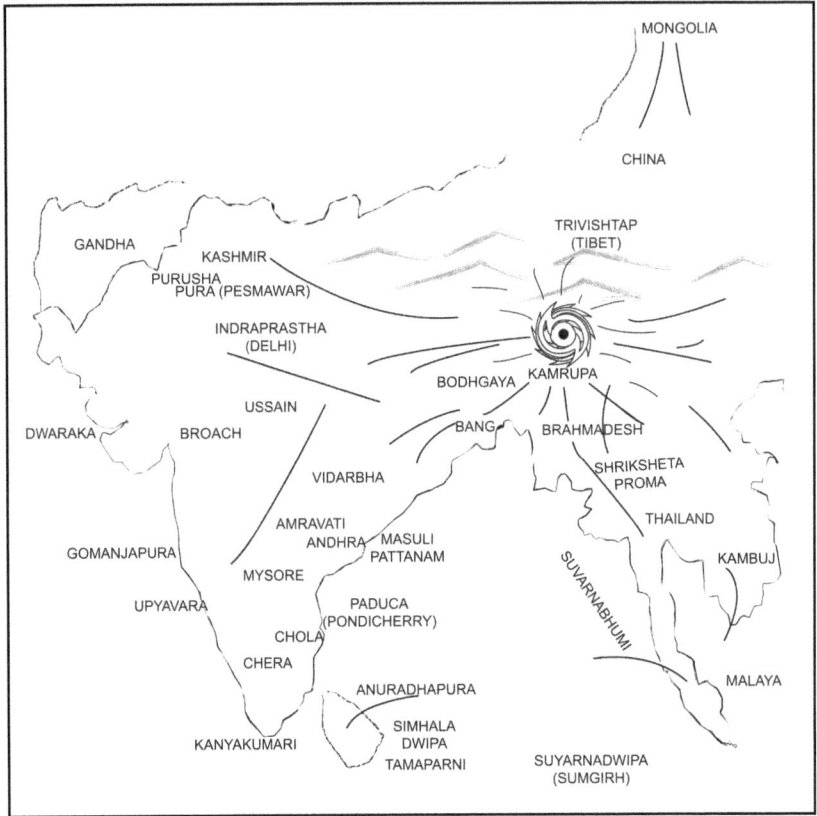

Figure 2.2. Showing the Northeast and Assam, as the center that connects the larger trans-Himalayan region, Southeast and East Asia, with India. Adapted from Joshi (2000). Made by the author.

island to itself, untouched by external agencies. If postcolonial scholars warn us of these myopias, it may surprise us that the Sangh are already engaged in worlds beyond the strict regionalism that Chatterjee alludes to. In this manner, the Sangh attempt a historical retelling and rethinking that not only culls from a mishmash of sources but also allows the region to be part of a larger transnational network of histories, ideas, and geographies.

If one is to take seriously Arjun Appadurai's (2000) idea of "process geographies," which include "action, interaction, and motion—trade, travel, pilgrimage, warfare, proselytization, colonisation, exile, and the like," then we also need to account for how various networks and bodies on the ground envision spaces (see also Lefebvre 1991; Mitchell 2002).

Appadurai goes on to note how established "area studies" are not geographical facts but are "best viewed as initial contexts for themes that generate variable geographies, rather than as fixed geographies marked by pregiven themes" (2000, 6–7). In the past few years, the emergence of Zomia—focusing on Asia's highland borderlands—a term popularized by Willem van Schendel (2002) (and latterly by James C. Scott [2009]), envisages such a zone linked through networks and processes that challenge the conventional grouping of area studies through institutional configurations. Instead, Zomia contests these dogmatic enclosures, particularly when highland Asia crisscrosses traditionally held Asian studies foci—Central, East, South, and Southeast Asia (see also Longkumer and Heneise 2019; Michaud 2010).

Such process geographies are not uncommon when examined from the view of the Sangh, particularly when their grand projections of Bruhattar Bharat/Greater India are in motion. For them, to envision their Greater India, the Northeast is central. Assam in particular is where the Mongoloid race was Indianized and made Hindu. This, according to Joshi (2000, 15), drawing from such books as *Place of Assam in the History and Civilization of India* by S. K. Chatterji (1970), is Assam's contribution to the synthesis of cultures and the fusion of races that took place in India. Indeed, the Northeast is the bridge between Southeast Asia and the Indian mainland. If one can find Indian culture and heritage all across Southeast and Central Asia, the Northeast, with its "Mongoloid" culture, was never isolated (Joshi 2000, 11). For example, Joshi (2000, 11) takes the figure of Ganesh, the elephant god, and charts his route (leaving traces in his wake) in a show of Indic cultural supremacy moving from India through Tibet, Nepal, and China, all the way to Thailand and Southeast Asia, including Malaya, Indonesia, Indo-China, Siam, and Cambodia, collectively known as "Dwipantara." He then provides enough Sanskrit place-names, events, material traces through monuments, and various Hindu temples from Burma (Brahmadesh) to Java (in Indonesia) to extend the vastness and precision of Indic markings. These instances are drawn from hard-to-access sources, though some have been primarily lifted from *India's Contribution to World Thought and Culture* (Chandra 1970).

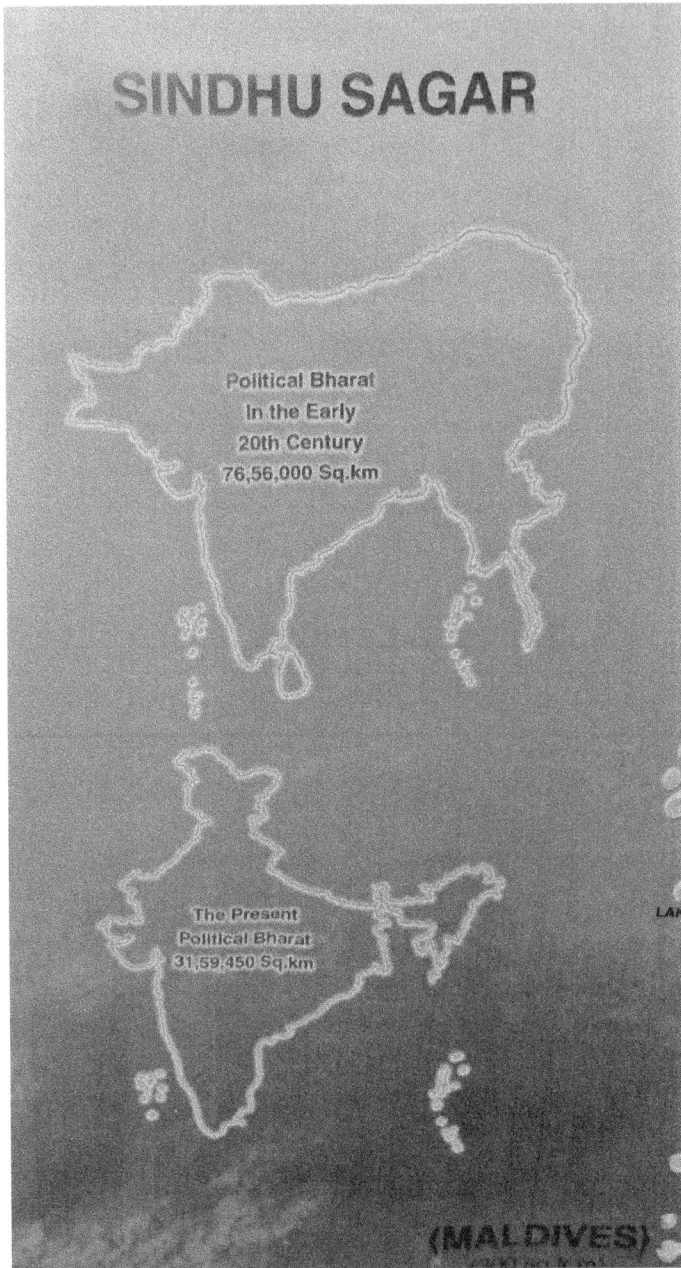

Figure 2.3. Map of Undivided/Greater India, hanging in Vidya Mandir, Jalukie, Nagaland. Photo taken by the author.

Mongolia too is not spared from this whirling history of ideas and events. To demonstrate the connection and that the Mongolians are ardent Sanskrit scholars, Joshi says, "It is surprising to an extraordinary degree when one goes into the interior of Mongolia the herdsman is interested in the literary theories of Dandin's Kavyadarsha [Sanskrit grammar] or wants clarification for some point in Panini's [Sanskrit philologist] phonetics" (2000, 14). One can see some humor in this. The route taken by these ancient sages, monastics, and travelers to China and Southeast Asia were usually via Assam, Manipur, and Burma. Introducing the various natives to the Indic reading worlds, they often carried with them the Ramayana (especially), Mahabharata, Puranas, and the Panchatantra (Joshi 2000, 12–13). Tim Ingold's idea of "wayfaring"—the wayfarer "sustains himself, both perceptually and materially, through an active engagement with the country that opens up along his path" (2011, 35)—comes to mind when reading Joshi's ebullient descriptions.

One can debate whether these observations are based on historical evidence, oral traditions, or fiction, or even question their credibility, but the larger point of these links and networks across Zomian landscapes is that these activities are meant to suggest a continuous cultural influence, making it seem all the more fabulous. While I propose that we pay attention to these cartographic styles of thought, resplendent with their ongoing toponymic labor, this is also an attempt by the Sangh to "salvage the subjugated truths that a scientific modernity has shrugged aside, to recuperate the wondrous and the fabulous that its disenchanted knowledge-practices have disallowed, and to pursue enchanted visions of the earth's past outside the professional disciplines" (Ramaswamy 2004, 13).

In arguing about loss and the labor of loss associated with places that are no longer geographically present, such as the lost continent of Lemuria, Sumathi Ramaswamy (2004) reminds us of how these place-worlds are constructed through the semantically charged category of the "fabulous." Although the Northeast is not a lost continent like Lemuria, its geographical indeterminacy however gives rise to alternate ways of thinking that are both imaginative and enchanting. These ways of thinking are not "alternative" in the sense of "transforming it into something 'other' than the familiar"; nor are they an attempt to create an alterity that replaces and dislocates (Jackson 1981, 17–18). Rather, they are alternate, an attempt to create something that is reconnected and relocated, made familiar and embraced.

NOSTALGIA AND PLACE

Vijay, a longtime worker with the Vivekananda Kendra in the Northeast, explained to me how he lost all his values at "home" (in Rajasthan) but has seen "all the value systems intact in the Northeast." "This is Ram Rajya [Ram's Kingdom], the golden period of society which we have lost there [the rest of India], but these value systems are still intact here. That is called tradition." Evoking the idea of relation, Vijay continues:

> If you look at the Hindu traditions or India's traditions, if anybody wants to see, I ask them to come to Northeast India. What is there in Mahabharata, in the Vedas, their interpretation you can find here rather than in other parts of the country. It has been manifested in temples and gods and in taboos, but in Northeast India, it is a way of life, and that is what the Vedic period is all about. That is what I am seeing here. So in this sense, we [mainland India] have lost it, but it is here, and in that way we are all united across India.
>
> *AL*: This Vedic period. Can you explain that a bit?
>
> *Vijay*: Those systems taught in the Mahabharata are in the Vedas. Mahabharata and other great epics are our guidelines. Our Upanishads are our guidelines for Indians. And those guidelines . . . If you see how they have described, if you want to look at these things, you have to come to Northeast India. Here, it is still intact.
>
> *AL*: "Intact" as in . . . ?
>
> *Vijay*: In the way of life. If you want to look at man and nature relationship, you have to come here. If you want to understand what is a woman, for that you have to come to Northeast India. If you want to understand the judicial system, for that you have to come to Northeast India. I feel that no other law is required here. Customary laws are powerful here. They work as a deterrent for many wrong deeds. No Indian law works like that. Those systems that we find in the Vedic period are still intact here. That time, there was no Indian Penal Code, during Mahabharata period. That was a social system,

and that system is here. That is how the society is governed. That is
why I feel it is very wonderful.

One must be alert to how such processes of place-making through the
trope of nostalgia, however benevolent they may appear, are imbricated
in power relations. It is not an empty sociological space where things
come into being but a deeply political one where cartographic designs are
shaped by the sentiment of one's ideology, nation, and glory. The idea of
Greater India and this nostalgia do not correspond to a benign gaze of
the observer but a colonial one, to resurrect the glory of India. Svetlana
Boym warns us about nostalgia as it fashions national futures: "Nostalgia
is paradoxical in the sense that longing can make us more empathetic
toward fellow humans, yet the moment we try *to repair longing with belonging*, the apprehension of loss with a rediscovery of identity, we often part ways and put an end to mutual understanding" (2001, xv; italics
added). Boym talks about how emotional bonding and creating an ideal
home may sacrifice critical thinking and "confuse the actual home with
the imaginary one" (2001, xvi; also Rosaldo 1989; and Chapter 5). Vijay
is involved in the process of longing for a past that no longer exists in
his home but is everywhere in Arunachal. One could argue this is an
imaginary construct, as it presents the region as timeless and unchanged.
It is imperialistic and paternalistic, because inherent in this viewpoint is
not simply the glorification of a period, the Vedic age, but also a national
revival based on mythmaking. It is fine for the rest of India to progress
and move ahead, but it is uncharacteristic and even unwelcome for the
Northeast to do so. If this loss occurs, it will be felt in both its national
and personal dimensions. Longing and belonging, in Boym's words, provide a sharp contrast to Vijay's language, where India can be found rest-
ing in these frontier places.

The Greater India project of the Sangh in the Northeast has remarkable synergies with the one that Susan Bayly (2004) discusses with regard
to its Calcutta progenitors. What began as an intellectual and nationalist
movement in the early twentieth century—the Greater India Society—
became closely associated with a kind of exercise in projecting Indic
cultural predominance spreading all over the Asian continent. Greater

India's focus, Bayly suggests, was to "document the intellectual and psychic complexities of colonialism [as they sought to illustrate] the capacity of south Asians to forge multiple and divergent visions of Indian identity, and to do so in ways that were translocal and supra-national" (707). She explains that they first of all wanted to challenge the dominant orientalist version of Indians as effeminate, weak, and as dreamers and mystics— aloof from the material concerns of the world. They questioned the history of India, largely viewed through the lens of conquest beginning from the Aryan, Islamic, and European civilizations (711, 712). They wanted to show that India's cultural colonialism had been established since time immemorial through monastic influences, adventurers, and "civilising missionaries" (712). Bayly also notes how this Greater India was envisioned:

> The terrain of this ancient Greater India was to be understood as comprising all the Asian lands including Burma, Java, Cambodia, Bali, and the former Champa and Funan polities of present-day Vietnam, in which Indians (or Indic "influences") had supposedly left their imprint in the form of monuments, inscriptions and other traces of the historic "Indianising" process. In some accounts, both Pacific societies and also most of the Buddhist world including Ceylon, Tibet, central Asia and even Japan were held to fall within this web of Indianising "culture colonies." (713)

The aim of the Greater India scholars was to illuminate the great truths of the Indian past and translate them into larger political capital not through violence and conquest (like the British and the "Muhammadan conquerors") but through "cultural colonization" that was explicitly "Indian centred" (Bayly 2004, 721). In this process, the Greater India scholars divulged their nationalist colors, combined with their cultural acumen of borrowing from a wide range of oriental and French Indological scholarship to pursue their agenda of glorifying Indian culture by subsuming Hindu and Buddhist (in Southeast Asia) influences under "Indian civilisational studies" (718). Thus, a distinct style of nationalist imaginings emerged that placed emphasis on the collective loss and displacement, while attempting to revive and celebrate Indic influences worldwide. The afterlife of these ideas would go on to shape eminent figures like Jawaharlal Nehru and movements like the Non-Aligned Movement (founded in 1961), led by

Nehru, Sukarno, and Nasser to emphasize transnational identities with the former colonial world, invoking a shared "inter-Asian cultural affinity and common spiritual heritage," rooted in "Indic" values (736–37).

Away from the corridors of power in New Delhi, Jakarta, or Cairo, these ideas of Greater India permeate the everyday spaces of ordinary RSS workers, who share in this transnational vision from the vantage point of Northeast India. Not only are the cultural influences valued, but, according to Abhishek, an RSS pracharak in Arunachal Pradesh, "India's philosophy of liberalism, spiritualism and universalism" must be emphasized through the idea of Hindutva, a principle rooted in the soil (see Chapter 3). Similarly, a VHP worker in Delhi, Ram, explained to me this idea of Greater India. When the globe-trotting Hindu culture is everywhere, how could the Northeast not be included? He said:

> James Mill wrote that we must be grateful to Hindus because they civilized us. Bharat made us civilized. When the Vedas were made here, they were living in the Stone Age and our sages went there. That's why you find a five-thousand-year-old Shiv temple in Canada, a seven-thousand-year-old Shiv temple in Siberia. How they went there? Hindu saints went there to get them civilized—to teach them language, how to eat, dance, sing, dress, speak. We have communication because of the saints. If we are to go with that definition—Bharatvarsh as a cultural idea—then the entire world was Hindu at that time, because of those values, which were finished by Christianity and Islam. If you find pre-Christian pre-Islamic culture, you will find a lot of similarity between Hindu values, Roman/Egypt/Maya culture, which have been destroyed by these two traditions. Hindus always believed in unity and the welfare of humankind—the entire globe as a family. That is the Hindu culture that was connected to those other groups.

Ram's exegesis far exceeds those of the inter-Asian collaborations; it is universal in scope and thus encompasses the globe as "one family." It is clear that the Sangh are also expansive in their approach to viewing the region within the larger frame of mythic time and through the gaze of world history. For them, the Northeast is encompassed within these territorial designs simply through the congruous historical message of universalism couched in the language of Greater India. How could it be otherwise?

CONCLUSION

I began the chapter with a marriage. The marriage of Krishna and Rukmini is a historical puzzle, a mythmaking exercise that has confounded
many who either argue for rapprochement for the sake of national integration or those who reject it as a tool used to impose and dominate. Reading
the Krishna-Rukmini story and the way it was packaged and performed
by those in Madhavpur calls us to exercise our analytical skills further by
reading between the lines and asking a range of geopolitical questions.
First, could one read the event as a larger lesson in what India means to
diverse audiences? Using the analogy of the marriage and indeed the language of subservience—that the abduction of our bride is fine as long as
it is for national integration—demonstrates unequal power relations. Second, Krishna's refusal to abide by cultural diktats or customary procedures,
and instead forcing those in the male hierarchy (Rukmini's father and
brother) to acquiesce to his authority, can be read as an exercise in power.
One cannot suspend the male gaze as the dominant discourse in the Gujarat mela in 2018 that I described, both in the language and the performance of the Krishna-Rukmini story. Viewing the West as the groom and
the East as the bride relays certain messages of kinship and marriage alliances anyone versed in Indian culture and society would not miss, where
they establish asymmetrical relations between wife-givers and wife-takers
with the former being inferior to the latter. There are clear demarcations
of power. Finally, the Northeast appears as the reluctant bride (symbolized
by Rukmini) brought to unify a country, after she has been subdued by
Krishna (the Indic figure of all-encompassing power). Now the region is
forever trapped and forced into this cosmological union. Indeed, the way
relations are understood—as both holographic and complex—magnifies
the scale to include any order of connection, even though it might seem
arbitrary and diffuse. Relations, however, as Strathern suggests, maintain a
degree of distinctiveness even amid their expansiveness. At the same time,
these distinctions can also be dissolved to render them the same. Sameness is then a trope, a practice, operationalized in the mela through the
slogan "One India, Great India" and replicated in similar fashion through
the act of place-making and naming.

Paul Carter, in the case of Australia, and Keith Basso, in the case of the Western Apache, argue that language plays a crucial role through which places are constituted. If we follow this idea of how people plot place-worlds, the narrative force makes them felt and visible. "If place-making," as Basso implies, "[is a] venerable means of *doing* human history, it is also a way of constructing social traditions and, in the process, personal and social identities. We *are*, in a sense, the place-worlds we imagine" (1996, 7; italics in original). The Sangh, along with various regional elites, have attempted to connect the region historically via the process of what Sheldon Pollock has called the "vernacularization" and the "Sanskrit cosmopolis" (1998, 6). The former is associated with the use of Sanskrit inscriptions, and the latter is constructed through the "space of cultural circulation [through] literary-critical imagination" all over South and Southeast Asia (6). The preponderance of the Sanskritic culture highlighted by different sources in this chapter favored the technique of the cultural supremacy of India across the geosphere. However, these imaginings also retreat to a safe but equally powerful nostalgia of longing and belonging through ideas of the Vedic age, an age that demonstrates a certain human condition and state of innocence. Primitivism and bizarre exoticism marry with an exercise in nationalism that confounds in its excesses.

The Northeast, according to the Sangh, helped inaugurate this global circulation eastward. Not only do names signify, but they also possess the land. The crucial practice of unmapping and mapping suggests a one-way process of recognition that undermines the historical reality of indigenous peoples with their own luxuriant tapestry of place-names, cultural distinctiveness, and political sovereignty, girded to their lands. Indeed, by marking these locations, the Sangh are making the convincing case of the region's unfailing and time-immemorial unity expressed through ideas of Akhand Bharat and Greater India that traveled through this region. How else would travel have happened if not through the Himalayas? If the weight of geographical evidence must stand the test of time, where else can one turn to but nature? The arborescent image of the region that I alluded to in the introduction also benefits from its association with its people. Not only is Hindutva, its ties to land and soil, effervescent, but it is also used to invoke notions of indigeneity that play on themes of blood and belonging, especially in the way Hindutva projects itself as the paradigmatic "indigenous" principle. If the region must be reconceptualized through spatial relations, the next chapter provides another way to think about its people, primarily through the discourse of indigenous religions. It is to this we now turn.

CHAPTER 3

HINDUTVA WORLDINGS
Whose Way of Life?

IN MAY 2018, I was asked to give a public lecture at Rajiv Gandhi University (RGU) in Doimukh, Arunachal Pradesh. The lecture was on my fieldwork in Arunachal and about the activities of the Sangh and Christian missionaries in the area. These were, of course, sensitive issues, and this became more potent when I began discussing my work and observations on Hindu nationalism in the region. As I presented, I could sense a palpable, edgy discomfort within the audience. At the end of the talk, a young academic, Margaret, stood up and said:

> Let's not mix our indigenous religion with Hinduism just because somebody
> wants to mainstream you. Let's first look at our own culture. Let's look at our
> own religion. . . . Let's not put a blind eye to this for some short-term benefits.
> Let us not mix indigenous and Hindu. This is what is being propagated here
> since our schooling. All the tribal kids have had mixed schooling. Some have
> studied with Christian missionaries, again shifted to Hindu missionaries, again
> shifted to government schools, again shifted to a radical institution where all
> religions are *bakwaas* [nonsense]. What happens to the orientation of this
> tribal kid? This crisis comes with everyone, but my problem is let us not put an
> oblique in these two separate religions. Let us understand them on their own.

Margaret then asked if I was aware of a survey of Arunachali religion that was currently circulating on Facebook. Margaret explained that in this religion survey—the origins of it largely unknown, she remarked—the percentages of Christians and Buddhists were shown separately, whereas those in categories of indigenous religions and Hinduism were conflated. There were many heated discussions on this Facebook post, described Margaret, with the vast majority of the Arunachali youth agreeing that this "whole idea of conflating indigenous religions/Hinduism was problematic because people will think this is how it is!"

The audience murmured for a while waiting for a fitting response. Construing my acknowledgment of Margaret's comments as agreement with her position, hand after hand went up. Someone stood up and introduced himself as Suresh from the English Department. Faces turned toward him, and a heavy silence pervaded the room as he attempted an answer to the issues Margaret had highlighted.

> Firstly, Hinduism is not a religion based on a book; nor did it start from a particular date. Christianity, Buddhism has a date but not in Hinduism. I am trying to draw similarities between the indigenous faiths and Hinduism. [In] Hinduism, we don't have a founding figure, similar to indigenous faiths. What do we worship in indigenous faith? As far as my limited understanding, people worship various aspects of nature, which is also similar to Hinduism. In Hinduism, we have *nag panchami*—we worship the snake. We have *govardhan puja*—we worship the mountain. We worship cow, animals. Hinduism and indigenous faiths worships aspects of nature. This may be one of the reasons why these people—I am not that person—made the oblique line [of conflating indigenous religions and Hinduism].

The issue that Margaret brings up has to do with what constitutes indigenous religion and who defines it. Suresh's comments draw on the dominant explanation based on a common relationship—that of nature (the "what" of the question)—but does not answer Margaret's probing of the why this conflation is being made and the machinations propagating it. Margaret's point is precisely how the "tribal" mind is affected and disturbed by these shifting categories—whether in census reports, social media, or the press.

Suresh's explanation does not go down well with Margaret. Margaret is a follower of an indigenous religion, having been educated in the Vivekananda Kendra Vidyalaya (VKV) in Arunachal Pradesh, started in 1977 by Eknath Ranade, an influential member of the RSS (Kanungo 2012). She is keenly aware of the activities of the Sangh (and Christian missionaries) and what they are doing in Arunachal Pradesh among "tribal children." She tells me that she never saw the VKV as a "Hindu mission" when she was a student, but once she started studying sociology at Jawaharlal Nehru University (JNU), she realized the extensive Hindu influence in the school. This was when she started questioning the promotion of "secular credentials" by VKV. With slight irritation in her voice, she addresses Suresh. She points to the fact that tribes in Arunachal Pradesh are considered "lesser Hindus," especially outside the state. These bitter, firsthand experiences, she explains, have to do with how Hindu society treats tribals, patronizing them and regarding them as "lesser persons, like they are doing us some favor."

Margaret and Suresh's debate is at the heart of this chapter. It grapples with the historical construction of these terms, how they operated in colonial discourse, and their contemporary manifestations and national and global resonances. In the previous chapter, I examined how the Sangh's notion of the Northeast of India is "reconstructed" in order to reflect the assimilation of this region with the rest of India. This envisioning of territory, alongside how the Sangh negotiate the complex interplay between national belonging and mapping, has been crucial in visualizing this region as part of Bharatvarsh "from time immemorial," to signal both a reconstructive and uncertain trope. Building on this idea of geographical inclusivity, in this chapter, I examine how the Sangh has sought to refine and evolve the notion of Hindutva to appeal to and be included within the concept of indigenous religion. I will show how notions of Hindutva, based originally on Savarkar's idea of civilizational identity, have been employed as a useful heuristic device to construct arguments of indigeneity and indigenous religion. This idea allows the Sangh to construct and make certain worlds possible—that is, *worldings*—through connections with ideas, interactions, and relations by showing how Hindutva is a way of being in the world.

This requires an examination, first, of how the concepts of Hindu, Hinduism, and Hindutva are used and understood. If we are to acknowledge the importance of locality, or "the soil," for Hindu nationalists in constructing ideas of nation, a second question emerges: How might the term *indigenous religions* be a useful category for Sangh activists and the indigenous elite? How does establishing a connection with indigenous religions enable them to envisage a unifying national identity? I will argue that while colonial history gave rise to "syndicated Hinduism" (Thapar 1985)—a means of consolidating various local practices into a single, coherent entity—a similar process can be understood regarding indigenous religions. While it was largely orientalists (European scholars) and Indian elites who undertook this earlier exercise of "syndication," in this chapter I will examine a similar process in the way the Sangh work with regional elites to syndicate their practices and traditions into a coherent religion.

One of the cornerstones of the rights of indigenous peoples propounded by the International Labour Organisation (ILO) in 1989, which would go on to influence the United Nations Declaration on the Rights of Indigenous Peoples (UNDRIP) (Niezen 2011, 5), revolves around the idea of protecting indigenous "ways of life . . . and [developing] their identities, languages and religions, within the framework of the States in which they live."[1] In his work on indigenous religion and human rights, Ronald Niezen (2011) emphasizes that the ILO's approach, and that of other transnational bodies working for indigenous people's rights, is significantly oriented toward "their assimilation into the body politic of states as a response to the imperatives of development (including 'spiritual development') and equality" (Niezen 2011, 6). It is striking to note, as I will discuss, how this discourse of "ways of life" for indigenous peoples can take on a particular edge, when dominant groups such as the Sangh can assimilate this narrative of indigeneity to argue that Hindutva too is "a way of life."[2]

It is important to distinguish the various ways in which the idea of "indigenous" is being utilized here. Tracking the numerous conversations, interviews, and unpublished and published materials produced by the Sangh and their sympathizers, I note that they use the term *indigenous* largely in three ways. First, they equate it with Hindutva, of the soil, premised in the language of nationalism. Second, they use indigenous religions as a way to define non-Christian groups, while at the same time giving these groups a coherent identity that is organized and increasingly institutionalized. In a way, both the Sangh and non-Christian groups borrow from the worldwide discourse of indigenous religions to draw on the overall importance of cultural and religious distinctiveness. Finally, they articulate ideas of the indigenous drawn from a wide array of sources that link it with its political resonance—that of self-identity borne out of marginalization. While it is not always explicit how they articulate this stance, aside from arguing that the Hindus are also victims through Mughal and British conquests, they do align themselves with indigenous religions in the Northeast, through which they are able to link ideas of indigeneity, using the discourse of religion. While the first two approaches demonstrate ways of operating as they negotiate their way in the region, the final approach is contentious in that applying such terms as *indigenous*—moving it away explicitly from a political, UN discourse— they are finding other ways to marry these ideologies through links with worldwide native groups.

Furthermore, Hindutva ideas of locality are operationalized through Hinduizing these indigenous religions under the large rubric of Indic civilization. This also enables a celebration of traditional culture through reversing colonial and Christian missionary understandings of animism and refocusing on the positive aspects of ties to land and nature. These concerns are crucial in the Hindutva understanding of (national) identity and its relationship to soil, as well as indigenous religions and their implicit recognition of the relationship of location and kinship to land. It is drawing on these similarities that enables the conflation of Hinduism/ Hindutva and indigenous religions, the conflation Margaret so deeply objected to. But it is also through drawing out these similarities that we are able to understand how the concept of Hindutva has evolved and the part that ideas of indigenous religions have played in this. Savarkar's initial conceptualization has changed over time, and one of the key contributions of this book is to show precisely how Hindutva is a malleable set of understandings that are both transforming and transformative.

HINDUTVA: WHAT IS IN A NAME?

As discussed earlier, according to the key architect of the idea of Hindutva, V. D. Savarkar, *Hindu* is a word that can be traced from the Sapta Sindhu (the seven rivers of the Indus River system), which has denoted a unified community of people occupying the Indian subcontinent, called Hindustan from the Vedic period, and succeeded in giving it "a local habitation and a name" (1969, 5). In his vision, Hindutva then was not solely a matter of religion but "a history in full," a civilizational identity. Hinduism, on the other hand, he argued, "is only a derivative, a fraction, a part of Hindutva" (3). Savarkar's use of these terms—*Hindu*/*Hinduism*—is something that other scholars have also pondered over, highlighting their complex nature.

David Lorenzen (1999), in his essay "Who Invented Hinduism?" notes two camps in this debate: (1) the constructionist camp, who argue that Hinduism was imagined or invented in the nineteenth century by British colonial administrators, missionaries, scholars, and the Indian elite and that before this date Hinduism did not exist as a substantive category (see also Hawley 1991); and (2) those scholars who argue that a Hindu religion expressed itself far earlier—through the Bhagavad Gita, the Puranas, and philosophical commentaries based on the six *darsanas* and debates between Hindus and Muslims around 1200–1500—and that it was "firmly established long before 1800" (Lorenzen 1999, 631; see also Lipner 2006). While these debates center on whether Hinduism can be imagined as a category long before 1800, the same is not true with the term *Hindu* as a geoethnic marker.

The term *Hindu* was recognized long before the nineteenth century, as it was first used by the Persians to differentiate the geographical area beyond the Sindhu, or Indus, River in present-day Pakistan. It was, some argue, used as a geoethnic category. The historian Romila Thapar suggests, "It was gradually and over time that it was used not only for those who were inhabitants of India but also for those who professed a religion other than Islam and Christianity" (1989, 222). Thapar's point shows that both the Brahmans (the priestly caste) and the lower castes were conflated within this category Hindu, which was, of course, contrary to the precepts of Brahmanism. The definition was bewildering for those on the receiving end of it for the simple reason that such diversity and multiplicity of practices were now conjoined as a singular tradition (Thapar 1989, 223).

If we accept Thapar's suggestion that the fluidity of the term *Hindu* illustrated different notions of how the community was represented by

Others (Muslims, British, Christians) and eventually how it represented itself internally—say, between different castes—then we can see how there is no one conception of this category (see also Gellner 2004). For instance, even recently, Mary Searle-Chatterjee observed that the term *Hindu* is frequently perplexing when perceived from a regional level. Research in north India suggests that the term is used primarily by the lower castes to refer to the upper caste, while for the upper caste, the term was reserved to connote those who were truly "Indian"—those without any religious allegiance to foreign traditions (Searle-Chatterjee 2000, 504). This demonstrates that the pervasiveness of the term *Hindu* is not without its problems when viewed from regional and oral perspectives. The concepts themselves—whether geoethnic or religious—are far from unambiguous or settled in terms of their associations, even though much has been written to delineate their usages.

While at first glance, it appears as though Hindu and Hindutva are primarily geoethnic and civilizational markers associated with common territory (rashtra), common birth (jati), and common civilization (sanskriti) (Savarkar 1969, 116), Savarkar confuses matters by associating Hindutva with a holy land. As discussed earlier, Hindutva is thus underpinned by a religious identity, Hinduism. Although Savarkar is not keen on the term *Hinduism* due to its invention by the "Englishman" (1969, 103), he does recognize its usefulness in trying to comprehend the bewildering display of diversity in India. "Hinduism," he says, "is the 'ism' of the Hindu.... Hinduism must necessarily mean the religion or religions that are peculiar and native to this land and these people" (104). But by using the term *Hinduism*, Savarkar is aware that it must include both the orthodox and the heterodox. The orthodox (influenced by the tradition of Shruti, Smriti, and Puranas), who form the majority, Savarkar suggests, could be called "sanatan dharma" (eternal way of life), an "ancient accepted appellation" (107). While those heterodox groups could be called Sikh dharma, Jain dharma, or Buddha dharma (107). These separate specificities should be retained, Savarkar suggests, for inclusive purposes, but when the need arises to address the whole, the generic term *Hinduism* or *Hindu dharma* can be used. By advocating this position, it removes the "cause of suspicion in our minor communities and resentment in the major one, [which] would once more unite us all Hindus under our ancient banner representing a common race and a common civilization" (107).

Significant for this chapter, however, is that Savarkar's understanding of Hindutva, Hindu, and Hinduism was never applied by him to the Northeast of India. Although Savarkar includes the Himalayas in his geopolitical vision of Hindutva, as I discussed in the last chapter, the "tribal" question was not acknowledged by Savarkar and only minimally by Golwalkar, his predecessor, who was more interested in the region in the context of Christian missionary activities. The question then is what about religions—such as indigenous religions—that are not recognized like Christianity, Hinduism, Buddhism? This question relates to the perennial problem that has plagued the study of religions, due to the European construction of these categories through colonialism (Chidester 1996; Cox 2007; Masuzawa 2005). Would they be classified as "Indian religions" or "religions practiced in India"? Would ethnic Naga, Mizo, Assamese, and Arunachali practices be considered "dharma," in the sense Savarkar uses it, for example? Or would they connote the heterodox traditions that Savarkar was willing to embrace as "minority communities" within the inclusive Hindutva vision? These pertinent questions then beg a further response: Who defines these? What motivations and intentions are at play? And finally, what does it say about power relations premised on the idea of the Hindu nation?

> We have found that the first important essential qualification of a Hindu is that to him the land that extends from Sindhu to Sindhu is the Fatherland (Pitribhu), the Motherland (Matribhu), the land of his patriarchs and forefathers. . . . This land is the birth-place—the Matribhu (motherland) and the Pitribhu (fatherland)—of that Tatvajnana (philosophy) which in its religious aspects is signified as Hindu Dharma. . . . Hindu Dharma of all shades and schools, lives and grows and has its being in the atmosphere of Hindu culture, and the Dharma of a Hindu being so completely identified with the land of the Hindus, this land of him is not only Pitribhu but a Punyabhu, not only a fatherland but a holyland. (Savarkar 1969, 68–69)

The key to extending Savarkar's definition of Hindu to the Northeast of India for the Sangh is by establishing the numerous other indigenous practices to form a common Hindu culture, thus fulfilling Savarkar's broad definition of Hindutva. Ramesh Babu, the Shradha Jaragan Pramukh of Akhil Bharatiya Vanvasi Kalyan Ashram, in Guwahati, provided an answer when he was invited in 2017 to celebrate the "eternal faith of the Bodos" (a tribe in Assam). Summarizing Savarkar's notion of Hindutva that conjoins territory, culture, and faith, Babu applied this to the Bathou faith in Northeast India:

> Thus, the Eternal faith of this land came to be known as Hinduism. The word Hindu means whatever is indigenous to this land. Therefore Hindu is synonymous to the word indigenous. When we pronounce the word Hindu we cover all indigenous faith of this land which is eternal. . . . Therefore Bathou faith [eternal faith of the Bodo tribe of Assam] and Hindutwa [*sic*] are one and the same. If there are similarities of Bathou with rest of the indigenous faith in India, it is well and good. If there is some uniqueness in Bathou belief, then that is your contribution to the great Bharateeya Sanskriti [Indian civilization]. (Babu 2017, 18)

Although Babu's explanation is conceptually imprecise (perhaps due to the speech being in English and unscripted), his idea of Hindutva conforms to Savarkar's discussion by conflating Bathou faith (akin to Hinduism as a "fraction") with Hindutva (the whole).

Hindutva, then, one could argue, is the par excellence understanding of civilizational identity that is indigenous to India. According to Savarkar, Hindutva "embraces all the departments of thought and activity of the whole Being of our Hindu race" (1969, 4). A further commentary is provided by the BJP. The Hindutva factor arose, according to the BJP ideological text on "cultural nationalism," because Hinduism was never organized. Rather, Hinduism incorporated all forms of beliefs and practices, without devaluing any of its deities and respecting agnostics and atheists alike. It had no beginning, founder, central authority, hierarchy, nor organization (BJP 2005, 112). This is a popular version that is widely understood, demonstrated by Suresh, for example, in his encounter with Margaret, and accepted by many scholars (Fuller 1992; Gold 2015) and Sangh activists (see Longkumer 2017b).

In the absence of any authorizing and coherent agent, the BJP text continues, Hindutva provided that organization, a kind of *external kinesis* to the internal workings of Hinduism. This main kinesis was a form of defense against those who wanted to destroy Hinduism, particularly the threat of the "Abrahamic faiths" (BJP 2005, 115–16). The Hindutva version of Hinduism, then, was a form of syndication that relied on a singular version, increasingly dominating the political sphere, in contrast to the "provincial" (Gold 2015) and everyday form of Hinduism that offered considerable latitude and flexibility. For this reason, according to the political scientist Jyotirmaya Sharma, "Hindutva is the dominant expression of Hinduism in our times" (2011, 7).

What are the implications of viewing Hinduism as highly politicized and nationalized? First, Hinduism becomes the "sole claimant of the inheritance of indigenous Indian religion" (Thapar 1985, 21). It allows a vast array of religions, previously critical of Brahmanical practices, such as Buddhism and Jainism, to be included within Hinduism, with a danger of their differences being denied, elided, or ignored. Second, by presenting an inclusive Hinduism and acknowledging an array of sects and a variety of beliefs and practices—ranging from location, language, caste, and tribal polities—the Sangh can effectively manage Hinduism "as a way of life" inflected with ideological motives. In the process, the Sangh have shaped, in the words of David Kopf, "an amorphous heritage into a rational faith" (1992, 676).

The following sections will elaborate on these questions in more detail. I preface them with some remarks on the messy translation of concepts. In the Northeast of India, the term *Scheduled Tribes* (STs) refers to historically disadvantaged people according to the Constitution of India.[3] While the appellation STs is used for many of the tribes in the region, the terms *janajati* (tribe, in Hindi), *tribal*, and *indigenous* are also used interchangeably. The terms *religion*, *tradition*, and *faith* also correspond and are sometimes taken to be similar (in English).[4] So too are English concepts like indigenous religion, indigenous faith and culture, indigenous traditional religion, tribal religion, janjati (tribal) faith and culture, and primordial/primal religion (both in the singular and plural) used according to the choices of individuals (see also Tafjord 2017). For consistency, I use the term *indigenous religions*. Aside from its wide usage, it also relates to the global category called indigenous religions and addresses some of the issues that such a term brings in its more evaluative, analytical, and practical usages (Johnson and Kraft 2017). Although these English-language terms have their roots in a Western understanding, once they are used in another context, often where English is a second language, they can take on new meanings, and making distinctions between these terms becomes unclear (Asad 1993; Chakrabarty 2000; Tafjord 2017).

LOCALITY AND ITS FORCE—IDEAS
OF INDIGENOUS RELIGIONS

Much of the discourse on indigeneity is increasingly compromised by the unequal political spaces (Tsing 2005). Indigenous peoples are seen as close to nature or "ecologically noble savages" (Baviskar 2007, 289). This image is championed by rights activists and utilized by indigenous peoples themselves as a strategic necessity to accrue political resources for survival. It is this space that has been usurped by the Sangh in arguing for indigeneity. They too, according to their arguments, have been historically conquered, suffered, and marginalized by invading Muslim (Mughal) forces from the fourteenth century onward and thereafter oppressed and denigrated by British colonial rule and Christian conversions from the seventeenth century (Hansen 1999; van der Veer 2002). Seen this way, the ILO definition in 1989 of indigenous peoples only confirms the Sangh's dignified presence within the world of indigenous peoples: on account of their "descent from populations, who inhabited the country or geographical region at the time of conquest, colonisation or establishment of present state boundaries. They retain some or all of their own social, economic, cultural and political institutions, irrespective of their legal status."[5]

It is no surprise then that such definitions can be utilized and compromised by dominant groups, thus disenfranchising minority communities for which these rights have been enshrined in the first place, as they contest the assimilative power of nation-states by making claims for autonomy and forms of sovereignty. A larger question that arises from this analysis is to ask if Hinduism is the world's largest "indigenous religion" (Longkumer 2017b). Similarly, how can Hindutva encompass 1 billion people in India, or more, and still make an appeal to being indigenous when this term strongly implies minority status (Karlsson 2006, 2001)? Indigeneity, indeed, is "*rooted* in and *routed* through" (Clifford 2001, 469;

my italics) particular spaces, both in its groundings and the expansive social networks one is exposed to.

There has been much discussion of indigenous peoples in India through the language of belonging, rights, sovereignty, and development (Baviskar 2006; Béteille 1998; Karlsson and Subba 2006; Roy Burman 1992; Xaxa 1999). The challenges surrounding these issues chart the numerous actors involved—from scholars and activists to the indigenous peoples themselves—utilizing the global discourse of indigeneity. Promulgated by international organizations like the United Nations, specific rights enshrined by the Working Group on Indigenous Populations have further emphasized the need for human rights and justice. Less has been written regarding indigenous religions, however. But the discourse of indigenous religions and its usage have been reconceptualized in the Northeast both by the Sangh and by the indigenous elite themselves to project a religion that is both grounded in the soil and has a transnational potential to seek collaboration with other indigenous peoples through an understanding of Hindutva. If both indigenous religions and Hindutva are "of the soil," the latter can lay claim to encompassing indigenous religions globally. This brings us to the question of indigenous religions. It is worth noting here that the Sangh is attempting to argue for indigenous religion as the basis for indigeneity and not indigenous religion as a second-order category for indigenous peoples (Niezen 2011).

According to James Cox, an important scholar in this field, a key feature of indigenous religion is that it must revolve, at a minimum, around locality and kinship relations.

> The primary characteristic of Indigenous Religions refers to its being bound to a location; participants in the religion are native to a place. . . . The single and overriding belief shared amongst Indigenous Religions derives from a kinship-based world-view in which attention is directed towards ancestor spirits as the central figures in religious life and practice. As such, Indigenous Religions are restricted cosmologically because their spirit world is organized around a system of lineage. Ancestors are known by name; they belong to a place just as their descendants do, and they relate to living communities as spirit conveyors of ancestral traditions. (2007, 69)

This is a position that has been debated by other scholars, such as Graham Harvey and Charles Thompson, who argue that the term *indigenous* is self-descriptive, that is, about "belonging to a place" (2005, 10). Religions, when combined with the concept of indigenous, can be read a particular way that is connected to land and enduring traditions rooted in rituals that have to do with elders, ancestors, and those who profess a close connection to the natural world (Cox 2007, 68; see also Harvey 2000). These descriptions are not uncommon, for example, among pagans and animists, who see their practices as embedded in networks of locality, kinship, and connectedness with nature. Cox's definition of indigenous religion also aligns with, through a different context, how Savarkar and others like Ramesh Babu understand Hindutva. Central to their conception of who is Hindu is locality (ties to one's land) and kinship (connections with patriarchs and forefathers).

The debate between Margaret and Suresh presents us with a larger set of questions: from Savarkar's early ideas, as he struggled to articulate the idea of Hindutva that is now being extended to the unfamiliar territory of the Northeast, to the different ways scholars employed textual and oral sources to understand the construction of Hindu/Hinduism, and to how census reports (which I will discuss later) provide glimpses of the differences and similarities in the way Hinduism and indigenous (tribal) religions are viewed. Similarly, if the Indian Council of Philosophical Research (ICPR) is keen to erase the differences between tribal religions and Hinduism (see below), what about those indigenous activists who are keen to maintain their traditions, like Margaret, who call upon all resources available to articulate their sense of location amid the bewildering ensemble of religious practices and ideologies? Margaret's trenchant critique of the Sangh deserves attention, particularly when some indigenous scholars, such as Gangmumei Kamei, provide energy and commitment to the cause of indigenous religions by acquiescence and uncritical appreciation of the Sangh's position.

Kamei was a well-known Naga scholar and activist from Manipur, with close associations to the Kalyan Ashram, the RSS body that works with tribes in the Northeast of India. He wrote extensively on the indigenous traditions of Northeast India (Kamei 2002; 2004; 2006) and contributed regularly to the Kalyan Ashram magazine *Heritage Explorer*, a monthly publication based in Guwahati, Assam. He highlighted the plight of the tribals, preserving their indigenous religions by using different resources that have national and international purchase, particularly by relating his work to the global indigenous movement.

Indigenous peoples are now, Kamei argues, more than ever, rekindling their traditions to protect themselves against the "proselytizing world religions" (Kamei 2006, 5). Kamei argues for the use of the United Nations Working Group on Indigenous Populations' (UNWGIP) Draft of the Declaration on the Rights of the Indigenous People (UNDRIP) to enable them to "follow, preach, and preserve their religion, Philosophy [*sic*], culture and national heritage" (2002, 4).[6] He emphasizes that the "real indigenous" people of India are those who still preserve their "religion and culture" of the soil, in contrast to those who have adopted an "alien religion" (2002, 10). These ideas, as I have shown, are not unusual for Hindutva audiences, as the centrality of their ideology concerns such binaries that Kamei alludes to. In her work on the *adivasi* (indigenous) people of western India, Amita Baviskar notes the increasing fluency by which proponents of Hindutva are able to equate themselves with indigenous peoples of India (2007, 281). "To be fully Indian and indigenous is to be Hindu," Baviskar argues, and shows how the adivasis are viewed as default Hindus by the Sangh, aided by the Indian state's classification of STs as Hindus, unless explicitly stated otherwise (2007, 282). At the UN level too, reports Ronald Niezen, while examining the different ways indigenous peoples are understood, India has adopted a "self-definition" of indigenous peoples primarily to project the view that it represents 1 billion indigenous people—"all citizens are sons and daughters of the soil"—and that competing claims to indigeneity cannot rival those of the Indian state (2003, 20–21). This "self-definition" is partly to lessen the impact of rivalry between groups to ascertain who occupied which land first and secondly to curtail antagonism that may develop when there is a more open definition of indigeneity (Niezen 2003, 73; Kingsbury 1998).

In practice, however, the "we-are-all-indigenous" idea promulgated by the Indian state is challenged by Kamei's and Baviskar's arguments, which appeal to the power of place and religion to determine indigeneity.

This inclusive position of the Indian state declared at the UN level fragments on the ground when groups make exclusionary claims. This tension between "being in place" and "being out of place" is very much at the heart of these discourses on indigenous religions. While ideas of being naturally rooted to place, argues Liisa Malkki (1992), provide a powerful vocabulary for the conception of nature, it might also have unintended consequences when deployed to exclude and render people "out of place."

This interesting interpretation of the UNDRIP is reminiscent of Savarkar's Hindutva. The emphasis on the preservation of religion is something, it might be argued, that is contained in the letter and spirit of the UNDRIP articles.[7] Kamei uses the term *indigenous* to refer to those non-Christian religions "of the soil," while Christian Naga nationalist groups like the NSCN-IM, for example, use UNDRIP to fight for their sovereignty and self-determination (Karlsson 2001; Longkumer 2017c). This demonstrates the diverse ways in which such rights may be mobilized for different ends even among the same community. For Kamei, his argument for the preservation of indigenous religions complements the UNDRIP articles: "The primal religion covers all the features of the indigenous faith or the tribal religion. And indigenous faith implies an ancient root and cultural heritage, the present consciousness and future continuance. The term, 'prior to the universal religion' expresses the ancient but do not necessarily represent the present status and the future" (2006, 15). He goes on to observe how the ancient and primordial name for Hinduism has been interpreted as sanatan dharma—the eternal way of life—and complements the criteria of antiquity for "indigenous tribal religions" that UNDRIP articulates. The similarity of tribal religions with Hinduism is thus the basis, he says, of a shared "essence," existing since "the beginning of time." Unlike Margaret, Kamei readily accepts the conflation of Hindu and indigenous religions and marshals evidence to point toward its benefits. For Kamei, indigenous traditions—both Hinduism and tribal religions—can be understood as "primordial religion" (2006, 15), to give a sense of antiquity, locality, and thus authenticity (see also Comaroffs 2009; Kuper 2003).

Kamei's text is broadly comparative and inclusive, ranging from the Maori of New Zealand, to the Zulu of South Africa, to the Cherokee of the

United States, to the traditional "cult of Sinkyo of Korea," and beyond. First of all, it suggests that these indigenous religions are all being revived via a common process of "searching for their roots" and that previously they were suppressed due to the presence of world religions such as Christianity and Buddhism. But Kamei also seeks to provide a robust defense of why "indigenous faiths" matter to India (2006, 19). This model of primal religions can be helpfully extended to both indigenous religions and Hinduism.

THE MAKING AND UNMAKING OF INDIGENOUS RELIGIONS

A document written by an RSS activist and intellectual, B. B. Jamatia, and published by the Janajati Faith and Culture Protection Forum (JFCPF), supported by the Kalyan Ashram, presents the key aspect of what it calls the "religious philosophy of the Janajatis of Northeast Bharat" in twelve points.[8] This covers everything from the importance of a "Supreme Being," to the soul, karma, rebirth, food, nature, anticonversion, and the importance of Mother Earth (Jamatia 2011, 21–22). It specifically makes several points about the importance of reviving and preserving indigenous religions based on two significant impulses: (1) the more a person stays in touch with Mother Nature, the more she is a loyal subject of Bharat (India); (2) the more a person is intimately tied to one's "ancient culture," the harder it is to be converted to "semitic religions" (2011, 13, 16).

There are several points in the document worth examination.[9] First, the document recommends that the indigenous communities of the region revive their religions based on the idea "culture is identity" (Jamatia 2011, 15). Losing culture comes from neglecting the ancestors and eventually forgetting them. Culture, it further goes on to say, is the "embodiment of our ancestors themselves" (15). Using the family analogy of parent and child, the document declares that abandoning culture is "deserting one's own parents" (15). Second, it focuses on eradicating the "evil practices in society" (15). Here it is asking for reform. Sacrifice of a *mithun* (Indian bison), for example, is expensive, and many cannot afford it, especially the poorer in the community. Not curtailing the economically exorbitant sacrifices allows, it says, "the alien religionist to convert our people" (16). Through this process of reform, an indigenous religious philosophy should be cultivated that leads "any sincere seeker of truth to salvation and finally to liberation from all bondages of worldly life, else it will be rather a hindrance towards spiritual development" (18).

Jamatia compares the abandonment of sacrifices with the reform of Hinduism in the nineteenth century, which focused on "evil practices like dowry, and child marriage" (19). Indigenous communities, he says, must also realize that the problem is not with their philosophies but with the "transfer of traditional knowledge" (19). This transfer has been affected by colonial forces (the Mughal invasion and British colonialism), which resulted in "social and religious erosion" (19), denigrating indigenous knowledge. Despite this, the text continues, "we the janajati people of Northeast Bharat including non janajati Hindus are still equipped with the religious philosophy of the highest order in the world" (19).

Third, the document cautions against the destructive power of "westernisation in the name of modernization" (18). It laments the loss of traditional customs and folklore, and now, with the advent of modern education, these changes are exacerbated particularly where indigenous languages are waning amongst the youth. To restore the loss, it suggests, weekly prayer centers should be introduced to counter religious conversion and to provide the youth with guidance on the "practical problems of life" (18). These reforms are also a way to make them more acceptable to the modern world, argued Tana in our interview. Tana is an indigenous intellectual from Arunachal Pradesh, who is an influential voice in the movement for indigenous religions.[10] Conversing in his large house in Itanagar, along with my RSS guide, Sandip, Tana gives me an example of how these reforms have happened over the years. He tells me that temples, altars, and priests are needed to remind the people that a religious system exists to support the community. These indigenous religions in Arunachal Pradesh—such as Donyipolo, Rangfraa, Meder Nello—need to be organized and made visible: "If, for instance, you want someone to see your religion, you can't suddenly make someone ill to show them how your puja is being performed. Sometimes illnesses may not come. Now that will not happen, as there are proper organizations." Tana's comment brings to light the processes through which indigenous communities in the Northeast are also becoming "religious," marking boundaries of their belief and practice, as a visible entity that can be seen.

I ask Tana to give me an example of how this visibility is envisioned. He points to the recent controversy regarding the adoption of a high god by the Rangfraa Faith Promotion Society, an indigenous religion of Arunachal Pradesh and Assam. This high god, it is said, resembles Shiva, a Hindu deity. The RSS magazine *Organiser* (and later reprinted in *Heritage Explorer*) reports on this process. In the article, the general secretary of the Rangfraa Faith Promotion Society, Latsam Khimun, explains that they needed a "religious tenor" to their reforms and thus decided to hold a painting competition, to choose an image for their deity. This is how Khimun narrates the event: "More than 100 people participated. The winning painting just happened to look like Shiva with some traditional imagery. The painting was sent to Jodhpur. From there came the first 300-kg marble sculpture of the Rangfraa in 1997" (2017, 14).

What is missing from Khimun's narrative, Sandip later confessed to me as we were driving away from Tana's house, is that those involved in choosing the deity (along with Khimun) are members of the Sangh—the VHP, Kalyan Ashram workers, and the RSS. Once the image was installed, the *Organiser* reports, the worshippers in the Rangfraa temple chanted "Jai Rangfraa, Jai Rangfraa, Jai Rangfraa" (Victory to Rangfraa). It describes how the voice of the worshippers grew, and the priests standing beside the Rangfraa "idol," who looks on like a "Mongoloid white Shiva," slipped into a trance, shaking (2017, 14). Some have criticized this depiction of Rangfraa as Hinduization/Sanskritization. Khimun, however, argues, "We think of Shiva as Rangfraa or Ishwar [Lord] in another form." He adds, "Ram, Krishna, Buddha, Mahavira, Christ and Muhammad Prophet are all Fraa or Bhagawan [god] and they are all our teachers, so no one has any right to claim exclusive possessions over any of them as such."[11] According to the VKIC vice president, Mananeeya Nivedita Bhide, these exchanges and influences have been central to the way tribal and nontribal societies have interacted for decades. Using the anthropologist Robert Redfield's (1941) "continuum thesis," Bhide argues that this continuity between tribal religions and Hinduism—through the adoption of Rangfraa from Shiva for example—is what provides their "unity" (2010, 60; see also Sackley 2012; Singer 1972; Srinivas 1952).[12]

This process of institutionalization, iconography, and the adoption of a central place of worship can be seen in the expansion of indigenous religions, such as Donyipolo in Arunachal Pradesh among the Adi (Scheid 2015); Rangraism among the Tangsa Naga (Barkataki-Ruscheweyh 2017); and the Heraka in Assam, Nagaland, and Manipur among the Zeliangrong Nagas (Longkumer 2010). Attempts at syndicating indigenous religions occur on two levels. First, using the language of nativism—that of soil, blood, and belonging—they are located in a space and time that speaks of what James Clifford calls "an absolutist indigenism, where each distinct 'people' strive to occupy an original bit of ground" (2001, 482). This hyperlocal reality can evoke the imagery of a "frightening utopia" (Clifford 2001, 482) that is a denial of all the "deep histories of movement, urbanization, habitation, reindigenization, sinking roots, moving on, invading, mixing—the very stuff of human history" (2001, 482–83). Second, there is circularity between the local and global at different levels—at a scholarly level Kamei and other writers are arguing for the preservation of indigenous religions to a local and national audience, while engaging with worldwide indigenous traditions. They use the UN language of rights to accentuate the pressures faced by indigenous peoples. These moments enable people to envision a world, weaving the different voices that make indigenous life-worlds possible.

One way to frame this global and universal world is through the words of Nivedita Bhide, the vice president of the Vivekananda Kendra in Kanyakumari, who offers a reading of Hinduism as both harmonizing-integrating and all-encompassing: Hinduism can be represented ideally as the "common principle of all native-indigenous traditions of various communities" (Bhide 2002, xxiii). The kind of idea Bhide is proposing becomes clearer when we examine the compatible relationship between Hinduism and indigenous religions, with paganism and animism. While recognizing these similarities and continuations, we must also be aware when these differences are glossed over and simplified.

ANIMISM, TRIBES, AND INDIGENOUS RELIGIONS
In 2018, the Indian Council of Philosophical Research (ICPR) canceled a seminar titled Rethinking Religious Pluralism and the Relationship

between Religions, which was to be held on 9 April 2018 at Jawaharlal Nehru University (JNU), New Delhi.[13] In a letter addressed to the organizer, Professor Puri of JNU, one of the reasons the ICPR objected to the seminar was because of "papers on tribal religious practices"—at least two papers about Naga tribal religion were listed in the seminar program.[14] According to the online newspaper *The Wire*, the chairman of the ICPR, S. R. Bhatt, is considered to be close to the RSS, and this does need to be taken into account. It reports that, according to Bhatt, the papers on tribal religions outlined in the seminar were not addressing "religious pluralism," and "we cannot have papers on adivasi [read: tribal] religion." The reasons for this are difficult to understand in what Bhatt and the ICPR have said publicly. Bhatt is reported to have said that there is a "difference between 'the religion of tribals' and 'what tribals think about religious pluralism,'" and the lack of "conceptual clarity"—the seminar was on pluralism, not on "tribal religion"—was one of the reasons for the cancellation.[15]

Mrinal Miri—one of India's most prominent philosophers, from the Mising tribe of Assam, and one of the keynote speakers—objected to the cancellation on several grounds. First, Miri argued that tribes are seen as having no religion to merit a seminar topic on religious pluralism. This argument over the lack of religion is reminiscent of eighteenth- and nineteenth-century colonial ideas, when British administrators and missionaries concluded that the indigenous peoples of Northeast India (and elsewhere) had no religion to violate and therefore were primed for missionary activities (Johnstone [1896] 2006, 43; also Chidester 1996). Second, it appears from the ICPR objections that only those "proper religions" are permitted for discussion, a definition that excludes tribal religions altogether.

If we are to unpack the notion that tribal religions cannot be included in the discussions of religious pluralism, it could be either because tribal religions are not religions, the point to which Miri objects, or because tribal religions do not fall under the category of pluralism; if you are to discuss pluralism, it requires separate entities. If we are assuming that tribal religions are synonymous with Hinduism, it may mean that this is not appropriate for the study of pluralism, but given this assumption is exactly what is being questioned, it brings us back to the same difficulty.

The fact that the ICPR did not wish the "debate" made public is interesting in itself.

Miri suggests that the ICPR objections not only arise from unfamiliarity with tribal religions, but more broadly, it is an attempt to deny tribals their own humanity. This is how Miri expresses his indignation: "The most that a tribal can be permitted to talk about in a seminar on plurality of religions is 'proper' religions, and not her/his own because the belief that there is such a thing is mistaken—the community of religions has no place for what the tribal thinks is her or his religion."[16] The fact that tribal religion as a category is dismissed by the ICPR demonstrates again the consistent claim made by the Sangh that tribal religion cannot be treated as something independent of Hinduism. The intervention by the ICPR in adjudicating discussions on religions in the JNU seminar is significant because it exposes the institutional weight behind what constitutes tribal religion and how these issues are envisaged in the current political climate. The ICPR's involvement moreover highlights the role Sangh ideas and activities play in educational institutions and among academic scholars (see the introduction). Virginius Xaxa (2005), the Indian sociologist, suggests this should not surprise us, when we consider previous connections between the Sangh and the work of the prominent Indian sociologist G. S. Ghurye, primarily around the question of whether tribes are Hindus.

Ghurye, an important Indian sociologist writing in the 1980s, argued that the tribes of India were "backward Hindus" (Xaxa 2005, 1364). The conclusion, based on secondhand census reports culled from various administrative reports between 1891 and 1931, also highlights how census materials can be used to categorize (see Cohn 1987; Guha 2003; Kapila 2008). Mr. Enthoven, the superintendent of the 1901 census for Bombay, expresses the difficulty in distinguishing "regular Hindu castes" from that of the "so-called Animists." He says, "No sharp line of demarcation can be drawn between Hinduism and Animism. The one shades away insensibly into the other" (Ghurye 1980, 2). This ambiguity seems less of a problem in the census of 1891 in which Sir Athelstane Baines, the census commissioner, reports that the religion of those who did not adhere to the "wider creeds" (probably referring to the main religious traditions of India) was termed "Tribal Animism" or "Tribal Religion" (cited in Ghurye

1980, 30). However, by 1921, Sedgwick, the superintendent of the 1921 census for Bombay, categorically states, "I have . . . no hesitation in saying that Animism as a [religious category] should be entirely abandoned, and that all those hitherto classed as Animists should be grouped with Hindu at the next census" (Ghurye 1980, 30). This means either tribal people are animists and therefore grouped as Hindus, or they represent a distinct religion on account of their isolation from the larger society.

While Ghurye's examination shows the ambiguous relationship between tribal religions and animism in parts of India, it must be noted that Ghurye omits the Northeast from his tribe/Hindu analysis. Ghurye himself suggests that this region is "still forming part of India (Bharat)" because it was an area acquired by the British and handed to the Indian government on independence (1980, 313). Ghurye, however, is a proponent of the view that tribal regions are part and parcel of Bharat, with any attempts to treat them as separate unwise for the future of the country. While it is debatable whether tribes can be seen as Hindu, the similarity appears to be that both tribal religions and animism are asserted as "natural religions" (Xaxa 2005, 1365).[17] The categorization within the census reflects much of the way the Sangh understand the tribals as Hindu. The Sangh's work appears to carry forward Ghurye's ideas into new areas.

B. B. Kumar, an anthropologist and now closely associated with Vivekananda Kendra Institute of Culture (VKIC), calls the issue of categorization a "census game" (2015: 10). In a speech delivered to VKIC New Delhi, which echoes much of the VKIC ethos of "cultural unity," Kumar blames the census for distorting the difference between tribal religion and Hinduism. Much like Ghurye's work, the census reports are examined by Kumar firstly to blame the British for these haphazard and arbitrary classifications and secondly to restore the continuum between what he calls "the distinction between the popular religion of the country and that of the Scheduled Tribes" (2015, 11).

To make his point more concrete, he suggests that the fluctuations in the census point to the arbitrariness of classifications. In the 1901 census, he notes, 72.03 percent of the Kachari were animists, while 27.97 percent were Hindus. In the 1931 census, the numbers were reversed. By 1961, 93.63 percent are classified as Hindus and the rest animists. He says that a similar pattern can be observed with the Mech, Mikir, Rabha, Naga, Kuki, and other tribal communities in Northeast India (Kumar 2015, 11– 12). Indeed, for scholars like Ghurye and Kumar, the boundaries between tribal religion and Hinduism are not as definite as the census makes them out to be. This amorphous classification system, then, works in favor of those who want to forge cultural unity by using exactly the same technique of numbers (or the "census game") inherited from the British. Kumar's willingness to accept the 1961 census showing 94 percent Hindus supports the ideological argument of the continuum between tribes and Hindus despite the disruptions—from British colonialism, Christian missionaries, and Westernization. The indeterminate nature of these classifications does not happen merely in the confines of documents and state census projects but also in the lives of ordinary people who have to deal with the casual ways these numbers and categories are interpreted. If the Sangh want to encompass indigenous religions and animists, it is worth examining the practical ways in which they are attempting to expand their ideological approach.

PAGANISM, NATIONALISM, AND GLOBAL INDIGENEITY

"Mitakuye oyasin" (we all are related) is a Native American saying, my informant Vijay Swami tells me, originally from the Lakota language. On a warm afternoon in May 2018, under the shade of a large tree, Vijay and I discuss the work he does, amid the bustle of a shakha organized by the RSS in Pashigat, in the Northeast state of Arunachal Pradesh. A hundred twenty young tribal boys participate in this shakha, where they are taught self-defense, learn about the Hindu nation and its key ideologies, and cultivate discipline through the rigorous twenty-day program. In the morning shakha, Vijay tells the boys about "native traditions" all over the world and asks them to say in unison, "Mitakuye oyasin"—to convey the message that these young boys in Pashigat are related to the Native Americans.

Trained in the Vivekananda Kendra, Vijay is an educationalist and closely aligned with the Sangh, having worked in the region for three decades. He tells me that in the Hindu tradition, too, "we say, 'Vasudeva kutumbakam'—the whole universe is one. So we are related." Upon researching different native communities around the world, Vijay came up with an idea. "We found that instead of doing research on different ethnic communities of Northeast India, why shouldn't we have a sort of a comparative and cross-cultural study between all native communities of the world?" That is how RIWATCH (Research Institute of World's Ancient Traditions Cultures and Heritage) came into existence, he says.

RIWATCH (with the motto "Nurturing the Roots") is an organization that is based in Roing, in the Lower Dibang Valley District of Arunachal Pradesh. They are a "community based research organisation with [a] mission of empowering ethnic communities to prosper sustainably by strengthening their value system" (RIWATCH n.d.). Vijay Swami runs the organization, along with twelve officeholders and board members. They have already opened a RIWATCH Museum in Roing and have the ambition of opening a research university. Their focus is also on study abroad and student exchange programs. In their undated annual report, they highlight the student exchange program to emphasize the connections with different indigenous and native traditions of the world: "Miss Maria Priscilla Alvarado Gomez was the first scholar from Costa Rica attached to RIWATCH to study the traditions of Idu Mishmis for a period of 3 months in 2008–2009. She found lots of common cultural threads with Natives of Costa Rica and Native Americans of USA" (RIWATCH n.d.).

RIWATCH is part of the International Center for Cultural Studies (ICCS) based in Pennsylvania. On their Facebook page, ICCS is described as an organization that "strives for a world where indigenous cultural heritage and traditions are valued for their intrinsic wisdom to strengthen communities and enrich life."[18] Originally conceived in Nagpur, in the western state of Maharashtra in 1994, under the guidance of Yaswant Pathak and then later Professor S. W. Bakhle, ICCS was established in 1996. Since 2003, they have conducted various activities, including conferences and workshops, under the forum World Council of Elders of the Ancient Traditions (WCEAT) (ICCS n.d.). The following gives a flavor of some of the themes and conferences they have organized:

> The first international conference was held at Mumbai in 2003 with the theme "Mitakuye Oyasin—We are all related". . . . The second conference was in 2006 at Jaipur with the theme "Spirituality beyond Religions". . . . The

third conference was held in 2009 at Nagpur with the theme "Renaissance of the Ancient Traditions: Challenges and Solutions".... The theme of this 4th Conference was "Nourishing the Balance in the Universe". The event was jointly organized by International Center for Cultural Studies (ICCS), Dev Samskruti Vishwa Vidyalaya (DSVV) and co-sponsored by the Council of Elders Mayas [*sic*], Xincas and Garifunas, European Congress of Ethnic Religions (ECER) and Children of Mother Earth. A total of 458 delegates from 33 countries including 178 from overseas participated in the conference. (Samvad 2012, 6)

The activities of RIWATCH and ICCS offer a platform for different indigenous communities to share their knowledge and to collaborate on an international scale. Centered on insider knowledge of indigenous peoples, the activities of these groups gain prominence when they collaborate with the RSS and other Sangh members. In the 2012 conference Nourishing the Balance in the Universe, Mohan Bhagwat, sarsanghchalak (chief) of the RSS, delivered the keynote address, where "he praised the efforts and resolve of the Elders in preserving their traditions and cultures. He recalled the priceless treasures of Bharat thought like 'Live and Let Live', 'Unity in Diversity', 'World is one family' & 'Let us ennoble the world' and remarked that these have extreme relevance today. Universal outlook is the hallmark of Bharatiya thought and the happiness and well-being of everyone is always sought" (Samvad 2012, 8).

The focus of RIWATCH and ICCS is presented as an ecumenical movement, though focused on a non-Christian and non-Muslim paradigm, where there is an attempt to find a connection between different native traditions—pagan, Native American, and Hindu. And this is the idea of Hindutva, exclaims Vijay. Hindutva, then, is central to the goals of ICCS and RIWATCH in light of the responsibility Hindu traditions have to the world, Vijay tells me. "If you look at the whole world's cultural heritage, there are only two civilizations that have been running continually for a long time. They are Chinese and Hindu. All other traditions (Egyptian or Incas) have been born some time and died their own deaths at some point. These living traditions, particularly Indian tradition, have the responsibility to help others to identify their own past richness and things." On its website, the ICCS further qualifies this point and adds, "Hindu society, being the oldest, and arguably most vibrant ancient tradition in the world, which can still be classed, in some sense as a flourishing civilization, naturally takes on the mantle of host."[19] The initiative of RIWATCH and Vijay's involvement in it speaks to particular issues surrounding the relationship between nature, Mother Earth, and nationalism that is underwritten by what the term *indigenous* implies and based against a Judeo-Christian (and Islamic) framework. This is a point reiterated in the ICCS's most recent conference in Mumbai:

> Elders, like Pat McCabe from the Diné Nation, raised in the Lakota tradition of the Native American peoples, spoke eloquently, while remaining hard-hitting in her keynote address that ancient traditions must come together in a real meaningful sense in order to push back against the socio-economic forces harming the Earth. The emphasis on feminine divine was the set theme, and a special focus was set on protecting, nourishing and living harmoniously with Nature. . . . The challenge seems clear enough. And the solution is equally as clear—that of a complete overhaul of the socio-political-economic framework in which our societies operate underpinned by a Judeo-Christian narrative.[20]

There are different ways of reading the summary of events described by the ICCS. On the one hand, the importance of ancient knowledge preserved and sustained through the ages among native and indigenous communities is worth acknowledging, with some newspaper headlines even lauding indigenous peoples as the "best guardians of the world's biodiversity."[21] Indeed, the movement to record indigenous knowledge has already been highlighted by the UN and UNESCO through the phenomena referred to as Indigenous Knowledge (IK), Traditional Knowledge (TK), and Traditional Indigenous Knowledge (TIK).[22] These forms of knowledge are seen as panacea to the worst kinds of modernity and consumerism, and the loss of indigenous knowledge is set against the "reach of technology and Christianity [which brought with it] the alarming prospect of an end of knowledge about ways of life that included unexplored pathways of human progress" (Niezen 2011, 125).

The unintended consequences of such challenging ideas are the ripples they create, widening the circle. Different groups take up these ideas, like Hindutva actors in Northeast India, by targeting a particular Judeo-Christian world view. This position is also reiterated by the ICCS statement, which leads one to a binary opposition of "us" versus "them," further entrenching antagonism. The way Hindutva actors navigate this quagmire in Northeast India is by working with indigenous religions to revive the pre-Christian gods and lay claims to the soil, not in (secular) Christian terms of dominance but through benevolence, where nature facilitates both loyalty to the nation and ties to "ancient cultures," an idea, argues Niezen (2011, 124–26), that is familiar in indigenous peoples discourses. Hindutva is able to link with global indigenous ideas of ancient cultures through paganism.

In a lecture given to the VKIC by the anthropologist B. B. Kumar, he notes: "Ancestor worship is an essential feature of our religion (generically known as Paganism; a generic term that includes Hinduism)" (2015, 33). In their official party text, the BJP reiterate this claim under the heading "Cultural Nationalism." The BJP draw on the idea of paganism as applied to those who worshipped the "God of the pagans, which in Latin means 'locality'" (2005, 94). Pagans are also referred to as "country-dwellers" or "heathens"; paganism was the old religion of pre-Christian Europe. It exists today in many forms, ranging from "Native Spirituality, Celtic Spirituality, European Traditional Religion, the Elder Faith, and the Old Religion" (BJP 2005, 94).

What is important though, the BJP text argues, is that paganism survived the onslaught of Christianization in Europe and is now undergoing a "massive revival" in the West, a point I explore further in Chapter 5. Similarly to Hindutva, which is undergoing a "reinstatement," the BJP text argues that paganism relates, crucially, to local gods and ancestors of the land based on ideas of polytheism (belief in many deities), pantheism (belief that the divine is everywhere), and finally that the divine is expressed as both male and female (2005, 96).[23] In summing up the basic overlap between paganism and Hinduism, the BJP text says: "In a sense at the basic level Hinduism is a Pagan religion. As Paganism allows for evolution Hinduism too allows for evolution. Since Paganism is belief in many Gods there is generally no fight over Gods. This is the greatest virtue of Polytheism. The highest merit of Polytheism is its capacity to integrate Gods. If Gods can work together, religions can work together" (2005, 97). Once Hinduism is expressed along these lines, then, it has the potential to relate with other native traditions that are intimately connected to land. An interview with Prudence Jones of the Pagan Federation by the scholar of religion Michael York, in 1991, focuses on this idea of allying with Hinduism. Jones points out that there is an important connection between Hinduism, Shintoism, and paganism as they are all "indigenous faiths" and are not dogmatic, like the religions of the book, Islam and Christianity, which are monotheistic—with a "Supreme Deity who has to be obeyed." Arguing for the need to organize themselves into one coherent body, Jones even suggests forming a "Worldwide Council of Indigenous Religions." She further suggests that European pagan religion, like Hinduism (which is indigenous to India), "is the native, indigenous religion of Europe."[24] For Prudence Jones, there is a clear ideological platform to align the UK Pagan Federation with Hinduism, affording them a larger political profile.

This interview is significant because it was reprinted in 2005 by the BJP under "Cultural Nationalism," appearing in local and national RSS magazines, such as the *Organiser* and *Heritage Explorer*. This interview was also referred to by several of my Sangh informants in recent years. It is emphasized to demonstrate the struggle of paganism—due to suppression by Christianity—and its revival as a lesson to Christians, who have suppressed their ancient cultures. The revival is seen as a challenge to the Judeo-Christian framework that dominated through imperialism and colonization, and now Hinduism, in its resurgence, is able to offer support to all indigenous traditions in the world. The common themes that link paganism, Hinduism, and indigenous religions are animism and kinship with nature (Harvey 2005; Rountree 2012), a discourse that is popular among Western pagan groups whose motto (to quote the first principle of the Pagan Federation) is "Love for and kinship with nature" (Rountree 2012, 305).

There are two ways in which the discussion surrounding paganism has developed. First is the discourse over the "closeness to nature" that scholars like Rountree (2012) and others (Fisk 2017; Harvey 2005) have articulated. They show how most modern paganism is intimately tied to nature, often articulated as "animism"—which includes all of "earth's visible inhabitants." These are "trees, rocks, rivers, mountains, caves, insects, animals (including humans), fire, snow, particular tracts of land or indeed the whole earth itself (or Herself)—are conscious and en-souled or en-spirited" (Rountree 2012, 308). In these texts, earlier and more negative uses of animism, based on E. B. Tylor's (1871) evolutionary idea—that animism is the basis of primitive religion that gives rise to polytheism and then monotheism—are abandoned for a more positive version that recognizes a world that is "full of persons, only some of whom are human, and life is always lived in relationship to others" (Harvey 2005, xi).

This "new animism" can be found in a host of scholars (Birt-Davis 1999; de Castro 1998; Descola 2013; Hallowell 1960; Harvey 2005; Ingold 2006) and also applied to local writers (Bhide 2010, 2002; Kumar 2015; Jamatia 2011) who are also interested in reconstituting the term *animism*. For instance, Nivedita Bhide, a veritable proponent of indigenous religions of Northeast India, explains that in the dictionary definition, "animism" actually means the "attribution of life (soul) to natural objects and phenomena" (Bhide 2002, xx). Bhide holds this as a positive description and links anima, soul, and atman (soul). Bhide concludes that Hindus believe atman pervades the entire universe: "If we go by the dictionary meaning of Animism, then all Hindus are animist, too" (2002, xx). She believes that the present crisis, where Hindus have been separated from animist tribals, is due to the colonial and missionary strategy of "divide and convert" (2002, xx).

Similarly, the turn toward nativism, with the appeal to roots that paganism encourages, inadvertently produces other kinds of connections having to do with land, identity, and authentic nationalism through "blood" and "belonging" (Gallagher 2009; Ivakhiv 2005). In the process of reclamation of land and tradition around a particular set of local symbols and ideas, many nativist traditions in Russia and the Slavic countries (post-USSR), for example, used a mixture of different traditions combined with nativism, paganism, animism, and Vedic sources of the Aryan race, against the Semitic religions. Paganism, for instance, is used as a way to link with "spiritual Aryanism in Europe" (Gallagher 2009, 585; Ivakhiv 2005, 213; Shnirelman 2017; see also Fisk 2017, 33). Adrian Ivakhiv (2005) argues that these movements are often related to disillusionment with modernity, Christianity, capitalism, and Zionism, characteristic features associated with a loss of identity. In fact, for the Ukrainian Native Believers, Christianity is to be blamed for taking away their original traditions, cultures, and values (Ivakhiv 2005). The solution for the Native Faiths, Ivakhiv suggests, is "a recovery of the original condition through a rebirth of the remnant forms of tradition and custom encoding those original relationships . . . by which human groups once lived in harmony with Nature" (2005, 216).

If we are to look at Hinduism as the "common principle of all native-indigenous traditions of various communities," as Bhide suggests, there is room to conceptualize the connection between Hinduism, indigenous religions, and Native Faiths in Europe and elsewhere, through connections with RIWATCH, the World Council of Elders of the Ancient Traditions (WCEAT), and the ICCS. Similarly, Meera Nanda argues that there is a relation between what she calls "neo-pagans" and Hindutva through the language of environmentalism, the critique of "Semitic monotheism," and their efforts to find connections between their pre-Christian European gods and Hinduism, the "living religion of nature" (2004, 2009). In his reply, Koenraad Elst, a sympathizer of the Sangh, accuses Nanda of overplaying the connection between Hindutva and neo-pagans. If this connection could exist, he says, it is through the WCEAT. This could be the beginning of an international network of likewise traditions, he notes (Elst 2015, 52–53). Both Nanda and Elst marshal rather thin evidence, and their critiques tend to be highly polemical. If the basic principle of Hindutva has to do with the soil and the gods and ancestors that inhabit it, it is possible for its affiliates/adherents to subsume paganism, nativism, animism, and indigenous traditions. This "resonance" provides a useful way of thinking, in the way Susan Lepselter uses it, describing and finding connections between the social, aesthetic, and affective dimensions and "often understanding that process as political" (2016, 4). This universalism is, of course, a challenge because many native and indigenous traditions have distinct practices that identify them as such. But by providing a broad canvas upon which anything can be etched and clarifying its identity by engaging with questions of indigeneity and indigenous religions, the evolution of Hindutva in the Northeast has created worlds that are possible and potentially universal.

HINDUTVA WORLDING

"Indigenous peoples all [speak many] different languages but in our meetings, we are speaking one language. Our relationship to Mother Earth is identical."[25] General Secretary Ban Ki-Moon quoted these words from a longtime indigenous activist, Tonya Gonnella Frichner, during the United Nations' first World Conference on Indigenous Peoples in New York in September 2014. Various scholars have observed that nation and culture are kindred concepts related to, or existing in, the "soil" (Clifford 1988; Malkki 1992, 29; Wagner 1981). Mother Earth is the ideal metaphor to carry home the message of the soil as it is "the centre of the universe, the core of their culture, the origin of their identity as a people. She [Mother Earth] connects them with their past (as the home of ancestors), with the present (as provider of their material needs), and with the future (as the legacy they hold in trust for their children and grandchildren). In this way, indigenousness carries with it a sense of belonging to a place."[26]

In the words of the anthropologist Liisa Malkki, "Terms like 'native', 'indigenous', and 'autochthonous' have all served to root cultures in soils" (1992, 29). This homology is evident in how the term *culture* is derived from the Latin for cultivation (Malkki 1992, 29; see also Wagner 1981: 21). The territorialization of nation and culture to the soil in arborescent forms is the subject explored in Chapter 1. Here, the metaphor of roots and soil continues to pervade much of the thinking of the Sangh, UNESCO, and indigenous peoples. In marking both the territorial nation and evoking the metaphysical valence of nation and culture as universalizing Hindutva, this became clear to me through my interaction with Abhishek.

Abhishek is a senior RSS pracharak (full-time worker) based in Arunachal Pradesh. He was the main organizer of the RSS shakha where the ideas of RIWATCH were on display. During the shakha, Abhishek talked in depth with Vijay, a leader of RIWATCH, and also gave a talk to the 120 tribal boys present. Abhishek has a PhD from Jawaharlal Nehru University (JNU) in international relations, focusing on Indonesia.

Through his work in Indonesia, he began to appreciate the extent to which Bharatiya culture (Indian culture) has had an influence, not only on their language but also the cultural influence that is pervasive in many aspects of their history, for example, in borrowing the Sanskrit concept *bhinneka tunggal ika* (unity in diversity), which became their national motto. It was through his work in Indonesia and the Northeast of India that he began to appreciate the "universalism of Hindutva," he told me. He acknowledged the importance of people like Savarkar, Hedgewar, and Golwalkar as important thinkers for the Sangh but reminded me that, although one must continue to use "their methodology" of "man making, nation building," we must also be prepared to "deconstruct their ideas to reconstruct our country." Parochial nationalism is therefore antithetical to the growth of the nation, he said. Using the language of humanitarianism, coexistence, and liberalism, ideas one may not immediately associate with Hindutva, he argued for Hindutva as universal, progressing from the individual, to society and nation, and on to the level of internationalism, culminating in universalism.

Probing a little further, I asked him, "How can the universalism of Hindutva be applied somewhere else, say, in China, Europe, or America?" Abhishek answered in one sentence: "Hindutva is an ideology that is relevant and universal in whichever country that acknowledges the soil as the core indigenous ideology from which everything else has cropped up." This arboreal language envisages encounters that connect and intersect with the wider world and "invoke or implicate worlding processes above and beyond a set of physical or situational conditions" (Palmer and Hunter 2018). Hindutva worlding is not simply about creating cultures but about worlds. In light of this, Hindutva worlding comes about through its physical grounding and metaphysical resonance—that of Mother Earth.

There is substantial evidence concerning how Mother Earth is used by the Sangh (and others) interchangeably with Mother Nature, goddesses, and the national symbol, Bharat Mata (Mother India) (Kraft 2017; Niezen 2011; Permanent Forum on Indigenous Issues 2010). The use of these images as icons will be explored further in Chapter 6. It is a way to fuse, according to Malkki, "people, culture, and soil on 'Mother Earth'"

(1992, 30). Reminiscent of the discussion regarding RIWATCH, the ICCS, and Hindutva, organizations like the Global Indigenous Caucus, in their New York meeting in 2009, issued the statement that "indigenous peoples of all over the world speak with one voice" (quoted in Niezen 2011, 128). This sort of universal voice, akin to that propounded by RIWATCH through the Hindutva worlding—"we are all related"—is often heard in the context of environmental issues. The language of indigenous spirituality becomes intertwined with ideas of how to care for Mother Earth and looks toward indigenous peoples' notions of care, stewardship, and guardianship of the world (Niezen 2011, 128–29). Critics however warn us of the danger of this view, which is often based on a particular European "grammar of conquest" (Brosius 2001; also Sale 1990).

Reacting against the generalized concept of the "sacred" through his work in Penan, Malaysia, Peter Brosius (2001), reminds us that indigenous peoples relate to the world in very specific ways, following a rich vocabulary inherited from the land and their ancestors. This is precisely Cox's (2007) critique, as discussed earlier. The universalizing of indigenous religions minimizes the location-specific, culturally rooted practices of people who relate to local contexts in ways that make universal generalization extremely difficult, if not impossible, as academic constructions. But in the realm of political articulations, these haphazard universalizing discourses are highly productive. Local knowledge is often usurped when their plight is taken up by activists to appeal to remote audiences in a language that has global recognition. This world-making, whereby the terms *sacred* and *Mother Earth* have powerful resonances, relates to the global circulation of ideas in a way that is generative. In Jamatia's description of indigenous peoples in the Northeast, these ideas take on a comparative salience. He says:

> The janajati people are forest dwellers, depending completely on forest produce for sustaining their lives. For countless generations, forest [*sic*] has been their home; therefore they are the most intimate to the Mother Nature [*sic*]. They are the simplest people on the earth. They are as holy and pure as the Mother Nature itself. They are, in fact, the most obliged and indebted to the Mother Nature than any other. So for them every portion of the Mother Earth and its creation (Nature) is pure and sacred (Jamatia 2011, 8).

If we acknowledge, following the anthropologist Tania Li, that identifying as indigenous or tribal is about *positioning*, "which draws upon historically sedimented practices, landscapes and repertoires of meaning, and emerges through particular patterns of engagement and struggle" (Li 2000, 150), we may view Hindutva in a similar light. The positioning of Hindutva and indigenous religions in the Northeast opens up the core issue of identification around similarities—land, nature, animism, and Mother Earth. Li's remarks become relevant insofar as Hindutva is a philosophy of indigeneity. It is hard to see how it could be excluded. Yet it must be stressed that Hindutva activists are not necessarily shouting to be heard when it comes to the UNDRIP or to be recognized as indigenous peoples. But what they are doing is aligning, or *positioning*, themselves with indigenous religions precisely to allow them to make certain worlds possible that might easily slip under the radar, in spaces that people might least suspect.

CONCLUSION

This chapter examines the way indigenous religions in India are constructed. It investigates how Hindutva activists seek to appropriate the idea of indigenous by showing how these categories are not simply descriptive but also politically charged. The homology between Hindutva and indigenous, "of the soil," demonstrates a particular synergy that is both productive and challenging.

It is productive for Hindutva and indigenous religions primarily because it brings together two traditions and two opinions—one that argues for difference and the other for similarity. But the dominant narrative appears to conflate the two as having a similar genealogy and a pattern of practices that are not simply descriptive but also political. The critique of the census and the arithmetic therein displays this with acuity. This conflation allows Hindutva activists to assimilate indigenous religions as Hindu, while also allowing indigenous religions to gain a larger political profile, especially when they are battling dominant Christian groups in the region, who see them as soft targets for conversion. It is productive too when Hindutva takes on a universal agenda of linking different native traditions around the world, through worldings, and creating a common, universalizing principle of shared cultural essences.

Using paganism, animism, and even UN ideas of indigeneity demonstrates the ways in which world politics, economies, communications, and cultures are all entangled and interrelated, a friction that continually persists and astounds (Tsing 2005). Tsing says, "Cultures are continually co-produced in the interaction I call 'friction': the awkward, unequal, unstable, and creative qualities of interconnection across difference" (2005, 4). What is missing in her description of "cultures" is the idea of "sameness," a technique that argues for the opposite of friction, a well-oiled machine, harmony. Hindutva is the harmonious echo that produces and aspires to fulfil worlds in which differences are celebrated and where sameness is the grammar. The image of the soil and how ideologies crop up from it provides the lasting arborescent finality of Hindutva worldings.

It is challenging because not all agree that Hindutva's assimilation of indigenous religions is right. Margaret's insistence on its separation, at the opening of this chapter, must be read from the perspective of someone who herself is a follower of indigenous religions in Arunachal Pradesh and has had experiences that make her question the benevolence of Hinduism. She expresses her anger and frustration at being seen as a "lesser Hindu," the same indignation that is visible in Mrinal Miri's reaction to the cancellation of a seminar by the Indian Council of Philosophical Research. Such institutions are keen to erase the differences between tribal religions and Hinduism. The cancellation of the seminar demonstrates that any attempt to treat them separately is unacceptable.

It is challenging, too, because Hindutva makes universal claims about indigeneity, even going so far as to use UN discourses of indigenous peoples. What happens when dominance, not marginality, enters the discourse of indigeneity? In a sense, the point made by James Cox (2007) concerning the locality of indigenous religions is valid here. Even though Cox's definition of indigenous religions might fit in with Hindutva ideas of belonging in India, specific studies of local contexts, as he has done among the Shona of Zimbabwe and the Arrernte of Central Australia, demonstrate that universalizing the local can only be done if the local is taken seriously and studied in its own right. Peter Brosius (2001), too, is skeptical of the discourse of the sacred—localized and distinct to Penan—when global movements usurp it for universal circulation that may not always compound with local articulations. This is where Hindutva ideologies, through their universalizing claims, connect with paganism as a universal form of indigenous religion and, paradoxically, its appeal to the local. Not only are ideas of Hindutva challenging how we think about certain concepts, its global circulations, and indeed its translations, but they are also making worlds that are possible through entering the discourse of indigeneity and indigenous religions. Here, experimental Hindutva thinking, through pursuing national and then transnational routes, is fashioning a certain sensibility that demonstrates that theirs is a way of life. But the question still remains: Whose way of life? In the next chapter, this question is illuminated through an examination of Christianity and prophecy.

CHAPTER 4

PROPHECY AND THE HINDU STATE

"ON THE MORNING OF 3 AUGUST 2015, I received a phone call from Eustar, Isak Swu's wife," recalled Jacob, the secretary of the prayer group Sumi Alakishi Kighinimi in Nagaland. Until his death in 2016, Isak Swu was the president of the National Socialist Council of Nagaland, Isak-Muivah (NSCN-IM), the largest and the most powerful of the Naga nationalist groups. We were sitting in Jacob's living room from which a hint of blue light was shimmering on the surface of the surrounding hills, as he told me the story.

"She had a piece of news that she wanted to share with me," Jacob recalled. She told him that Swu had been asked to put his signature on an important document. Because he was unwell and in the hospital, she had some time to ponder over whether her husband should sign it and to ask for prayer support. She was scared, Jacob confessed to me, primarily because she did not know if the framework agreement was a sincere document from the government of India. They were referring to the framework agreement signed between the government of India and the NSCN-IM to find a settlement to the protracted Indo-Naga political situation, which began in 1947. Jacob informed me that he had immediately assured her, "Grandmother, I will pray and provide an answer to you. I will phone all my Nagaland for Christ prayer warriors and will start praying right now." Jacob then contacted each member of the prayer group and asked them to stop what they were doing and to focus on praying. Jacob pointed to a corner in the room with a rug neatly rolled up. He called it his prayer place. On their knees, they prayed from 6:00 A.M. to 8:00 A.M., but no revelation came. They continued praying again between 8:00 A.M. and 10:00 A.M., but still no answer from God. Then Jacob said to his friends on the phone: "Aay, today we need to pray extra hard like Joshua. He stopped the sun and moon when they were fighting against the Amalekites. We have to pray like Joshua and Elijah—who got the fire: four hundred false prophets of Ahab's group or Elijah? Those praying to their false gods or to their Lord Jehovah?"

These words borrowed from the Old Testament story of Joshua and his victory against opposition and barriers were given to encourage the members, Jacob explained. "At eleven thirty A.M. the revelation started coming to us," said a relieved Jacob. "Then I phoned Isak's wife and told her that all is fine and that this [the framework agreement] is God's doing. And then Uncle Isak put his signature on the document." Isak Swu, according to many accounts, was a deeply religious man and was associated with the Sumi Alakishi Kighinimi along with Eustar Swu, his wife. Asking for God's revelation and guidance was therefore nothing new.

That evening the representative of the government of India R. N. Ravi, chairman of the Joint Intelligence Committee, and Thuingaleng Muivah, the general secretary of the NSCN-IM, added their signatures to the framework agreement, in a ceremony at the prime minister's residence. The agreement is seen as a "political" document that assesses the "unique history of the Nagas," an acknowledgment first made in 2002 by the BJP leader Atal Bihari Vajpayee. The framework agreement lays the basis for the government of India and the NSCN-IM to continue negotiations toward a final agreement on the Indo-Naga situation. One of the ways in which the two entities attempt to go forward is by accepting that the "Nagas are not Indians but a different entity with equal status, having separate and distinct identity with unique history and cultures." The agreement, then, is a "preamble" to any final solution.[1]

In an important sense, the opening story highlights the role prophecy, as revealed knowledge, plays in bringing about Naga sovereignty and the way this knowledge is then used to interact with the Indian nation-state. Is there room for revelation and prayer when deliberating about the nation-state? Both Muivah and Prime Minister Narendra Modi spoke at the event in 2015. Their speeches provide optimism and assurance in the face of considerable challenges in overcoming the seventy years of conflict in the region, instead evoking the language of democracy, public good, and governance. Jacob's story, however, about God's revelation through prayer and the influence it had on the signing of the framework agreement, allows us to observe a different side to this political moment, one that acknowledges the presence of gods in the process. Bruno Latour's delightful description captures moments such as these well: "When men of good will assemble with their cigars in the Habermas Club to discuss an armistice for this or that conflict and they leave their gods on hooks in the cloakroom, I suspect that what is under way is not a peace conference at all.... Real peace is unattainable if negotiators leave their gods, attachments, and incompatible cosmos outside the conference room" (2004, 456, 457).

While the focus of this book is primarily on the region's interaction with Hindutva forces, in this chapter I want to examine the role of the Indian state more widely. The material this chapter presents on prophecy—as revealed knowledge—discloses a certain understanding of India, however crude it may be, as a Hindu state that has denied the Christian Nagas their birthright: that of sovereignty. For example, a widespread understanding of the Indian state during the period when armed conflict was at its highest from the 1950s onward was a fear of "Hindu domination" (Luithui and Haksar 1984, 125). According to the NSCN-IM propaganda, the reach of the Hindu state extends to the Indian military, who were seen as occupiers, and included the influence of Bollywood, traders, and teachers, whose colonialization of the Naga lands are insidious. The most direct violence is unfolding, the propaganda says, when their mission is to supplant "the Christian God, the eternal God of the Universe" (Shepoumaramth 1995, 273). Therefore, on the other hand, there is a sense more widely across India that the current BJP government and the RSS are the culmination of the "Hindu forces," viewed as the full realization of a Hindu state. While the next chapter interrogates the way Christianity is viewed by the Sangh, in this chapter I want to reverse the gaze by looking at how Christians view Hindutva and the Indian state, in this moment, through the Indo-Naga conflict and the discussions over sovereignty.

The event narrated above is about harnessing the collective power of prayer, revelations, and prophecies in order to benefit the Naga nation as viewed in relation to the Indian nation-state. It brings to focus the notion of cosmopolitics as a "common world" (Latour 2004; Stengers 2005) with different human and nonhuman actors and what this relationship says about the shared history of people brought together by the tempestuous history of colonialism and its aftermath. We first need to think about what happens in prophecy if we understand it to imply revealed knowledge about the future that needs to be navigated in the present. Here, it is helpful to examine the archiving of prophecies and what they say about prophecy's cumulative tradition in Nagaland. The archive here is used to indicate oral and written sources that incorporate stories, visions, revelations, dreams, and prophecy that speak to the Indo-Naga conflict (see also below). I choose to use the term *archives* in the manner of various subaltern historians and anthropologists. In highlighting the margins, an archive compiled by indigenous activists and nationalists—an archive that is not officially recognized or, for that matter, that does not officially exist—allows us to think of the archive as a "political act to become historically relevant," an act that means indigenous peoples are now also writing themselves into the history of the nation-state (de la Cadena 2017).

In what follows, through these archives, I would like to paint an alternative history of the Naga movement for sovereignty as a starting point to think more broadly about Christianity in the region and its interaction with the Indian state.[2] I will not follow the traditional linear history of the Naga struggle, which has occupied many writers and many a bookshelf.[3] Rather, there is a far more interesting and complicated relationship between the rendering of the past, present, and future through the use of prophecy and what it says about the Indian nation-state. I aim to offer a more nuanced telling of the situation, which sheds light on these unlikely archival sources, using them to question the narrow confines of the linear history of the nation-state. The prophecy archives demonstrate the cosmopolitical vision of Christianity that seeks to escape such confines. I argue that prophecies rise to the surface when there is much political uncertainty. Certainly, the Indo-Naga conflict has decades of traumatic memories etched deep onto the landscape. It is in these moments where hope as a method (Miyazaki 2004) continues unabated. Using recent works on prophecy (Empson 2006b), I argue that prophecy produces new knowledge that supports the fashioning of hope in these uncertain times through the "agency in abeyance" (Miyazaki 2004, 97), not as passive surrender but as a productive gaze that waits for God's response.

THE ALGORITHM OF PROPHECY

What then is prophecy? Primarily we think of prophecy as foretelling the future (Leavitt 1999). But for my interlocutors, prophecy is about interpreting and negotiating the world in which they live by synthesizing the past, present, and future. In a straightforward sense, prophecy is about decision making, authority, and ideas about causality and time (Empson 2006a, 1). Drawing on the widespread phenomena of prophecies in Mongolia and their relationship to state and society, Rebecca Empson (2006a) presents four salient points about prophecy that have close parallels with the Naga case.

First, Empson suggests that prophecy is direct revelation or vision that comes through divine inspiration from a deity. Although the human voice is the medium, it is the deity that does the talking (see also Csordas 1997). Second, prophecy can be differentiated from divination, which tends to be specific to the individual or of a personal nature. The kinds of prophecies that interest me in this chapter are congruent with Empson's observation that prophecies may appeal to a larger constituency like "society," "the nation," and "the people" (2006a, 4). Third, the nature and practice of prophecy tell us something about political change and uncertainties and how knowledge enables the formulation and reformulation of ideas in the present to better grasp the imminent future (Empson 2006a, 5). The kind of uncertainty that comes with "reading" the political climate means that certain prophetic explanations that reveal a truth about the world tend to be privileged over other explanations (2006a, 5). Unlike mere speculation, it is important to distinguish prophecy as knowledge that is fulfilled, though not necessarily in the way we expect, and what gives it authority and certainty. Finally, prophecies can be read as a form of collective belief that mobilizes and harnesses the power of the nation into action. This is not to suggest that all members of the nation are consciously aware of these prophecies, but it implies that prophecies, however small the incision may be, are already affecting the nation through the actions of the few.

THE PLACE WHERE PROPHECY HAPPENS

Sumi Alakishi Kighinimi (SAK) is a prayer center that has been active for over twenty years in praying for Naga sovereignty. SAK's main purpose is to make known God's message and acknowledge God's hand in guiding the Naga nation and the Indian state. For them, prophecy is about the nation; it is a collective practice that is enacted beyond the individual. It is a task, the members tell me, that comes with immense sacrifice. One of the tasks they have been required to perform since 1997 is to publish letters to the prime minister of India in the local newspapers or send them by fax (and sometimes deliver them in person or via other state dignitaries). Known as "prophetic messages," they utter God's revelation to all parties involved in deliberating Naga sovereignty. During my recent meeting in 2016 with Jacob and Shikato, the main representatives of this prayer group, they told me that one of their prayer warriors has seen—through a vision—Narendra Modi, the present prime minister of India, reading their "files." Their hope is that Modi will one day pray with the prayer group. When I asked if this was indeed possible, Shikato said, "It is up to the Lord; whatever the Lord says we will do. Modi is also human, like us, but from God's side, there aren't any categories and God will speak to anyone."

Prophecies around sovereignty are not solely confined to the work of SAK or of prayer houses, for that matter, but circulate around many Naga areas and domains of Naga life. When talking to activists, nationalists, prayer warriors, and intellectuals about the Naga nationalist movement, it became clear that prophecies regarding sovereignty were prevalent, starting as early as the 1940s and 1950s, during the beginnings of the Naga movement for sovereignty.[4] While the SAK are the most active in pub-

SUMI ALAKISHI KIGHINIMI
(Sumi Peace Prayer Cell) Ghathashi
P.O. Pughoboto, Dist. Zunheboto : Nagaland
Theme: *"Blessed are the peace makers" Mt. 5:9"*

Ref. No. 1   Date 13.11.97

-1-

PROPHETIC MESSAGE

While fasting and praying at Nagaland Peace Prayer Centre, GHATHASHI on 13th Nov. 1997, God revealed His prophetic message through His Servant, the prophet conveying to the PRIME MINISTER OF INDIA, NEW DELHI. Time - 09:55 AM, Date - 13.11.1997.

THE WORD OF GOD EXPRESSLY SAYS:-

1. I am prepared to establish the kingdom of Nagaland.

2. I am aware that Nagas have committed "Nagaland for Christ" to preach My gospel. Accordingly I have been dwelling in Nagaland since long time.

3. No other nation on earth has so far declared their country to be governed through Me (Christ through the Holy Spirit) but only the Nagas claimed My reign dedicating "NAGALAND FOR CHRIST" invoking my spirit to function among the Nagas.

4. "Unless you settled Naga issue during your tenure of leadership, you shall not be allowed to return to power again" says the Lord God. "And I will drive thee from thy station and from thy state shall he pull thee down" Isaiah 22:19

5. You shall not listen to any words and prejudiced accusation from any corners. Unless Nagas are set free straight away, the Union of India shall be split.

6. Recollect how many Prime Ministers of India have perished and how many topped because of not liberating Nagas as warned by me.

Figure 4.1. Sample Prophecy File. Courtesy of Sumi Alakishi Kighinimi. Reprinted with permission.

lishing their prophecies—in newspapers, for example—other prophesies that are from individuals without any organizational backing or collective also find their way into the public eye, sometimes through newspapers, prayer meetings, events like Naga National Day celebrations, or in churches and printed materials, like letters and compilations. During the course of my fieldwork, I have been given these letters, testimonies, stories, and written pamphlets, which in Gyanendra Pandey's (2012) words are "un-archived," in the sense of not having an institutional identity, but nevertheless provide powerful words that cut through the absences, gaps, and silences of received history.

This algorithm of prophecy is often in written and oral form. Most of the written prophecies, both from the SAK and other sources, that I have analyzed are in English, though a few of them are written in tribal languages, and some are translations from those languages into English. These prophecies, for diverse audiences, navigate the orbit of the state using modern technologies, which allows their message to be read and communicated far and wide through newspapers, the internet, and WhatsApp. For example, when I arrived at the prayer center, the first thing the SAK did was to give me a copy of the letters given to the prime ministers of India. It was not a perfunctory exercise for them; handing over the letters explained the need for a scholar to have access to these documents, and it also highlighted the potential mediatory role I am to play in "declaring these messages to the whole world," which then form "our evidence, our record," a task I am reminded of time and again by the SAK.

PROPHECY AS KNOWLEDGE

"We are giving you these prophecy files in an envelope," declared Jacob. In early December 2014, I met Jacob and Shikato and drove to a village called Ghatashi, a few hours north of Kohima, the capital of Nagaland. As we arrived, seven prayer warriors—three women and four men—greeted us. They offered us refreshments and we introduced ourselves. I was presented with a faded yellow envelope, with a red cross adorning it; the materiality of the envelope and the weight of its contents felt unnerving. This was the first time I would glance at these prophecy files—the time, space, and the words felt like the weight of Naga history. Other letters, pamphlets, and newspaper clippings found their way to me, either in person or through acquaintances I knew who acted on my behalf to gather material about prophecies. Some were photocopies in faded ink; others had been typed on old typewriters; some had been written in hand. White, pink, yellow, and blue papers provided the blank canvas upon which history was composed. The black typed letters soon formed a ubiquitous surrounding around my study as I attempted to read, interpret, and analyze. These words were not the only conduit that mediated the experience of reading and writing; prayer and the accompanying power of words left sonic traces. After we spent the day in Ghatashi in the warm winter sun, and having gorged myself over lunch with local pork, rice from their paddy fields, fermented soy beans, and fresh vegetables from the garden, I was invited for prayer as I was packing to leave. In silence, I followed the prayer warriors inside the prayer house, a ritual performed many times over, and stood among them in a circle as the words said in unison, three times—"Jehovah tshe, Jehovah tshe, Jehovah tshe" ("Praise Jehovah")—filled the room, creating an ambient resonance with the empty space around, wave after wave of words encircling us with their vibrations. The prayer was loud, with different voices mixing and in a language I did not understand, but the scene was familiar to me, having seen these prayers in many places all over Nagaland. When they spoke of prayer in their stories, I recognized the tone, the voice, and the habit and sensed the way space and time provided openings for communication with God.

There is a "method for ascertaining truth" (Povinelli 1995) that my informants acknowledge. Many versions of prophecy might surface, depending on the person, but eventually one "truth" must prevail and be acknowledged as *the* prophecy—in fact, Shikato told me, for the SAK, prophecy is "that that will be." There is a process of filtering to avoid confusion, and the process involves "asking" God at least three times, using the repeated process to ascertain true from false prophecy. The process works in a particular manner, which allows us to view prophecies as moving from possibility to probability. I have consolidated the different ways prophecy is ascertained into the following.

First, the process involves referring to the Bible and legitimating a given prophecy's message. For the prophecy to be authoritative, whatever prophecy is received by a person, they will have a vision of the Bible and its words. Some prayer warriors are illiterate and cannot read the Bible, so God speaks Bible verses alongside the prophecies, which are then checked by those who can read. Thomas Csordas explains, regarding the efficacy of the Bible and prophecy, that "if scripture is the word of God, . . . prophecy is its direct extension in the present: the living word of God among his people" (1997, 328). Second, the prayer warriors insist on having nothing to do with money—not seeking it or handling it in the prayer center—as they believe it corrupts and they need to be "pure and unadulterated." Since money influences power, eventually, the SAK say, it drives people to complacency and "sin." They point to numerous "fake prophecies" influenced by money, where knowledge of future events is told to suit the customer, creating a chain of dependency, which disassociates "truth" from "power." Third, the collective is crucial to the deliberation of prophecy. When all the members are together, the prophecy is clearest because the same prophecy is revealed to two or three people at the same time. Distance and time constraints also take their toll on members, precisely because God calls the prayer warriors from disparate professions and locations—some are government officials, some teachers, some mothers, some farmers—although in general members are from the same tribe and speak the same language.[5] Gathering in one location, though, can be a challenge.

Finally, accompanying prophecy is prayer and fasting. Sometimes it is for forty days and forty nights, an event reenacted to remember the forty years during which the Jews wandered the desert in Exodus in search of their promise land and the forty days and nights Jesus fasted in the desert. Prayer, therefore, is a form of communication where a dialogue occurs between God and the prayer warriors (Luhrmann 2012), but it is also a kind of "undertaking" for God. Sometimes these diktats are demanding. One time, Jacob told me, God asked the SAK to pray seven times a day, with seven prayer points (for a period—though he did not tell me for how long). During that time, they were sequestered and not allowed to leave their house or the church where they were praying. Such demands mean that not only are their prayers heard, but it establishes a loyalty that is absolute. Similarly, fasting is an "undertaking" that brings prayer warriors closer to God's house. Viheto, a member of the SAK, made a comparison between fasting and catching a mithun (Indian bison), an animal common in Nagaland. "Say you have to catch a mithun—even if you have seventy-six youths pulling the mithun, it's impossible as the mithun's stomach is full. Don't feed the mithun for seven to eight days, and then the mithun will come to your house without any issue. Same with fasting." Fasting brings them closer to God and makes them more amenable to realizing "God's will and path and getting to God's house."

There is a kind of egalitarianism, they say, during these prophecy sessions where there is no leader, prophet, or one person whose prophecy people rely on as the sole arbiter of authority. In this sense the term *prophet* is never used. The title prophet usually refers to a "messenger of God" and in the Jewish, Christian, and Islamic tradition often implies a "special" person who sets up a new community (Baum 2005, 9; Overholt 1989). But the emphasis in these prayer houses is always on the message and never the individual. In fact, I was reminded time and again that there are no prophets, only prayer warriors. God chooses individuals to relay the prophecy based not on one's ability to read or write but on the ability to see the truth. Prophecy is therefore uttered as speech from the person's mouth, but the actual talking is from God. As Thomas Csordas in his study of the Catholic Charismatic Renewal and their use of prophecy says, "*Prophecy* is a first-person utterance in which the 'I' is God; the human speaker is merely the deity's mouthpiece" (1997, 322; italics in original).

On the one hand, the SAK and their many prophecies might be construed as marginal. In fact, the relationship between the SAK and the Baptist churches is not always agreeable. The SAK have told me that they have sent all the prophecy files to the Nagaland Baptist Church Council (NBCC), the central body of the Baptist church, though the NBCC have not acknowledged their activities yet. SAK members also explained that the church authorities do not take them seriously because "we are uneducated, and have no formal institutional authority like the church pastors and elders." On the other hand, one might suggest that the practices of the SAK and other groups are only religious ideas and have no recourse to or consequences for substantial political events. They are not, after all, called upon by the people to represent the Nagas in the fraught public arena of independence and sovereignty. But I want to suggest that these distinctions are unhelpful, particularly when the cosmos influences the workings of politics in unprecedented ways. The SAK believe their importance arises because these prophecies speak to power, or to recall a utopian phrase, "speak truth to power"—such as the Indian state—from a position of marginality. Their numbers and context—small in number, largely from the village, professing little formal education, and having no particular institutional or honorific titles—present us with a group that has limited power. Yet the SAK point out that they are able to proclaim prophecies without being subjected to reprimands or threats to their life. This "protection" exists, they say, because their motivation and revelation come directly from God.

In one way, one can understand the archive of "prophecy material" as an index of historical struggle (Foucault 1982) over the right to sovereignty. The prophecy material fits this modality of function and method. It adds to the rich texture of Naga history and of the region in a way that complements other versions of history and, furthermore, brings to light certain absences and silences with its raw and unedited voice. But the key point of divergence from historical archives is the issue with an ahistorical actor, that of the voice of a deity who constantly enters conversation with people over questions of sovereignty.

PROPHECY FILES

"Did we tell you about our visit to Delhi to meet the prime minister of India, Atal Bihari Vajpayee, in 1999?" Intrigued, I asked Jacob to tell the story. They were instructed by God to go to Delhi and visit the prime minister's office on 21 May.

> God instructed us to give seven Bibles and seven letters to the prime minister [PM] of India. What words we are to take only God tells us, and we then keep it in the prophecy file. In the beginning, without any permission, we went to Vajpayee's office, and without any appointment, we went to his office and entered the PM's office and said to him that we give this present [the file] in the name of the Father, Son, and the Holy Spirit. All of us were instructed to wear our shawls, slung across our shoulders. We didn't speak to him. The Lord said, "When you go to Vajpayee's office, go and give him the Bible and the file, and I will make you speak only three things—and in the name of the Father, Son and Holy Spirit we give you this file." Vajpayee said thank you. Bodyguards were all shocked and instead asked, "Where could we buy these shawls?" So this is a miracle—without any appointment.

As evidence of this momentous event, Jacob later sent me the photograph taken, he said, of three of them standing outside the PM's office. Draped in their traditional shawl, they stand there tall, looking at the camera without any inhibitions. The recollection of the story, like a statement, according to Foucault, could indicate an incision, a tiny emergence: "However banal it may be, however unimportant its consequences may appear to be, *however quickly it may be forgotten after its appearance*, however little heard or badly deciphered we may suppose it to be, a statement is always an event that neither the language nor the meaning can quite exhaust" (1972, 28; my italics). This event—the kind of miracle that allowed strangers to walk into the PM's office, the most guarded space—is not arbitrary but rather reliant on the individual commitment to be open to grace: "Receptivity to miracles are the products of a ritual, liturgical structuring and study within a shared community" (Marshall 2010, 214). In this sense, God is a "permanent parousia, or presence, the witness to which performs a new state of being" (2010, 214).

The files are organized according to numbers ranging from 1 to 12, based on the sequence of prime ministers starting from 1999 (Atal Bihari Vajpayee, Manmohan Singh) up until 2016 (Narendra Modi).[6] There are a number of key characteristics. First, the time and date of the prophecy are assiduously recorded (see sample prophecy file, fig. 4.1). Second, each letter starts with the proclamation "While fasting and praying at Nagaland Peace Prayer Centre, Ghatashi on [...] God revealed His prophetic message through His Servant, the prophet conveying to the PRIME MINISTER OF INDIA, NEW DELHI. Time—[...], Date—[...]". Third, the messages follow a pattern that explicitly gives the power of speech to God—"The word of God expressly says"—before delivering the points. This convention is so powerful that the pronoun *I* in these prophecy materials is "not the proximate human speaker" but attributed to God. Placing the emphasis on God demonstrates the point that the divine plan is larger than individuals or any community (Csordas 1997, 328). This prolegomenon is repeated ritualistically within each entry indicating a level of organization, reflection, and purpose to these declarations, akin to official documents, with a proper insignia and address (fig. 4.1). Each prophecy letter consists of ten to seventeen points, and one can discern at least four main themes. In these archives are intricate modalities of speech, an intimate knowledge of the biblical world as a form of response, and the careful exegesis of history stitched with an awareness of the current political climate. In these spaces, history is written to breathe life into the content of power and belonging.

MISSION AND SOVEREIGNTY

The first theme is demonstrated by a typical letter given to the Indian political leadership (here to Atal Bihari Vajpayee). In the letter (file 1) it says:

1. I am prepared to establish the kingdom of Nagaland.

2. I am aware that Nagas have committed "Nagaland for Christ" to preach My gospel. Accordingly I have been dwelling in Nagaland since long time.

3. No other nation on earth has so far declared their country to be governed through Me (Christ through the Holy Spirit) but only the Nagas claimed My reign dedicating "NAGALAND FOR CHRIST" invoking my spirit to function among the Nagas.

These points, related to the idea of chosenness, are expressed with the georeligious idea "Nagaland for Christ." Naga nationalists, especially the NSCN-IM, believe that "Nagas are a chosen people with a chosen destiny, guided by God along their migration from Mongolia to their present land of habitation to form a Naga nation, and destined to be messengers of the Christian God to their neighbors, particularly the Hindus (in India) and Buddhists (in Myanmar)" (Lotha 2009, 16). The route of migration—from Mongolia to China, Thailand, and then Nagaland—is not an accident, they suggest. Why did the Nagas stop in this area? Why didn't they venture further? They believed it is because this is how God chose it.

According to groups like the NSCN-IM and numerous mission organizations, the territorial fact of Naga settlement in their present location cannot be attributed to human factors but to the larger cosmic narrative of God's plan. It relates closely also to the first American Baptist Foreign Missionary Society (ABFMS) pledge of expanding beyond the Naga hills and extending the influence of Christianity all over Asia (see Longkumer 2018b). Mary Clark, an early ABFMS missionary, expressed this georeligious expansion as follows: "These Mountains should be spanned and the kingdom of our Lord extended from the Brahmaputra to the Irawady, and from the Irawady to the Yangtze" (1907, 135). Nagaland is an area surrounded by non-Christian religions, so why is it that American missionaries Christianized Nagaland? Because God has chosen the Nagas, they say, and the missionary zeal to convert neighbors is connected to a form of "spiritual capital," which in turn will be activated and realized through territorial sovereignty. In economic terms, the investment (missionary activities) is being recouped with profit (sovereignty). For Jacob, the missionary covenant of sending ten thousand Naga missionaries, promised during the formation of the Nagaland Missionary Movement in 1970, has not always been easy because of Indian rule. Once the Nagas are liberated from its shadow, missionary activity will develop further, quickening the process of missionizing, finishing what the ABFMS were unable to do—connect with those in unreached areas in Asia—and eventually spreading to the whole world. Even unborn Nagas have already been anointed to preach to the whole world, the SAK explain. This is how Jacob put it: "Missionaries will go to the whole world—Japan, America (North/South), Greenland to New Zealand. Hinduism, Jainism, Buddhism, Taoism, Shintoism, Communism, Islam, Zoroastrianism, Sikhism, Baal, Kemot, Asshayat, Nehoyat [unclear names], Judaism [will be transformed by Christianity]. Jesus as the son of the God will be preached all over the world" (Longkumer 2018b, 170).

Political settlement and missionizing the world are thus two sides of the same coin (see Ao 2012; Longkumer 2018b). The narrative of mission and nationalism here—transnational activity for the realization of the national—is an interesting tension that remains at the heart of these prophetic messages. On the one hand, it is acknowledged that Naga sovereignty is connected to the work of mission and making the region Christian. On the other, there is also a sense that the Nagas and Indians have a shared history that cannot be side lined, primarily because Nagaland is still within the Indian nation-state. This relates to the second theme of these prophecy files, the shared future between the Nagas and the Indians.

SHARED FUTURES

Many Indian leaders appear in these prophecy files—M. K. Gandhi, Jawaharlal Nehru, Indira Gandhi, Morarji Desai, Rajiv Gandhi, Narasimha Rao, Atal Bihari Vajpayee, Manmohan Singh, and Narendra Modi. These leaders are recognized as those with power, as many of them held the position of prime ministers when these prophecy materials were composed. In the prophecy files, there is an acknowledgment that the Nagas and the Indian state are embroiled in the same goal of independence, though the former is unrealized and the latter fulfilled. Here is one of the messages the prophecy file declares: "Having recorded bloodshed, suffering and afflictions of millions Indians [*sic*] under British regime pained me. You are my creation. If my creation shed blood and suffered I counted their worth and set them free from the yoke of British regime" (file 1).

In these files, God invokes the watershed moment in Indian history—the year of independence in 1947—and similarly reminds the Indian leadership of the shared goal of independence, as a right. Commemorating the fifty years of Indian independence in 1997, God says to India: "Now your freedom is 50 years old. That in commemoration of the 50 years Indian Independence Jubilee celebration, you should set free the Nagas. Because in the like manner I have created Nagas, counted their bloodshed, sufferings and afflictions. Hence I am prepared to liberate the Nagas. Therefore, liberate the Nagas" (file 1). The year 1997 also marks the year peace was established between the government of India and the NSCN-IM. This fifty-year commemoration recognizes the shared history among the Nagas and the Indian state, particularly when A. Z. Phizo, the leader of the NNC, met with M. K. Gandhi on July 19, 1947, in Bhangi Colony (Delhi).

Gandhi, the NNC (2004, 39) recalls, was understanding of the Naga situation, making three important points that find their way into these prophecy materials. The first is Gandhi's acknowledgment that "the Nagas are not Indians and Nagaland is not Indian territory." When Gandhi agreed to meet the NNC delegation, this statement was explicitly written in the agenda as a topic of discussion, requested by Gandhi's secretary, Mr. Pyrellal. Second, he said that neither he nor anyone in India would force the Nagas to join the Indian Union. When the NNC told Gandhi that they were going to declare independence on 15 August, Gandhi said to them, "Why wait until August 15? Why not declare it today?" Finally, Gandhi embraced his philosophy that "might is not right" and even declared, "If force were to be used [in the Naga areas] then I will sacrifice my life for you and I will ask them to kill me first before a Naga is shot" (NNC 2004, 39).

After this meeting, several things happened. Gandhi was assassinated in 1948, and Jawaharlal Nehru's uncompromising stand on national integrity and unity became paramount. This brought about the beginning of military conflict with the NNC in the Naga hills in 1954. From the NNC point of view, it would seem that Nehru shattered the shared future of the Nagas and the Indian state, contrary to Gandhi's position. One of the prophecy messages issued in November 2015 expressly addresses Narendra Modi, reminding him of Gandhi's position. God says, "Do not put your hand in any religions. . . . Be like Mahatma Gandhi and follow the constitution and stand up for your country. If you put your hand in religion . . . I will depose you from your office, and you will be ousted from your position and I will set up another Government in your place" (file 11).

The mention of Gandhi is interesting as he is often seen as a friend of the Nagas because he acknowledged Naga independence. But a further curiosity is the phrase "do not put your hand in any religions." When I asked the SAK about this phrase, they mentioned that concerns have been revealed to them through prayer and prophecy over the rise of the BJP and Hindutva activities, related directly to the anxiety felt in the Christian regions of India. I asked them to describe these concerns, and they pointed to the BJP announcement that Christmas Day will be Good Governance Day and the issue around the beef ban, a challenge to their religious and cultural sovereignty. This has obviously brought about apprehension in the many Christians states in the Northeast of India with various church bodies, such as the Young Mizo Association (YMA) and Nagaland Baptist Church Council (NBCC), saying, "What good is there when 'Good Governance Day' is hurting the sentiments of Christians who celebrate the birth of Jesus on that day?"[7] Similarly, the beef ban has met with resistance in many Northeast states. They argued that eating beef is central to their diet and identity. In Meghalaya, a majority Christian state, the ban was opposed by considerable numbers, even organizing a "beef party" by civil society during the visit of the president of the BJP, Amit Shah, and leading to the resignation of BJP Christian workers over "this imposition" as recently as 2017.[8]

Uncertainty over the Hindutva agenda is voiced by the well-known Naga writer Easterine Kire. She writes in the local newspaper—the *Morung Express*—that "the determined attempt to transform Christmas day to Good Governance day and declare it a working day equals religious persecution. It puts the government above faith. Faced with that kind of choice, most people would choose faith over governmental diktat." She further questions, "Can the world's biggest democracy really hope to create better citizens by interfering with their holy days?"[9] Indeed, as Christophe Jaffrelot (2017) has noted, since the BJP came to power in 2014, there has been a rise in what he calls "cultural vigilantism."

The key characteristic of "cultural vigilantism" is the campaign and promotion of "another pet theme of Hindu nationalism" (Jaffrelot 2017, 56). This vigilantism has targeted Muslims over "love jihad" (the claim that Muslim men seduce Hindu women into marrying in order to increase converts to Islam), held the Ghar Wapsi (homecoming) campaign, aimed to reconvert Muslims and Christians into the original "Hindu fold," and supported the beef ban by creating militia and umbrella movements known as Gau Raksha Dal (GRD; Cow Protection Organisation) to defend the "sacred cow" of the Hindus (2017, 56). In the prophetic messages to Modi, God both express the anxieties just mentioned and critiques the current system of oppression by asking Modi and, by extension, the Hindutva movement to desist from interfering in religion. The realization of India as the fulfillment of a Hindu state is therefore not a far-fetched idea for the SAK, particularly if the pattern of Hindu hegemony continues through this cultural vigilantism.

After the Nehru and Gandhi years, it was Narasimha Rao, the Congress leader, followed by Atal Bihari Vajpayee who continued, in earnest, deliberating on the Naga conflict as a political issue. (The prophecy files began only from Vajpayee's tenure.) Now the figure of Narendra Modi preoccupies these prophecies. The SAK often point to the sincerity of Modi, because it was under him that the framework agreement was signed. He also appears, according to the SAK, to be proactive in solving the Naga issue. This is how a prayer warrior of the SAK, Vitoli, explained it: "Congress government nothing happened. It is interesting that only with a BJP Hindu government backed by the RSS that this is happening. It is only them who are interested in solving this Naga issue. Our time is measured not by humans but by God." There appears to be anxiety and uncertainty over the activities of the BJP-Hindutva nexus. Prophecy file 12 (from November 2016) is shown in figure 4.2. The hand of God upon Modi and the commandments issued to him suggest that Modi and the RSS are instruments waiting to be used by God. The fulfillment in this message is twofold—benefits will accrue to both the Nagas and India. In fact, another prayer warrior, Shikeye of the SAK, is of the view that the "RSS do not know what they are doing":

> Those RSS who say that they will solve the Naga problem—[it] is actually not them who are speaking, but the Holy Spirit is working through them. The Lord Jehovah has already appointed seven angels in the PM's office, and they are reporting the discussions to us. And two of those angels are helping the Nagas. So even ordinary believers cannot hear these angels. So we are praying, and like prophets, we are working with the Holy Spirit . . . They [RSS] are not supporting us, but unknowingly God is using their tongue, and the Lord is leading them in mysterious ways.

The work through adversaries like the RSS illustrates the manner in which God works through history for the SAK, where God is an agent in the world (see Bialecki 2014). The fact that for God there are no categories—all people are empty vessels waiting to be used—suggests a particular theological understanding that, at least for the SAK, usurps the usual temporal narrative of the progress and development of the Indian state. It foregrounds God's agency by negating individual choices and deliberations. This tension is at the heart of these prophecy narratives, because humans become mere instruments in this divine theatre, but at the same time, humans are seen to be willful agents that make conscious deliberations on their actions, a point I return to below.

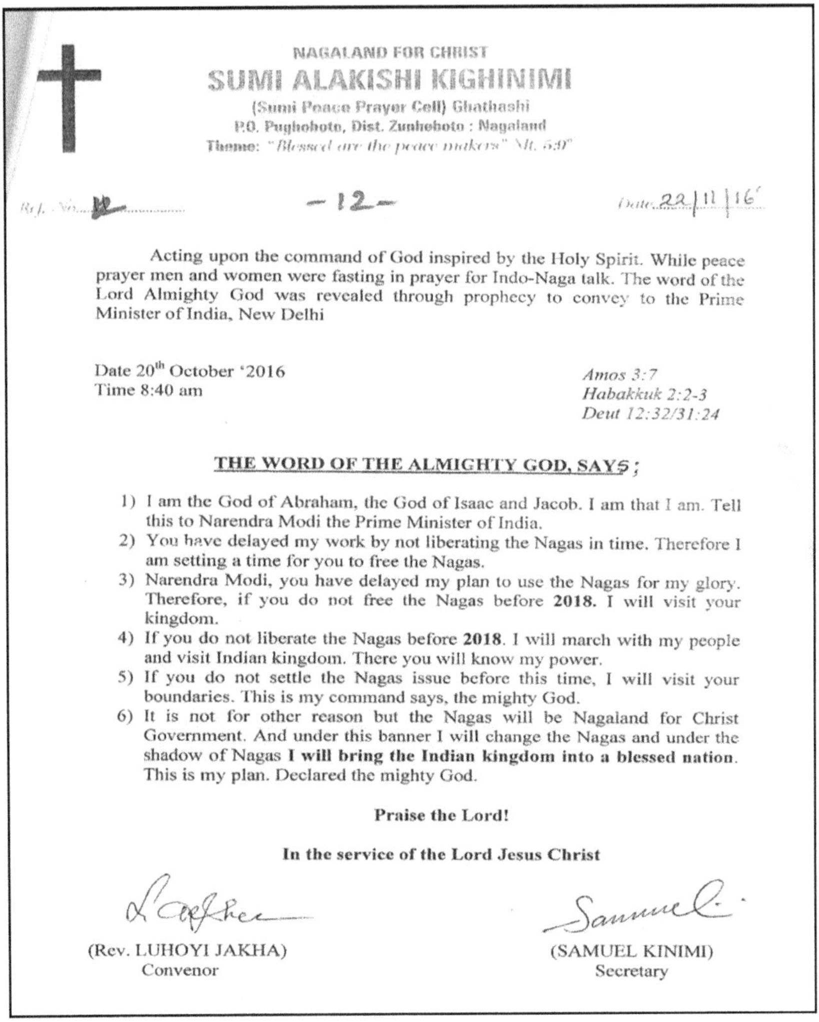

NAGALAND FOR CHRIST
SUMI ALAKISHI KIGHINIMI
(Sumi Peace Prayer Cell) Ghathashi
P.O. Pughoboto, Dist. Zunheboto : Nagaland
Theme: "*Blessed are the peace makers*" Mt. 5:9"

Ref. No. 12 — -12- — Date 22/11/16

Acting upon the command of God inspired by the Holy Spirit. While peace prayer men and women were fasting in prayer for Indo-Naga talk. The word of the Lord Almighty God was revealed through prophecy to convey to the Prime Minister of India, New Delhi

Date 20th October '2016
Time 8:40 am

Amos 3:7
Habakkuk 2:2-3
Deut 12:32/31:24

THE WORD OF THE ALMIGHTY GOD, SAYS;

1) I am the God of Abraham, the God of Isaac and Jacob. I am that I am. Tell this to Narendra Modi the Prime Minister of India.
2) You have delayed my work by not liberating the Nagas in time. Therefore I am setting a time for you to free the Nagas.
3) Narendra Modi, you have delayed my plan to use the Nagas for my glory. Therefore, if you do not free the Nagas before **2018**. I will visit your kingdom.
4) If you do not liberate the Nagas before **2018**. I will march with my people and visit Indian kingdom. There you will know my power.
5) If you do not settle the Nagas issue before this time, I will visit your boundaries. This is my command says, the mighty God.
6) It is not for other reason but the Nagas will be Nagaland for Christ Government. And under this banner I will change the Nagas and under the shadow of Nagas **I will bring the Indian kingdom into a blessed nation**. This is my plan. Declared the mighty God.

Praise the Lord!

In the service of the Lord Jesus Christ

(Rev. LUHOYI JAKHA)
Convenor

(SAMUEL KINIMI)
Secretary

Figure 4.2. Sample Prophecy File. Courtesy of Sumi Alakishi Kighinimi. Reprinted with permission.

CONFLICT IN THE MARGINS

With Gandhi's assassination in 1948 and Nehru's intransigence over Naga territory, the "shared future" of the Nagas and Indians took a different turn. One argument is that the intense military operations that began in 1954 and the resistance to them by the Nagas made Christianity into what it is. If prophecy flourishes under uncertainty and political indeterminacy, the period from the 1950s onward was when prophecies became a collective source of knowledge concerning state mechanisms that undermined the process of sovereignty through military might. In response to these conditions, Christianity took on a more revivalist form—marked by greater religious and emotional zeal, reassessment of one's family and life, and the work of the Holy Spirit—welded to the political nature of the future of the Nagas. The Indian security forces committed various atrocities, including village groupings and RGV (regrouped villages), a tactic borrowed from British Malaya and enforced by the British. In fact, one could argue that the corresponding surge in revivalist activities as a reaction to these atrocities could not be more apparent.

RGV was a tactic to separate the local villagers from the "insurgents" by grouping small villages together into huge, closely guarded settlements manned by the Indian army, who would control who goes in and out, monitor their agricultural activities (which meant that food production largely ceased), and oversee strict surveillance to identify anything deemed antinational (Lintner 2012, 67). The mode of surveillance and panoptic gaze embodied by the RGV, according to Michel Foucault, induced in the individual "a state of conscious and permanent visibility that assures the automatic functioning of power" (1995, 201). Away from the gaze, though, another form of power was at hand. The power of the Christian revival allowed the Nagas to freely express their anxieties and frustrations amid the brutal military operations and the surveillance of the state in managing their livelihoods. No longer did the self-perpetuating power of the panoptic gaze hold its shape. In fact, as I argue elsewhere, the nationalist movement and the revivals went hand in hand—both exhibiting intense emotions in response to the material conditions created by the security forces (Longkumer 2018a).

The most influential revivalist and a former NNC activist, Lanu Longchar, vividly recalled the situation in the 1950s to me: "Village life, without knowing, came together. Unlike the olden days without the love of God, the revival brought together people. Revival affected the moral law and the governance during that time. During that time NNC was also beautiful—like the revival, it was grassroots. NNC was like church work—it was beautiful." But what was crucially important—and the memory of those still alive bear witness to this—is the force of the atrocities committed by the Indian military that further invigorated the Nagas. Although Indian military might was on full display (in contrast to Gandhi's "might is not right")—mobilizing close to a one hundred thousand soldiers in 1956 to fight a tiny guerrilla force of a few thousand (Maxwell 1973)—the question of Christianity was still on the minds of the Indians who felt its strengthening power. For example, Buddheswar Gohain, a Mahasabha (Hindu nationalist sympathizer) activist in the erstwhile North-East Frontier Agency (NEFA), bemoans the influence of Christianity and suggests that education should be freed from Christian influence, "even with the help of military when essential" (quoted in Thomas 2016, 122).[10] Even the Niyogi Committee Report in 1956, set up to check Christian missionary activities in Madhya Pradesh, bought into the conspiracies of the Cold War between the former USSR and the United States, purporting that (American) missionaries were supposedly being supported by foreign powers (the United States) to overthrow the Indian state. This logic was also applied to the Northeast of India and Burma: "The recent hostile attitude of the Karens, Nagas and Ambonese points in the same direction," and the need of the hour is to check the activities of missionary expansion (Thomas 2016, 123). Nehru feared that the United States' close alliance with Nepal in the Himalayan region would spill over into neighboring areas, such as Nagaland (Gopal 1979, 207).

With the American Baptist missionaries now expelled from the Naga hills by the government of India, the Indian military continued its attack on villages, targeting churches and pastors. The historian John Thomas compiled accounts of these incidents, and I quote from them to illustrate the manner in which the brutal attack on Christian institutions fueled anti-India/Hindu rhetoric and feeling.

> On 22 April 1956, the village of Khensa was raided by 400 troops and five of the prominent church leaders were publicly executed. On 6 June 1956, the village of Longpha was raided. The deacon of the church, Mr. Imtilepsuk and seven other church leaders were tied to posts, tortured and shot dead by a firing squad. . . . Incidents such as these were always made into public spectacles and the symbolism of many people being tortured by being tied on

a post, with hands stretched, like a crucifix did not fail to make an impression on the people. For instance, at the junction of two roads in Mokokchung, five men were tied to posts, wrists to wrists, hands stretched in crucifix fashion and shot dead in full view of the public. Moreover, church buildings were generally turned into torture chambers and church altars were desecrated. (Thomas 2016, 123)

The very forces being used supposedly to integrate the nation—the security apparatus—served to widen the gulf between the Indians and the Nagas further, with the former representing the Hindus and the latter the persecuted Christians.

Similar to the Nagas, Mizo autonomy, and what it meant to be part of post-1947 India, was brought into question by the encroaching power of the Indian state. Christianity's influence and power in providing a space of resistance for the Mizos led to the Mizoram Independence War (1966–86). In 1966, the Mizo National Front (MNF), an organization that was set up to provide relief for the famine caused by bamboo rats ravaging crops and food stock, decided to defy the Indian state and fight for independence. They launched Operation Jericho: "The operation was called Jericho, because we were kept oppressed within the fortress of Indian governance and administration and we wanted to fight it with righteousness, faith and hope" (quoted in van Schendel 2016, 88). The MNF launched this campaign due to what they saw as the inept response of the Indian state to the famine. But they saw the growing hegemony of the Indian state—through the imposition of the Assamese language—as undermining Mizo suzerainty over their language, culture, and religion.

With the coming of the English Baptists and Welsh Presbyterians in the late nineteenth century, Christianity slowly took a foothold in Mizoram. By the mid-1940s, Christianity and Mizo identity were already becoming solidified to the extent that Mizo writers were expounding the idea of "the Mizo nation for Christ," where "the land and the people already belonged to Christ" (Pachuau 2014, 126). This is when Christianity became their new *sakhua* (tribe spirit), characterized "as one that focuses greatly on being filled in the 'spirit', on the longing for a constant state of *harhna* ('revival') which is an 'indicator of life' in the church, and while not everyone may be a recipient, the condition is an acknowledgement of the spiritual state of the people" (232). Externalizing this condition to the national sphere, the war of independence between the MNF and the Indian state was seen as a "struggle that was pitched as one protecting a 'Christian' culture against a 'Hindu state'" (133).

This sentiment is found explicitly in the MNF declaration of Mizo independence. It states that the marginalization of the Mizo people under Indian rule is happening through "religious assimilation and Hindu indoctrination." Instead of the state's official policy of secularism, they note, Indian state activities were leading to the suppression of Christianity. It continues: "We, therefore, the representatives of the Mizo people meeting on this day, the First of March in the year of our Lord 1966 appealing to the Supreme Judge of the world authority of the good people of this country, solemnly publish and declare that Mizoram is and out of right ought to be free and independent, that they absolved from all allegiance to India and its Parliament" (quoted in Lintner 2012, 112).

The strong association of Christianity with Mizo nationalism in the 1960s is something that is also seen in the Naga case, which similarly and increasingly took on a georeligious flavor. In the NNC declaration, it says:

> To say that Nagas are not Indians is God's own creation. Man cannot go against it.... So it was that on August 14, 1947, Nagaland declared her independence with the motto, "NAGALAND FOR CHRIST". It is quite probable that the heathen would have laughed at such declaration, but the national faith of Nagaland from the very first day of its national existence had acknowledged Christ as the Supreme Ruler of both heaven and earth with a commitment, "Thy kingdom come to Nagaland." (quoted in Lotha 2009, 280)

The nature of this proclamation, I have been suggesting, comes from the particular material conditions created by the Indian military machinery. Even here, God acts, according to the nationalist worker Shapwon Heimi (2007), to bring peace between the Nagas and the Indians after talks broke down in 1968 and the cease-fire was abrogated. Intense military operations against the NNC, now splintered and deflated, continued, and to "protect the Nagas," the Shillong Accord was signed in 1975, which required the disarming of the NNC cadres and a de facto acceptance of the Indian constitution and union. God spoke through Chaplain Vephi Dozo of the NNC: "I don't want bloodshed between Indians and Nagas, so I brought peace to Nagaland in order to solve the Indo-Naga conflict through peaceful means.... The Shillong Accord was not the outcome of human wisdom, but I (almighty) had done it [*sic*] before it was signed" (Heimi 2007, 40).

The Shillong Accord has been a controversial agreement primarily because it admits, at least in theory, that the Nagas have succumbed to the pressure of the Indian state and that now the Nagas are Indian citizens. The fact that this prophecy is told in this manner—absolving human actions of responsibility—suggests two further points. First, because this prophecy makes the position of the NNC paramount and God's predetermination of this decision indissoluble, God favors the NNC. The abeyance of human agency, secondly, could suggest that God brought peace to reaffirm the shared future of the Nagas and the Indians. From this moment, at least in the recorded prophecies, there also appears to be a split in allegiances. The archive compiled by Heimi in 2007 favors the NNC prophecies, while groups like the SAK confirm the leadership of Isak Swu and Muivah of the NSCN-IM. It could be said that with the emergence of different factions, the prophecies also fragment to the extent that different interpretations emerge. It challenges the neutrality of God's allegiance. This problem was not sufficiently answered in my interviews with various prophecy groups, but all prophecies are in agreement that Naga unity and sovereignty is the central guiding concern. The theme that exemplifies this motif of sovereignty is that of fulfillment. Threats and warnings, if not obeyed by the Indian state and their leaders, turn into punishment and thus fulfillment of God's judgment for these prayer groups.

FULFILLMENT

One of the prayer warriors of the SAK, Logevi, told me that in one of the files given to Prime Minister Atal Bihari Vajpayee in 1999, God said: "You have tortured the Nagas enough; therefore, I will send the enemy to the state that is the apple of your eye and scatter your people here and there, and the state shall shed blood." I have already recounted the meeting between the prayer warriors and Atal Bihari Vajpayee. Seven days after meeting with Vajpayee, Logevi tells me, the Kargil War of 1999 between India and Pakistan started. Therefore, he continues, "if the Indian state delays in liberating the Nagas again, the Lord is telling that India's kingdom will be divided and will be given to other foreign nations." There are a number of things to take heed of in Logevi's words. "The state that is the apple of your eye" is a reference to Kashmir, the Indian state that has been the focus of three wars with Pakistan. (Its territorial boundaries are now contested among three nation-states: Pakistan, India, and China.) In fact, during the 1962 Indo-China War, China won a swift war and occupied parts of Kashmir and Aksai Chin, which is still claimed by India. If the Nagas are not liberated by the Indian state, then, like the Kargil War between India and Pakistan, potential exists for the dissolution of the Indian state. One of the prophecy files (file 2) emphasizes the point:

> If you don't heed my command I will divide India into six (6) parts. I will cause heavy flood to kill thousands and destroy countless dwelling places, I will send hot wind to kill many through ailments and destroy plants and vegetations [*sic*] through insects showered in rain. I will cause sanction on foreign aid to India. I will destroy many Indian Leaders. However if you hearken unto my voice, I shall bless you. And I will drive thee from thy station, and from thy state shall he pull thee down (Isaiah 22:19 [The Christian Bible]).

Other events are recorded that have been fulfilled due to obstructing Naga sovereignty. When Nehru and Phizo disagreed over Naga sovereignty in 1952, Nehru reportedly said: "Whether heaven falls or India goes to pieces or blood runs red all over the country, I don't care. I shall not set the Nagas free and I will not meet the Naga leaders for that matter." Nehru's subsequent death on 27 May 1964 and the advent of the peace process on 24 May 1964 are two highly significant events within the prophecy archives. First, they are seen as an indictment of Nehru's intransigence toward the Nagas. Second, Nehru is told about the peace process a day before he dies by B. P. Chaliha, a member of the Peace Mission. The fact that, close to death, he is informed of the very thing he deemed impossible— that India and the Nagas can sit together as two nations—is recorded as "divine judgment" for not letting the Nagas free. "I will exterminate the

Naga rebels. There will be no mercy," said Prime Minister Morarji Desai on 14 June 1977 after meeting Phizo at the Indian High Commission in London. Soon after that, he had an air crash (but survived) in Jorhat (Assam) and lost the prime ministership (Heimi 2007, 61–62).

Prime Minister Indira Gandhi's assassination at the hands of her Sikh bodyguards also figures prominently in the prophecy archives. According to these archives, the untimely death of the daughter of Jawaharlal Nehru (prime minister from 1947 to 1964), can be read as a lesson in divine retribution for standing in the way of Naga freedom. Her son Rajiv Gandhi, another prime minister of India (1984–89), also met an untimely death. Blood runs thicker than water—and the sins of the father are inherited, suggests the archives.

The Indian writer Dessan Tagore, in his volume *Israel in India*, spends a considerable part of the book analyzing Indira Gandhi's stance on Naga nationalism. This is a book that is widely circulated among different nationalist groups—a copy of the book was given to me in the NNC office in Kohima Village, while the SAK and other documents I have collected also mention it. Published in 1986, the book is a highly polemical didactic account of the "spiritual weakness of India" as witnessed in what Tagore terms "idol worship" (referring to Hinduism), the debilitating "caste system," and the wanton greed associated with the proliferation of "Indian spirituality" through "spiritual leaders" in the guise of gurus. Tagore describes these phenomena as deceiving Indians and Westerners alike. The main theme of the book, though, concerns the Nagas and what he says is a "secret, sadistic policy to exterminate them" by the Indian state for over 40 years (1986, i). Nagas are not Indians, he says, because the "Nagas of the North East India, 3 million of them, are the Israel, the children of the Most High God" (i). Tagore further explains the comparison between the Nagas and Israel through biblical examples.

Like the punishment meted out to the Egyptian people for obstructing the Israelites in their quest for freedom, Tagore too laments the uncompromising stance of Indian leaders regarding Naga independence. It is more than political wrangling that led to the present predicament, he says; it is the "raging spiritual conflict between the Nagas, the Israel in India, and the pagan Hindu rulers who want to keep them captive" (1986, i).

Indira Gandhi is at the center of this. Her assassination is a prophecy that was narrated to me by a prophet belonging to the Shisa Hoho, a national prayer center, and repeated again by Tagore when he is refused an audience with Indira Gandhi to raise the issue of Naga independence. Led by what he calls "his Spirit," Tagore decides to write a letter to Indira Gandhi and shares its content with a Naga friend, Ray, who celebrates Tagore's veracity and honesty. Tagore recalls: "What impressed Ray more than anything else in this letter was the ultimatum given to Indira, that if she would not set the Nagas free and if she, through her military forces, continues to persecute and kill them, living judgement would befall her and *she would die.* None of the idols, in whom she has put so much faith, can save her." (1986, 38; italics in original)

After Indira's death, when Tagore repeats his prophecy with Ray and Phizo (the leader of the NNC) at his London residence, all acknowledge the power of God in intervening on behalf of those who opposed "idol worship." Phizo tells Tagore of Indira Gandhi's meeting with a Naga woman who had forewarned her that she would be punished if she did not stop persecuting the Naga people. Both Tagore and this woman, Tagore reflects, were inspired by the same "spirit"—his own warning given to her in 1983 in Delhi and this Naga woman from Kohima. He says that this woman "witnessed to her about Jesus Christ. . . . Mrs. Gandhi was so moved by the lady's witness, that she thought of becoming a Christian. But in the end, she didn't. And everything the Naga woman said to her began to implement. She was soon assassinated. The idols could not save her" (Tagore 1986, 139).

The prophecy does not stop there, as in 1986 Tagore goes on to note that Rajiv Gandhi would meet a similar fate should he not withdraw the military from Nagaland and Punjab and let the Nagas and Sikhs go free, along with "other minorities." He even declares to his friend Ray that he will write to the prime minister and warn him, as he had his mother (1986, 112). In a letter written by an American, Peter Johnson, to the president of India in 1991, given to me by Rev. V. K. Nuh, who has archived many of these prophecies in his *Naga Archives and Research Centre*, Johnson reminds President Venkataraman of Tagore's prophecy and even concludes that the deaths of the three prime ministers of the Nehru family—Jawaharlal,

Indira, and Rajiv—were each due to the "ill founded SOVEREIGNTY over the Nagas." Only by letting the Nagas go free would the divine mandate be fulfilled; otherwise, the Indian state is constantly defying God—and this, the writer reminds the president, is futile. In connecting with the theme of fulfillment, I am arguing that covenant and obedience are not simply two ways to fulfill God's promise as a form of quid pro quo but allow us to analyze the place of agency—whether human or divine—in actualizing the effects of where prophecy lies and what it says about the present.

COVENANT AND OBEDIENCE

Michael Walzer (1984), in his important book *Exodus and Revolution*, argues that wherever people have read the Bible and experience oppression, the Exodus story provides succor and inspiration for resistance. Thus, the narrative of bondage, wilderness, covenant, and the promised land is a paradigmatic template through which the Naga story could also be understood, as it has been among African Americans, Latin Americans, and even the Puritans, Calvinists, and Dissenters in Europe (Coffey 2013; Cone 1969; Croatto 1981; Glaude 2000; Gutierrez 1973; Said 1986).

In light of Walzer's thematic exploration, there are a number of important points about the Exodus story that have been applied to the prophecy material. First, as the prophecy materials make clear, the two opposing forces—Egypt (India) and Israel (Nagas)—form an important part of this Exodus narrative. The prime ministers of India are pharaohs, and while the figure of Moses is not always clear, in some interpretations, Isak Swu takes that mantle. Second, Exodus is an account of deliverance through obedience. Disobedience leads to subjugation. The Nagas who shed blood and kill fellow human beings in the name of sovereignty find themselves under the Indian state. Only once violence ceases and obedience to God is absolute, then God, like the ultimate warrior, will vanquish the enemies and liberate the Nagas. It is only through covenant that this freedom will be realized.

The covenant that surfaces again and again is the idea of Nagaland for Christ. It is a contract between God and the Nagas, and in this, the idea of mission is both cosmic (the migration of the Nagas to their present location is due to divine design) and national (that Nagaland for Christ will be fully realized once Nagaland is free from India). In an important sense, this covenant is a "founding act, creating alongside the old association with tribes a new nation composed of willing members" (Walzer 1984, 76). According to Walzer, Exodus is not simply a story but a history of a people forged through a common experience of tumultuous change, oppression, and marginalization. These experiences bring into focus the existential dilemmas confronting the Nagas. On the one hand, the cosmic dimension of their location was already predetermined; on the other, the covenant of Nagaland for Christ is interpreted as a voluntary act made by the Nagas. The promise to send ten thousand missionaries is an act of human volition. Recalling a vision where he was part of a conversation that God was having with the angels, my SAK informant Jacob tells me that God said: "See the Naga people: they don't know how to wear clothes, eat properly, but see that they want to live for my name, and they want to establish my kingdom here on earth. Was it Japan, Russia, America, UK, Australia? Those hi-fi countries didn't proclaim for Christ. No, it wasn't."

This covenant is closely related to purity and obedience. In Exodus, it is the worship of idols (like in Egypt) that the Israelites were warned to forgo. Leaving these strange gods behind and showing allegiance to a single God is an absolute demand. One can recall the making of a golden bull, an idol, by the Israelites at the foot of the mountain when Moses was atop for forty days. Seething with rage, Moses descends and smashes the tablets and asks his supporters to show support, while demanding the killing of those who disobeyed God by constructing an idol (Walzer 1984, 55–61). The narrative of Tagore, who highlights Indira Gandhi's weakness by referring to the "idols she worships," demonstrates the parallel construction of Egypt/India as lands of idols, while Israel/Nagaland are places that worship the one true God. As an illustration of this wider trope of idolatry, explored further in Chapter 6, I present an example of the kind of prophecy that circulates in Nagaland, taken from a prayer meeting held in Phek Town on 9 October 1993. Spoken by Asu Tetseo, "a humble prayer lady at Phek Town," the pamphlet asks: "To every Town and Village of Nagas, ask whether you are a real Naga? No Nagas will serve other nations. No Nagas will be idle. No Nagas will worship idols. For Nagas are not Egyptians but second Israel." But here, this creative tension and the ability to recognize idolatry is what allows for "true freedom" to exist, one that lies in servitude to God.

Organizations like the Shisa Hoho, which means "doing in obedience," and SAK told me that sovereignty will "come only after purification and obedience to God—acting and practising according to this ideal. God's demand means obedience, and prophecy plays an important role in bringing about that sovereignty, which is the idea of faithfulness." Hear again the prophecy in Phek town in 1993, which says:

> The land of the Nagas has been purchased by Blood, Sacrifice and Sweat. Your beloved brothers who suffered and died in water, in hunger and in thirst and in fire and by sword and bullet. Remember! Yet their bones are not perished but shouting—Is there no fighter for Nagas? The Lord says, "The real armour of Naga sovereignty are [*sic*]: LOVE, PEACE, UNITY, FAITHFULNESS and SINCERITY. But not Sword, Spear, Dao nor Gun".

This echoes Anderson's (1999) idea of the "goodness of nations," which commemorates the dead in material and symbolic memory—but their death is connected with the unborn and living to illustrate their sacrifice as "national goodness." Yet the future and its anticipated consequences are clearly laid out for the Nagas to see where the past not only haunts the memory of the living but the living must also obey God to participate in the goodness of nations. Obedience then comes with action.

This became clear to me when I was talking to members of the Shisa Hoho, as we were discussing the "Hindu government," the BJP/RSS nexus, and the reflections of recent prophecies on current conditions. Isn't it ironic, I remarked, that Naga sovereignty is being deliberated on by the BJP, which has imposed Good Governance Day and the beef ban and is famously close to the Hindutva organizations who have attacked Christians in many parts of India? They remarked that making progress on the matter of sovereignty alongside a powerful Hindu-majority government is the last thing they expected, but it says more about the power of God and not governments: "We have to work through our adversaries to realize God's dream for us." This kind of unconditional surrender to God—obedience—is what requires a careful understanding of the current political climate, both in acting on behalf of the Indian state and for Naga sovereignty. Recently (the exact date is unclear) members of the Shisa Hoho were commanded by God to go to New Delhi. Twelve of them walked around parliament from 4:00 to 7:00 A.M. for seven days to sanctify the parliament. When I asked why, they replied that the parliament is where many of the laws are deliberated and passed. They also want a favorable outcome to the recent framework agreement signed by the NSCN-IM and the government of India. When I asked if onlookers saw this as odd, they replied that no one interfered with their walks around the parliament, not even security personnel. The fact that it was early in the morning also helped, they said. "Even on the seventh day, we blew trumpets around the parliament, and people watched—the trumpet is the sound and sign of triumph and victory."[11]

COSMOPOLITICS AND THE PLACE OF PROPHECY

I have been suggesting that the "common world" of gods and humans is an important facet of contemporary Indian political life. Although one can suggest that the political praxis displayed in the signing of different accords over the years illustrates the workings of the state and bureaucracy in the name of governance, what elides modern political discourse is an analysis of how the cosmos effects the workings of politics. This cosmopolitical relationship is, therefore, useful in attempting to understand how prophecy works.

The idea of cosmopolitics has been developed primarily by Isabelle Stengers as a way to question the normal way of doing things and to "create an opportunity to arouse a slightly different awareness of the problems and situations mobilising us" (2005, 994). Bruno Latour summarizes what Stenger's cosmopolitics achieves: "The presence of cosmos in cosmopolitics resists the tendency of politics to mean the give-and-take in an exclusive human club. The presence of politics in cosmopolitics resists the tendency of cosmos to mean a finite list of entities that must be taken into account. Cosmos protects against the premature closure of politics, and politics against the premature closure of cosmos" (2004, 454). Where does prophecy fit in with the idea of cosmopolitics? Prophecy, as I have been suggesting, is revealed knowledge about events that will happen or are happening. It never sits in isolation. The subject is that of sovereignty and how one is able to discern the movements across time and space that allow a better articulation and appreciation of the way things are. National governments come and go, prayers warriors may change and pass, but the substance of these prophetic materials acts as cumulative knowledge that is circulated and passed on from generation to generation. It is a source of knowledge, however, inflected by tradition and Christianity; it remains resolute. Having this knowledge then brings about questions of knowing with certainty even though one could argue that that which is in the future cannot bring resolution because it has not happened yet. When the SAK say that prophecy is "that that will be," there is a certainty that it has already happened—as if we can actually see it fulfilled. So does this suggest that human agency is perpetually in abeyance?

From the outside looking in, prophecy might demonstrate a risky strategy in speculation that, if not properly assessed, will lead to misunderstanding. Here, it might be tempting to suggest that to minimize human error, one strategy is to ignore human agency and exploit "structures as moral alibis for their contingent actions" (Herzfeld 1997, 113). God then is the ultimate agent, and human agency is simply dormant as a risk-avoidance strategy (Miyazaki 2004, 105). But, as I have shown, prophecy is hardly based on the logic of risk and speculation. Rather, it is based on trust that the deity's all-knowing power has the ability and capacity to act in the right manner in the interest of the people. The question that remains, though, is, what happens when prophecy appears to be unfulfilled in the straightforward sense? At least in the context of the prophecy material I have examined, it is unhelpful to adjudicate what has been fulfilled/unfulfilled or even failed (Kravel-Tovi and Bilu 2008). It is more helpful to evaluate how the nature of prophecy itself reveals new ways of understanding knowledge in the present.

Rebecca Empson's work in Mongolia among the Buryat examines one such feature of the ever-changing nature of prophecy even though certain prophecies—like "the time of great calamities"—fail in terms of full disclosure (i.e., "no time is the *actual* time of the great calamities") (Empson 2005/2006, 57; italics in original). Therefore, the "time of the great calamities" is the "known" future, but there is no *actual* "time of the great calamities" (57). While some might view the failure of the prophecy to be realized as evidence that it is false, the question is, rather, what this tells us. Empson argues that, in fact, because "the time of the great calamities" is viewed as knowledge, it enables people to define and redefine their present predicament. This ability of prophecy to aid in defining and redefining the present is, Empson suggests, exactly why it is valuable (57–58). One can take a similar view of Naga sovereignty and the "solution" that has been widely anticipated since the beginning of the Indo-Naga conflict in 1947, when the shared future of the Nagas and the Indians started, to the recent statement issued to Narendra Modi that a solution to the Indo-Naga conflict had to be realized by 2018. The framework agreement that I started this chapter with continues to be a document with many possibilities. And the main concern for these prophecy groups is that the framework agreement will include Naga sovereignty. Even if a "solution" to Naga sovereignty did not materialize in 2018, what is being fulfilled is that "this allows for a widening of the range of possible associations to the concept, generating new meanings that are *more persuasive* than that of the original prophecy" (57; italics in original).

Using Empson's idea of the perpetuating idea of prophecy as a generator of new knowledge, what sort of ritual experiences are replicated to produce hope both in realizing the original prophecy of Naga sovereignty and in fashioning a body politic that repays God's faithfulness in the face of adversity? In his work on Fijian Christianity and gift giving, the anthropologist Hirokazu Miyazaki (2004, 97–107) examines the way people create moments of hope. For example, in gift-giving rituals, he observes how the formality of the ritual is important in deliberating on the nature of the gift, what it says about Fijian culture, and the nature of the exchange. In the very nature of exchanging gifts, there is an element of risk that the gift will not be received by the gift receivers, leading to failure (though in practice, he notes, this situation is rare). There is a process of mutual exchange that occurs during the gift-giving process: the givers declare the smallness of the gift, while the receivers praise its largeness. But the moment of hope, both for the giver and the receiver, occurs when there is uncertainty over the nature of the gift and its reception. It is only once the gift is dutifully given and graciously received that there is fulfillment. This moment of hope happens through what Miyazaki calls "agency in abeyance" (2004, 97). In the gift-giving analogy, for a moment, the gift giver's agency is in abeyance because the gift is being given and nor is it in the hands of the gift receiver. This moment of uncertainty is, however, necessary for the gift's fulfillment.

What Miyazaki's analogy of hope and fulfillment suggests when applied to the prophecy material is that one's openness to prophecy is a "moment of hope" in which the gift is given (the openness of individuals) and received (the response from God) and where fulfillment is attained. Recall how this openness is cultivated through ritual action, such as prayer, fasting, and Bible study, which enables the prayer warriors to seek knowledge of Naga sovereignty through a series of questions in their prayers, which are then known through direct revelation from God and mediated by dreams and visions. Asking God, as Jacob and the SAK did in the opening section of this chapter, is another form of gift exchange, or as Esther Goody points out, it allows "two partners to enter into a social exchange" (1978, 23). During this moment of hope, there is an abeyance of agency, and agency is given to God, which, according to Miyazaki, is when "all present ceased to emphasize their own or others' actions and instead looked to God for a response" (2004, 105). When applied to prophecy, for example, that crucial moment, in the act of abeyance, is where the exchange itself creates the possibility of experiencing the efficacy of divine agency (Miyazaki 2004, 105). This prophetic moment, like the Fijian gift-giving ritual, suggests that the cumulative nature of these prophecies, expressed and reflected upon through generations and connected through time and space, enlarges as it awaits a response for its immanent fulfillment. In one sense, as this chapter suggests, the nature of the prophecies looks toward a better understanding of knowledge, as it generates new meanings in the present to better prepare for the future. What must be kept in mind, however, is that the key is not whether prophecy is true or false but that every event, every statement, every incision, however small, adds to the ever expansive repertoire of knowledge.

CONCLUSION

This chapter has demonstrated the importance of prophecy in deliberating about Naga sovereignty. I have suggested that in the Indo-Naga conflict, the relationship between people, God, and government is a significant aspect of how one understands the life of politics. Prophecy, both as a source of knowledge and a mode of deliberation with the Indian state through prophetic messages, is a vital aspect of the workings of politics. It must not bracket out the workings of the cosmos but must be mutually constitutive, especially in the way cosmopolitics, as a technique of thinking and feeling that is transformative, is vital to how we understand the idea of fulfillment in these prophecies. I have argued that sovereignty is constantly in the process of becoming, which requires the Naga nation to maintain their covenant and obedience to God. A seasoned Naga activist said to me recently: "Even if it is seventy to eighty percent, that is all right for our people for now. Leave it to the future generation to make a better decision on sovereignty and to add to what we have achieved. Don't worry; sovereignty is up here [*pointing upward*]. Let us maturely rejoice in what we have become; we are not more than what we are, but we are not less than what we are. Hallelujah!"

I have suggested that the cumulative tradition of prophecy provides one way for the Nagas to enact resistance in the face of obvious adversity and to manage the power of the Indian state, now exemplified by Hindutva forces. In other words, how are we to recover a politics of hope that, in Dipesh Chakrabarty's expression, is to resist and escape the "best human effort at translation across cultural and other semiotic systems, so that the world may once again be imagined as radically heterogeneous" (1992, 22)? The Australian philosopher Mary Zournazi's sentiment of hope provides a way to accommodate participation, which does not "narrow our vision of the world but instead allows different histories, memories and experiences to enter into present conversations on revolution, freedom and our cultural sense of belonging" (2002, 18). If we are to carve a space where heterogeneous life worlds are imagined and lived, and if we open ourselves to different histories that shape divergent political cultures, then hope as a method (Miyazaki 2004) broadens our sense of engagement. The language of prophecy provides one such engagement. Like the gift givers' presentation of the cultural forms that precede the experiencing of the moment of hope, in the Naga case, God's ultimate response is dependent on the practitioner's covenant and obedience. In other words, the capacity for humans to control the effects of their action in the world brings about a recon-figuring of the relationship between humans and God. This assertion of agency through human action, however, remains perpetually incomplete—for humans are not always obedient nor will the covenant be realized fully. It is only when human effort and its limitations are acknowledged that there is the abeyance of agency and a looking for God's response.

As an indigenous methodology to "ascertain truth," prophecy honors and illustrates "most eloquently the inadequacies of conventional assump-tions about power relations" (Pasternak 2017, 50). In other words, however peripheral and unconventional prophecy might present itself, it works against the grain in two ways—as an archive that preserves the workings of groups and individuals entangled with a deity and as a cosmopolitical vision that speaks truth to power, which illustrates, rather than simply theorizes, the nature and practice of sovereignty. In this sense, one can ask: How is the hope for sovereignty kept alive generation after genera-tion even though it appears unreachable? Could sovereignty, conveyed in the language of Christianity, provide the Naga people with hope as a modality of engagement with one another, with their God, and with the Indian nation-state? Raising these questions is to acknowledge that the process through which history is unfolding not only speaks about the state of the Naga areas but, in a way, speaks to the larger concerns in the Northeast. The BJP and the RSS—represented as the culmination of the "Hindu forces"—ironically appear as the most sincere in proactively "solving" the Naga issue, even though, one can argue, they could be the least likely force in supporting the Nagas, due to the Nagas' Christianity. In re-iterating Vitoli's comment that "our time is measured not by humans but by God," we are presented with a dilemma for those trying to understand Hindutva and how their role is magnified in the prophecy material to be used as "instruments of God." Like the biblical motif of using enemies to punish but also revive the Israelites to be obedient and remember the covenant with God, the Nagas appear to mirror events in the Bible. Here, then, the role of Hindutva forces makes sense. In the next chapter, I high-light this tension from the gaze of Hindutva actors and how their accep-tance of Christianity in the region is one that is formulated according to their own vision.

CHAPTER 5

"CHRISTIAN HINDU" AND
NATIONALIZING HINDUTVA

IN JANUARY 2015, I was surprised to receive a WhatsApp message from
Among, a friend in Delhi, that said: "Have you seen this?" The message
contained a poster:

> Your Christianity is a Samasya [problem] so our mission is Gharwapsi
> [homecoming]. From now onwards, no Christianity, only Hindutva. No
> Bible, only Bhagvad Gita. Either convert or else leave our Hindurashtra
> [Hindu nation] soon. We will erase Christianity by 2021. Hindu Rashtr
> Banake Rahengey.

The poster's title, in bold, had the RSS (Rashtriya Swayamesevak Sangh)
name on it, and certain expressions, like the last sentence, were highlighted
in orange. Translated into English it reads: "The Hindu nation will be a
reality." Even without understanding all of the Hindi expressions, my
friend, who is part of the evangelical circle of Christians in the capital,
was worried. This poster was advertised by the Dharm Jagran Manch, a
branch of the RSS formed when plans were made to launch the Gharwapsi
(homecoming) of Christians/Muslims into Hinduism. In defending their
decision to issue this poster, the leader of the Manch, Rajeshwar Singh
Singh, said: "We have not done any conversion. We have ensured 'ghar
wapsi.' Why they [political parties] did not utter a word when Hindus are
converted? What's their objection when we ensure that they come back to

the religion?"[1] Among, as a Christian living in Delhi, was concerned about whether this was a one-off incident or a long-term program of the Hindu right. Did I know, she asked, whether my RSS informants were involved in any of these activities in the Northeast? To my mind, it seemed unlikely that RSS activists in the Northeast would want to issue an open statement like this in a region where Christianity has substantial numbers. But the question remained: How indeed do Sangh activists respond to the question of Christianity in the Northeast?

Among is not the only person who has an interest in this issue; many Christian communities from the Northeast are equally perturbed by the way in which the Hindu right has recently turned to the Northeast, with a large Christian population, as a problem that it now seeks to address. As a reflection on these issues, this chapter will consider how the Sangh interprets Hindutva and its vexed relationship with Christianity. A lot of ink has been spilled on the constitution of Christianity and its relationship to Hindutva. In the previous chapters, I have shown how questions have arisen in the Northeast over the notion of Hindutva and its central tenets of nationalism associated with territory, emotional attachment to the name (Hindustan), the coherence and unity of language with Sanskrit and Hindi forming its core structure (or Hindi-Hindu-Hindustan as the RSS would see it), and finally the idea of the shared blood and race providing the mechanism for national unity (Savarkar 1969, 82–89; see also Hansen 1999, 78–79). These tenets have been questioned primarily due to the existence of asymmetrical nationalisms in the Northeast that are incongruous with the idea of Hindutva and indeed India. Even the idea of pitrubhoomi (holy land), which formed the cornerstone of the Hindutva ideologue V. D. Savarkar's ideas of religious belonging within India, cannot be so easily evoked by Hindutva activists in the Northeast.

Savarkar claimed that for one to be Hindu, their pitrubhoomi—the holy and sacred sites of one's religion—had to originate "out of the soil of India" (1969, 110). Even if non-Hindu religions like Christians and Muslims had patriotic feelings and were culturally Hindus, they would remain "partial Hindus." Only by giving up their religious beliefs, would they be admitted back into the Hindu fold (1969, 115). But here is the problem for the Hindutva activists in the Northeast: Savarkar's original ideas simply do not work due to Christian nationalists' own preference for exclusion from India. This puts into question another core aspect of Hindutva: that of territorial and cultural congruence. So how does the Sangh rework Savarkar's notion of holy land in light of this Christian presence?

To answer this question, my primary field of ethnographic enquiry is Nagaland based on my discussions with the Janajati Vikas Samiti (JVS, also known as Kalyan Ashram), an RSS organization that works mainly with tribal people.[2] What follows is an analysis of the JVS's attempt to dismantle the edifice of Christianity by reconstructing its basic premise.[3] They see this dismantling as necessary due to the pernicious effect of Christianity's destabilizing force, its ability to bring rupture to Bharat. The Sangh argues for Christianity's place in the Northeast by invoking the idea of restoring order through national patriotism—the ultimate goal of Hindutva. In this way, they make three points worthy of examination: First, Christianity's association with Western ideals has meant a loss of "original" culture. Here, the Sangh ask if indigenous culture can be recovered to cultivate a Hindu national self. Once this "authentic" self is salvaged through an appeal to pre-Christian traditions, the notion of Hindu/Indian is possible. Second, I will assess the relationship between Christianity and Sangh ideas of what it means to be Hindu/Indian, where Christianity is seen as challenging the territorial integrity of Bharatvarsh, or Mother India (also Bharat). This challenge is regarded by the Sangh as territorial "secessionism"; their aim is to prevent it and unite the country. Third, to limit its cultural force, the Sangh characterizes Christianity solely as "the profession of belief" precisely to be able to encompass it within the broader spatial domain of Bharat. I will argue that the boundaries between Hindutva as cultural nationalism and its religious underpinnings are usefully maintained in the context of Nagaland because they allow Sangh activists to relegate Christianity to mere belief, "as a state of mind rather than as constituting activity in the world" (Asad 1993, 47).

By deploying the language of belief, Sangh activists are able to reconstitute the limits of Christianity and incorporate it into Hindu civilization on their own terms, akin to what Jacob Copeman and Aya Ikegame call "expansive containment," that is, "extending in order to include and

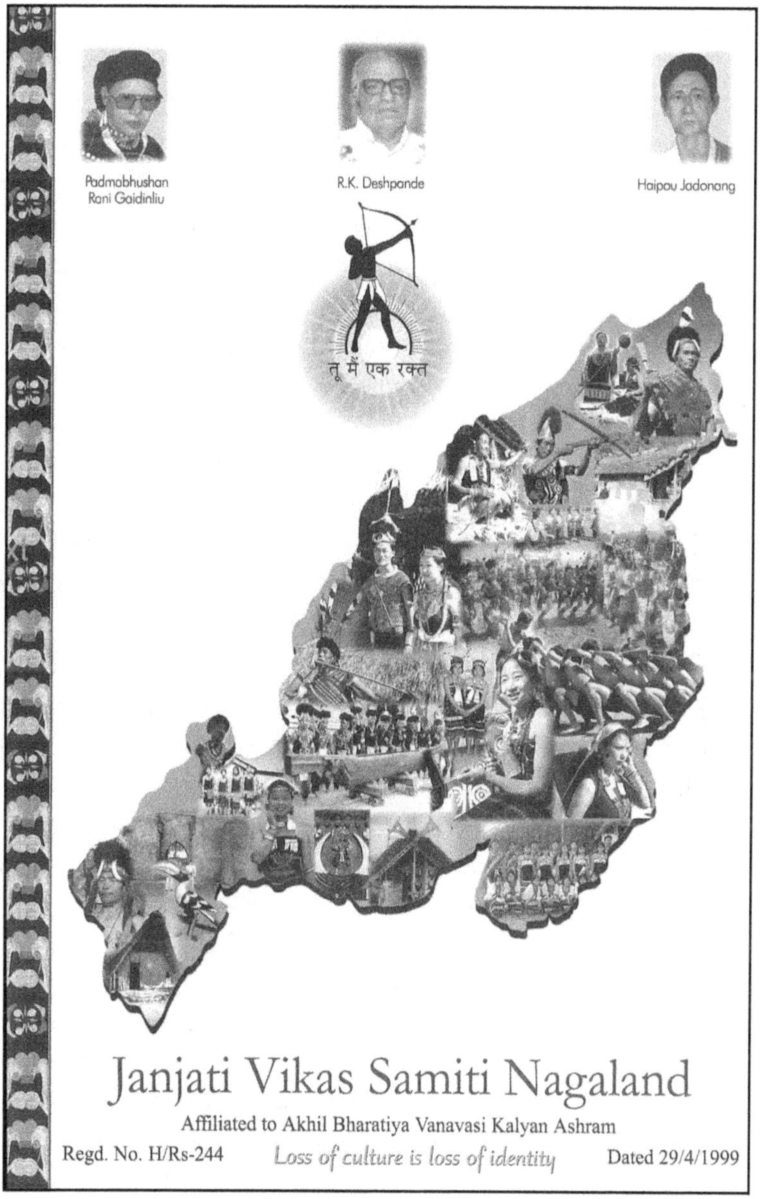

Padmabhushan Rani Gaidinliu

R.K. Deshpande

Haipou Jadonang

तू में एक रक्त

Janjati Vikas Samiti Nagaland

Affiliated to Akhil Bharatiya Vanavasi Kalyan Ashram

Regd. No. H/Rs-244   *Loss of culture is loss of identity*   Dated 29/4/1999

Figure 5.1. Janjati Vikas Samiti, promotional pamphlet. Courtesy of the author.

including in order to extend" (2012, 15). The Sangh's version of Christianity can thus be encompassed within the civilizational and familial characteristic of Bharat, or Mother India. Finally, in this context, I will examine the ethnographic construction of a "Christian Hindu." I will illustrate how the JVS develop this construction by examining the broader tension between locality and religious allegiance and by following the Sangh's territorial logic: like Christianity that demands exclusive religious allegiance, so do the Nagas demand exclusive territorial independence. Once this allegiance is recomposed to its more inclusive Hindu ideology, integration, not secessionism, will be achieved.

INFORMANTS AND WORLDS THEY CREATE

It is a cold December evening in Kohima. I sip my tea on the street corner waiting for my RSS informant Jagdish to arrive. People mill in the vicinity of makeshift tea stalls, along with gas burners and woks, where vendors serve hot Chinese-style noodles to hungry customers.

December is a busy month in Nagaland: the annual cultural Hornbill Festival draws in thousands of tourists every year; offices are shut early, schools are closed, and people make plans to visit their ancestral villages to mark Christmas and to celebrate the occasion through feasts and community events. From where I sit, there are visible signs of Christmas: the shops are festooned with decorations, colorful toys, and other trinkets that will find their way into homes as presents. The ubiquitous star of David is foisted on bamboo poles, on top of houses and shops, giving off a red-neon effect, as far as the eye can see.

I have known Jagdish now for over ten years. Jagdish, who was also introduced in earlier chapters, is an RSS pracharak (full-time worker) who has been in Nagaland since 1975. Originally from Uttar Pradesh, Jagdish is the main RSS representative in Nagaland; over recent years, he has regularly visited (and advised) the then governor of Nagaland (2014–2019, another RSS worker), union ministers, and important national dignitaries. It is through Jagdish that I have come to know many of the other RSS and VHP workers in the Northeast. Not only is Jagdish an indefatigable organizer who is the main strategist of the JVS in Nagaland, but he is also involved (unofficially) in mediating between the state BJP unit and the central authorities. He is both locally connected and a prolific writer—in Hindi and English—regularly contributing articles in local and national presses and to the main RSS magazine, the *Organiser*.

"Namaste, Arkotong-ji," he greets me as we order tea from the nearby street vendor. Amid the sea of people, Jagdish stands out in his white Indian lungi, with his *sikha* (a tuft of hair on the back of his shaven head) half covered by his khadi shawl. These visible sartorial and ritual markers and his choice of welcome and gesture are, he insists, part and parcel of his Bharatiya (Indian) identity, which resists the normative Western aesthetic preferred in Nagaland—a preference that, he continues, is annihilating indigenous cultures. He tells me, "Even the NSF [Naga Student Federation] president called me one day and said to me, 'Are you teaching us about Naga history?' He threatened to beat me, but I kept quiet. But I know Naga history." While Christianity, as discussed in the previous chapter, provides the moral force for many in the region, how do JVS activists encapsulate Christianity within the larger territorial and civilizational space of Hindutva? Answering this question is not straightforward. In what follows, I will first take up Jagdish's conflation of Christianity and Westernization as a starting point to understand the larger agenda of the JVS, and later I will explicate what he means by "Naga history."

DISMANTLING CHRISTIANITY: DELEGITIMIZING ITS FOREIGNNESS

In 2004, when I first contacted the JVS to ask them about their work with the indigenous religious movement that I was studying—the Heraka—I often visited their offices in Dimapur, Nagaland. On one such visit, I saw a poster displaying the picture of an American by the name of Stephen Knapp, highlighting his tour of Northeast India hosted by the JVS. When I asked the person in charge of the office, Ramesh, about the poster, he said that since the Nagas were converted by the American Baptist missionaries, I should make it a point to look at Knapp's website, primarily to learn about "the problems of Christianity."

In what follows, I draw on Knapp's discussion to point to the larger rhetoric employed by the Sangh to explicitly link Christianity and Westernization as two deliberate forces that have had a detrimental effect on the Nagas. As I have shown in Chapter 4, the indigeneity of Naga Christianity and the concomitant political imagination provide them with a sense of belonging that contradicts the Sangh's representation of Christianity. But why is Stephen Knapp central to this debate? Not only was I told on numerous occasions of his work, but the JVS were keen to point to the error of Christianity, by employing the very person from where the ancestry of Naga Christianity is established—that of the United States—and to demystify the allure of Christianity/Westernization that many Nagas, allegedly, blindly ape. Moreover, Knapp's work as an apologist for the VHP places him in a unique position of having been both a Christian and now an advocate for the place of Vedic culture in an era of globalization. Knapp's glorifying of Vedic culture, by abandoning the Christian West for the JVS, speaks volumes that can be reiterated in the Naga context.

During his tour, Stephen Knapp, the president of the Vedic Friends Association, was accompanied by the vice president of Indigenous Voices International, S. D. Youngwolf, a member of the Southern Cherokee tribe, as they toured Nagaland. In Knapp's account, available on his website, he recounts how Youngwolf talked about the dangers of Christianity obliterating native cultures and traditions, based on his own experience in North America. Knapp informs us that in Nagaland this

> news often had a big impact on the views of the people who heard us. With both of us giving our talks, it was like a one-two punch, countering the propaganda that the people there had heard and are often given, and providing them more reason to have pride in their own culture. They were also impressed that two Westerners had enough respect for them to participate and interact with them and their culture.[4]

Interestingly, Knapp does not note on his website how many attended these talks. Knapp observes how the people in the West are increasingly looking for "deeper levels of spiritual development, often by researching and adding the ways of Eastern culture to their lives."[5] From the land of the missions—nineteenth-century America—comes this insight into the darker implications of how Westernization and Christianity have marred the landscape his ancestors walked upon. I quote him at length:

While I was there [in Nagaland], I personally saw a "Christian" Christmas party at the Sabarimata Hotel where we were staying. . . . Therein they [Christians] would dance, smoke, drink and then easily associate with those of the opposite sex. Being in a hotel, they could also "follow their path of salvation" in private rooms upstairs for more intimate affairs. So, although Nagaland is a dry country and alcohol is not allowed, I saw that for Christians liquor was easily flowing. In fact, although Christian pastors have banned local alcohol, it is common knowledge that no pastor is without his liquor. . . . Is this the sign of the type of progress that adopting a new western form of religion can bring? . . . Another example is that in Nagaland they have also started beauty contests to expose or exploit many girls' beauty, all in the name of progress, where modesty had been previously honored. Because of the increase in promiscuity, HIV/AIDS has risen dramatically amongst the Nagas where it was unheard of before. Plus, the incidents of Naga boys raping Naga girls is on the rise where previously it rarely happened. With the idea of accepting Christianity also comes the idea of adopting western forms of lifestyle and habits.[6]

This passage unabashedly denigrates the Christian identity that the Nagas have adopted. Knapp cannot be singled out in this; many of the Sangh activists express a similar view, including local non-Christian activists who write for the RSS *Organiser*, penning articles with such titles as "Westernisation Threat to Naga Culture" (Zeliang 2005). Indeed, there is a constant effort by the Sangh to portray Christianity as conspiring for world domination by forcing illicit practices, such as alcohol and sex, onto naïve populations (see Froerer 2007; Kim 2005).[7] Knapp apparently views Nagaland as the example par excellence in the Northeast of what happens when the stable world of "traditional culture" gives way to the valorization of a West that represents all that is hedonistic about society. Here the West is an abode and exporter of moral decay, a binary that contrasts the Orient (the East) as noble, dignified, and peaceful with an Occident (the West) that is violent, rapacious, and heedless (Carrier 2003, 10), reviling the latter and celebrating the former. This is a familiar idea in Sangh writing that praises the spiritual superiority of Hindu traditions over the materialism and degradation of the West. But this is an idea that can also be traced back to the reformist tradition in India in the nineteenth and twentieth centuries and the interaction between the East and the West, particularly the influence of the Hindu reformist Swami Vivekananda's construction of "spirituality" upon, and as, nationalism (Chatterjee 1993; McKean 1996b; van der Veer 2001, 74). This kind of "ecumenical Hinduism" is visible primarily in Vivekananda Kendra's work in Arunachal Pradesh, which we have already discussed.

Later, Knapp offers a glimpse into his motivations for writing this diary. Playing the role of apologist for the JVS, and for the sake of the larger Vedic culture that unifies the entire region under one umbrella, he seems to bemoan the loss of culture being experienced by the Nagas. Christianity is squarely written off as violent, war mongering (Bible in one hand, gun in the other), and destructive to local cultures due to its foreignness, arguments visible also in the Sangh criticism. In a moment of direct repudiation of Christianity, Knapp writes: "We have a very substantiated history of that right here in America regarding the way they treated the natives when the Christians first arrived. Yet, it is often the case that you do not know what you have until you've lost it, and you find the new culture of religion is not all it was propped up to be."[8]

CHRISTIANITY AND COLLECTIVE LOSS

Knapp's rhetoric about the obliteration of local cultures and indeed the yearning for a "traditional past" can be summed up, according to the anthropologist Renato Rosaldo's formulation, as "imperialist nostalgia," which

> occurs alongside a peculiar sense of mission, "the white man's burden," where civilized nations stand duty-bound to uplift so-called savage ones. In this ideologically constructed world of ongoing progressive change, putatively static savage societies become a stable reference point for defining . . . civilized identity. "We" (who believe in progress) valorize innovation, and then yearn for more stable worlds, whether these reside in our own past, in other cultures, or in the conflation of the two. . . . When the so-called civilizing process destabilizes forms of life, the agents of change experience transformations of other cultures as if they were personal losses. (1989, 70)

The kind of "loss" that the Nagas, and indeed indigenous peoples, are experiencing can be viewed through the notion of the "vanishing savage," where people like Knapp and the Sangh criticize the destructive intrusion of missionary work and the imperialist regime of domination.[9] This irretrievable loss of a bygone era is palpable in Knapp's and other accounts that bring to the forefront the destructive recesses of so-called progress (here the Christians). If a hero figure is needed, the recovery of this "savage culture" is made possible by Hindutva forces aiming to achieve a calibration with national identity.

Destruction, absence, death, and ignorance are common descriptions that are summoned when talking about loss, as Knapp's account helpfully evokes. Ideas about loss can also represent a fixation with origins, romantic escapism, and a search for the exotic. Contributing a postcolonial reading of the negative accounts of this kind of loss, the historian Ajay Skaria remarks,

> We have learnt to be suspicious of narratives of loss. And rightly so. In their colonial, nationalist, or liberal forms, narratives of loss are about a transition from homogeneity to differentiation, from the originary fullness of autonomy to a degraded condition of subalternity. These narratives suffer from a pervasive nostalgia, a yearning for unity with the homogenous past, a desire for the closure of difference, and any politics associated with them would be profoundly conservative and restorative. (2000, 298)

And it is here that the Sangh's work is at its most trenchant and deliberate. The connection between Knapp's impassioned pleas to protect indigenous culture finds a natural partner with the Sangh, whose own work among the tribals speaks of a kind of "imperialist nostalgia" centered on the idea of loss. Unlikely as it may seem, the Sangh would take succor from recent theories that examine loss and its effects on the human imagination particularly when considering how "evocations of loss . . . also make possible the politics of hope" (Skaria 2000, 298). A more eloquent rendering is provided by the historian Sumathi Ramaswamy when considering the case of the lost continent of Lemuria in the Indian Ocean. In suspending her postcolonial suspicion, she says, "Apprehensions of loss mobilise the imagination, provoke political action, and interpellate whole fields of knowledge" (2004, 8).

Although the appeal to a "primitive past" is attractive to the Sangh, as it allows them to recover the "authentic" national self of the Nagas, this kind of posturing itself can be seen from the vantage point of the present, where the tropes of "nostalgia" and "authenticity" are continually debated and negotiated among indigenous peoples through the "performance of identity" (see Canclini 1995). In this sense, Renato Rosaldo's evocation of "imperialist nostalgia" can easily extend to Sangh ideas of nationalism that partake of the recovery of loss as a positive feature while challenging postcolonial warnings to be "suspicious of narratives of loss." To ground such abstract postcolonial theorizing on loss and recovery with some empirical evidence, it is helpful to turn to Tana's thoughts on this matter.

Tana, whom we met earlier, is a karyakarta (worker) from Arunachal Pradesh who has been associated with the Vivekananda Kendra for many years.[10] Discussing at length the place of Christianity in Arunachal Pradesh, Tana said: "Nagaland is a lost cause. Mizoram and Meghalaya to an extent too—nothing is left for them." Here he is singling out the three Christian states to suggest that with Christianity comes a complete loss of culture: "If culture should have been promoted, it should be in a place where something is already there. You cannot promote where there is nothing. From another angle, it could also be the case that if there is nothing then something needs to be *replanted* as well." Whereas, in Tana's words, "Christianity completely destroys the converted person by altering his world," in a place like Arunachal indigenous culture is still visible because the people have resisted the onslaught of Christianity and Westernisation. One must take note of the caustic nature of Tana's remarks, which I would assert stem from his being active with indigenous movements that resist Christian conversions, particularly from missionaries from Nagaland. While people like Tana, Stephen Knapp, and the Sangh deplore the loss of culture in places like Nagaland, for them there is still a glimmer of hope amid the loss.

This recovery is possible, according to the Sangh, by navigating the contours of place and "place-making" (Basso 1996). If the key is to demonstrate that Nagaland and the Northeast have been part of Bharatvarsh since time immemorial, they have to go some way to establishing these connections. As discussed in Chapter 2, place-making then is a modern project that attempts to salvage that which is lost where the intricacies of power and imagination have shaped the encounter that produced loss in the first place. This idea, of course, is not new to Hindutva literature, in which the foreignness of Christianity is precisely used as an argument to exclude Christians from belonging in India. Given the Sangh's attempt to dismantle the fabric of Christianity and its association with destabilization and the creation of "collective loss," we now need to consider how the Sangh start restoring the cultural balance.

RECONSTRUCTING NATIONAL IDENTITY

The key point that needs to be established is the notion of Hindu, a point that has been discussed in Chapter 1 and in detail in Chapter 3. For our purposes here, it is necessary to reiterate some of the main points, primarily to clarify the ambiguity of the term and also, according to JVS, to remove any misunderstanding and suspicion of Hindu as a category referring solely to a religious community. In my conversations with JVS members, *Hindu* is an indigenous term that captures the idea of sanatan dharma, defined by them as "eternal religion and culture." Those who adhere to sanatan dharma, according to the JVS, are taken as Hindu, who "have different ways of worship and different names for gods." Moreover, Hindu, unlike Christianity and Islam, is a way of life and not a way of worship. In short, Hindu is a conglomeration of different forms of worship and philosophies.

The use of sanatan dharma by the Sangh is not new and has historical precedents that are widespread throughout the Indian scriptural tradition (Dimitrova 2007, 90). Indeed, it is important to note that sanatan dharma has been differently constructed in different periods, and for different purposes and by different people, suggesting that it is less than "eternal" (Dalmia 1997). It was used primarily as an orthodox resistance to reform movements of the eighteenth and nineteenth centuries that remained as a "signifier of various practices and structures that were perceived in particular regional and historical contexts as encapsulating 'traditional Hinduism'" (Zavos 2001, 121). Over time, and especially in the 1920s, it was usurped by Hindu nationalism in an effort to consolidate the different groups into a modern Hindu identity with a "meaningful constituency of Hindus" (Zavos 2001, 121; see also McKean 1996b, 82–84). The use of the term *sanatan dharma* by the JVS in the Northeast reflects the common understanding of Hindu as defined by the VHP, which "embraces all people who believe in, respect or follow the eternal values of life, ethical and spiritual, that have evolved in Bharat" (quoted in Bhatt 2001, 180–81). Although this definition is a broad canvas upon which any practice could be etched, there are subtleties in the way they approach the subject of non-Indian religions, that is, Christianity and Islam.

In emphasizing the common Hindu identity that is beyond "mere worship," the goal of the JVS, as I was told, is to stress that "Nagas are our blood brothers" and by extension part of this Hindu orbit that is familial, territorial, and civilizational. This strategy is significant in this context. In my conversations with JVS activists, they never refer to Hinduism (or even the word) as religion, precisely because they want to foreground the idea that Hinduism is more than internalized belief (or worship). It is "social, political, economic, and familial in nature" and can encompass India (the secular state) in India (the Hindu homeland). For them, the idea of Hindutva is visualized as a nationalist concept, not a theocratic or religious one (Cohen 2002, 26–27; also van der Veer 1994, 134). Their primary aim is to establish a sense of national unity and to share in the cultural resources of Bharat. They particularly narrate a version of history that pits the Nagas against foreign rulers, especially the British and later the Christian missionaries, and extols the worthiness of rejecting foreign powers, which has broader resonances with Hindutva strategizing.

NARRATING A LOCAL HISTORY OF RESISTANCE

JVS's version of Naga history begins with the British conquest of the Angami villages of Khonoma, Mezoma, and Kekrima in 1878 and their resistance. To demonstrate this broader theme, Jagdish's Naga history comes into play here. He highlights how the Chang Naga community in eastern Nagaland and then the Zeliangrong people in the South fought against British expeditions. Particular mention is made of a Rongmei Naga leader, Jadonang, hanged by the British in Imphal (Manipur) on 29 August 1931, for sedition by proclaiming a "Naga Raj" that would oust the British, and then the imprisonment of his successor, Gaidinliu, in 1934. Why focus on these examples? Here is the crucial aspect according to Jagdish: "They said that our indigenous faiths are ours; we don't like any foreigners' religions." The JVS's reasoning goes something like this: the resistance demonstrated by the Angami, Chang, and especially Jadonang and Gaidinliu represents the true spirit of the Nagas, not those exhibited by the Christianized Nagas who formed the Naga Club in 1918, the first articulation of a Naga political identity to resist integration with India.[11] This club, JVS assert, only divided and cultivated mutual suspicion between the Nagas themselves and between the Nagas and Hindus/Indians.

In contrast, the Sangh laud leaders like Jadonang and Gaidinliu because they vehemently opposed Christian conversion in their native areas. They reformed their indigenous religion to deal with the onslaught of Christianity and colonialism on their own terms (see Kamei 2004; Longkumer 2010). The Sangh have integrated the actions of Jadonang and Gaidinliu into their history, particularly Jadonang's recorded admiration of Gandhi's civil disobedience movement (Mukherjee, Gupta, and Das, 1982, 67–96), Nehru's respect for Gaidinliu (calling her the rani, or queen, of the Nagas [see Chapter 6]) as he rallied for her release from prison in 1947, and her subsequent close relationship with the Indian government—to encompass them in the larger Indian national struggle for independence.

However, Christianity remains an integral part of Naga identity if for no other reason than the large numbers calling themselves Christian—and this is problematic for the JVS narrative. It is difficult for the JVS to argue against Christianity as being integral to the people's identity. Unable to dismiss Christianity completely, how do the JVS argue for territorial integrity given the "foreignness" of Christianity, which goes against Savarkar's original Hindutva posturing? The JVS argue that Christianity brought about a separation between religion and culture. Using this argument, the JVS relegate Christianity to a cognitive sphere of belief, removed from Hindutva's nationalistic space, which provides the material, social, and religious landscape in which to situate one's belonging. This then allows the JVS to domesticate the foreignness of Christianity as a tactic of national inclusion.

RELIGION AND CULTURE CONTINUUM

The JVS have questioned the secular understanding of religion, claiming that it is not something separate from culture. This separation occurs, they say, only when religion is organized around worship. As Jagdish explains: "Culture is religion in action. Culture and religion are inseparable—they are two sides of the same coin. When Christianity came, with planning, they tried to separate culture from religion. And that is why wherever Christianity went, culture automatically died. And a separate culture developed, which is based on hedonic consumerism, free from spirituality." Christianity has long been associated with creating an ineluctable split between religion and culture in a variety of contexts (Dumont 1971; Keane 2007). Indeed, in much of the colonized world, separate conceptual categories, such as religion, culture, law, and politics, familiar to the Euro-Americans, did not exist. Translating them into local contexts was fraught with difficulties. This separation, and indeed the creation of religion as a category, was a uniquely post-Reformation European phenomenon (Mazusawa 2005). With the rise of modern science and the privatization of religion, religion came to be seen as a state of mind rather than a practical activity (Asad 1993, 47). Lord Herbert developed the well-known theory of natural religion, which posits that religion is natural and common to all human experiences. Talal Asad suggests its "emphasis on beliefs meant that henceforth religion could be conceived as a set of propositions to which believers gave assent" (1993, 41). What this allowed for was a universal definition of religion that tended to privilege belief as cognitive, ultimately a private and subjective phenomenon. This shift to considering religion as belief centered fundamentally altered the worldview of seventeenth- and eighteenth-century Victorians, and this would then reverberate into the margins of the British Empire (see Longkumer 2016b; van der veer 1994; Viswanathan 1998).

For example, early missionaries in the Naga hills from mid-nineteenth century made a clear distinction between Christianity ("true religion") and ancestral custom ("false religion"). Ancestral custom—such as drinking rice beer, animal sacrifice, venerating ancestors, head taking—was anathema to any Christian idea of progress; such practices had to be discouraged, the missionaries believed, among new converts. But Christianity, the missionaries realized, also needed to be relevant within the local culture to be effective. Therefore, they gradually and painstakingly distinguished between "local culture" (which included language, food, festivals, songs, and poetry, albeit purified) from "pre-Christian religion" (spirits, gods, shamans, divination, priests, sacrifices, rice beer, omens) (Longkumer 2016b). An instance among the Tangkhul Nagas in Ukhrul, Manipur, is pertinent here. Baptist missionaries working in the area used these conceptual categories—religion and culture—to mark difference: "Many of the church members and workers had participated in the great tribal feasts, which include sacrificing to evil spirits, apparently not realizing the inconsistency of such action with their profession of Christianity. When the issue was clearly drawn, seven of the little church of thirty-five remained steadfast. . . . The remaining members . . . seemingly have returned to heathenism" (Clark 1907, 155). A similar process was unfolding in mission fields across the world. Webb Keane analyzed this problem in Sumba, Indonesia, as follows: "Those who advocated the localization of Christianity had a reason to seek out differences between religion and culture. But in doing so, they risked participating in the purification process that had contributed to secularization in the West, by confining religion to a distinct sphere apart from other domains of social life" (2007, 106). Christianity, in these cases, is treated as an objective, inner activity that can coexist with some aspects of the outer domain of culture, as long as the latter does not clash with the former. In Nagaland, Mohan, a JVS worker, attempted to universalize the problem of Christianity and its contact with indigenous cultures, in part to provide a rationale for the JVS's action: "When missionaries came, they said their ancestors have been practicing evil and that their traditions, worship, and festivals must be stopped since it equates with 'devil worship.' So when the ways of Christianity were adopted, the harmonious community living ends and divisions occur. Community participation also becomes ruptured because these Christians are only interested in individual salvation. Once Christian converts come, then community activity ceases." Mohan is making the argument, which is symptomatic of JVS opinions, that rupture from land and custom brings about a different kind of allegiance. An allegiance that is "foreign" and fosters "cessation" must be transformed into something that is benevolent and celebrates Hindu national identity.

On face value, it would appear that the JVS polemic would not allow for such a reparative connection with culture. For them, Christianity is primarily belief-oriented worship, for it separates foreign beliefs (Christianity) from locality (Naga culture). Therefore, it is highly significant that Christianity severed links with the Naga past. This renders Christianity ineffective and spurious—it is only a cognitive exercise—because it has no sociopolitical relevance in Bharat. Due to the strong dematerialization of Christianity from culture, it leads to disenchantment (or hedonistic consumerism), a definitive feature, as the JVS see it, of secular modernity, or Westernization. To stop the further secularization of Naga culture, lest its roots be lost, the JVS proposes two solutions. To preserve the coeval nature of both religion and culture, as indigenizing mechanisms, in the Naga context requires (1) a return to the eternal religion and culture (sanatan dharma) and (2) to remember that Naga ancestors were all Hindu. In other words, they want to claim Nagas as Hindus despite their Christianity.

NATURE LINKS AND CIVILIZATIONAL IDENTITY

Although the JVS argue that Hindu as a nationalistic and civilizational identity has little to do with worship in the above secular sense, the term *Hindu*, for many Christian Nagas, has negative, religious connotations. As discussed in Chapter 4, the unwelcome restating by the JVS of a view of Hindutva's "synthesising apperception" (Khare 1976, 261)—a kind of coercive assimilation of Jain, Buddhist, and Sikh practices into a unified Hinduism (Cohen 2002; Copeman 2012)—appears to have set the stage for a Christian response. For them, Hindu is the very opposite of what it means to be Christian. Hindu is a false religion for it worships idols and venerates nature, which in Christian terms is demonic because it gives agency to those forces instead of exclusive allegiance to one God. However, the Sangh, while upholding the idea of Christianity as foreign, suggest that this is a misunderstanding of Hindu and one given by nineteenth-century Christians.

The JVS claim that precisely because the pre-Christian Nagas worshipped the sun and moon, sacrificed to ancestors, deities, and spirits, and venerated the natural world, they are Hindu. "Refer to any texts on pre-Christian Naga animist practices and you will find an affinity with Hindu culture," asserted one JVS worker. Indeed, the Sangh regularly evokes the idea of tribals and Hindus worshipping nature, as discussed in Chapter 3. Certain early accounts apparently substantiate JVS claims. For instance, the early American missionary Edward Winter Clark equated the polyvalence of the Ao Naga deity Tsüngrem with the Hindu deity Ram. Further, "the sun and moon are regarded as deities, and are occasionally worshipped, as are also the spirits officials and ancestors" (Clark 1907, 57). Equivalences such as these have powerful resonances for the JVS through the discourse of sanatan dharma.

At the center of this debate is the relationship of the janjatis of Northeast India to Mother Earth, or India as mother (*maa* or Bharat Mata, Mother India). Notice this injunction from Jagdish as he attempts to link faith in Bharat with one's history and culture, which is exemplified by the notion of Bharat Mata.

> And everybody having faith in Bharat Mata, having a regard for Bharatiya history, and pilgrim places, they are all taken as a patriot. If I regard Phizo and Aliba Imti [past NNC presidents] as my own forefather, then you should also regard my *bhagwan* Ram as your own forefather. This Tsüngrem [Ao Naga high god], if I take as one of the gods, we accept that you will have the same regard for our gods. No clashes: you go on your own way; I go on my own way. Same river leads to the same ocean. So similarly, through your Tsüngremong and Moatsü festival [Ao Naga festivals] Sekrenyi and Ukepenopfü [Angami Naga festival and deity], Tuluni [Sema Naga festival], and all these lead to the same god. So that is the Indian/Vedic philosophy.

The power of these ancient symbols, such as Bharat Mata and its link with anthropomorphic representations of Mother Earth, evokes the "body-cosmos" (Eck 1998b, 170; see also Ramaswamy 2001) of India's sacred landscape as tangible and relatable. This kind of ecumenical Hinduism links with the logic provided by L. Khimun, a Tangsa Naga from Arunachal Pradesh and the general secretary of the indigenous Rangfraa Faith Promotion Society. It runs something like this: since the janjatis are jungle dwellers, they are closest to nature through their dependence on the forest for their livelihood; because of this they are "spiritual" in the sense that they are as "sacred" and "pure" as Mother Earth; due to this relationship, they worship her (Khimun 2012, 14). Similarly, according to Khimun, Hindus worship the elements of the earth (fire, water, air, and sun) and thus revere Mother Earth—often depicted as the goddess Kali maa. These similarities mean that the Hindus, like the janjatis, are also indigenous. Here Mother Earth is the ideal representation of sanatan dharma in the whole of Bharat (Khimun 2012, 20). Christianity, as a modern idea, on the other hand, has severed links with nature and abandoned many of its customary traditions, which the JVS claim made the Nagas Naga and part of Mother Earth and Hindu in the first place. In this way, the JVS project is to highlight the indigenous aspects of the Nagas' faith, whether this is within or outside Christianity. The important point is that, according to the JVS, it is their roots that make Nagas Hindu.

JVS activists say that when they visit non-Christian villages, Nagas remark, "We are Hindus, and we have been waiting for a Hindu missionary. Why didn't you come earlier?" Jagdish offered me a history lesson that goes some way to explaining what he means by returning to one's roots. I paraphrase his lengthy lesson, not as an accurate portrayal of historical events but as illustrative of a larger point based on his dictum: "You say that you are civilized, but I say that because of Christianity, you are losing your civilization." He said that when South Africans became Christians, their land was taken from them through deceit, guns, and mission work. Some were more diffident, however, and retained their indigenous faith. In the midst of Christian persecution, they still retained voodoo as a religion, and that is how it survived. Similarly, Christianity in Europe attempted to suppress the pagan religion—reading Dan Brown's *The Da Vinci Code* allows us, he says, to see how indigenous faith has persevered against the odds. "The priory of Scion, Archimedes, and Einstein all practiced this faith. Some leaders even became priests and bishops and popes to hide their religion," he explains.

Although one may not want to give too much weight to a fictional account of religion as conspiracy theory, as in Brown's book, for Jagdish, it stands as fact and a fact that can hardly be proven otherwise despite my observations about its fictitiousness and contested historical revisionism. The point though is clear. For Jagdish, pre-Christian practices in Nagaland and elsewhere have been suppressed for years, and like Jagdish's aforementioned history making, these pre-Christian routes must be resurrected. The context however is different both in terms of geographical terrain and in terms of the Hindutva ideology that I have been discussing throughout this chapter. In the case of the Christians in Nagaland, how do the Sangh maintain broader civilizational links in response to the Nagas' own preference for exclusion from India? Some distinction between Nagas and Christianity must be maintained if the JVS are to have any success in responding to the Nagas' indifference to the national unity of Bharat. What does this do to the larger project of Hindutva in Nagaland? Can non-Hindus be part of India? The simple answer for the JVS is yes, but only by assimilation and acceptance of the territorial sovereignty of Bharat. I was told that if Christians accept this principle, they are "Christian Hindu" (the criteria is different for Muslims [see Bakhle 2009, 168–74; Varshney 1993, 231]). Discussions on this are varied in the history of Christianity in India, and the next section will explore some of these debates.

CHRISTIAN HINDU AND THE NATIONAL FRAME

According to Sebastien Kim's work, there were basically two camps: one becomes a Christian outside the "Hindu social fold" (the discontinuity thesis) or within it (the continuity thesis) as "the tent put up by our Western friends . . . can never be our permanent habitation" (2005, 89). But within these two powerful movements, there was always an attempt to find a "meeting place" that tried to articulate a Christian theology within a predominantly Hindu cultural context.

Some, like Kaj Baago, the Protestant theologian from South India, articulated a "Hindu Christianity," in which one leaves institutional Christianity and accepts Hinduism and Buddhism as one's own (1966a, 331–32). His argument was that Christ transcends religions and cultures and that it should not be bound by the church, which after all is a colonial legacy and incompatible with the Indian context. He suggests that people be open to the idea that "the gospel should be allowed to grow within Hinduism" (quoted in Kim 2005, 91). As radical as his position would seem, Baago was increasingly concerned about the place of Indian Christians, particularly since the ideology of Hindutva was growing in influence. This growth was based on the Hindutva identification of Indian with Hindu, an assimilation that called for a choice: you were either Indian or a Christian (Baago 1966a, 1966b; see also Brown 2003). Others, like M. M. Thomas, argued for a "secular fellowship" to bridge the gap between Hindus and Christians, by way of becoming "truly 'religious' without being 'communal'" (1972, 88). Combining his liberal theology with a secular position in a plural India, Thomas believed in the ideals of secularism in which the values and differences created by these religions would dissolve and give way to a human community and where the universality of Christ would be affirmed. Both these positions stirred debate, partly because, as some argued, it was impossible for the two positions to be compatible within Christianity. If one's allegiance to Christ is decisive, this allegiance must take visible social form, overriding the person's commitment to the Hindu community (Newbigin 1972, 78).

Among the Catholics, this meeting place would take on a similar tone, inflected by their exclusive theology of "no salvation outside the church" (*extra ecclesiam nulla salus*). Brahmahandhab Upadhyay (1861–1907), an Indian Catholic convert, argued that it is possible to adopt a "Hindu-Catholic" identity that synthesizes Hindu notions of ethnicity and Catholic notions of "sacramental rebirth"—or, in other words, the physical and mental composition is Hindu, but the immortal soul is Catholic (1991, 24–25). But Upadhyay's concerns were overtaken by Raymond Panikkar's articulation of "Hindu Christianity" (distinct from "Indian Christianity"), which argued for an "unknown Christ of Hinduism" (1964). This kind of "fulfillment" theory (Sharpe 1977) that Panikkar was proposing was seen as a negative strategy: that Hinduism was seen simply as "preparatory" to Christianity (Swarup 1994, 182–98). However, these discussions would go on to influence the development of a Hindu-Catholic approach that saw Hinduism consist primarily of *samaj dharma* (customs, ritual purity, food, etc.) and Christianity as *sadhana dharma* (the way of salvation) (Kim 2005, 115). Christianity in turn can accommodate the material conditions of Hinduism without conflicting with its true, inner essence. Thus, this method of inculturation and syncretism became the dominant model of the "middle way" articulated by Catholics (Vandana 1993).

This kind of Catholic synthesis, however, argues the anthropologist David Mosse, led to the retention of Hindu religious beliefs alongside the cultural forms inherent in villages, despite being inhabited primarily by Christians. For example, he argues that the caste system persisted in such places, despite its disavowal by Christians. Christian converts are said to be given a "new identity," one aside from, and more fundamental to, their caste. However, to maintain power and political influence, both the Catholic leaders and caste leaders have been complicit in maintaining a "high-caste Hindu hegemony" (Mosse 1994, 87–92, 101). It was the offer of escaping the caste system through Christianity that proved attractive to Dalit Christians, or former untouchables. Dalit Christians are hesitant to buy into a Christian Hindu view because of their past, where "Brahmanical Christianity" was advocated (a combination of Vedic texts and Christian belief), which did not have space for Dalits (Jeremiah 2012).

The status of Dalits is an interesting example. Nathaniel Roberts, in his recent examination of Dalits in South India, notes that the conversion of Dalits to Christianity in the nineteenth century was not an issue for Hinduism as Dalits were not recognized as Hindus. Largely due to the post-1909 demographic struggle between Hindus and Muslims, Dalit inclusion in the Hindu fold became important as a key strategic move by M. K. Gandhi, among others, not merely as a means of competing demographically with Muslims but also as a central question of national identity for Hindu majoritarianists (Roberts 2016, 8).

This broader discussion of political theologies is helpful in bringing into view larger Hindu-Christian conversations regarding the problem of belonging in India. It suggests that these debates are not isolated but are reincarnated in different forms in the Northeast. Let us return to the Northeast in light of these discussions. First, the Northeast to a large extent is not a caste society but a "tribal one," wherein discriminations based on caste, and what it means upon conversion, are not the pressing issue they might be in other parts of India (see Jeremiah 2012; Mosse 1994; Roberts 2016; Robinson 1998). Also, so far, the problem of belonging articulated here has not confronted Christian demands of territorial sovereignty. We have discussed Christians incorporating Hinduism within an Indian identity but not Christians demanding territory on the basis of their Christianity. This is what makes Nagaland and the demands by Naga nationalists based on Christianity such a compelling case study. Negating Christian Naga claims of territorial sovereignty is an explicit means of absorbing the Nagas into the Hindu national self through the ethnographic construction of a Christian Hindu, where the Hindu part becomes the source of a different territorial claim.

CREATING NATIONAL CHRISTIANS

The post-Enlightenment notion of religion as belief can have strategic uses for proponents of Hindutva. The difficulty with Nagaland, as I have already explained, is that they do not fall into the neat JVS nationalistic paradigm of indigeneity. So the JVS are confronted with a double task: How do they persuade the Nagas that like the Hindus they are also are rooted to the land? And how do they convince the Nagas that this rootedness to the land is part of Mother India, or the holy land—precisely what the Nagas have sought to contest for over sixty years?

The following polemic by Mohan, a JVS informant, reiterates this point:

> Bharatiya culture came into clash with Christianity and Islam because exclusively they said only Jesus, only Bible, only church, and no salvation out of the church; Muslims said out of Quran and masjid no salvation. We said, no, Jesus Christ is also one of the gods. Muhammad is also one of the prophets, one of the incarnations of god. We accept them as gods, but Christians reject us; clash comes there. But integration also comes here, that you will feel part and parcel of Bharatvarsh [land of Bharat]; Bharatvarsh is a land of yours; Nagaland is mine and Delhi is yours; whole country belongs to you, whole country belongs to me. So, you should say that I'm a Bharatiya; I'm an Indian. At the same time, when you are following your own faith, that is an integral part and parcel of Hindu faith. So that emotional culture is our motto: Nagas should also say that I'm an Indian.

The dogmatic orthodoxy of Christianity and Islam is contrasted with the fluid heterodoxy and orthopraxy of the Hindus, which can encompass the many strands of these sectarian religious truths within the stream of Hindutva as a civilization. In the words of a JVS activist, Rajiv: "You have only Jesus Christ, but we have thousands of gods. It is not a demerit that we have many gods. But it is a demerit that you have only one God."

On a practical level, this sort of negotiation—Christian and Hindu—was narrated to me by Jagdish. He gave an example of five Konyak Christian Naga girls, who were sponsored by the JVS to study and live in a hostel in Gorakhpur, in the Indian state of Uttar Pradesh. These girls were refusing to participate in the morning prayer rituals. Their refusal was later explained to Jagdish:

> [The girls said,] "*Bhaiya* [brother], our father said that we shouldn't do any satanic pujas—if we do, it is sin and we will go to hell. So how can I pray? This is not Christian prayer. Then I [Jagdish] said: "I'm a Hindu but I go to the church, read the Bible, and have dozens of biblical literatures. By going to the mandir, you don't become Hindu; by going to a particular puja, you are not going to get *pap* [sin]. When you are at home, pray to Jesus Christ; when you come here, follow this practice."

The girls eventually "got it," Jagdish explains enthusiastically. With a sparkle in his speech, he narrates the following events. After three months, he went back to the hostel where, alongside these five girls, now there were nineteen Naga girls from different tribes. They had their bath, put on clean clothes, and went to the mandir (temple) and took a copper pot, which they brought back with *prasad* (gift of food to deities) for Jagdish to eat. Clearly Jagdish was impressed as he told me, "This is not indoctrination into Hinduism; rather, they are privileged as they know Hindu and Christianity. Being a good Christian doesn't involve neglecting puja and touching elders' feet and saying, 'Namaste.' It is part and parcel of Bharatiya culture. Wearing jeans is not part of this culture, but wearing *salwar kameez* [Indian dress] and *mekla* [traditional Naga clothing] is. In this way, the students achieve assimilation and emotional integration."

The gradual manner in which emotional integration is achieved is vital to the project of Hindutva in Northeast India. On the one hand, Jagdish is not too concerned if these girls maintain an introspective Christianity in their lives, which is largely consistent with the Sangh ideology. His primary concern, on the other hand, is that these girls publicly demonstrate their willingness to participate in Hindu national identity through Hindu rituals, a kind of nonsectarian practice that transcends the exclusive religious allegiance instilled by their Christian parents. In stating this, it might be useful to counterpoise this discussion with the kind of Christian missionary tactic that the Hindutva activists decry.

If one were to rewind to the days in which American missionaries worked in the Naga hills, their insistence was on inward conversion, of the heart—the idea that conversion was an *event*, a rupture from the local setting where the material conditions, such as dress, social norms, and traditions conflicted with the new message of Christianity. This meant that the new Christian identity was largely irreconcilable with local culture, a debate that I highlighted earlier. This kind of rupture is precisely what the Sangh and the JVS have argued against, instead advocating for a new kind of Christianity, one that can assimilate, as with the example of the Konyak Naga girls. Inverting the formula that the American missionaries introduced—where inner conviction leads to the gradual dissipation of outer Naga material forms—Hindutva activists emphasize maintaining the material aspects as preserving national identity, assuming that this will, in time, give way to a change of heart. This approach resonates with Gandhi's argument that the best way to eliminate non-Hindu behavior was to instill the practice of worshipping Hindu gods, or, to use a Christian example, as Blaise Pascal reportedly said: "Kneel down, move your lips in prayer . . . and you will believe" (quoted in Roberts 2016, 140).

This under-the-radar kind of activity suits groups like the JVS. For them, the process of conversion may require a hundred years, but they will persist at it. "Imagine," said Rajiv, who coordinates the education program for the JVS,

> now we have sent four hundred students to schools and hostels, and some are doctors, engineers, teachers in Nagaland. What happens when this number increases to thousands, lakhs? Then these students will share their experience of studying in places like Gorakhpur, and then the Naga public will have a different picture of the Hindus—not like the earlier picture of the Hindu represented by the cruel Indian military, corrupt businesspeople, IAS [Indian Administrative Service] officers, and the CRPF [Central Reserve Police Force]. Naga people will come to learn that Hindu society loves them.

Unlike the overt forms of nationalism exhibited by the Dharm Jagran Manch in the opening part of the chapter, this strategy of conversion, or expansive containment, adopted by the Sangh in the Northeast will, I suspect, not entirely convince friends like Among, even though their activities on the surface may be construed as benign. It is in this respect that the work of the Sangh through organizations like the JVS has managed to offer a novel way of approaching the subject of emotional integration through the use of religion and culture that is attempting to nationalize Christians over the *longue durée*.

CONCLUSION

In this chapter, I have shown how the Sangh approaches the question of the vexed relationship between Christianity and Hindutva. This approach creates some difficulties, particularly in light of Savarkar's claims that Christianity's foreignness is the basis for its exclusion from belonging within India. Applying this to the Northeast is complicated, however, not least because of the many people who assert a strong national Christianity based on difference and exclusion. I have shown how the JVS, notwithstanding Hindutva's original position regarding Christianity, reconceptualize this position and adapt some of the key contradictions. In effect, the JVS dismantle Christianity based on its foreignness and delegitimize it as "hedonistic consumerism," succinctly articulated by Jagdish when he said, "You say that you are civilized, but I say that because of Christianity, you are losing your civilization." Couched in the language of loss and nostalgia, the JVS employ a language of place-making that envisions a new future for the Nagas by channeling the collective loss brought about by Christianity to make possible the recovery of a Hindu national self.

The JVS make claims to the discourse of religion and culture to emphasize the civilizational links, particularly with those who do not feel that they belong in Bharat, or Mother India. They persuasively maintain that national behavior unites people rather than individual and sectarian worship, which causes conflict. But how does one deal with a religious tradition that is practiced in vast numbers without excluding them from Bharat? This integration comes through their construction of a Christian Hindu. This construction is not new, however, as the dual aspect of belonging has been articulated throughout the history of Christianity in India.

Indeed, this separation between religion and culture worked in favor of the Christian apologists who could see it working out in the context of a syncretic religious identity: where Hinduism represented the material and social aspects and Christianity provided the cognitive and spiritual recourse. Hindu commentators were perturbed by these divisions because, they argued, Indian culture and Hindu religion could not be so easily distinguished, and these two entities—Hindu and Christian—could not be united as each was a distinct entity. Furthermore, Hindu commentators saw this as an ultimate aim to eventually convert the Hindus into Christians through the process of syncretism, where only those practices that did not clash with Christianity were taken instead of the adoption of Hindu culture and religion en masse and in situ.

In the case of the JVS in Nagaland, although they recognize that religion and culture cannot be separated and blame Christianity for the original rupture, they now have to dismantle and then reconstruct these ideas for the purpose of relinking the religion-culture continuum. Christianity for the JVS, then, is represented as mere belief, or of the heart, and so can be incorporated into the broader Hindu national self, which provides the material and social landscape in which to situate one's belonging. The material dimension of being Hindu does not mean that one becomes a religious Hindu from another region of India; it simply emphasizes that Hindu is the acknowledgment of physical reality itself. Therefore, in a way, JVS activists demand a different kind of Christianity—one that is not divisive, is in touch with its pre-Christian roots, and celebrates the performance of (ancestral) identity as patriotic duty. In other words, they take on the Christian apologist position in an attempt to create a Christian Hindu identity on their own terms as a kind of expansive containment, to indigenize Christianity by encompassing its basis of difference for a sociological construction of sameness and repairing the religion-culture dynamic.

From this chapter, one can argue that national unity is constructed as natural, evoking the idea of sanatan dharma (eternal faith and culture) and all people share this singular force. Whether this is a fiction created by certain groups is not the point. Rather, it must be noted that there is an underlying drive to create a sense of sameness that incorporates the margins into the dominant Hindu culture. Here, Savarkar's notion of holy land takes on a different meaning: for him, it was the exclusion of certain groups that became central to imagining a Hindu nation. But for the present Hindutva in the Northeast, the holy land is not about exclusive religious belonging but one that must incorporate the territorial vastness of Bharat and its practices in an act of inclusivism that is both strategic and essential to the future of Hindutva. The next chapter highlights this tension between national belonging and resistance through the figure of a woman and her iconicity.

CHAPTER 6

RANI GAIDINLIU

A Semiotic Challenge to the Nation-State

IN 1966, RANI GAIDINLIU, a Naga leader, after a decade underground fighting for a Zeliangrong homeland, finally surrendered to the Indian authorities. In her surrender, she highlighted two points when talking to the officiating negotiator, S. C. Dev, the deputy commissioner of Kohima (the capital of Nagaland), which would go on to shape the remainder of her life aboveground. First, she had fought for the independence of India along with Mahatma Gandhi and Jawaharlal Nehru and to drive out the British. Second, she was an Indian and a Naga through and through. She declared that advocating for the preservation of her culture and tradition made her an indigenous Naga, as opposed to the alien Christianity that many had adopted in the region, and her association with the freedom struggle made her an Indian. The Nagas and Indians, she said, were not separate but formed the "great Indian nation" (Dev 1988, 76–77). Over the next few years, she gradually became a national icon, lionized by the Sangh in particular, as she traveled the length and breadth of the country becoming the "face" of tribal India. However, in her home region of the Northeast and especially in her adopted home state, Nagaland, she remains controversial. Since 2016, fifty years after her surrender, she has suddenly been thrust into the limelight by the Sangh as a national symbol for resisting British imperialism and Christian conversion and glorifying indigenous traditions, bringing to fore the complex life of the region and of a woman. Her body politic is etched onto the skin of the Indian nation-state.

Who then is Rani Gaidinliu, and why is she such an enduring presence in the Sangh imagination? It should come as no surprise that various nationalist figures, such as Subhas Chandra Bose (Copeman 2013), B. R. Ambedkar, and other tribal leaders in the Northeast, have been co-opted by the Sangh for nationalist inspiration.[1] Rani Gaidinliu is especially important because of her status as a tribal, non-Christian figure, who can be incorporated into the Hindutva version of India. Her conciliatory personality is particularly relevant to counter the recalcitrance of Naga nationalists and churches in acceding to the idea of India. There is no one way to imagine and remember Rani Gaidinliu, but the Sangh method has been most pervasive in the collective Hindu imagination, because her life provides fruitful "raw semiotic material" (Ghosh 2011, 10) in India and the world over.

The idea of "raw semiotic material" applies to Rani Gaidinliu precisely because her life as an icon can be represented in diverse and multivalent ways.[2] I will examine the ways institutions and movements like the Sangh use icons as signs (semiosis) to evoke certain meanings that act as powerful sites to generate symbolic and cultural capital (Ferguson and Gupta 2002; Peirce 1996). Although James Ferguson and Akhil Gupta's work deals primarily with the state, it could easily apply to powerful institutions like the Sangh, who organize the practice of citizenship as an affective political site around icons. Because these icons are visible in public spaces, politics then takes the form of a "cultural regulation of publicity" (Cody 2011, 45). By interrogating the activity around icons, the main aim of this chapter contributes to the book's central theme concerning how the Sangh understand the region—an understanding that is not only integral to the nationalist history of India but also, through Rani Gaidinliu, highlights the complex discussions around gender, nation, and iconicity that are taking place in India today.

This chapter argues that while the Sangh project of animating her iconicity is circulated and accepted as indexing certain notions of Rani Gaidinliu as "freedom fighter," "devi" (goddess), and "tribal leader," her iconicity has largely failed to appeal in Nagaland precisely because the

Sangh have transformed her image into one of divine possibility. This fabrication, from the human to divine, is at the heart of this chapter. The second important aspect that I explore in this chapter is the precarity of being a woman within this national space, an argument that requires elaboration.

Cultural theorists such as Victor Turner (1974) have argued that in all ritualized movements there is a liminal space that allows escape from scripted obligations. Turner suggested that "in this interim liminality, the possibility exists of standing aside not only from one's own social position but from all social positions and of formulating a potentially unlimited series of alternative social arrangements" (1974, 13–14). Turner's model is helpful in thinking about Gaidinliu's life, though I might modify "interim" to one of "perpetual liminality." On the one hand, she is celebrated as a devi, freedom fighter, nationalist, woman, tribal, non-Christian, sister, and daughter. On the other hand, in conversation with many people in Nagaland she is denigrated as an enemy of the nation, "sorcerer," "black magician," and "puppet of the Sangh Parivar." These variegated opinions obfuscate aspects of her personal life and what she means to ordinary villagers in Assam, Manipur, and Nagaland. She has largely become what people make her to be. This is precisely the challenge for what Ghosh has termed "bio-icons" because, as she explains, "their 'lives' [are] told and retold for instruction; exemplary prototypes, they are often deployed as pedagogy. Hence, outpourings of biographical fragments (biographies, gossip, anecdote, legend, or lore) habitually accompany icons whose message wavers; in the allegations, refutations, and revisions, a wildly oscillating biograph can dislodge the image from its hegemonic encoding" (Ghosh 2011, 46).

In what follows, I explore how Rani Gaidinliu has become an icon for the Sangh, for whom she is the ideal representation of Northeast India. In the midst of all the region's fragmentations and resistances to the nation-state, she represents the stable and loyal patriot. The verdant iconicity of Rani Gaidinliu represents the Sangh ideology of "One Nation, One Culture," indexed through the feminine subject who becomes the "geobody" of Bharat (Ramaswamy 2001; Winichakul 1994), meant to inspire the masses into action. But this hegemonic encoding is challenged in other accounts, particularly by Christians. This chapter provides the historical context in which this tension emerged and the extent to which Rani Gaidinliu's life continues to provide a fruitful way of thinking about the Indian nation-state.

To consider these issues, the remainder of the chapter is divided into four sections. First, I explore the life of Rani Gaidinliu and her notoriety among the British. Second, I examine what Rani Gaidinliu means to the Sangh in their effort to incorporate her image and legacy as the icon of tribal India. Third, I show how the Rani Gaidinliu Library cum Memorial Museum (RGLMM) embodies semiotic tensions concerning Naga civil society and the perceived threat of Hindu saffronization. Finally, I reflect on what this means for the life of icons in contemporary India, focusing especially on how the female body is incorporated into the geobody of Bharat.

DAUGHTER OF THE HILLS

In popular accounts, Rani Gaidinliu was born under auspicious signs. Under clear skies, lightning flashed during her birth, frightening the villagers and stopping only five days later (Mall 2014, point 1).[3] Gaidinliu's mother, Karotlenliu, saw an angel in her dream who told her that the baby would be a girl. It came with a warning though. Either the mother or the child would die; if both survived, the girl would be extraordinary. The goddess Cherachamdinliu, the daughter of Bhuban cave, is said to have entered the womb of Karotlenliu, being born as Gaidinliu on 26 January 1915.[4] Gaidinliu was born in Lungkao, a Rongmei village in Tamenglong District of the state of Manipur. Throughout her life, she was accompanied by the goddess Namginai, who was another daughter of Bhuban and guided Gaidinliu in her activities. It was through Namginai that Gaidinliu was led to Bhuban cave, and it was there that both Gaidinliu and Jadonang, a collaborator and kin, received instructions from the god Bhuban (Longkumer 2010, 30–34). The early life of Gaidinliu and her activities with Jadonang have received attention elsewhere (see Kamei 2004; Longkumer 2010, 2017a; Thomas 2016), but here it is necessary to provide a brief outline of events.

When she was a teenager, Rani Gaidinliu met Jadonang, who was already starting to form ideas of the Naga Raj (a regional sovereign government) by making connections with other southern Naga tribes like the Angami and thus threatening the British colonial order. There are different stories associated with Jadonang and Gaidinliu's kin relationship (see Kamei 2004), but what developed was a close connection, akin to an older brother and younger sister. The first accounts from administrative records that we hear of Jadonang's activity are from around 1931 in Manipur. It is said that he started a "new religion," instigating his tribe, the "Kabui Nagas" (now known as the Rongmei), to overthrow the existing British administration. He is credited with "supernatural powers," treated as a "Messiah," and universally spoken of as the "King" or "spirit King."[5]

Such revolutionary fervor encourages the Sangh to link Jadonang's activities with the Indian national struggle. While one can be tempted to make these links "national," it is not always explicit if Jadonang or Gaidinliu thought of their fight against the British as one within the "national frame." It is more likely that theirs was a fight against paying house taxes in their region of Manipur (a considerable imposition by the British); the use of labor for the First World War in Europe, where the British were recruiting for the Labour Corps; the abuse of power by the local leaders in exploiting the *pothang* system; and internal animosities against neighboring tribes, such as the Kukis, who they saw as their enemies (Longkumer 2017a).[6] While we must exercise caution in interpreting these events as "national," some accounts do suggest that Jadonang, due to the presence of Congress workers from neighboring Silchar in Assam, was aware of M.K. Gandhi and his fight against British colonialism. In fact, the historian John Thomas mentions that Jadonang was keen to meet Gandhi when the latter was planning a visit to Silchar in 1927 (2016, 81). Gandhi did not make it to Silchar, and the meeting never took place. Other historians have been quick to link both Jadonang and Gaidinliu with Gandhi (Mukherjee, Gupta, and Das 1982), with her RSS biographer Jagdamba Mall even claiming that Rani Gaidinliu and Jadonang met Gandhi in Guwahati on December 26, 1926—an account he received directly from Rani Gaidinliu (Mall 2014, point 66).

Mall quotes Rani Gaidinliu further: "When the entire country has taken to the streets, then we too, must partake in this struggle for freedom and must sacrifice our all to free the Naga society and Bharatvarsh.

Taking inspiration from Mahatma Gandhi we must immediately dedicate ourselves in completing this pious task" (2014, point 10). This nationalist reading, with all of its vested interest, is significant in the context of the Sangh. In Rani Gaidinliu's biography, meeting Gandhi is projected as positive; yet in conversations with RSS workers over the years, Gandhi and Nehru are lambasted as "stooges of Mountbatten and the Muslims." I return to this nationalist understanding of Rani Gaidinliu below. Here I want to focus on Rani Gaidinliu's capture by the British and her subsequent incorporation into the nationalist imagination.

In 1931, Jadonang was captured and hanged by the British after being implicated on false charges of "human sacrifice." Gaidinliu, his close collaborator, escaped with a large number of followers to the North Cachar hills in Assam. Gaidinliu was then captured by the British. A fellow Naga, Dr. Haralu, was accused by her followers of conniving with the extra assistant commissioner Hari Blah and Captain Macdonald of the paramilitary force the Assam Rifles, and this led to her captivity in Pulomi village in the Naga hills in 1932. She was eventually brought to Manipur to be interrogated by J. C. Higgins, the political officer of Manipur, and J. P. Mills, the deputy commissioner of the Naga hills. In Captain Macdonald's report, he describes the young Gaidinliu, fatigued and bedraggled after evading colonial forces for a year. When captured, they dragged out the "biting, scratching girl for whom they [the village] had uselessly worked so hard and killed so many cattle [to feed her and her followers]."[7]

The myth, mystique, and notoriety of Gaidinliu's reputation occupied some of the colonial administrators and anthropologists during this period. A few years after Gaidinliu's capture in 1932, the anthropologist Ursula Graham Bower, who spent considerable time in Zeme Naga villages in the North Cachar hills, writes about her with literary flourish:

And the girl [Gaidinliu] who faced the Political Agent that day was not only the figurehead of as pretty a mob as ever graced Chicago, but was herself the hub of a money-spinning God-racket. The Agent sent her home, as too young to jail. She made an immediate dash for the north, her gang and the faithful, and a few days later the whole Kacha [Zeme] Naga country was alight. (1952, 43)

Gaidinliu was imprisoned for life—at around the age of seventeen—for assisting Jadonang, with the additional charge of instructing her followers, after her arrest, to murder a Kuki chowkidar (watchman) of the Lakema Inspection Bungalow in the Naga hills, suspected of aiding Gaidinliu's capture.[8] She was transferred several times between 1932 and 1945—from Kohima to Imphal, Guwahati, Shillong, Aizawl, and then Tura before she was released. It was in 1937 when Rani Gaidinliu was in the Shillong jail that Nehru heard of her and her exploits. The panegyric prose of Nehru quickly captured the imagination of the nationalist movement, and it was here that Gaidinliu moved beyond the narrow confines of her prison cell.

MEETING THE QUEEN: GAIDINLIU AND NEHRU

In 1938, an article appeared in an American periodical called *The Living Age*, in which Jawaharlal Nehru republished an essay he had contributed to the *All India Congress Committee Newsletter*, entitled "Gaidallo Ranee." He recounts his visit to Sylhet, Assam, where many Nagas from the surrounding hills visited him with greetings and gifts. Through them, he hears the story of Gaidinliu. He writes how a young Gaidinliu (he mentions her age as nineteen) hears of the "news of Gandhi and the Congress" when the civil disobedience movement was spreading through the length and breadth of the country: "She dreamed of freedom for her people and an ending of the galling restrictions they suffered from, and she raised the banner of independence and called her people to rally around it." He notes how her movement was quashed by the mighty imperial forces and how she was imprisoned, where she still languished, unknown to the average Indian and to the outside world. Nehru continues:

> What torment and suppression of spirit they have brought to her who in the pride of her youth dared to challenge an empire? She can roam no more in the hill country through the forest glades, or sing in the fresh air of the mountains. This wild young thing sits cabined in darkness, with a few yards, maybe, of space in the daytime, eating her fiery heart in desolation and confinement. And India does not even know of this brave child of her hills, with the free spirit of the mountains in her. . . . A day will come when India also will remember her and cherish her and bring her out of her prison cell.[9]

How prophetic is Nehru's clarion call in a contemporary India that celebrates her image as unifying a country amid the forces seeking separation. Indeed, this letter by Nehru and his reenvisioning of Gaidinliu—from a peasant girl to a national icon—was debated in Allahabad in the All India Congress Committee in 1938. Gaidinliu's case was subsequently taken up by Lady Astor, a member of parliament (MP), and deliberated on even by the governor-general of India, Lord Wavell.

Nehru rallied support from Lady Astor, who enquired about Gaidinliu in 1939. Writing to Colonel Muirhead, the parliamentary undersecretary for India and Burma, under the government of Neville Chamberlain, Lady Astor made the case that Gaidinliu should be freed because the danger had passed with the demise of Jadonang, who was seen as the main instigator for the revolt and murder of the traders. She also asked the government to consider some form of "reformative treatment" rather than permanent imprisonment. Muirhead, however, presented the case that Rani Gaidinliu was still an imminent threat and her release would only bring simmering tensions to the surface, which would be counterproductive for law and order in Manipur and the province of Assam. Nehru was amused when Lady Astor informed him about the position of the British government over Gaidinliu and even quipped: "The girl must be an unusually interesting person" if she still presented a threat to Manipur and the Assam Province, and the maintenance of peace in Manipur and Assam "had a very insecure foundation if it rested on a girl in the twenties being kept in prison indefinitely."[10]

Unable to gain support through Lady Astor, the issue was taken up again by the Sylhet Mahila Sangha, an organization working for the "upliftment of women folk," and petitions were made again to the governor-general of India, Lord Wavell. The Mahila made the claim that Gaidinliu and her movement were emboldened by the "civil disobedience movement" in full swing in 1932. Emphasis was placed on the reverberating effects of the national independence movement in the hill areas and that she be released due to her ill health as a result of solitary confinement.[11]

Nehru's commitment to Gaidinliu and her Naga cause is intriguing, particularly if one is to take into account his fervent opposition to Naga independence a decade later, which I have explored in Chapter 4. Here, one can see the strong sense of national unity that Nehru championed throughout his premiership postindependence: Gaidinliu represented the more accommodating vision of Nehru's India rather than her counterpart, A. Z. Phizo, the president of the NNC, who was determined to achieve independence from India. The tension between these two images—both advocating independence but from different perspectives—will be discussed a little later.

FROM FREEDOM TO UNDERGROUND

When Rani Gaidinliu was eventually released in 1945, she remained quiet in her adopted home of Yimrup in Mokokchung District of Nagaland (then the Naga hills). She reappeared again in the public limelight in 1952, when she was finally allowed to return to her home village of Lungkao in Manipur after about twenty years in exile. There she was active in local affairs and launched her vision to unite the Zeliangrong people, comprised of three kindred tribes—Zeme, Liangmei, and Rongmei—scattered in the states of Assam, Manipur, and Nagaland. Under the Zeliangrong People's Convention (ZPC) she met with the president of India, Rajendra Prasad, during his visit to Imphal in 1952. The historian Asoso Yonuo summarizes Gaidinliu's thoughts:

> Till now the Government of Assam and the Government of Manipur had completely ignored the development of Zeliangrongs in Manipur, the North Kachar Hills and the Naga Hills. They were more stringently suppressed by the oppressive and repressive policy and measures than what was done to them during the period of the British rule, and they felt that they were treated as "colonial and unwanted subjects," and that the authorities had desired to keep them illiterate, uncivilized, and backward, so that they might remain isolated from the mainstream of the Nagas and not pose a serious threat to the Government by not joining hands in the force of the Naga freedom movement led by Zapu Phizo, the President of the Naga National Council. (1982, 151–52)

This vision of a Zeliangrong homeland clashed with the NNC vision of Naga sovereignty. While the NNC activities were largely concerned with seeking an independent homeland for the Nagas outside India

(Chapter 4), Gaidinliu's agitations were primarily concerned with finding a homeland for the Zeliangrong within the Indian Union. Due to these differences in opinion and to fight against the Christian conversion of her people, Gaidinliu helped organize the Heraka movement, a viable non-Christian tradition, and went underground in 1960 with the formation of the Zeliangrong Government of Rani Party. During this time, Gaidinliu was popularly known as Amuipui (our mother) and taught the army cadres, I was told, to "love their religion, culture, and preserve their traditional and customary practices."

One of the cadres of this Rani Party, Mihuibe, remembers their time vividly. Their daily routine would start with the sunrise prayer and a military-type salute to the sun, accompanied by song and dance. The movement was inspired and led by dreams, visions, and prophecies from Rani Gaidinliu—central to the indigenous life worlds of the Zeliangrong—and accompanied by an unseen god, Haideurang. Water would flow from dry rocks; certain pathways were closed or opened depending on certain messages from God; Rani Gaidinliu would observe the pattern in the sky before moving her army—if the sky showed dark patches, conflict was imminent, and it was best to avoid certain routes. She would also read from a curious "magic script" she always kept beside her bed, as a source of knowledge about future events (see Longkumer 2016a).

During this six-year period her underground activities would go on to shape much of the religion known as the Heraka, which she professed and expanded, becoming an ally of the Sangh, particularly post-1966. The Rani Party resisted the modular forms of nationalism the NNC were promulgating (boundaries of the nation, having a constitution, a government), aided by a "foreign" religion, Christianity. The contrast between the two is therefore significant. The Rani Party was composed primarily of villagers with little formal education and relied heavily on dreams, visions, prophecies, and communicating with Tingwang (the Zeme high god). Their concern was primarily with Christian conversions (which they equated with imperialism) and the neglect of the Zeliangrong regions by the Indian state. Their fight for the Zeliangrong homeland was therefore to alleviate these hardships. Unlike the NNC, the Zeliangrong movement was an attempt to bring together the fragmented regions, a consequence of imperial design, into one administrative block, within the Indian Union.

In contrast, the NNC were largely seen as "lettered," educated in Christian mission schools and exhibiting sophistication, associated with the growing urban centers of Kohima and Mokokchung. Their transnational links—first with the British and the Americans and then during their fight for independence making connections with Pakistan and China—meant the NNC's nationalism was strategically positioned in the realm of international politics early on. Furthermore, the rise of the NSCN—a breakaway group from the NNC—in the 1980s connected with a strong regionalism, linking with other national movements in Burma and India (such as the ULFA and the PLA of Manipur) (see Lintner 1990) I discussed in earlier chapters.

THE NATIONAL GAIDINLIU

In exchange for her surrender and giving up arms in 1966, she was given a house in Kohima, Nagaland, a monthly stipend, personal aides, a jeep along with a driver, and several bodyguards from the Indian government. According to the words of her personal aide—Iheule—"Ranima is pure queen [*heguangpui*] because she lived freely, got ration and a house from the government. Because of this, we believed Ranima is the queen of the Nagas." During this time, the RSS and the VHP sought to make connections with her and the Heraka movement. According to her RSS biographer, Jagdamba Mall (2014, preface), Ranima's greatest achievement was to establish a close relationship with the "greater Hindu society," which included Bharatiya Vanvasi Kalyan Ashram, Vishva Hindu Parishad, Rashtriya Swayamsevak Sangh, Rashtra Sevika Samiti, and Vidya Bharati. When invited by these organizations to participate in their national programs, Mall recalls, Rani Gaidinliu would always seek God's approval before consenting. Rani Gaidinliu, in Mall's account, is represented as highly patriotic, pious, and judicious in all her dealings, despite the "terrorism of the church" constantly threatening her life and activities. Rani Gaidinliu's involvement with the larger Hindu society is significant, not least because, for the first time, a tribal leader from the Northeast was felicitated and celebrated as a national icon, over and above other (Christian) leaders, something that continues to this day under a BJP central government. But it also shows a different side to Rani Gaidinliu, one that is hard to penetrate and understand due to the overwhelming number of articles and books written about her by the Hindu right and sympathizers to the extent that we increasingly see an image of a Hindu freedom fighter par excellence.

During the Emergency (1975–77) called by Indira Gandhi, elections were suspended and certain civil liberties were curbed by the government in the interest of national security, which led to protests by the RSS (among other groups) and the wide-scale arrest of many of their cadres. One of them from Uttar Pradesh slipped the net and arrived in Nagaland. Jagdish, one of my main informants, had family connections in Kohima— his sister and brother-in-law ran a small business—and sensing it would be better to keep a low profile, he arrived unnoticed in 1975. Traveling the length and breadth of Nagaland, Jagdish had the impression there was much misunderstanding between Naga society and mainstream Hindu society. He saw the existence of a Hindu-Naga society largely suppressed by the church and the national movements. In Chapter 3, I elaborated this point, how the idea of a Hindu/tribal-people discourse is understood by the Sangh through the lens of indigeneity. The existence of a Hindu-Naga society, then, was largely hidden from view. Jagdamba Mall recalls how in the 1960s and 1970s the majority of the people in the top positions of government and military were Hindu officers in Nagaland, and yet he says they were unaware that "a Zeliangrong Naga woman from a type V bungalow numbered A.F.96 at Kohima's forest colony, was worshipping Bharatmata, day in and day out" (2014, point 42).

Gaidinliu is recognized more so outside her hometown than within it. The Nehru Memorial Museum and Library in New Delhi organized an exhibition and seminar in her honor in February 2016, entitled *Rani Gaidinliu: A Life of Selfless Service*. During the centenary celebrations, a prominent woman activist from Nagaland, Elizabeth, was invited to a function in the Constitution Club in New Delhi by a "Hindu organization." In my interview with her, she said the chief minister of Nagaland requested she attend the function, as the human resource development minister, Prakash Javadekar, would be the chief guest, and she would, he said, experience a different view of Rani Gaidinliu. She was surprised to see and hear from the many Hindu welfare organizations who had met Rani Gaidinliu during her lifetime gathered in this club. Elizabeth told me she met many corporate business leaders who were giving their money to help spread the Hindu religion while also financially support-ing the tribals of India, and in particular in the Northeast. Many in the audience welcomed Elizabeth and even told her they had visited Rani Gaidinliu's home village in Tamenglong, as an act of pilgrimage. She con-fessed to me, in an embarrassed way, that these community organizations and donors knew more about Rani Gaidinliu than Elizabeth did, a fellow Naga. She went on to say:

> I wasn't aware so many Zeliangrong children had been educated through their societies (or through them). Many of the children performed in chaste Hindi and Sanskrit—in songs, poems. And here I saw in many of these Ze-liangrong areas where there has been poverty, there have been many sponsor-ships [*sic*] by the Hindu welfare organizations for decades. So they have been building up on this. Like how Naga missionaries are going over to Burma and doing various activities, similarly they have been doing the same with us here in the Northeast and Nagaland.

This exposure to other points of view for Elizabeth is not something many Nagas are privy to, as there tends to be a more insular view of what Rani Gaidinliu represented. For many Indians, outside the North-east, Rani Gaidinliu represented an exotic tribal. But the Sangh publicize her story as a tribal woman who fought the British from the young age of sixteen. The ritual telling of this narrative has become fixed in the imagi-nation of many of those who have heard of her or have met her, gradu-ally plotting a certain order. Rani Gaidinliu received invitations from the upper echelons of political society, such as by Rajiv Gandhi, asking her to be one of the members of the Committee for Observing the 40th An-niversary of Freedom and Jawaharlal Nehru Centenary in 1986 and to be part of the Quit India Movement Golden Jubilee Celebrations in 1992 by Prime Minister Narasimha Rao (Zeliang 2012, 12). She also cultivated a close bond with Indira Gandhi over the years, and in one encounter in 1977, recounted by the historian Asoso Yonuo, both Gaidinliu and Indira were moved to tears as Rani Gaidinliu narrated the early part of her years evading the British and her subsequent imprisonment and underground activities (1982, 196).

From these accounts, it appears the weight she carried cuts through the national arena, across parties and sections of people, but she also had an effect on ordinary people who wanted to share a part of her life with theirs. For example, in January 1991, S. K. Biswas, undersecretary to the government of Nagaland, recognized her timeless aura and wrote to her: "You do not know me but who does not know you in the whole of India." Referring, of course, to her involvement in the "struggle for Freedom," Biswas writes:

> I am an autograph collector and collect them for posterity. Today I have got autographs/letters . . . of more than 3,600 great personalities of India and other countries. This is the largest collection in India and finds mention on PP22–23 of Limca Book of Records 1991 edition. I am enclosing a photograph of yours with the request that you may autograph it both on the photo side and the reverse side with date (Zeliang 2012, 15).

One can see the obvious imprint of a bureaucratic culture of signatures extending onto the form of the autograph. And Rani Gaidinliu, I suspect, would have been open to admiring fans. Aside from ardent autograph collectors, she was also invited to the Hindu Mahasabha session in New Delhi in December 1991, along with a statement that said because of "your deep attachment with Hindu Mahasabha, we are sure you will undertake the long and arduous journey" (Zeliang 2012, 15–16). During Raksha Bandhan, rakhis were also sent to Rani Gaidinliu by members of the Rastra Sevika Samiti, in acknowledgement of her "dedicated service to our beloved motherland" (Zeliang 2012, 15–16).[12] These anecdotes are repeated here to give an indication of the popularity of Rani Gaidinliu across large sections of the population in India, ranging from the quotidian collector of autographs to those participating in the national life of India. It is however with the Sangh that she became most involved.

GAIDINLIU THROUGH PICTURES

Rani Gaidinliu was already on the Sangh radar as early as 1969 when she met the second RSS chief, M. S. Golwalkar, during the Jorhat Hindu

Conference in Assam. Golwalkar presented her with an "idol of Lord Shri Krishna," and Pujya Shri Swami, another religious leader, presented her with a "shriphal" (wood apple). She addressed the audience by narrating her life story and emphasizing that the indigenous traditions in Nagaland were being threatened and that conversion was rife. She challenged Hindu society to rise up and curb these activities (Mall 2014, point 44). In 1979, she was invited to the Second World Hindu Conference, organized by the Vishva Hindu Parishad (VHP) at the time of the Mahakumbh (a Hindu pilgrimage that occurs on the banks of the Ganga River) at Prayagra (in the Indian state of Allahabad) on 24–26 January 1979. There is an extensive visual record of Rani Gaidinliu with her aides and with other personalities, such as photos at Sangam (the junction where the Ganga, Jamuna, and Saraswati Rivers meet) with Ashok Singhal, the international president of the VHP. She also tours Varanasi and takes photographs in front of the Kashi Vishwanath Mandir, an image that will grace many magazine covers.

Figure 6.1 shows one of the few occasions when Gaidinliu is standing on her own, in traditional Rongmei dress, garlanded, with the Kashi temple in the backdrop. If one is to feel the historical significance of this photograph as acquiring what Walter Benjamin calls a "hidden political significance," it is important we do not view this photograph as a "free-floating contemplation" (1999, 220) or as "paltry paper signs" (Tagg 1988, 12) but how it stirs the viewer and brings to light new ways of interpreting this image. In many images, Rani Gaidinliu is surrounded by male leaders, women aides, or well-wishers. By contrast, in this photograph one can sense a quietly confident, gentle figure, perhaps striking a pose to demonstrate her individuality rather than the cynosure she has become. This image is present in many homes and RSS/VHP offices (along with her iconic image), demonstrating what Pierre and Marie-Claire Bourdieu call "sociograms"—which provide a "visual record of extant social roles and relations" (2004, 601). In this sense, she speaks to an audience through specific accoutrements—the garland and the temple in the background—and the choice to be represented in this manner, perhaps distinctly aware of her Hindu admirers, while also conscious of how her suspicious Christian kin at home might view this.

Figure 6.1. Rani Gaidinliu in front of the Kashi Vishwanath Mandir, Varanasi. Courtesy of the author.

There are also photos of her emerging from having had a dip at the Sangam River along with her Heraka followers and students, probably staying at hostels for tribal children near Allahabad, who had come to visit Gaidinliu and also to attend the Kumbh Mela pilgrimage (Zeliang 2012, 53–69). These photos depict a woman who is adored by those surrounding her, sometimes on the verge of devotion, akin to what Christopher

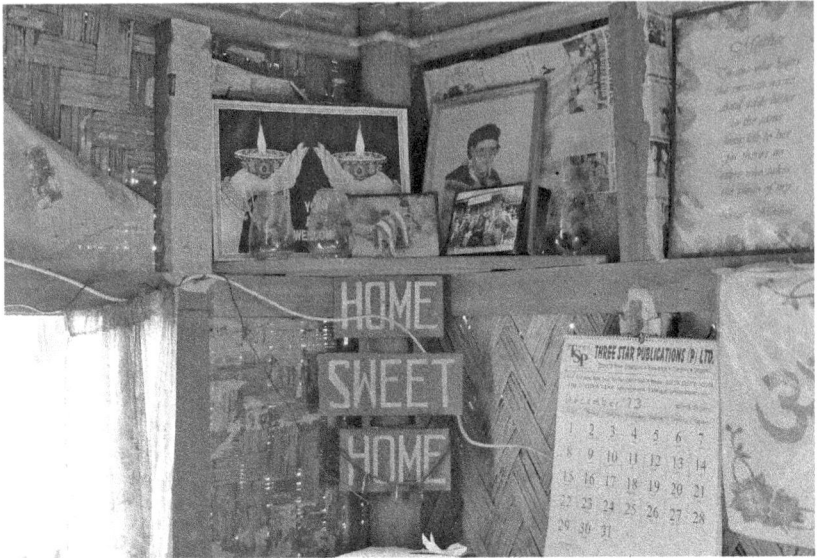

Figure 6.2. Image of Rani Gaidinliu in a home. Photo taken by the author.

Pinney calls "proximal empowerment." Pinney's work on photographs in India argues that photos are used to index relations to mobilize an idea of "proximal empowerment through which persons, objects, and images can come close to divine power" (1997, 171). Gaidinliu appears unperturbed by any of the attention, sunglasses, traditional Rongmei dress, and always impeccable in her necklaces made of conch shells and headscarf—the iconic image now universalized. Images have a way of framing the face, the body, fixing a pose into a trace that lingers. This image is then transformed into a perfect product, stylized and represented for audiences, carrying the weight of the message and, in due course, fixed into the mind's eye, permanently lodged as a devotional object that is infinitely replicated, without losing its aura. This iconic image now manifests and circulates in many homes and offices, providing that idiom of "proximal empowerment" (see fig. 6.2), even to the extent the Assam Rifles, a paramilitary Indian force, bring forth her image in new contexts to martial their troops toward nation building and to offer lessons on her status as the "first female freedom fighter," while conveying their message of "friends of the hill people." This is relevant in a context where armed

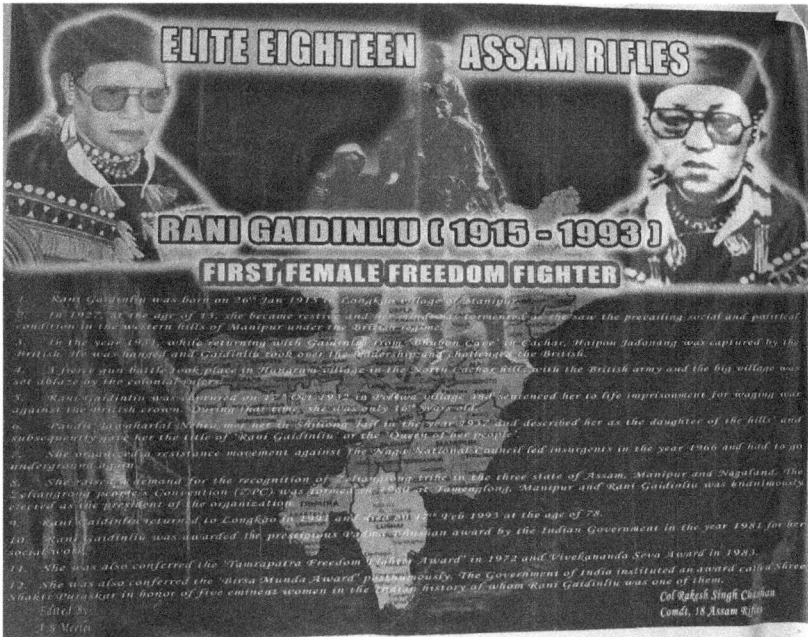

Figure 6.3. Banner of the Assam Rifles representing Rani Gaidinliu. Photo taken by the author.

conflict has been ongoing since Indian independence and where paramilitary forces like the Assam Rifles have been engaged in counterinsurgency. Contrary to their message, the Assam Rifles have been accused of widespread human rights abuses that make the blending of the image of Gaidinliu, freedom fighter, and friends even more paradoxical.

Jagdamba Mall offers additional commentary on Gaidinliu's activities to illustrate her card-carrying Hindu status, mindful of the sacrality of these sites marking the territory of Bharat Mata but also showing her universal appeal and spirit to be open to all faiths, in contradistinction to the "narrow-minded" Naga Christianity that advocates a single path to the divine: "While on the way to the conference, she had stopped at Varanasi and performed puja with the help of a renowned panda (priest) with Gangajal (the holy Ganga water) on the Dashashwamedh Ghat there. She went for the 'Darshan' of Lord Shiva at Kashi Vishwanath temple, and Lord Buddha at Sarnath, thereafter" (Mall 2014, point 46).[13]

Gaidinliu's status as a Hindu is the main issue for the Sangh. They claim it on numerous occasions in their publications, which suggests a clear strategy on their part to focus on Gaidinliu's predilection and commitment to Bharatvarsh. She is quoted as saying, "I am Bharatiya [Indian], all Nagas are Bharatiya and Nagaland is the integral part of Bharatvarsh [India]" (Mall 2014, point 50). The Sangh claim her for their larger Hindutva narrative, where she becomes the spokesperson for the Northeast in articulating such important policies as the Religious Freedom Bill of 1978 and the opposition to the visit of Pope John Paul II in 1986. The Sangh accrued social capital and extend their spatial universe when such tribal leaders as Gaidinliu issued a press release in Kohima in support of the construction of the controversial "grand Ram Temple." Rani Gaidinliu wrote a letter (date unclear) to the central government to permit the "Hindu samaj" to continue with the demolishing of the Babri Mosque and to build a Ram temple in its place (Mall 2014, point 50).

Not only is she represented as a national personality, but she is also made into a person of devotion, a move that makes her "spiritual." This is how Jagdamba Mall expresses this idea. Imagine a scenario, Mall says, where a Naga child would ask about Rani Gaidinliu and the parent would reply: "She is Rani Gaidinliu. She is Hindu, an Indian freedom fighter. She has been given Tamrapatra and Padma Bhushan and she opposes Naga separatist organisations and Church proselytization." He continues:

> At the very sight of Rani Maa, Naga Hindus became agog with happiness and they felt inspired. Her Kohima residence (at A/F 69, Forest colony) was a great tourist attraction worth seeing. Any outside tourist or traveller must meet her. They will take her autograph and a snap [photograph] with her. It happened so, because she had become a symbol of Indianness. The aged, the young, the children—all of them showed their respect toward her by calling her Rani Maa. Kohima had become a shrine due to her presence (2014, point 62).

If icons have the ability to foster different representations, perceptions, and embodiments, as I have been discussing, then Rani Gaidinliu fulfills the task of an icon. The harnessing of the power of the Hindu right in projecting an image of Rani Gaidinliu has certainly been successful to the extent that her image—stable, sanguine, pious, and even spiritual to the extent of requiring darshan—and turning her abode into a shrine speaks to the particular language of an icon. In the following, I will trace the effects this has had on the Christian imagination in Nagaland, where icons and certainly objects/persons that are imbibed with power require a more guarded and suspicious stance.

LIFE OF AN ICON

When I interviewed one of the VHP organizing secretaries, Ravi, in New Delhi in 2016, he said:

> She [Ranima] is popular with VHP workers all over the world, not only in India. She is still popular among RSS workers all over the world and the VKA throughout the country and those people who are aware of our freedom struggle. Those people who are aware of the people who fought for the welfare of our religion, they know Ranima and are proud of her. In other words, they rather worship her.

Ravi's comment points to the popularity of Rani Gaidinliu among Sangh workers. Moreover, she is also (as he emphasizes in a different segment of the interview) an "icon," who they "rather worship." Bringing Rani Gaidinliu into the orbit of icons, Ravi says that he feels unfortunate not to have met her, but more so because he did not have the chance to exchange darshan with her. It is clear that Ravi venerates Rani Gaidinliu as special, equating contact with her with offering darshan to a deity or a holy person. The iconicity of Rani Gaidinliu brings about interesting questions regarding what Bruno Latour and Peter Weibel (2002) have termed "iconoclash." Due to the different and conflicting visual traditions in India, there is indeed uncertainty regarding the meaning of "pictorial referents" (Probst 2012, 10), which continue to divide opinion. It is this clash of icons that brings about a fruitful way to engage with iconoclash, which, according to Bruno Latour (2002), is the collision between visual, material, and mental presuppositions regarding images and the method employed to suppress these images and their mediators. Rather than iconoclasm, which involves the physical breaking of images in defiance of representations of the divine, iconoclash concerns ambivalence about whether an icon is constructive or destructive (Latour 2002, 16). It is more guarded, attentive, and reflective about the effect images have. This is a point that I will elaborate below concerning the problem of the presence of Rani Gaidinliu as icon in Nagaland and what it says about the nature of the semiotic nation-state.

Icons, following Bishnupriya Ghosh's work *Global Icons*, are a certain genre of signs that enable a nation to form "social bonds" situated in their "historical materiality as intermedial signs we have encountered *before*" (2011, 10; italics in original). This suggests that icons are privileged associations that are imbued with power, allowing them to be accessible and to affect large swathes of people. It demonstrates that icons, mass-mediated, are largely open signifiers with meaning inserted into them by diverse audiences and consumers. Icons can be made to represent semiotic challenges. This, as we shall see, is particularly true in the case of Rani Gaidinliu.

Images of Rani Gaidinliu are circulated widely in media ranging from photographs, portraits, television, murals, websites, and smartphones—what Mirca Madianou and Daniel Miller (2012) call "polymedia," as a multivalent device to communicate widely. The polymedia are also carefully orchestrated to fill the spaces in public institutions and organizations like the offices of the Kalyan Ashram, VHP hostels and office, bookshops, homes, and as calendars that legitimize her status alongside other great leaders, such as M. K. Gandhi, M. S. Golwalkar, or K. B. Hedgewar. Situated side by side, such collections of images form what Raminder Kaur (2005) calls "iconographies-of-power." Initially interpreted as being a national figure, with viewers encouraged to pay obeisance to her life story and struggle for freedom, her image has become "spiritualized" over time and made into a devotional icon, fashioning a narrative pathway that speaks to the power of representation achieved by the Sangh. For instance, Rani Gaidinliu as icon is brought alive in screen media through documentaries that portray the singular message of national integration.[14] Ironically, however, her iconicity, though acknowledged and received by the Sangh with the "trappings of divinity" (Cashman 1975, 3; Amin 1984), remains contentious in the very place that we might think her image would be celebrated most: Nagaland.

A strongly Baptist Christian state, Nagaland has resisted her status as icon primarily because of its people's aversion to images of devotion

Figure 6.4. Image of Rani Gaidinliu in a VHP hostel, Haflong. Photo taken by the author.

(except among the Catholics, who form a small minority). The process that made her image an object of devotion for the Sangh clashes with the Nagas' own Christian ideas of venerating images as idols. Although there is an attempt by Christians to purify the landscape by ridding it of all mediations and attaining direct contact with the one true God, the question remains: "How can we reconcile this request for a totally aniconic society, religion, and science with the fabulous proliferation of images that characterises our media-filled cultures?" (Latour 2002, 18). Rani Gaidinliu's image circulates within the media-filled culture evoked by Latour. All of these underlying religious overtones bring to the surface the tension over precisely what the icon of Gaidinliu indexes.

THE DEBATE: ICONOCLASH

After Narendra Modi launched Rani Gaidinliu's birth centenary cele-brations in August 2015 in New Delhi, which included venerating her as a freedom fighter, various groups in Nagaland reacted negatively. For instance, they disliked the idea, pursued by the Sangh, that her portrait be displayed in the Nagaland Assembly, the chief minister's office and resi-dence, the ministers' offices and residences, and the Raj Bhavan (the official residence of the governor). There were also proposals during Narendra Modi's visit to Nagaland in December 2014 to establish an

independent Rani Gaidinliu Central University with a special department dedicated to the promulgation of the "eternal religion and eternal culture of the Nagas" and for renaming Nagaland's only airport Rani
Gaidinliu Airport (Longkumer 2015b). All of these developments have
made the Nagas nervous, not least due to their Christianity and coupled
with a wider sense that the forces of saffronization, which, with the growing presence of the BJP, are strengthening in Nagaland. The selection of
an openly RSS governor, P. B. Acharya, by the BJP, and the ascendency
of non-Christian communities like the Heraka, affiliated with the Sangh,
further substantiate the fear of a saffron wave moving across Nagaland
and the Northeast of India. The recent electoral successes of the BJP in
Assam, Tripura, Nagaland, and Manipur, explored in Chapter 7, have further exacerbated these fears.

In a number of articles in September 2015 by Naga church and civil
society groups, these fears were articulated on paper—particularly in the
local newspapers. Targeted in particular were attempts by the Indian state
to materialize Rani Gaidinliu's body onto the imprint of the Naga nation.
One controversy centered on the building of the RGLMM in Kohima,
the capital of Nagaland. The timing of these responses is indeed interesting, because before the launch by Modi of Rani Gaidinliu's birth centenary
celebrations, the atmosphere had been uncontroversial. Her actual birthday on 26 January 2015 was celebrated without much opposition. Even the
RGLMM had been initiated under the previous government in Nagaland
of the regional Naga People's Front (NPF) in 2010. It was a priority project proposed by the Art and Culture Department of Nagaland between
2010 and 2011 to the Ministry of DoNER (Development of Northeastern Region), and Kohima was selected as the site because Rani Gaidinliu
lived in the capital for twenty-seven years (1966–93) and "breathed her last"
there.[15] In their concept note submitted to DoNER, the Art and Culture
Department played on her image as a "freedom fighter" who fought for the
"unique Naga cultural traditions."[16] Work was already under way on the
RGLMM before the controversy broke out. Why did the Nagaland public
react in this way only after Modi launched the centenary celebrations?

What the Nagas object to is a rewriting of history by the Sangh
around Rani Gaidinliu as the "national icon." A month after the August

celebrations in New Delhi of her centenary, the Angami Public Organisation (APO), a tribal body, submitted a memorandum to the governor
of Nagaland, P. B. Acharya, saying that Gaidinliu's status is questionable, firstly, because she opposed the NNC and its call for a sovereign
state and, secondly, because her status as a freedom fighter is an imposition from outside that has no recognition within the state of Nagaland.[17]
The plans for the RGLMM are being contested, and thus construction
is halted, primarily because it is seen as symbolizing a larger agenda for
those who want to celebrate Gaidinliu while undermining Naga sovereignty. It is no coincidence that opposite the RGLMM lies the memorial
to Phizo, the leader of the independence struggle. If symbols are loaded
with political messages, this juxtaposition is striking.

The APO further justified their right to demand a halt in the development of the RGLMM because they are the traditional landowners,
and sharing "our land" with an "alien," such as Gaidinliu, was not acceptable to the Nagas of Nagaland. They further note, and this appears to be
the crux of the issue, that "promoting a culture of eulogizing her" would
go against the cultural sentiments of the indigenous Nagas, as "she was
not comparable with A. Z. Phizo," who is seen as the father of the Naga
nation. Moreover, the APO reiterates the position the churches in Nagaland have taken, that the Nagas do not "venerate idols."[18] Unlike the
Hindutva position of making the human divine, the corollary—making
the divine human—is an interesting aspect of Christianity in one sense,
but it is not generalized beyond Christ, which points toward Christianity's exclusivity in contrast to Hindutva's ability to diversify icons for their
political use. The APO statement is further supported by the Nagaland
Baptist Church Council (NBCC), the apex church body for the Nagas
in Nagaland. In a sharp response to the birth centenary celebrations, the
NBCC released a statement—"Who Is Our Spiritual Leader?"—to the
local press, addressing the Hindu right directly:

> The Nagaland Baptist Church Council has made its position clear that
> Christianity in general and Naga Christians in particular at no point of her
> history acknowledged or have recognised any living or dead person in her his-
> tory as spiritual leader sans Jesus Christ, the Son of the Living God. Nagas

were never Hindus nor was Heraka ever recognised as the traditional religion
of the Nagas other than as a cult. How the Hindus find their connection
with Heraka is a mystery and a suspect [*sic*]. This gives us the impression that
Hindu as a religion would stoop this low to find ways to disturb the peaceful coexistence of a community. The Naga politicians are answerable to their
constituents who are majority Christians as they return from the celebration.
What answer will you give when you are swayed away by people of other religion? Our state is in turmoil and the constitutional head of the state should
be more interested in solving the depleted condition of the state than acting
like the big missionary of a particular religion.[19]

I quote this at length to illustrate the firm opposition to the RGLMM
by the church but also to elaborate on three points. First, the role of the
church in denigrating Gaidinliu is not new, and the church, to a large
extent, has often branded her as "satanic," due to what they see as her
practicing "black magic," which, according to the church's version of history, led to her imprisonment by the British. This view is summarized by
the APO president, who said, "Gaidinliu was anti-Naga and anti-Christ."
The president also declared that she sacrificed "scores of people for her
interests and also forcibly converted people into her religious sect," and
her powers swayed the people under her influence.[20] Second, the NBCC
highlight the role of the governor ("the constitutional head of the state"),
P. B. Acharya, in acting like a Hindu missionary. Acharya, as we may
recall, is an RSS worker and happens to be the secretary of the organizing committee for the centenary celebrations. He has come under attack by the churches and civil society for abusing his position as governor
to propagate the Hindu religion. His public declaration to build a temple
in Nagaland and his issuing of Bharat Mata posters in the Republic Day
function in the Raj Bhavan (the official residence of the governor) have
not endeared him to the state. They see him and the RSS/VHP projection of Rani Gaidinliu as a "pan-Naga Hindu spiritual leader" as promoting the ideology of the Hindu right, so it can "spread its Hindutva
tentacles."[21] Even the honorific suffix -*maa* is viewed suspiciously, seen
as having Hinduizing overtones.[22] The final point that relates to this discussion is about the idea of iconoclash. It is not simply the destruction

of images but the clash of images at stake here, situated in the "fabulous proliferation of images" that "attract intense effect, spawn spectacles, or motivate collective action" (Ghosh 2011, 3).

ICONS AND IDOLATRY

The lives of icons in India are active, bristling, and energetic. They enter the rich conversation of worship (Eck 1998a), images (Davis 1997), photographs and chromolithographs (Pinney 2004), political economies (Jain 2007), performance and politics (Kaur 2005), and charismatic figures (Amin 1984; Ghosh 2011). The agency of icons has a vital historical precedent in South Asia, whether to transform the individual's relationship with the divine, to mobilize the collective (Appudurai 2004), as pathways to sensual pleasure (Pinney 2001), or for people to repurpose them for political action (Gorringe 2017; Jaoul 2006). In contrast, the general culture of icons having agency is not as widespread in the Northeast historically and does not permeate the workings of religion, culture, or politics, especially in the Christian states.

In order to remedy this lack, during early RSS activities in Assam, Dadarao Parmarth, a pracharak, quickly realized that icons popular in other parts of India would not work in Assam.[23] So they adopted the local sixteenth-century scholar and reformer Sankardev to spread the RSS brand of nationalism. He was placed alongside such RSS leaders as K. B. Hedgewar and M. S. Golwalkar. Similarly, they consolidated the figure of Gopinath Bordoloi as a "freedom fighter" and presented him as a "Hindutva hero" because he fought against Mohammad Ali Jinnah, who had attempted to incorporate Assam into East Pakistan. In Manipur, it is Tikendrajit Singh, a prince of Manipur who fought the British in 1889, and in Meghalaya it is U. Tirot Singh, a Khasi chief who fought the British in the eighteenth century.[24] In Arunachal Pradesh, it is Talum Rogbo, the main organizer of the indigenous religion Donyipolo, who is seen as a "tribal hero" by the VKA and included in the illustrations of Bharat Mata (Scheid 2015, 145). These sociograms speak to a certain nationalist narrative of bringing these icons within the larger orbit of the cosmopolitical landscape of India.

This is precisely why Rani Gaidinliu's icon causes difficulties for the Christian Nagas: real agency (belonging to God alone) cannot be fabricated with that of humans. Icons, for example, in Hinduism, treat the physical embodiment of a deity as a divine person (Davis 1997, 23). The deity is accorded respect, treated graciously, offered food and water, and adorned with clothes and ornaments, and petitions are made to the deity to "grant them his all-powerful grace" (Davis 1997, 23). The ability for icons to have divine agency goes to the heart of the recognition of Rani Gaidinliu, who, on the one hand fits within the cultural ethos of the Sangh but, on the other hand, clashes with the religious belief and practice of the Naga Christians. The discourse mediating this clash is idolatry.

Richard Davis (1997) suggests that idolatry is principally a category of discourse, which derives from the Greek, "adoration of images." Idolatry, therefore, is a direct charge, a polemical tool to denigrate false gods, while "dialectically affirm[ing] a community of faith that is distinct from and superior to those it classifies as idolaters" (Davis 1997, 205). Idolatry in various ways has been central to certain religious communities, such as Islam and Protestant Christians, while also used to propagate a civilizational discourse in the formation of empires that saw monotheism as the apogee of human progress. But as many scholars have shown, the story is far from simple (Keane 2007; Pietz 1985). The Gaidinliu episode is a "visual puzzle" (Latour 2002, 18). For it is not the wanton destruction of images through violent physical acts that is at stake here but the ambiguity, enigma, and discourse over idolatry that fabricate images. In the words of Latour,

> We can define an icono*clash* as what happens when there is *uncertainty* about the exact role of the hand at work in the production of a mediator. Is it a hand with a hammer ready to expose, to denounce, to debunk, to show up, to disappoint, to disenchant, to dispel one's illusions, to let the air out? Or is it, on the contrary, a cautious and careful hand, palm turned as if to catch, to elicit, to educe, to welcome, to generate, to entertain, to maintain, to collect truth and sanctity? (2002, 20; italics in original)

But all of this seems absurd to many of those for whom Rani Gaidinliu is revered as a local leader and by some as a national freedom fighter. Why can't they celebrate her life without overpoliticizing this issue? Elizabeth told me there is nothing wrong in Gaidinliu having "dreams for her people" by advocating for the preservation of her traditional culture, regardless of who that "god would have been." Acknowledging the strong resistance to her image by the NBCC, Elizabeth, a Catholic, was more conciliatory: her view is for a more secular outlook, a place in Kohima, funded by the central government, to create a space for learning, like the Nehru Memorial Museum and Library in New Delhi. It can be a "multidisciplinary center for intellectual exchange that does not mean the library will be stacked with books on Hinduism," Elizabeth tells me, and a vibrant resource center for learning. In conversations with Nagas and Sangh workers during the time of the controversy, not all take up the position of the NBCC or the APO in demanding the RGLMM be closed. One RSS worker, Ramesh, even pointed out the absurdity of this affair.

He said there are plenty of icons of Don Bosco, Mary (mother of Jesus), Jesus Christ, Francis Xavier, and Mother Teresa constructed all over Nagaland and in Kohima—so why the resistance to Rani Gaidinliu? In what way are these "Christian figures indigenous to Nagaland"? Ramesh's question is taken up by the Zeliangrong People's Association (ZPA), who argue with the same logic that institutions named after important figures do not need to correspond with whether one is indigenous to Nagaland—Indira Gandhi Stadium and Little Flower School (a Roman Catholic School) being cases in point.[25] Rani Gaidinliu's Zeliangrong people have ancestral land in the Peren District in Nagaland, linking her more closely to the land than any of the aforementioned names. Some see the bestowing of titles *Rani* or *maa* as equivalent to a Hindu agenda, though the ZPA claim this was given by Nehru out of love and respect for the "cause she stood for. Nothing more nothing less should be read beyond this." The ZPA express disbelief that Naga Christians are more than willing to use "alien names," such as Matthew, James, Peter, and David, but find it insulting when Rani is uttered. Similarly, the ZPA suggest declaring Rani Gaidinliu as anti-Naga and anti-Christian is wrong because she was merely defending her "Naga indigenous religion" against the NNC proclamation of "Nagaland for Christ," which is based on the teachings of a "foreign religion." What she stood for, they say, was "secularism," where "every religion including the Naga indigenous religion and culture should have a rightful place." The statement then asks: "So who is anti-Naga?

Those who tried to destroy Naga culture and religion or Rani Gaidinliu who tried to preserve Naga culture and religion?"[26]

Much of the bad press is associated with her being a non-Christian who opposed the NNC and the church. Due to the dominance of these forces in Nagaland, then, her image has naturally suffered. But the question Ramesh asks is, shouldn't a woman who is a Naga be celebrated instead of being tarnished? I posed Ramesh's question to Elizabeth, who suggested there are three factors for Rani Gaidinliu's rejection among the Nagas: (1) she is not a Naga nationalist because she opposed Phizo and the NNC; (2) she was born on the other side of the border—in Manipur; and (3) Kohima is the center for Angami national heroes, while she is Rongmei.[27] Several people I spoke to reflected on this issue. Some said Rani Gaidinliu's image/memorial/statue could be established in her hometown of Tamenglong in Manipur or New Delhi, given that the center says she was such a vital national freedom fighter. But, they asked, why in Kohima and why beside Phizo's memorial?

In conversation with a Baptist pastor in Dimapur, he said it reminded him of the Ayodhya controversy: the Ram temple had to be built in that

Figure 6.5. Memorial for A. Z. Phizo, Kohima. Photo taken by the author.

Figure 6.6. Rani Gaidinliu Library cum Memorial Museum, Kohima. Photo taken by the author.

very location where the mosque was, even though they could have built it anywhere in Ayodhya. This resonates partly with what is happening in Kohima, but unlike the Ayodhya case, Gaidinliu's memorial is not replacing any other religious site; nor has it gained mass popular support; things have remained largely quiet after the flurry of initial objections in August–September 2015. Yet the RGLMM represents what Deepak Mehta in his work on Rama and Ayodhya says is both a "site of national regeneration and a pastoral landscape" (2015, 12). In both Mall's biography and the ensuing controversy, the topography of Kohima is indexed with the presence of Gaidinliu as if in a shrine.

The final point I would like to take from this discussion is the status of Rani Gaidinliu as a woman. It is in this space of gender where a critical debate can happen regarding icons and their place in a society that is largely patriarchal. Here the cartographic depiction of Rani Gaidinliu as devi (goddess) follows a predictable trajectory forged by the Hindu right of the place of women in the national imagination. Understanding this goes to the heart of the anxiety over the position of women in contemporary India, and more specifically in tribal communities in the Northeast.[28]

GEOBODY OF THE NATION

Gaidinliu is said to have been reborn as the goddess Cherachamdinliu, the daughter of Bhuban cave. Cherachamdinliu and Gaidinliu are thus seen as the goddess Durga (Mall 2014: point 2). Throughout her life, Gaidinliu is often recorded as conversing with devi and even acknowledging devotion to Bharat Mata, to set Bharat Mata free from the slavery of the British and to protect Naga identity (Mall 2014, points 5, 18). The feminine deity is ever present in Gaidinliu's life. The first biography written by her longtime confidant Ramkhui Newme, in Hindi, entitled *Rani Maa Gaidinliu*, recounts how Gaidinliu was always accompanied by another deity, the Goddess Mother.[29] During the early days of her movement, she recalls how the Goddess Mother appeared before her and the villagers: "Between 2–4 P.M. the wind picked up speed suddenly. It blew for a long time and people saw a man-like figure riding on a horse and suddenly disappeared. The wind stopped. Suddenly a lion was visible and Goddess Mother was riding on it. The villagers were frightened. Goddess Mother rode round Gaidinliu's house and then retreated to a mountain" (Newme 1990, 41). The manlike figure we find out later is the Zeme high god, Tingwang, while the Goddess Mother, in the Zeme version, is the goddess Namginai, Gaidinliu's friend. It is striking to note the resemblance in this narrative with Durga's. She too comes riding on a lion and resides on Mount Meru. The image of Durga portrayed in the two biographies of Rani Gaidinliu tells us something about Gaidinliu's life and how both authors chose to associate her with Durga.

Durga, in classic Indian tradition, is associated with Devi-Mahatmya (Great Goddess) who is "lauded as the supreme female divinity of whom all other goddesses are partial manifestations, or else the existence of a single female reality is affirmed as the unique source of all goddesses—and often nondivine female beings, such as human women, as well—who are described as her portions" (Pintchman 1994, 119). This idea of devi is central to Hindu cosmology (Hawley 1996, 2), evoked throughout the ages and even envisioned by Nehru as representing India (Kovacs

2004; McKean 1996a, 147). Even her RSS biographer, Jagdamba Mall, calls Rani Gaidinliu devi, who proliferates under many forms—as Durga, Namginai, Cherachamdinliu, and Goddess Mother. These are what Tracy Pintchman calls "her portions" (1994, 119). One can take this image further and apply it to Bharat Mata (Mother India), an idea taken from Bankimchandra's celebrated hymn of his motherland.

The song "Bande Mataram" (Salutation to the mother) imagines Durga as the mother, with her ten weapons of war. This song has become the patriotic slogan for the Sangh (McKean 1996a; Sarkar 2001, 163–90). Furthermore, the pairing of Durga and Bharat Mata was constituted in the twentieth century as a territorial deity presiding over India (Gupta 2001; Ramaswamy 2001, 103). Bharat Mata, according to Ramaswamy (see also Gupta 2001; Kovas 2004; Sen 2009), presents various sides to her personality—mother, daughter, angry warrior, passive woman, lover. What Ramaswamy is ultimately concerned to show is how the map of Bharat Mata transforms the nation's territory from "geographical space into an intensely human place" (2001, 97).

Ramaswamy argues that cartography plays a role in imagining the nation as a deeply gendered space, where the somatic being, here embodied as Mother India, gives rise to a bodyspace that incorporates a "strategy of spatializing" (2001, 98): "The circulation of such bodyscapes of Mother India enables Hindu nationalist parties to make specific claims regarding ownership to land, the exercise of sovereignty over it, and legitimacy of rule—claims that maps have enabled everywhere in the modern world" (2001, 103). But such images as Bharat Mata and Durga are not without their own problems when available in the political sphere of action. Bharat Mata acts as iconography of the motherland for Hindu nationalist leaders, such as Uma Bharati and Sadhvi Rithambara, who use vituperative speech to instigate Hindu men into violence against "non-Hindu others" (Sen 2015). As Durga, she is a martial figure, slaying demons, and she retreats into the safe space of domesticity, where she is a dutiful wife and mother, which in turn links to women as carriers of both national honor and traditional culture (see Banerjee 2006; Kovacs 2004; T. Sarkar 1995; Sen 2009).

The linking of woman and the nation imagined through female bodies has marked the history of violence across the world (Blom et al 2000).

On the one hand women represent preserving national honor, but on the other hand they are denigrated through assault and rape. In India at least, argues Banerjee, women are not excluded in the highly charged masculine narrative of the nation, primarily because the Sangh continue to draw on images of women as "heroic mother, chaste wife and celibate masculinized warrior to negotiate their way in this landscape" (2006, 63) dominated by male compatriots and, I would suggest, set within a male gaze of female representation. Similarly, Rani Gaidinliu is seen as a martial warrior, fighting the British and then the Christian nationalists.

Ramesh, my RSS informant, asked me to imagine the situation in the 1930s when Rani Gaidinliu rose to challenge the mighty British Empire. "Do you think just anyone could have mounted a challenge?" he asks. He continues, "When we assess her life, then she has extraordinary qualities, more than Lakshmibhai, more than Rani Durgavati [a sixteenth-century queen who fought the Mughal Army in present-day Madhya Pradesh] because they were having all the things at their disposal, but Ranima had only a *dao* [a traditional hacking knife]." Lakshmibhai, the Rani of Jhansi—who is depicted riding a horse with her son (heir to the throne) strapped onto her back—fought for her kingdom rather than capitulate to the British (see Hills and Silverman 1993). She was the celebrated warrior who embodied masculine Hinduism, according to Savarkar (1969, 147). However, Sikata Banerjee reminds us that this celebration of Lakshmibhai came, for Savarkar, with a caveat. This warrior status was only possible after removing all markers of her sexuality, embodying two models of "woman in the nation": first, the "heroic mother" (fighting for her son's birthright) and, second, the "masculinized, celibate woman warrior" (Savarkar 1969, 67).

Rani Gaidinliu in the modern Sangh imagination is Maa, mother, to the nation. Without children and an immediate family of her own, she becomes a universal mother, a heroic mother, who fought for her children (here Bharat). In his speech, Modi affectionately called her Maa and offered obeisance at her feet, with the hope she will continue to "inspire us, energize us." Rani Gaidinliu is represented as androgynous—her image shows a strong-looking, masculinized woman. Many of her followers remember her as having male traits, like consuming lots of meat and having a martial spirit, epitomized in leading an armed resistance in the 1960s. In producing these stories, the Sangh do not explicitly link her to Durga/ Bharat Mata, but they lend weight to their agenda through a process of retelling and circulation. Rani Gaidinliu is also depicted as a woman unencumbered by any male demands—no husband—and viewed as independent and single, an image that goes contrary to most traditional societies where family and having children are the paragon of societal acceptance and honor, particularly for women. This transforms her into a celibate warrior—the highest honor for a woman in the Sangh imagination.

Even her sexuality is under discussion. She is presented as asexual and indeed without any sexual organs, according to another male RSS commentator, Jagdish. This corresponds with the way women who participate in the Hindu right are portrayed: as chaste and suppressing the desire to be sexually active and for love, relationships, and marriage. Female sexuality is viewed as dangerous. If not curbed and denied, it could threaten the very foundation of the nation (see Afshar 1987; Blom, Hagemann, and Hall 2000; Nagel 1998). In the 1930s, when Rani Gaidinliu was imprisoned, recounts Jagdish, the jailers attempted to rape her, but "her vagina was plain, as there was no sexual organ." To spite her, the jailers would throw poisonous snakes and scorpions, but she would tame them and play with them instead. The jailers trembled in fear, Jagdish said, because now they knew she could kill them by cursing them. The power of this seventeen-year-old girl was something to be reckoned with, suggested Jagdish, and the jailers respected her.

This Hindutva gaze, warns Banerjee, means only certain women fit their notion of womanhood; others simply disappear or are silenced from raising issues of social power within the patriarchal setup (2006, 77–78; see also Kovacs 2004, 384). The nation (and its association with the goddess) is thus the object that empowers women to participate to the detriment of her social situation within immediate family circles, where daily life is lived. A woman's agency is thus secondary to the nationalist cause (Kovacs 2004, 377). In this way, the Sangh have shored up the ideal template of womanhood bound up with family and nation. But in the case of Rani Gaidinliu, the ideals of family life cannot be applied, and in this the Sangh notions of womanhood are contextually adaptable.

There are also attempts to bind the Northeast with the image of Bharat Mata, deploying the very tools of what constitute ideal womanhood. It must be remembered that unlike other parts of India where goddess worship proliferates, in Northeast India, it is generally not the case. Therefore, how does one introduce a foreign concept into the region without alienating the people altogether? One way the Sangh have accomplished this is through the *strategy of spatializing*; it offers situational and practical resources for mobilization and also to define place as a deeply human experience.

Popular images of Bharat Mata maps are circulated all over Northeast India portraying Bharat Mata as Durga (beside a lion) and with different freedom fighters from all over India. Recently, the Sangh have attempted to repackage the image of Bharat Mata. She is replaced with young tribal girls from the Northeast. Engineered by the BJP spin machine in Tripura for the upcoming elections, the usual portrayal of Bharat Mata with a saffron and red sari has disappeared and been replaced by tribal dress, along with the flag of India. This is an attempt to appeal to the different constituencies of the Tripuris: Reangs, Chakmas, and Debbarmas. They plan to introduce this idea to the whole of the Northeast by customizing (with the flag and lion but with a different girl and tribal dress) the image so that the alienated tribes of the region feel part of Bharat and claim Bharat Mata. According to a news report, "In the Tripura posters, the mother goddess and national deity will not be of strictly mystical origins. The BJP has recruited women in their twenties to pose for the posters, smiling and clutching the national flag . . . chanting 'Bharat Mata Ki Jai'."[30] This is a claim further reiterated by the BJP chief Biplab Deb in Tripura: "Portraits of Bharat Mata in traditional tribal attire will be alongside her portraits in her traditional sari, especially in areas inhabited by indigenous communities. This is driven by the idea of integration."[31] In this sense, the Sangh have "converted the citizen subject from a neutral observer of the cartographical image of India into its devoted patriot" (Ramaswamy 2001, 105). Although one can argue the citizen subject can hardly be neutral, the point here is that the image of women, old and young, as bearers of traditional and national culture, is important to the visual iconography.

Figure 6.7. Image of Bharat Mata with a tribal woman from Tripura. Circulated by an RSS worker in Tripura via WhatsApp. Courtesy of the author.

Young women in their tribal clothes symbolize the preservation of identity and, with it, a tradition that must be protected, a key Sangh policy toward tribal India. They represent the repository of a pure interior, a preserver of an enduring tradition. Tribal women, in particular, act as ciphers of pastoral tranquility, signified by simplicity and truthfulness. The iconography of Rani Gaidinliu is now available in most mediascapes, depicting a woman in a certain sartorial order (see figs. 6.1–6.4). She projects a way of being intrinsically "tribal," "woman," and a "bearer of tradition." Her body is represented as a "semiotic of (alternative) modernity" (Chakrabarty 2001, 34; see also Tarlo 1996). The female body remains a "key social hieroglyphic" that in this case demonstrates the visibility of a tribal woman via particular "para-linguistic codes: bodily markings (posture, gesture, insignia, clothing and headgear), movements in space and time, and non-verbal and visual signs" (Ghosh 2011, 275).

This idea of Bharat Mata, though central to Sangh ideology, does not sit well with those whose allegiance is not with Bharatvarsh and also those whose theological monotheism (such as Christians and Muslims) forbid idolizing other gods. I posed this problem to Ravi, an activist of the VHP. He said that it is hypocritical when Christians (Catholics?) call 40,000 nuns their mothers and not their country. Mother, he continues, is not a religious figure but a sentimental figure, and he finds it difficult that they cannot say, "Bharat Mata *ki jai*" (Victory to Mother India). This slogan is primarily patriotic and has nothing to do with worship, argues Ravi. It is those whose commitments are outside their country who have a problem with this victorious slogan. He continued:

> If I say, "Jai," it is not worship; it means praying for "victory." Can any Indian pray for the victory of America and Pakistan and defeat of this country? Can we see them as patriots? Those people who worship Victoria [queen of Britain] or Babur and Humayun [Muslim Mughal Kings], who were attackers of this country, have problems in saying, "Bharat Mata ki jai." Remaining Christians and Muslims have no problem, as they are patriots.

This goes to the heart of what this Bharat Mata iconography represents, particularly if we are to revisit the debate about Rani Gaidinliu and RGLMM representing some kind of idolization that has no place in Christian Nagaland. Charu Gupta makes the case that in the Bharat Mata temple at Benaras, the creator of the temple, Shivprasad Gupt, wanted it to represent the map of India as that of the motherland, as a nationalist sentiment. M. K. Gandhi even praised the temple without "gods and goddesses," where only "a map of India [is] raised on marble" (Gupta 2001, 4292). In inaugurating the temple, Gandhi envisioned a composite space, where all communities and castes could come and worship. But in practice, the temple has been associated with "Hindu religious idiom and deity" (such as the hymn "Vande Mataram" inscribed on its gates—an ode to Durga, "I praise thee, Mother"), where the goddess Bharat Mata invariably represents a Hindu icon that identifies national identity with "Hindu piety and activism" (Gupta 2001, 4292). Thus, the Bharat Mata temple could be seen as a confusion and conflation between Hindu/Indian/nation (2001, 4293).

In order to escape this quagmire and to make sense of this entanglement, Ravi suggests that seeing India as a goddess is optional. For him and the Hindu community, he says, it is a cumulative tradition handed down through generations, but equally it is a vision not imposed on all. Even the worship of mothers is a natural thing they have inculcated through generations because "she has given birth to me." "But I know others [Muslims and Christians] don't share our values, and so that's the difference: but we don't force them to worship their mothers." Although eloquently articulated by Ravi, for many Christians and Muslims there is an intimate relationship between the victorious slogan of Mother India and the religious side of venerating an icon, akin to worship. Ravi's claim becomes all the more contentious when we realize how hard it is to disentangle the two, as demonstrated by the NBCC text "Who Is Our Spiritual Leader?" and by Muslims who have a similar point of view. In a recent statement by the Darul-Uloom Deoband, the leading Islamic seminary of India, on the controversy over chanting "Bharat Mata ki jai," the seminary said they "love Bharat Mata," but Muslims cannot chant "'Bharat Mata ki jai' because it is against Islam and 'tauheed' [the idea of worshipping one God], which forms the core of Islam."[32] Words are not benign, but loaded with affect—any slippage threatens the frailty of nationalism.

CONCLUSION

In her work *Global Icons*, Ghosh (2011) shows that the more an icon is in the public, the more her figure is animated and the more "intense the affect of revelation." "If the visual design of the iconic images makes for the icon's sensuousness," Ghosh argues, "the rhetorical and narrative capacities of the 'life story' constitutes its affective charge" (2011, 185). In this sense, the life of Gaidinliu, in perpetual liminality, provides us with a glimpse of how the life of an icon is repeatedly animated and reanimated for the many who celebrate and contest what she represents.

Kajri Jain (2007) has argued that the power of images and icons to move political sentiments in India is due largely to the cumulative power and popularity of devotional images in the realm of Indian religiosity. The secular intelligentsia's opposition to these devotional practices in their own political activities has meant a steady decline of their membership in parliament and appeal among the masses and a growing rise of the Sangh, who embrace such visuality to their advantage. While the visual representation of Bharat Mata images and the orchestrated effort to mobilize local variations are cases in point, it is also the fact that the ability of the Sangh to harness local and cultural rituals and symbols to garner consensus for a Hindu India is promulgated vigorously in the Northeast of India and elsewhere.

Rani Gaidinliu as devi, devoted to Bharat Mata, falls into the Sangh paradigm of an ideal citizen subject who portrays loyalty and dedication to the country. She can now be reconstituted as a national icon that serves the country with devotion and shares in the ideals of Sangh womanhood. But her iconography oscillates between a martial figure (in her young age fighting the forces of empire) and a devi (in her old age as a national icon), who is seen as the protector of dharma (world order). Indeed, Durga traditionally is associated with the Divine Mother, who intervenes on behalf of creation and removes evil and restores dharma (Kovacs 2004, 377). Anja Kovacs's work among the militant women's organization the Durga Vahini (Durga's Army), associated with the Sangh, discusses how the organization is willing to entertain only certain aspects of Durga—such as combating demons and integrating martial ideas even by resorting to violence against such enemies as Muslims and Christians—to restore dharma. They, however, obfuscate her other characteristics of indulging in meat and blood and intoxicating drinks and as an independent entity who controls her own sexuality (2004, 378).

Rani Gaidinliu, though, takes on the more traditional aspect of Durga in preserving sanatan dharma through the celebration of tradition and culture. In this way, her image is used to resist the forces of Christianity. This softer image works for the Sangh, who naturalize Gaidinliu as one who is "closer to nature," laced with an environmental message. On 24 August 2015, Prime Minister Narendra Modi, along with numerous dignitaries (a who's who of the political elite in New Delhi and the Northeast)[33] attended a ceremony to inaugurate the birth centenary celebration of Rani Gaidinliu at Vigyan Bhawan, organized primarily by the VHP and the VKA. In his speech, Modi offered "respectful obeisance" to Rani Maa, as he called her, saying that her life "inspires us all."[34] He continued, "She worshipped Nature, she treated Nature as God. The teachings of Rani Maa are teachings related to the love of Nature." Understanding her philosophy, he continued, allows us to come closer to finding the answers to "global warming and other environmental issues." Rani Gaidinliu—from a child in the throes of colonial revolt, to captivity, to release, to armed resistance, and finally in her final avatar as a national icon—is now repackaged to summon the forces of nature to come to humanity's rescue. She becomes the restorer of dharma, the ultimate nature translator.

In light of the Sangh attempts to create links with the Northeast through land, identity, nature, and such icons as Gaidinliu, the next chapter will look at the practical impact of building these links and the connection with the increase in electoral wins for the BJP that has swept the region in recent years.

CHAPTER 7

CITIZENSHIP, ELECTIONS, AND THE
BHARATIYA JANATA PARTY

IT WAS A WARM APRIL evening in the Dasrath Deb Bhawan in Agartala, the headquarters of the Tripura State Communist Party.[1] My research assistant, Aheli, and I talk to a worker of the Communist Party of India (Marxist) (CPI-M) about the recent elections and their disappointing loss in February 2018. Taking advantage of the evening breeze on the balcony, he shows us a video clip on his phone of a BJP mob in Belonia, in southern Tripura, taking down a five-foot-tall fiberglass Lenin statue, only recently inaugurated by Prakash Karat, a senior CPI-M leader. "It's dangerous to be a Communist in Tripura now; I'm from Belonia, and I'm scared to go back; that's why I'm staying in Agartala." When I asked his senior colleague, Bishwajit, about the incident in Belonia, he replied dismissively, "Statues are just symbols; it is ideology that matters."[2] Bishwajit was exasperated by these recent events, which were covered extensively by the national press and circulated through social media. However diffident Bishwajit's reactions are in the context of the CPI-M electoral loss, the change in the political landscape of Tripura has perturbed many in his party and, more generally, has raised challenging questions regarding the future of the state.

In March 2018, Tripura elected a BJP government, beating the incumbent CPI-M, which had governed Tripura continuously for twenty-five years. The BJP won thirty-six seats in the sixty-member assembly, while their alliance partner the Indigenous Peoples Front of Tripura (IPFT) won eight seats, forming the government together with a tally of forty-four. The CPI-M followed by winning sixteen seats, and the Congress (the opposition party in the last government) was completely wiped out. This was an extraordinary feat, especially considering the pre-2018 political landscape where the BJP's political presence was negligible.

During and after the elections, the media in India portrayed the elections in Tripura as a straight fight between the Left and the Right. It focused on how two cadre-based parties—the CPI-M and BJP—competed in the fraught arena of electioneering. Narendra Modi, the BJP prime minister, even labeled the victory as "epoch-making."[3] Storming the last "Red Bastion" of Communist power in the east and northeast of India is an important milestone for the BJP. Although the celebrations and analyses have largely focused on the way the BJP managed the elections—from appointing key people, to the campaign blitz focusing on the involvement of national leaders, to the mobilization of Sangh workers (primarily the RSS), to the role monetary inducements, social media, and data analysis played—little attention has been given to the way the BJP made alliances with the IPFT. Nor have analyses considered the way the political landscape in Tripura shifted due in part to the lackadaisical and complacent attitude of the CPI-M regarding indigenous politics, the desires of the aspirational class, and questions over migration and land.

This chapter focuses on the central question of citizenship. Through an examination of elections, we can understand how the fashioning of identity has implications for the territorial future of the region. It examines the way these political alliances were brought about and what this means in a landscape dominated by such national parties as the Congress and the CPI-M over three decades. While the victory of the BJP must not be underestimated, other combined factors also contributed to their victory. One important factor is the role of "indigenous politics." Indeed, an anthropological analysis of the "vernacularization of democracy" (Micheluti 2007) will provide crucial insights into how a redefinition of indigeneity, territoriality, and ethnic and monetary politics was central to the success of the BJP in the Northeast. While the regional political alliances have shifted generally toward the BJP, I draw particular attention to the state of Tripura to tease out the nuances around the politics of citizenship, partly as both the CPI-M and the BJP are seen as "Bengali Hindu" parties by indigenous groups. I argue that although the BJP is often acknowledged to make astute alliances with indigenous peoples' parties all over the region, playing on their mantra of being a national party with a regional outlook, there is a larger Hindu majoritarian strategy at play.

Secondly, the larger territorial issues of the region highlight the complex modalities of "homelands" played out across the three nation-states of India, Bangladesh, and Myanmar. The historian Willem van Schendel (2005, 2018) argues that much of the desire for these homelands has occurred due to the complex geohistorical makeup of these tenuous borderland spaces, accelerated through the formation of modern nation-states and also due to the algorithm of ethnic politics. There are numerous territorial aspirations across India-Bangladesh-Burma/Myanmar borders such as "Adibashistan (which would unite Garo people across the Mymensingh-Garo Hills border), Rajasthan (which would do the same for Rajbongshi people living in Cooch Behar, Jalpaiguri and Rangpur, Swadhin Asom (an independent Assam), Great Mizoram (united Mizos living in India, Burma and the Chittagong Hill Tracts of Bangladesh), United Bengal" (van Schendel 2005, 90), and Greater Nagalim (uniting the Nagas from Myanmar and India). Against these developments is the idea of Akhand Bharat (undivided India). How do ethnic politics situated in this complex territorial amalgamation play out when competing against a national and singular idea of a Hindu universe?

In Chapter 3, I examined the way Hindutva represents the ultimate indigenous principle and how the Sangh both vivify questions of locality and link that to international discourses on the rights of indigenous peoples through "nativism." Interestingly, in the discourses circulating during elections, there is a similar idea and claim put forward by the BJP/RSS concerning the absorption of indigenous peoples (and Jains and Buddhists) as default Hindus, with the offer of citizenship to Bangladeshi Hindus, further complementing their vision of Akhand Bharat at the expense of indigenous peoples' land and politics. Akhil Ranjan Dutta (2017) argues that in Assam the BJP utilized the discourse of indigeneity (Khilongjiyas, also Khilonjia) by bringing together the different "Assamese people" and tribal constituents into a common platform. Ambiguity over what constitutes Assamese people—is it language, ethnicity, certain cultural markers?—played into the hands of the BJP, who engineered the distinction between "citizens" and the "indigenous people of Assam." While the latter is now captured by the term *Khilongjiyas*, the former became a movement to grant citizenship to Bangladeshi Hindus and has increasingly ostracized the Bengal-origin Muslims as "outsiders" (Dutta 2017, 19). Here, Hindu majoritarianism continues to flourish despite claims the BJP regionalizes its politics to accommodate local interests. It is this gray area concerning what Hindutva represents within the discussion of indigenous peoples that enables the BJP to operationalize its ideology within these borderland regions of the country. Entangled in this matrix of alliances and demands is the BJP, and understanding their role in the region will provide a clearer context for their work in Tripura.

BJP: A NATIONAL AND A NATIONALIST PARTY?

The BJP's poor performance in the 1996 Lok Sabha elections exposed its inability to project itself as a "national party" (Gillan 2007, 31; Hansen and Jaffrelot 2001; McGuire and Copland 2007; Palshikar 2015). According to Michael Gillan's post-1996 prognosis, the BJP needed to radically refashion its ideology if it wanted to be viable in the east, northeast, and the south of the country, where its presence remained limited. First it had to position itself as "*the* ascendant, preeminent *national* party political force" (Gillan 2007, 32; italics in original). In order to accomplish this, it needed to articulate a strategically viable ideology of accommodating regional voices, without disowning their main Hindu nationalist base. Whether it was issues related to territory, identity, or national security, the BJP had to be ready to engage groups within a broader ambit than their previous ideological positions had allowed. Consequently, if coalition politics, and indeed the varying magnitudes of subnational concerns, had to be addressed, the BJP made astute symbolic gestures; they substantiated their presence in a region long marginalized.

In the Northeast of India, the BJP's position has always been a challenge due to the tension between the grand visions of India sharing a unifying cultural essence and those whose interests lie in seeking to be distinct (among the Naga, Metei, Mizo, Assamese, and Bodo) (Baruah 2007; Longkumer 2018a; Prabakhara 1994). The BJP's position thus is deeply hostile to any "separatist aspiration" based on sovereignty. This position is not unique to the BJP but also shared among other national parties (see Chapter 4). The second important factor is the migration of Bengalis from erstwhile East Bengal, East Pakistan, and now Bangladesh.

The Assam Movement (1979–85), for example, began over questions of "illegal immigration" from Bangladesh, foregrounding issues of land, resources, and the politics of identity for indigenous Assamese people by protecting and providing constitutional, legislative, and administrative safeguards (Barbora 2019; Baruah 1999). While bordering states to Bangladesh like Assam, Tripura, Mizoram, and Meghalaya have over the years been affected by "illegal immigration," the question that remains is, are these centered on the polarizing of the Hindu-Muslim-indigenous dynamic, or does ethnic nationalism transcend these religious binaries? The BJP in Tripura largely views the Hindu immigrants as refugees, escaping persecution from Muslim Bangladesh, and needing "refuge" (see also Bhaumik 2016; Gillian 2002; Ramachandran 1999; van Schendel 2005). For indigenous parties, an illegal migrant, regardless of religion, is still illegal. These ethnic nationalisms in the Northeast, though suspicious of the Indian state, see in the BJP and their efforts to make alliances a party willing to tackle a common problem: that of illegal immigration. So how has the BJP gone from a small presence to forming governments or alliances in the majority of the northeastern states?

ALIGNING THE MARGINS

The Assam elections in 2016, seen as the turning point in BJP electioneering and the opening of the doors to the Northeast, saw the BJP gain a majority and form the government, winning 60 seats on its own and 86 seats through alliances with the Asom Gana Parishad and Bodoland People's Front, in the 126-member Assam Legislative Assembly. This victory provided momentum to the BJP as they sought to establish themselves as a party that would address developmental inequality, the long-protracted issues of ethnic nationalisms, and illegal immigration from Bangladesh. Indeed, for the BJP, capturing the Northeast accords well with their ideological conceptualization of Akhand Bharat. In a highly polemical and partisan account of the Assam elections, two BJP campaign managers proclaimed: "That for the fulfillment of the ideological vision of 'Akhand Bharat' (undivided India) and for the nation to be culturally and nationally integrated in spirit and not just geography, the North-east is crucial. For the BJP, it is not a peripheral state but the heart of India" (Sethi and Shubhrastha 2017, xxv). This ideological vision has to be realized in pragmatic ways.

I chart three general factors that highlight the way elections were fought in the Northeast and how the BJP fashioned itself as a national party with a genuine stake in the region, emphasizing their integrationist stance of Akhand Bharat. First, the media attention focusing on the elections in Assam in 2016 and then in the four states of Manipur, Meghalaya, Tripura, and Nagaland in 2017–18 was unprecedented. Not only did Narendra Modi travel to various parts of the region during the 2018 elections, but he also went to unexpected and remote places, such as Tuensang, a district in eastern Nagaland close to the Myanmar border. When I met Raj in Delhi, a data analyst associated with the elections in Manipur and Tripura, he told me how Ram Madhav, the BJP general secretary in charge of the Northeast, instructed each analyst to engage with TV news channels like NDTV and Rajya Sabha TV during the elections in Meghalaya, Tripura, and Nagaland in 2018. The aim for the BJP was to make the entire country care about the Northeast elections. Raj said they wanted people to see the region as a success story for the BJP, a story of how the BJP won the Northeast. Through this, Raj said, they wanted people from across India to be directly invested in the region:

> There has been a concerted effort on our part to make the Northeast visible and part of the larger Indian political narrative—not a marginal voice but a dominant one. We want people to care and to counter the isolationism. We use elections as a means of doing this. Once you put the Northeast on the election agenda in major news outlets, people will be talking about it. Right now, if you go to a random village in Bihar and go to a chai shop, you will probably see people talking about the Nagaland and Meghalaya elections.

The second aspect was the use of social media and data analytics, or "Hindutva enterprise" (Udupa 2018), a phenomenon widespread in India.

Partho, a BJP worker in Tripura, told me the use of Twitter put the spotlight on Tripura. Rajat Sethi, a close aide of Ram Madhav from the India Foundation, played a key role in organizing the social media platform in Tripura.[4] Sethi created, according to Partho, around one thousand local social media activists who would tweet and retweet news instantly, creating a ripple effect focused on key BJP campaign issues. Raj told me they used demographic profiling drawn from surveys, electoral voters lists, and trends from previous elections. This method was novel in the Northeast, he emphasized, and they made use of the data to focus on certain constituencies, speak to particular issues, and know which candidates to support. They brought what they learned from the 2014 victory. After the BJP success, Arvind Gupta, the BJP's head of national technology, said: "We had data on each of the 543 constituencies. We knew how many mobile and Internet users were present in each constituency. The same holds true for social media users. Alongside, we used analytics to understand which polling booths had voted for the BJP in the previous elections."[5]

Raj explained he was in Manipur and Tripura during the 2014 elections for a total of eighteen months. In Manipur, he argued, the BJP lost the narrative battle in terms of attracting the urban ethnic Meitei voters. Most of these went to the Congress. The majority Meiteis of the Manipur valley wanted the introduction of the Inner Line Permit (ILP)—requiring "outsiders" or nonindigenous persons to the state to apply for a permit—prevalent in Nagaland, Mizoram, and Arunachal Pradesh. The BJP, however, could not guarantee this because of their conviction concerning integration and therefore the free movement of Indian citizens. Another important aspect was the 2015 Naga Framework Agreement signed with the NSCN-IM, a Naga nationalist group. The Meitei and Kuki ethnic groups were worried the framework agreement would split Manipur into half, with most of the Naga hill areas forming the NSCN-IM's vision of Greater Nagalim. The Meiteis and the Kukis viewed the BJP as siding with the Nagas simply because they were the other signatory on the agreement. In both cases, Raj and the data analytics team understood the voting patterns and the issues concerning the people. But the issue of Greater Nagalim (and in the case of the framework agreement its secrecy) and the adoption of the ILP are so complex that the BJP simply could not control the narrative. The national imperative clearly lost to the local variable of ethnic mobilization and competition. For the subsequent elections, the BJP had learned lessons.

The final key factor was anti-incumbency. While the Congress Party was the dominant force in the Northeast for many decades, people were tired of their corruption, lack of vision and development for the region, the growing inequality with the rest of India, and the inability to solve the prolonged ethnic conflicts. The alternative third front, the North-East Democratic Alliance (NEDA), a BJP-led coalition formed in 2016 to unite non-Congress parties, played a vital role in negotiating with the different partners and providing a united regional front.

In both Tripura and Manipur, the anti-incumbency factor appears however to be significant. In Tripura, the anti-Left movement meant the BJP were in a prime position to dominate, as they were the only party untainted with the history of the state. In Manipur and Meghalaya, despite the Congress emerging as the single largest party with twenty-eight out of sixty, and twenty-one out of sixty assembly seats, and the BJP following with twenty-one and two seats respectively, the anti-Congress coalition made up of regional parties and the BJP—NEDA—went on to form the state government. In Nagaland, Rakesh, a BJP political analyst based there during the elections, told me how the political instability created by three power brokers—Neiphiu Rio, T. R. Zeliang, and Shurhozelie Liezietsu—helped the BJP, as the public increasingly grew tired and despondent. The BJP were seen as the only stable party amid the bickering and power tussle between these three leaders of the regional Naga People's Front (NPF), with Rio splitting the NPF to form the Nationalist Democratic Progressive Party (NDPP).

We, however, need to be cautious about portrayals of anti-incumbency as the inherent logic of regional politics. In some cases, it could be the fluctuating political behavior based on "personal promises and expectations going unfulfilled" (Wouters 2018b, 16; see also Béteille 2012) that determine political allegiances. The BJP played a tactical game by committing to an alliance with the NPF and the NDPP, who incidentally are both members of the NEDA. The NPF and NDPP bought into the BJP's power game because their split exposed their political vulnerabilities. Both also desired an alliance with a party in the center. The NDPP, however, agreed to a prepoll seat-sharing arrangement with the BJP and won a combined twenty-nine seats, with the remaining twenty-seven seats won by the NPF. The seasoned Manipuri journalist Pradip Phanjoubam (2018) captured this historic moment with this phrase: "How BJP won without winning in Nagaland."[6] Historic because the BJP won twelve seats in a strongly Christian state: "The BJP can now be known as the Bharatiya Jesus Party!" a BJP activist told me. This is despite the vehement resistance and denouncement of the BJP as a Hindutva party by the influential Nagaland Baptist Church Council (NBCC). Phanjoubam is convinced the appearance belies the state of affairs on the ground, with the BJP riding on the coattails of the regional NDPP.

These general factors leading to the presence of the BJP in the Northeast can only tell us part of the story. Far removed from cold, hard data analysis, this is what Lucia Michelutti (2007) calls the "vernacularization of democracy." She argues that through this process, "new social relations and values" are produced, which in turn shape "political rhetoric and political culture" (2007, 641). This idea of political sociality privileges relations over representation (Piliavsky 2014; Spencer 1997) and party ideology (Gellner 2009; Holmberg 2008). If we follow this logic, in one sense, "decisions on voting are made according to highly localised sets of relations" (Holmberg 2008, 11). The political anthropologist Jelle Wouters, discussing Nagaland, suggests any elections and democratic networks must understand the difference in voting patterns: "If many in India's heartland prefer to vote their caste, most Nagas prefer to vote their clan, village, or tribe (usually in that order of priority), and so similarly privilege 'primordial', partisan, and parochial loyalties over broader civic considerations" (2018b, 3). This contradiction in political sociality—the individual versus the community—lies at the heart of the Indian democratic experience that is fundamentally inexplicable.

Michael Gillan's work on the BJP, and their ability to fashion themselves anew, has paid particular attention to the vernacular politics of the region. Tarun Gogoi, the Congress chief minister of Assam, after the 2016 defeat wryly remarked: "They [the BJP] want it all. They want to show that they are an all-India party" (quoted in Sethi and Shubhrastha 2017, xxv).

But the region's complex history of ethnic, religious, cultural, and linguistic alliances and upheaval cannot simply yield to an incoming force that has in its sights the idea of "nation first." The BJP's experimental laboratory has for the time being achieved success, realizing its ideological moorings are anchored here in an uncertain and tempestuous terrain.

For the BJP to succeed further, its "majoritarian outlook," warns Sethi and Shubhrasthra, "would need to give some political space to a 'minority darshan' or philosophy" (2017, xxx). Would giving space to minorities—such as the tribes of the region—allow the BJP to become a centrist party? Suhas Palshikar's (2015) idea that the BJP cannot be a centrist party must be considered when evaluating the majoritarian politics of the BJP and Hindutva in light of the region's political sociality. Palshikar's view could indeed be valid, but in the Northeast, the pattern is idiosyncratic. It might be more relevant to ask whether the BJP will continue to remain a national and nationalist party. Hindutva ideas did play a role in some states, but not explicitly so in others. The BJP won seats due to paying attention to local issues and contexts, but they still need to declare their vision of the Northeast as an inalienable part of Akhand Barat. This may require the BJP's approach to undergo further ideological nuancing. How else would you draw candidates from Christian areas of Nagaland, Manipur, and Meghalaya to a party that traditionally worked for Hindu interests?

Both Phanjoubam's analysis of Nagaland and Richard Kamei's analysis of Manipur suggest the electoral outcome is contextual and "cannot be explained within the political narrative currently governing the [Indian] nation."[7] In the case of Manipur, Kamei argues, "People who have voted for the BJP in the state have not done so due to its Hindutva narrative. In fact, it is possible that the hill communities perceived the actions of the Congress regime in the state as akin to right-wing politics."[8] The political spectrum of who is on the Right is locally conceived. In Manipur, it is the Congress who are linked with the majoritarian valley population and marginalizing those outside their territorial orbit. Therefore, data analysts and macropolitical interpretations dovetail in translating these prescriptions as success stories, when it is this reality that needs to be understood before making any conclusions. It is to this messy process of the vernacularization of politics in Tripura that I now turn.

THE HISTORY: CONNECTIONS, LOSS, AND BETRAYAL

In the grounds of the famous Ujjayanta Palace, once the official residence of the Tripuri royal family and now a state museum, there are a number of poignant human depictions sculpted in clay.[9] They depict the trauma of war and partition, as people escape the violence and seek peace and hope in a new land: a man with a child on his shoulder, a mother holding a child on her hip while she grips a suitcase, with remnants of her worldly possessions.[10] They appear weary, worn, bereft, and desolate from walking, leaving homes and loved ones behind. A woman gives water to a man from a gourd, quenching his thirst. There are no names, no ethnic markers explaining the context; it simply represents the human drama unfolding and the unforgiving and tempestuous nature of human movement. It is striking how these depictions of melancholia, hope, acts of solidarity, and munificence are now at the heart of debates over the changing demography of the state, couched in the language of betrayal, theft, and loss.

Tripura was a princely state, ruled by the Mankiya dynasty for centuries until it became part of the Indian Union on 15 October 1949, two years after India's independence. However, the princely state of Hill Tippera (Tripura in India) and the British district of Tippera (Comilla in Bangladesh) were spatially demarcated in 1854, prior to which both regions were linked through common histories and cultures (Sen 2018, 54).[11] The transformation of this space into an "imperial frontier" in which mapping, cadastral surveys, census, and ethnic classification lent themselves to the dictum "classify and conquer," was practiced all over imperial Britain, not least in the Northeast of India (Ludden 2003; Sen 2018; van Schendel 2018; Zou and Kumar 2013).

While this territorial demarcation evolved in the nineteenth century, the transformation of this space into East Pakistan/Bangladesh and Tripura through the rigid policing of borders has largely failed (and the demographic makeup of Tripura testifies to this reality). It is within the contemporary frame of identity politics that this imperial frontier has energized the territorial sequestering of ethnic enclaves, further entrenching claims to self-determination based on questions of indigenousness and immigration. Historians and social scientists have encouraged us to examine the social construction of imperial spaces and frontiers through war, tribute, land management, cultural and religious exchange, and linked histories. They continue to interrogate the arbitrariness of these locations in the emergence of the modern nation-state. Yet we must also be mindful of the way these boundaries now serve indigenous politics to protect against dominant forces usurping the fabric of indigenous peoples' identity, be it language, dress, food, and land.

In the merger with India, Tripura became a union territory in November 1956 and then attained full statehood on 21 January 1972 (Bhaumik 2009, 2016). But there were two important events that shaped the geo-ethnic dimension for years to come. The first was the partition of the subcontinent in 1947 into West Bengal and East Pakistan, and the second was the Bangladesh War of Independence in 1971. Between 1947 and 1971, it is thought that 609,998 Bengalis, displaced from East Pakistan, came to Tripura for rehabilitation and resettlement (Bhaumik 2009, 67). The state during this time, largely dominated by the Bengali elite, aided in expediting these processes, as most of the new population, or "refugees," were kin across the border. This led to the large-scale loss of tribal lands, through settlements. For example, in the 1941 census, tribals constituted 53.16 percent, and in just ten years that figure dipped below 37.23 percent of the population (Bhaumik 2016, 9).

There are two issues worth pointing out briefly regarding the spatial construction of Tripura, its connection to Bengal, and the exclusion of tribals and Muslims within this territorial imagination. First, according to R. K. Debbarma (2017), a certain conception of Tripura related to Bengal is a homeland ideology that is part of the Bengali Hindu narrative. Muslims, who are largely absent in the standardized version of the census, constitute the second largest community and are also excluded from this Bengali Hindu ideology. They have become the Other and the "infiltrator" (Debbarma 2017, 208–9). In his speech to the United Nations Working Group on Indigenous Populations in 2002, Bijoy Kumar Hrangkhawl of the INPT explains: "It is notable that, at that time the Bengali Hindu used to represent less than one percent. After partition of India all the Muslims were compelled to leave Tripura and Bengali Hindus are ruling with absolute majority."[12] "Within a span of over two decades [since partition in 1947]," Debbarma argues, "the new state enforced its definition of 'outsider' (Bengali Muslims), 'anti-national' (Tripuri ethno-nationalists) and inscribed a new text on the landscape" (2017, 211). Second, in the process, the Bengali Hindus have dominated the administrative and political landscape to such an extent that rival conceptions of homeland are summarily dismissed. Tripura is now rehabilitated as the land of innocent and simple tribals and nontribals (read Bengali Hindus) and its "irreversible link to precolonial Bengal" a matter of fact (Debbarma 2017, 212). Therefore, the question of shared history and spatial encompassment of parts of Bangladesh—including Comilla, Sylhet, and the Chittagong Hill Tracts—is partially acknowledged by the indigenous parties, the BJP and the RSS. They in fact see in this spatial complexity designs for their ideas of Akhand Bharat (undivided India) complementing the ideology of homeland espoused by Bengali Hindus.

Bijoy Kumar Hrangkhawl, one of the architects of Tripura's tribal politics (of the INPT), told me in his house in Agartala that the "tribals are victims of ignorance." Because of the lack of formal education and the low rate of literacy among the tribal population, Hrangkhawl said, the Bengalis took over the government structures and eventually tribal lands due to "their cunning ways." It must also be remembered, according to Hrangkhawl, that Bengalis have lived in Tripura for a long time. The partition and the post-1971 years were not the only moments when migration happened. In fact, the Tripura kings encouraged Bengali migration into the state for their own interests. The Rajmala, the Tripura's royal chronicles, mentions the influence of the educated and trained Bengalis in modernizing the royal administration (Sandys 1915). Regional relations too were significant—in terms of war, tribute, and cultural exchanges—with the Moghuls from the eleventh century, when Tripura became a tributary state to the rulers of Bengal; with the British in the seventeenth century; and in their boundaries with the Lushais (present-day Mizoram) and the Kukis (Bhaumik 2016; Sen 2018; van Schendel 2005).[13]

Since 1886, the royal administration of Tripura made land reforms attracting peasant farmers from the eastern districts of undivided Bengal, on the border with Hill Tipperah, to rent fallow land or forests (known as *jungle-avadi* lease) for cultivation. Because land ownership patterns were largely unregulated, and the Bengali peasants were more advanced in their methods of cultivation, they soon produced a surplus. This gave them additional capital, which was used either to buy tribal land or loan out money to tribals against the mortgage of land within a set period. If this period elapsed and the debt was unpaid, tribal land was repossessed by the Bengali moneylender—an activity seen as exploitative by Hrang-khawl. This move from communal ownership to individual proprietorship of land affected the socioeconomic balance in favor of the Bengalis. But as long as the tribes had adequate land to cultivate, and the pressures from the Bengalis were limited to certain pockets, "land alienation of tribals did not become a major problem" (Bhaumik 2009, 67). The situation altered once India's independence happened and the merger of Tri-pura occurred in 1949.

The "refugees" who arrived from East Pakistan/Bangladesh were more "conscious of politics," said Hrangkhawl. This is how he explained the dominance of the Bengalis:

> Influx took place, illegal immigration took place, and since they are in power, they didn't take strong measures as in other states like Nagaland or Manipur. The government was in their hands; all the administration was in their hands. Till today also we are not that conscious. Our people are simple. This is the main reason why many mainstream officials came from West Bengal. The main administrators were all Bengalis. Naturally, they will invite their own people.

The dominance of the Bengali elite became more complicated because, although the Sixth Schedule is in effect in Tripura, which gives tribal areas an autonomous status in the form of the Tripura Tribal Areas Autonomous District Council (TTAADC), it has not been implemented adequately.[14] Although nontribals cannot own land in TTAADC areas, the district magistrate can make exceptions. For example, under the Congress administration (1963–77), "land cooperatives" like the Swasti Samity in northern Tripura started claiming large swaths of tribal lands (set aside by King Bir Bikram Kishore Debbarman [1908–47] as tribal reserves totaling around 2,050 square miles) with the conniving participation of bureaucrats. The Communists in fact mobilized the tribals and took the matter to court, only to be ignored by the institutional bureaucracy (Bhaumik

2009, 68). The Communists too were not innocent. They made Land Allotment Committees that adjudicated land ownership and gave them to nontribals in TTAADC areas. The results of this were obvious, remarked Hrangkhawl: "In the subcommittee, all political people are Bengali members and they will give to their own party people." In reality the significance meant the recalibration of vote banks. In simple arithmetic terms, nontribal voters gradually became the majority once they settled in tribal regions. And due to their numbers, Hrangkhawl told me, they dominated the state assembly, municipal district council, and *panchayat* (local government).

GETTING THE ALLIANCE RIGHT

In a political landscape dominated by the Communists for over three decades, the various parties had to mobilize, collaborate, and make difficult alliances. If one were to analyze the politics of "nation first," or "community first," both the BJP with its strong integrationist ideology and the IPFT with its equally robust mobilization of indigenous politics could appear to be willing bedfellows. Both practice the politics of inclusion and exclusion in different ways that mark their kind of politics as "nationalist." It is helpful to be reminded of this challenge, particularly when examining right-wing politics, as their "geographical imaginations" tend to veer toward ideas of homeland that are "chauvinistic, essentialist, and exclusive, as opposed to ecumenical, open and inclusive" (Castree 2004, 141).

Indigenous Peoples Front of Tripura (IPFT) was formed in 1996, after the government banned the armed National Liberation Front of Tripura (NLFT). A year later IPFT merged with Tripura Upjati Juba Samiti (TUJS) and Tripura National Volunteers (also Tribal National Volunteers) (TNV), another armed nationalist movement, and renamed themselves the Indigenous Nationalist Party of Twipra (INPT) in 2002. In the 2003 state elections, the INPT won six assembly seats in the Tripura Legislative Assembly and formed an alliance with the Congress Party but lost overall to the CPI-M, who formed the government until the elections in 2018. Since 2003, various factions emerged within the INPT as a result of internal feuds and ideological differences.[15] In 2009, N. C. Debbarma revived the IPFT (NC) and went on to form an alliance with the BJP in 2018 to fight the "Left front," consisting of the CPI-M, the Communist Party of India, the Revolutionary Socialist Party, and the All India Forward Bloc.

The alliance between the BJP and the IPFT was particularly delicate. This was due to the demand by the IPFT for a separate tribal state, Twipraland, similar to Nagaland and Mizoram, a position that is not supported by the INPT. In the run-up to the elections in February 2018, the BJP-IPFT alliance officially announced in their "common minimum programme" that "the IPFT will not raise the demand for Twipraland or a separate state."[16] R. K. Debbarma, an historian of Tripura, argues that indigenous politics in Tripura revolves around the deportation of the Bengalis to Bangladesh for any redress to occur for the indigenous peoples, a position maintained steadfastly by the INPT. The IPFT demand for Twipraland, interestingly, undercuts this position by conceding to the politics around deportation, no longer questioning the legitimacy of Bengali presence in Tripura.[17]

Statehood would mean a return to a majority tribal rule; the current position of the TTAADC is limited, the IPFT argue, because it is still under the Tripura state dominated by Bengalis. According to a Bengali BJP minister, Joydeb, their party disagrees with the IPFT's demand for statehood. The IPFT knows their stand is not possible, remarked the minister. The BJP would never advocate for any idea of separation. Secondly, the presence of the Bengali majority in the state assembly will automatically oppose such a move. The tribals have only twenty reserve seats in the sixty-member assembly. The remaining forty are in the general category, including ten reserved for the scheduled castes, also dominated by Bengalis.

The issue of statehood has certainly divided opinions in the state, even among the tribal organizations. The main difference is between "deportation" of immigrants who came post-1971 (based on the cutoff date of 25 March 1971, coinciding with the Bangladesh War of Independence) and "statehood." INPT is for deportation and the amendment of the Sixth Schedule by giving full-fledged land rights to the scheduled tribes in the TTAADC areas. Secondly, they want direct funding from the Centre for the TTAADC, and not via the state as it currently stands. Thirdly, they want the inclusion of Kokborok as a recognized language in the Eighth Schedule of the Constitution of India. The IPFT, on the other hand, want the TTAADC areas to be reorganized as a state, Twipraland, for the tribals because there is a fear "refugees" will slowly populate the TTA-ADC areas as they did in the rest of Tripura. Statehood is to protect the tribals from further encroachment and dilution of tribal authority, stated the IPFT leader, Kumar. This, however, is not simple, as many of the tribals also live outside the TTAADC areas, and, for instance, Agartala, the seat of the Tripuri royal family, is excluded from Twipraland. Many nontribals also *live in* the TTAADC areas, which further complicates the idea of having an exclusively tribal state. Kumar explained the need for protection against the growing tide of migration as a long-term strategy:

> They [refugees] are not indigenous people. If they find it difficult to stay, slowly they will go back to their own places in Bangladesh because the borders are still open. They may go to West Bengal. Our target is if we get this power, in the near future, they can think for themselves [i.e., think of leaving]. They cannot go and do business in our area, for instance. They cannot buy land. All laws will be followed. They will get disturbed.

While some fear statehood will bring another partition-like scenario and many people oppose this model, the IPFT suggests a more gradual process, but one, equally, that reminds the current Tripura state that tribal demands are here to stay. Because of this recalcitrance of the IPFT, many of the INPT activists joined the BJP. Pritam, a tribal BJP MLA, reflected on the tribal votes and representation in the assembly by saying they are united on tribal issues across parties. "The party" is no longer the dominant authority.

While the BJP depended largely on Bengali voters, who would never agree to separate statehood, they also realized going it alone in the state would run counter to the image they wish to project of a national party with a regional outlook. Similarly, the IPFT needed this alliance. Firstly, they acknowledged theirs is a party with limited resources, and they could not compete with the BJP in terms of its national reach and deep pockets. In any election, money is a factor. Secondly, although the twenty seats reserved for the scheduled tribes represented an important constituent for the tribals, over the years, only seven to eight of these seats has a tribal majority. The rest are of mixed demography. The IPFT leader, Kumar, explained the scenario:

> Can you imagine? ST seats but majority voters are Bengali. This is the main problem we are facing now. Slowly they [Bengalis] have migrated and registered. They have become vote banks. If I become too vocal about refugees, they may not give me a vote. I lost twice because of that. To win the election, you have to join with a national party, Congress, BJP, or CPI-M. If you are a candidate of these national parties, then they will give you vote [*sic*]. They have some feelings toward regional parties—my people will vote for me, but these people will not vote for me. They are conscious people. Therefore, all our regional parties are not doing well. It is difficult to win. They [Bengalis] are a big stumbling block.

This means the dynamics of Twipraland are complicated too for the IPFT. Since the Bengalis comprise 70 percent of the state population but control only 30 percent of the land, and the tribals are 30 percent of the population but control 70 percent of the land, the Twipraland issue hits a sensitive nerve, which comes back to the history of Tripura and of migration narrated earlier. But how did this injustice demonstrate itself in the February 2018 elections? While the Bengalis have dominated all of the national parties—CPI-M, Congress, Trinamool Congress, and the BJP—it was the CPI-M that bore the brunt in 2018 due in part to the disillusionment felt by the people toward them.

FOR THE PEOPLE
The full moon looks like a burnt roti.

Written during the Bengal famine of 1943, this poem by Sukanta Bhattacharya evokes the idea that for a hungry person, the beauty of the full moon is inconsequential. The poet and the words are quoted to me by an eloquent Marxist philosopher and one of the primary functionaries of the CPI-M in Tripura, Bishwajit. He uses the poem to reflect on the nature of socialism, the political dynamics in the state, and how to reconcile their loss in 2018. "We couldn't capture the aspirational class," he told me in a classic Marxist analysis of the way things went wrong for the Communists. This analysis, which many in the state sympathetic to the Left front reiterated, focuses on the growing consumerism of the middle class. Citing Lenin's argument that the middle class simply acts as a pendulum, Bishwajit explained that they swung toward consumerist values this time, while in other times they swung toward the working class. Because the middle class have no "class identity," he reiterated, they voted for the BJP because they were promising the voters wealth creation, luring them into the philosophy of consumerism.

Partho, a former Communist youth leader, now a BJP worker, explained there was a strong perception that if a person wanted a job, they had to join and work for the CPI-M party. In other words, "the party" had supreme authority over jobs and a stranglehold over the organization of the state economy. The unemployment rate in Tripura is one of the highest in the country—19.5 percent according to the National Sample Survey of 2015–16.[18] Modi and the election campaign played on this disenfranchisement and spoke about various schemes, such as Ujjwala Yojana (Stand Up India) and Mudra Yojana (Start Up India), specifically targeted at the youth but also toward women, Partho explained. While these strategies can be explained in ideological terms by the Communists—as gimmicks, as surplus value, or control over the forces of production—it is difficult to deny that they appealed to the ordinary voters who were tired of the Communists' grandstanding.

For the Communists, with their strong ideology of socialism, class/caste/tribe/religion distinctions do not matter. For them, it is always "man" first. This is how Bishwajit explained the sentiment to me: "We recognize a person as a man, not as a tribal, not as a nontribal, not as a Hindu, Muslim. He is a man. Scientifically, I can say all people belong to the group *Homo sapiens*. They may be Mongoloid origin; I may be Caucasian origin, but we are all men. Everybody is equal." This man-first ideology meant they had to cater, equally, to both the tribal and the nontribal, particularly in terms of land distribution. This idea also meant the Communists never allowed ethnicity to determine how state politics was articulated and performed (Bhaumik 2016, 10). Initially, the undivided Communist party worked among the tribal population from around the 1940s even providing leadership in their armed struggle as they were facing uncertainty after the end of princely rule (Bhaumik 2009, 106). This movement was known as the Tripur Jatiyo Mukti Parishad (or also known as Gana Mukti Parishad) formed in 1948, with such early leaders as Dasaratha Deb and Biren Dutta (Bhaumik 2009, 106; Debbarma 2013, 14).

Between the 1940s and the 1960s, Communist workers—both tribal and nontribal—set up schools through the formation of the Jana Siksha Samiti in 1944 and provided education to the underrepresented sections of the community (Debbarma 2013, 14). Early tribal leaders like Dasaratha

Figure 7.1. Image of tribal Communists in Tripura. Photo taken by the author.

Deb and S. Debbarma wanted to "rouse the tribal people towards democracy" and "challenge the Bengali domination of princely bureaucracy."[19]
While this success translated into greater political mobilization among
the tribals, it was only from the mid-1960s onward, according to Bishwajit, that the movement began appealing to the Bengali population, and
given the growing influx of Bengalis from Bangladesh, by 1961 the tribals
had decisively become a minority in the state.

Bishwajit reminded me it was actually under the Congress (1963–77)
and later with the TUJS alliance (1988–93) when much of the refugee
settlement program happened on tribal land. As discussed earlier, the
Tribal Reserve Area, which was earmarked by the late King Bir Bikram
for the tribes, soon became a Bengali settlement. The Congress was using
the "refugee vote" to edge past the Communists. But in practical terms,
expressed the Communist leader, the Bangladeshi migrants also had to be
housed somewhere, due to their philosophy of man first. However, when
there was a rumor in the 1970s that these illegal landowners would be
pushed back to Bangladesh, there was uproar in the state by the "refugee
Bengalis," which further strained the Bengali-tribal relations, represented
by two armed groups, Amar Bengali and the TNV, respectively.[20] This
eventually led to the 1980s conflict, known as the Massacre at Mandai
in which close to 350 Bengalis were killed. This led to ethnic riots between Bengalis and tribals in which 1,000 people, mostly Bengalis, died
(Bhaumik 2002).

Over the years, though, the CPI-M also began to adhere to majoritarian politics by building their base around the Bengali population, thus
coming to be seen as a *bhadrolok* (gentleman) party with only a superfi-
cial concern for tribal welfare (Bhaumik 2002). The strong Communist
base in the tribal areas could have been maintained if Dasaratha Deb,
the tribal leader, was made chief minister when they won the elections
in 1978. The Central Politburo in West Bengal instead chose a Bengali,
Nripen Chakrabarty, who was described by the tribals as "the refugee
chief minister" (Bhaumik 2002). This demonstrated, as various tribal activists told me, a disregard for tribal leaders and went with the majoritarian logic of Bengali dominance. This paternalism has continued among
the BJP as well, argued a young tribal BJP worker, Ayan: "The land is

ours but the Bengalis disrespected our rights and oppressed us." "The BJP and the RSS assured us," he said, "that if the tribal constituents win more than fifteen seats, the CM post is ours, but they didn't give us [*sic*]." For this reason, tensions are heightening. The other issue has to do with the official recognition of the indigenous Tripuri language, Kokborok, as the second language, appearing in the Bengali script, not the Roman script indigenous people wanted (Bhaumik 2009, 78; see also Longkumer 2019).

Although the Communists wanted to be seen as a party for the tribals, in reality, the INPT activist Hrangkhwal told me, they are a "Bengali party with Bengali interests" because they do nothing about the "infiltration of Bangladeshis." They are relatives from across the border whose appearance and language are the same, he said. The rise of the TUJS and the TNV in the 1960s (and the NLFT, which followed) squeezed the Communists' influence in tribal belts. This meant the Communists had to turn toward nontribal support but found themselves in a complex bind, according to the journalist Subhir Bhaumik: "If Partition gave the communists a great chance to build a political base by utilising the nationality question, it also created an arena for bitter ethnic conflict which subsequently reduced their base" (2002). The rise of the TUJS and TNV, alongside the INPT and IPFT, further started to erode the Communists' appeal in the tribal areas that saw them suffer in the 2018 elections.

THE STARS HAVE ALIGNED: THE BJP, LIKE
A PHOENIX RISING FROM THE ASHES

The anti-incumbency factor was so strong that the BJP and the IPFT became the only viable option for many in the state. Hrangkhawl, the INPT leader, expressed the need to oust the Left, even if it meant sacrificing their chance of winning. He categorically asked his cadres to join the IPFT, because they were allies with the BJP and saw they had a good chance of winning. Even in his home constituency he did not stand, fearing a split in votes between the IPFT and his party would mean the Communists would come back to power. A former INPT worker, Ayan, now a BJP activist, told me he joined the BJP to work toward ousting the Communists. He also wants to work toward empowering the TTAADC, instead of obtaining the statehood demanded by the IPFT, which for him

Figure 7.2. BJP election slogan with Narendra Modi, Agartala, Tripura. Photo taken by the author.

is a more pragmatic option. For the first time, extolled Pritam, Christian missionaries and the RSS worked together against the Communists. This collaboration of anti-Left forces is no better exemplified than by a poster of a determined and muscular Prime Minister Modi with the slogan in Bengali: "Let us change; BJP government in Tripura this time."

One of the RSS activists, Roy, explained to me the challenge for the BJP was to get from 1 percent of the vote to around 40 percent. Prior to 2018, the BJP had no MLAs in the state assembly. Therefore, they had to break into the Congress and Trinamool Congress (TMC) vote bank that provided the initial base because of their political capital in the state. Out of the current thirty-six BJP MLAs, at least fifteen of them were from the Congress and the TMC, a strategy that had worked well for Modi when he co-opted many Congressmen to the BJP during the 2014 elections (Jaffrelot 2015, 157). One of the leading Congress MLAs, Dipesh, joined the BJP out of frustration at the way the Congress Party was being led by Rahul Gandhi. The situation in West Bengal was the tipping point, he said. The Congress allied with the CPI-M to defeat Mamata Banerjee's TMC in the 2016 West Bengal elections.[21] According to Dipesh, the Congress Party's rationale has always been to fight against "communal" forces, which in this case was the BJP, but instead, they focused their energy on tying up with the CPI-M. This move, he said, upset the entire rank and file of the Congress because

> for the last twenty-five years, wherever CPI-M has existed, there has been bloodshed, mayhem, arson, looting, murder. Thousands of our Congressmen were killed. . . . Many of them—parents, guardians, sons, brothers, sisters—had to flee the state for Bangladesh, Assam, or elsewhere. It is a pathetic story. Now, how can we swallow or digest that you are joining hands with a murderous party and you shook hands with those murderers that have been tainted by the blood of Congressmen? That forced us to resign. Our ideology was to defeat the Communist forces in our state. And we had said even if we have to change our religion, even if we have to hug Christianity, even if we have to hug Mohammed, we will do so, but our main fight is to defeat the CPI-M.

This anger and frustration led to the conclusion that the only party untainted by the Left was the BJP and the TMC. It is indeed a difficult choice, explained Dipesh, because he still sees himself as a Congressman. After thirty-six years it is difficult to alter one's DNA, a feeling other Congress Party members also have. But the national calibration went against the state principles. Because the Congress was in alliance with the CPI-M in the center, through the United Progressive Alliance (UPA), which brought together center-left parties in 2004, this meant the national was prioritized over the regional. Dipesh even suggested it was the "Congress national high command that ensured the CPI-M remained in power in Tripura." One can read Dipesh's reaction as a culmination of sitting on the sidelines and being maligned by the central Congress leaders. He and the state party members realized if the Congress continued to contest in the state elections, the vote would be split between them and the BJP, bringing the CPI-M back into power. "For the people of Tripura, we had to sacrifice," responded Dipesh. It would seem the inchoate nature of Congress politics at the national level hurt those in the regional corners.

In terms of electoral calculations, with the BJP hovering only around 1 percent, the 46 percent addition to this bank of votes from the anti-Left parties made them a real contender. While most of the Congress joined the BJP, the TMC dynamic also played a part in this dramatic increase. Ideologically, the TMC was closer to the Congress. They were also attracted by the charisma of Mamata Banerjee, the leader of the TMC and the chief minister of West Bengal, a state the Bengali elite of Tripura historically looked up to. But again, the TMC plan was counterintuitive to the situation in Tripura. For the TMC, it was no longer the Communists who were a threat; now it was the BJP. Mamata Banerjee was supportive of their fight against the Communists in the state, but later on, her stance changed, and she made the call to ally with the CPI-M to defeat the BJP.[22] The national-regional dynamic concerning the Congress and the TMC meant the floodgates were open for the BJP. "People even call us," remarked Dipesh, "Congress to BJP via Trinamool." But what does this mean in terms of the "ideological win" associated with Tripura?

Across the political spectrum—from the Left, Congress, BJP, IPFT, INPT—it would seem this was not an ideological win in the way the Sangh would have liked: that the politics of persuasion, of Hindutva ideology, and the vision of "one language, one nation, one religion" overcame the regional politics of resistance and dissent. It was an anti-Left vote, expressed by different party denominations. Dipesh, the ex-Congressman, remarked he did not join the BJP because of its ideology, but "to screw up these leftists." He even cautioned that the shift in votes—46 percent of the Congress votes—did not reflect the "vote percentage for the BJP." It must be remembered the electorate gave their votes only in this election. In Nagaland too, as Phanjoubam observed earlier, the BJP vote share dramatically increased only because of the support of the regional party, the NDPP. For a party to go from 1 percent of the vote share to the majority mark overnight and to form the government speaks more about the politics of convenience.

In any discussion related to the BJP, the question of Hindutva came up in Tripura as well. While in Meghalaya, the issue surrounding Hindutva deterred the mainly Christian voters from supporting the BJP, in Tripura, it appeared to be different. A Christian BJP MLA from the south of Tripura, Pritam, said that in his constituency the majority of the BJP workers are Christian—from the *mandal* (assembly constituency) to the *pristha pramukh* (grassroot party workers). As an ex-Congressman, he was approached by the current BJP chief minister, Biplap Deb, to contest in the February 2018 elections. While he agreed with the main developmental agenda of the BJP, he was particularly concerned about the violence meted out on Christians in many parts of India. The BJP leadership in the state promised him the minority Christians would be protected and not harmed. The BJP even gave a ticket to a Christian deacon in central Tripura (Burbo Mohan Tripura) who went on to win. In the current BJP-IPFT alliance, there are five Christian MLAs.

This certainly allows the Hindutva agenda to be seen as "inclusive," a point made by Dipesh, saying that "Hindutva embraces all," even to the extent of wanting to give citizenship to persecuted minorities—Hindus, Christians, and Buddhists—from Bangladesh. It is interesting to note that in Tripura, throughout all the interviews, the topic of Hindutva did not have the same ideological edge as in Meghalaya, even though the RSS were involved in both states. For example, in order to prove the RSS are working with the tribals and Christians, Pritam said he studied the Hindutva ideology carefully and concluded it is only militant organizations like the Bajrang Dal who would harm Christians. Interacting with the RSS and also listening to their speeches convinced Pritam the RSS were not sectarian and were primarily working for "tribal development." Even core Hindutva ideas were downplayed by Mohan Bhagwat, the RSS Sarsanghchalak (chief), when he visited Tripura and said, "The Muslims in India are also Hindu."[23] Pritam may believe the RSS are "not sectarian," but their "inclusivity" suggests an ideological position nevertheless. The RSS presence and activities therefore played an important role in Tripura.

There are approximately 150 RSS shakhas (units or cells) in Tripura and an intellectual forum called Boddhik Toli, where my RSS interlocutor, Roy, is a member. What people must remember, Roy suggested, is the RSS was working long before the BJP even came to power in Tripura, particularly under difficult circumstances, where the Communists would threaten anyone associated with the Sangh. Roy said, "When a political party comes to power who share in the same ideology as the RSS—of Akhand Bharat (undivided India)—then our interests naturally align. After Narendra Modi came to power, our confidence was enhanced." Roy explained, one could divide the work of the Sangh into a timeline—pre–3 March and post–3 March 2018, when the BJP government was installed in Tripura. "The amount of members who came out openly was unprecedented," said an ebullient Roy. During the elections, around three thousand local workers were mobilized to be involved in the elections—this was called Lok Jagaran Manch (People's Awakening Platform). Roy explained:

> The structure was thus: In each legislative assembly constituency [*mandal* level], there is one coordinator, one assistant coordinator. Under them they have a booth each. Each booth has a coordinator and assistant coordinator. Each constituency has about fifty to sixty booths. Under them, there is a team of eight to ten people. Their work is to communicate person to person, go from household to household and speak to them about their comforts, discomforts, address their problems, and so on. We never told them to vote for the BJP. We talked about the condition of the country and the state. Then they can think of whom they want to vote for.

This process is akin to what Pradeep Chibber and Susan Osterman (2014) call "vote mobilisers," whose commitment is beyond simply voting for a candidate but involves monetary contributions, door-to-door canvassing, and the distribution of election and party leaflets and pamphlets. This kind of micromanagement was successful particularly in the West Tripura District, where there were fourteen assembly seats, and where Roy was in charge. The focus on individuals and families was so carefully managed and directed—ranging anywhere from health care to jobs to schools—that, according to Roy, they managed to work with most families. In the tribal districts, it was trickier primarily because of the Christian population and also because of the mistrust of any Bengali trying to campaign. In tribal areas, therefore, Bengali workers were not present; it was primarily those from outside—Assam, Uttar Pradesh, New Delhi, and Gujarat. "Around two thousand BJP/RSS workers came," remembers Pritam, the south BJP MLA. Articulating a familiar RSS strategy of assimilation in tribal pockets, Pritam said:

> One thing good in RSS is they go to the village; they eat there, and they sleep there. The people coming from outside don't need any good rooms, good food. . . . Wherever there is a poor family, they will sleep in that house; they

will eat there. In that way, the attachment comes. Our people are soft, and they think these are the real leaders. That is also one reason that the BJP has come.

Pritam's description highlights the RSS's ability to use their skills at the grassroots level, while also suggesting the villager's perception of the RSS as "real leaders" had an emotional effect. The BJP/RSS appear as benevolent caretakers, taking on the host's lifestyle with ease. Pritam's description displays the power dynamics in these rural encounters that belie the purely disinterested nature of RSS activities. Their influence, however inadvertent it may be, played a role.

The RSS were also involved in assessing candidates—since they were the ones working in local constituencies. Pritam told me there were three levels of assessment done on the candidates—first by the local RSS, then by the BJP central intelligence, and then finally the national party. The micro-, meso-, and macrolevel of scrutiny meant all factors are evaluated—acceptability in the community, record of transparency, effectiveness as a worker, and synergies at a state and national level. Two candidates, explained the BJP MLA, were a total surprise even to the BJP workers at the state level—the first was a Christian leader Burbo Mohan Tripura from Gomati Constituency and the other was a Santana Chakma from Pencharthal Constituency, a Buddhist area. Both were first-time contestants and came from a social work background. Aside from the utilization of their vast network, the RSS/BJP always insisted they were not "communal" and wanted the best candidate to win, even to the extent of nominating Christian and Muslim candidates.

"Page observers" (in Hindi *panna pramukh* and in Bengali *prishtha pramukh*) were used at the microlevel management. This is a model developed in Uttar Pradesh and one that worked successfully in Manipur and Assam, explained Partho, the BJP worker. Like the RSS model of Lok Jagaran Manch, the page observers were in charge of looking after forty to sixty voters—the list of voters on the first two pages of an electoral roll. Tripura employed forty-two thousand page observers consisting of local workers, *vistaraks* (full-time workers) from outside the state, some short-term (fifteen days) and others full-time (six months). The page observers were instrumental in managing the electoral roll at a microlevel,

answering questions from health care, education, employment, and anything concerning the individual or the family. Once these concerns were
brought to the candidate, she or he would try to highlight these issues
immediately. Along with page observers, a similar tactic was developed by
Sunil Deodhar, the chief strategist of the BJP, which targeted commuters
by employing "Modi doot," or Modi ambassadors. These ambassadors,
wearing Modi t-shirts, worked regularly at six o'clock in the morning on
the busy railway line between Agartala and Dharmanagar. They had two
leaflets written in Bengali and Kokborok and would distribute them to
the commuters. Speaking to *The Wire*, Deodhar said, "From the trains,
on an average, I would get about 700–750 mobile phone numbers out of
which 200–300 would have WhatsApp. We made Excel sheets, started
sending them messages. Then, we divided them assembly-wise."[24]

Partho told me the data collected in these train encounters—ranging
from better salaries (seventh pay commission [a centralized system of re-
viewing and recommending salaries to the government]) to improving
education and employment prospects—went into the BJP-IPFT vision
document. In other words, they were able to translate everyday conversations and anxieties into policy, by speaking directly to the voters. While
the BJP-IPFT alliance has been a success in capturing the imagination
of the voters, the contentious issue surrounding the status of Hindus and
religious minorities was debated while I was in Tripura, because it goes to
the core of the migration issue along communal lines.

CITIZENSHIP BILL

In this election, one saw the growing division of votes along religious
motivations, argues Bishwajit, the Communist leader. Paralyzed by the
Hindutva wave, the Muslims have largely voted for the Communists. In
his constituency, for example, Bishwajit told me he won largely due to
the Muslim vote, even though he felt uncomfortable admitting this to
me. The BJP made a big deal out of this, calling him "mia," a deroga-
tory term referring to a Muslim Bangladeshi. But he insisted India is a
"secular country" and like any Hindu, a Muslim also has the right to call
India their "Bharat Mata" or "Mother Land." There is a feeling, he sug-

gested, that with this Hindutva *hawa* (wind), the Muslims feel insecure, and therefore, they voted for him for protection. Indeed, the increasing division between Hindu and Muslim, as seen in the Citizenship Amendment Bill, is particularly striking in Tripura.[25]

The proposed "amendment" on the Citizenship Act of 1955, introduced by the BJP in the Lok Sabha (the lower house of parliament in India) on July 15, 2016, seeks to provide citizenship to non-Muslim minorities— Hindu, Buddhist, Jain, Parsi, Sikh, and Christians—from Muslim majority countries like Afghanistan, Bangladesh, and Pakistan. It says these minorities "shall not be treated as illegal migrants for the purposes of this Act." The bill further proposes to reduce the requirement of eleven years to acquire citizenship by naturalization to six years of ordinary residence for such immigrants.[26] This amendment was part of the BJP's election manifesto during the 2014 general election, where they promised to welcome Hindu refugees and provide shelter.[27] There has been various opposition to this bill, and it has been labeled as "communally motivated humanitarianism" and a challenge to the secular fabric of the nation.[28] To adjudicate citizenship on the basis of religion, here primarily to non-Muslims but largely focusing on Hindus, however, should not surprise those who are keen followers of Hindutva ideology. This is the line taken by various indigenous commentators, particularly in Assam, where this debate has been the trickiest and the most complex.[29]

In a piece published in Assamese in the local newspaper *Amar Asom* and republished in English in the online magazine *Raiot*, the writers note the "amendments themselves are consistent with the grand vision of the RSS of the Akhand Bharat, the homeland of the Hindus."[30] What this amendment is attempting to do, argue the writers, is to polarize the Assamese and Bengali-speaking Hindus against Muslims, even as the BJP in Assam (with support from various Bengali organizations) are suggesting the Bengali-speaking populations of the Barak valley assimilate into the Assamese linguistic and cultural orbit.[31] This tactic, they suggest, is classic Hindutva posturing. In fact, a senior member and the current finance minister in the BJP government of Assam, Himanta Biswas Sarma, could not have been more blunt:

> The BJP has a reason to grant citizenship to Hindus who migrated to India
> from Bangladesh after they were subjected to persecution in the neighbour-
> ing country. India is the largest Hindu-inhabited country in the world. So it
> is natural for harassed Hindus to seek shelter here. Muslims and Christians
> from countries like Bangladesh can go to other Islamic and Christian coun-
> tries in the world. But Hindus cannot go to such countries. Thus, the BJP
> is going to do humanitarian work by providing shelter and citizenship to
> them.[32]

Sarma's zero-sum-game approach based solely on religious indices is hard
to understand in a region shaped by historical and cultural alliances across
borders and among peoples. These polarizations (Sarma includes Christians while the Citizenship Amendment Bill focuses on non-Muslim minorities) based solely on religious identities become alarming when they
make clear who the enemy is in an already fraught landscape, through
the Hindutva construction of homeland (pitrubhoomi). Sarma's views,
though construed as volatile by some observers, nevertheless speak to the
larger "Bangladeshi issue." Unlike Sarma's views of privileging one over
the other, in Assam, Meghalaya, and Tripura, states affected by the "Bangladeshi issue," there is a general refusal to abide by these religious groupings. "Bangladeshi" is a geographical tag and not explicitly a religious one.

In discussions with the various indigenous parties—such as the INPT
and the IPFT—the feeling is generally that the dominance of the Bengali must be halted, and redress must occur in terms of accommodating tribal interests. With a strong majority of assembly seats, Bengali
interests are already in an unassailable position in terms of power. This is
expressed in different ways—the INPT want deportation of the Bangladeshi refugees as a result of the 1971 war (the exact date is 25 March as a
cutoff for excluding anyone who arrived after this), and the IPFT argue
for statehood, Twipraland. Whatever their aims, the two came together
to form the All Tripura Indigenous Regional Parties Forum (ATIRPF)
to oppose the bill.

Speaking at length, Dipesh, the BJP minister, explained that the
bill is a sensitive issue across Tripura. He told me his ancestral home is
Kishoreganj (part of Dhaka division), a district in central Bangladesh.

He still has family ties there. Previously the Hindu population in Bangladesh was 32 percent; now it is reduced to 9 percent, he remarked with sadness.

> Many Hindu family's properties have been forcibly occupied by the majority population there—that is Muslims. . . . Once a Hindu girl steps into the college, she is forcibly made to change her religion to Islam. My government is fully aware of that. Now the atrocities are being rendered not just on Hindus but also Buddhists, Christians, Jains, et cetera over there. They are in a horrible state of affairs. Out of fear or out of atrocities meted to them, chunks of the population of Hindus have come to Tripura, Assam, and other parts of the country. Even the Chakma tribes, for whom the religion is Buddhist, are forced into conversion. These are the places where Modi ji understands, and that amendment being brought in by the central government has not yet been passed; it has been forwarded to the select committee. [This bill is now an act, passed 11 December 2019.] I think it is a welcome move.

While the BJP position clearly favors a kind of settlement, to provide citizenship to thousands of religious minorities, without explicitly saying only Hindus, a goal of their ideas of Akhand Bharat, this is a position that has already seen widespread resistance in the region. "What is the solution in terms of land distribution to these new citizens"? I asked. The minister said they will not receive "an inch of land" in the TTAADC areas, and instead they will be settled outside these areas. Roy, the RSS activist, took a different line and explained to me that this whole issue of Bengalis coming to Tripura is a sentimental one; it is not about land per se. There is ample land available. He said the tribals are 30 percent yet control 70 percent of the land, while the inverse holds true for the Bengalis. Besides, he explained, the area of Tripura he lives in, is part of "greater Tripura," which at one point included Sylhet, Comilla, and Chittagong Hills Tracts in Bangladesh. "I belong to Tripura then as I do now—we are inhabitants of Tripura who have just shifted base," he argued. Even the Tripura king was Hindu (he used to do Durga Puja!), he said. The Christians of the region are closest to the Hindus, which means for Roy that the people in the Northeast can work together to build an India beyond these state and nation-state boundaries, a vision of Akhand Bharat. Although the RSS have a positive view toward religious minorities, such as Christians, Buddhists, and Jains, the same is not true of Muslims.

Partition in the subcontinent happened primarily based on religious demographics. But Bharat did not become a Hindu Rashtra; it welcomed people of all faiths, Roy explained. To prove Hindus are not communal, Roy pointed to the statistics: Muslims in India are actually growing, while in Bangladesh and Pakistan Hindus are decreasing postpartition. "Where are these Hindus going from Bangladesh?" he asked. They are coming to Tripura.

> Tripura's Bengalis are cent percent [100 percent] uprooted from Bangladesh. My birth is in Tripura, but my parents came from Bangladesh. Hindus are coming here under these circumstances; they are compelled to come. We had to leave all our homes and property as they were and flee. It is not like we sold the property, gathered money, and moved. We left it like that. It's the case with all of us. Those who are coming like this . . . What is Bharat? Bharat is a country for Hindus—you can say, for sanatan dharma, which includes Buddhism, Sikhism. When these people are coming to Bharatvarsh, they are treating this as their motherland. If we don't let them live here, then whom will we give? Should we give to those who are saying Pakistan Zindabad? That is our basic concept—persecuted Hindus will be given citizenship.
>
> You see now, there are roughly fifty-two Muslim countries in the world and about seventy Christian countries. Till date, there was only one Hindu country in the world, Nepal. Now even that is no more after the coming of the Communist regime. In this condition, if Hindus cannot come to Bharatvarsh, then where else will they go?

Roy's emphatic articulation of this point can be found in the archives of the RSS and BJP, a view escalated during the 1990s when the campaign to construct a Ram temple at the disputed site of the Babri Masjid (mosque) in Ayodhya gained momentum (Gillian 2002, 77). Focusing on the perceived incompatibility of "illegal migrants" with the exclusivist conception of national identity, the BJP launched a nationwide campaign in 1992–93 around the illegal immigration and dispersal of Bangladeshis across India. Arguing how this mass influx had brought about socioeconomic tensions in the Northeast, in West Bengal, parts of Bihar, and affecting even places like New Delhi, the BJP pointed to the increased lack of stability, security, and the strain this has brought to the national economy (BJP 1992). Categorized as unregulated "infiltration," the BJP focused their attacks on the Congress for harboring and encouraging these developments, while promoting themselves as the only party capable of guaranteeing "security" and "stability." Territorial integrity—both in terms of keeping these "illegals" out and in securing the borders of Punjab, Kashmir, and the Northeast—became for the BJP a campaign that was particularly strident against Muslim "infiltrators," viewed suspiciously as forming "part of an 'undeclared' policy of Bangladeshi colonization and invasion of selected districts in order to establish Muslim majorities and facilitate another partition of the nation" (Gillan 2002, 86; see also Ramachandran 1999; van Schendel 2005). For the Sangh, according to Michael Gillan (2002, 86), changing the demographic character (toward Muslim "domination") along border states like West Bengal and the Northeast is to undermine the territorial integrity of a Hindu Rashtra.

Tripura, however, is dominated by the Hindu Bengalis, and the preponderance of the population concentration along the Indian border is therefore not only Muslim; nor is it always Hindu. Although the Hindutva groups are eager to assimilate and erase local indigenous religions for pan-Hindu ones (see Chapter 3), there are also border areas where Buddhists and Christians (in Chittagong Hills Tract in Bangladesh and Tripura and Mizoram in India) dominate. Similarly, along the Bangladesh/Meghalaya border, there are predominantly Garo Christians on the Indian side, bringing into question the long-held view that the partition of Bengal happened primarily along Hindu/Muslim lines (van Schendel 2005, 46–48). Nor did the partition solely bisect Bengalis; there were also clear discontinuities between Bengalis and non-Bengalis, particularly along the Meghalaya, Mizoram, Tripura, and Assam corridors. Furthermore, where the border separated the Bengali from the non-Bengali majority areas (in the case of Tripura and Assam for instance), "it was often the case of Bengalis (both Muslims and Hindus) on one side and non-Bengali Christians or Buddhists on the other" (van Schendel 2005, 47). This breaks down the normative partition view of the Hindu/Muslim divide and also brings to focus the "ethnic bias," questioning the "history of the region [being] that of the Bengalis and marginaliz[ing] all others" (van Schendel 2005, 47).

The BJP and the RSS are largely aware of these histories, as many of their workers are based in the border areas of Bangladesh/Mizoram among the Chakmas and Reangs (known as the Bru in Mizoram). The BJP are in fact using this corridor to enter the electoral landscape of Mizoram and making their presence felt in a strong Christian state, with the aim of taking over the last of the northeastern states in the upcoming elections in November 2018.[33] For their idea of Akhand Bharat to work, it is not only Hindus who must be resettled in Tripura, as the BJP minister articulated above, but also persecuted Buddhists and Christians from Bangladesh must be given refuge. The election of Santana Chakma, from a Buddhist region in North Tripura, a first-time BJP MLA and now minister of social welfare and social education and animal resource development, shows the seriousness of acknowledging the Buddhists (but encompassing them within Indic civilization [see Chapter 5]), while also accommodating Christian MLAs in the BJP-IPFT alliance. This highlights how the BJP are portraying themselves as a nonsectarian party and moving away from core Hindutva ideals. But this is largely tactical, because these alliances are mainly to work with marginalized minorities in Tripura and elsewhere in the Northeast of India so they can present a common front in resisting the Muslim onslaught from Bangladesh. For example, Roy's earlier articulation that there is "ample land available in Tripura" is an idea that extends, according to scholars (Ramachandran 1999; van Schendel 2005), to the whole of the Northeast by both the Bangladeshi elite and the Indian government.

Culled from various newspaper reports in Bangladesh, Sujata Ramachandran suggests "many Bangladeshi intellectuals are encouraging the migration of Muslims into the north-eastern parts of India. . . . These scholars, it is revealed, invoke a theory of lebensraum or living space, to submit that unmitigated population growth along with restrictions of geographical space, compel migrant mobility 'in search of land'" (1999, 237). The phrase used in India is of a "demographic invasion." In a report to the president of India in 1998, the governor of Assam described a sinister design to create "Greater Bangladesh and provide *Lebensraum* [living space] 'by severing the entire land mass of the North-East, with all its rich resources, from the rest of the country'" (quoted in van Schendel 2005, 196). Both these ideas are couched in the language of settler colonialism and expressed in terms of conquest and xenophobia, which have become a part of the vocabulary of these borderland spaces. Where once the linked history of the region was unquestioned, now the unmitigated salience of the language of nationalism dominates the landscape creating friends and foes. The complexity of this matrix—along religious, ethnic, economic, and political lines—characterizes the landscape of the region that must comprehend the way politics is about a human place in flux.

CONCLUSION

In May 2018, my research assistant, Aheli, and I visited the India-Bangladesh border in Tripura, locally known as the "international border." Our taxi was stopped and checked, and we were questioned about our purpose for visiting Tripura. Assured that we were legitimate Indian citizens, we were allowed to pass through the first gate and directed toward a parking lot. We then entered the area where the border check posts are, with military personnel patrolling on both sides. Traveling the length and breadth of the Northeast of India, my identity as a Naga and a researcher often raised suspicion. In the interstate border areas with Assam/Nagaland, Assam/Manipur, Assam/Arunachal Pradesh, or in the interior Naga villages in Assam, for example, the Assam police and the Indian military frequently harassed me, simply because of my identity as a Naga or because the car I hired bore a Nagaland number plate. Strangely, here, none of these identities mattered. After a long time, I felt relaxed around military personnel; a young Border Security Force (BSF) man from Bihar even told us as we were milling around, "Don't worry, we are here to protect you." We immediately asked, "From whom?" He smiled, clutching his AK-47, and in Hindi said, "Against those people," nodding beyond the check post into Bangladesh. Here, Naga, Bihari, and Tripuri faded into the background—we were all "Indian" against those "Bangladeshis."

Once the ritual lowering of the flag closed the India-Bangladesh border for the day, we met some young IPFT workers who had arrived with

Figure 7.3. India-Bangladesh Border, Agartala, Tripura. Photo taken by the author.

their minister, Mevar Kumar Jamatia, the minister of tribal welfare and forest. Jamatia was hosting some dignitaries from Maharashtra as guests of honor. As we walked toward the car, the IPFT workers started expressing their antipathy toward the Bangladeshi immigrants, who they say have changed the demography to such an extent that they now feel threatened, and "our survival is at stake."

As they discussed the issue of Twipraland, it became obvious they believed it was only this that would safeguard them against dominant Bengalis. They warned me, "as a tribal brother," to be wary of the Bangladeshis. "They will do the same to you in Nagaland," they said, "as they have done to us." As we were leaving, a young man in a suit with a suitcase and an older couple passed by. I wasn't sure whether they were Bangladeshis who had crossed over to Tripura for business or Tripura residents returning from business in Bangladesh. All I heard was "*Chutia* [idiots], infiltrators, go back," and then the young IPFT activist spat on the ground. Borders are places where identities are contrasted; feelings reverberate inward toward homes, communities, and cities. Historical memory once nurtured by human connections brings about new challenges that go deep into the hearth of the nation.

The election campaign and the focus on the BJP success have dominated the political landscape in Tripura and the Northeast in the last few years. In Tripura the issue of "identity politics" related to land and migration preoccupies much of the discussions. The BJP juggernaut, with its vision of Akhand Bharat, specifically in relation to questions of citizenship, has brought about tensions with those whose own ethnonationalisms revolve around the construction of homelands, demarcating clear boundaries and going against the dominant ideological grain of "nation first." What appears on the surface to be a success story for the BJP—with a sweep of the electoral mandate in Tripura along with their alliance, the IPFT—appears to be largely an anti-Left reaction, leaving us with a wider set of issues having to do with questions over Bengali migration into Tripura. If part of the attraction of the BJP in Tripura is their willingness to address immigration, as many scholars, activists, and commentators have noted, how can the BJP truly address this issue when its base includes immigrants—their own chief minister is seen as a refugee—and is reliant on the very Bengalis these indigenous movements are defining themselves against?

Here is the inexplicable tension that confronts the BJP as a national and nationalist party. On the one hand, they are driven by their ideological motivation of inclusion and of envisioning Akhand Bharat as central to their designs in the region. On the other hand, the local political algorithms do not always complement the national arithmetic. It is here, especially in the Northeast, that the limits of Hindutva are tested. Either they are adapting to the fluctuating geoethnic realities by regionalizing themselves, or they are steamrolling on with their agenda without recourse to those very people with whom they seek alliances. From a position of power, however, it appears the BJP presence in the region forms another piece of the puzzle, slowly being assembled to give a picture of a Hindutva landscape.

HINDUTVA BECOMING AND THE
GREATER INDIA EXPERIMENT

I BEGAN THE BOOK by examining the fraught landscape of Hindutva politics in Northeast India. In doing so, I tried to capture the emotion and passion that occupied my ethnographic research as I traveled the length and breadth of the region interviewing, interacting, and seeking out spaces, ideas, and thoughts that went into the making of this book.

This book is about the Greater India experiment, as a cultural, geopolitical, and visual narrative that is articulated throughout the pages of this book. It is also about Hindutva becoming in Northeast India based on a set of ideas that argue for a singular Indic identity—rooted in Hindi, Hindu, and Hindustan—amid multiple ethnic identities and affiliations vying for autonomy and sovereignty and challenging the "idea of India." It is the coming together of these forces that make Hindutva in the region interesting and unique. I have argued that this Hindutva laboratory is experimental in its implementation but yet guided firmly by their core ideology. Observing the way these ideas navigate the landscape known as Northeast India contributes to the way Hindutva and the region itself are undergoing change in unprecedented ways. Not only is the book an ethnographic examination over the long term, but it also contributes to existing scholarship on the Sangh Parivar, their ideologies, and the way they organize themselves in different parts of India, still ideologically driven and increasingly pervasive, even in the most unlikely of spaces.

While my work is focused on Hindutva, I am also trying to understand the Northeast through its different interlocutors. Viewing the region through Hindutva eyes, moreover, contributes to different histories
told from a certain perspective that, on the one hand, acknowledges the
diverse and fractured landscape but, on the other hand, offers newer read-
ings that confront the region's perception as separate and isolated. Questioning this historical myth of separation, Hindutva actors find ways to
argue for unity and locate the region's imprint through civilizational ties.
Although their activities in many parts of India may come across as violent and vituperative, in the Northeast, it is Hindutva victimization that
allows them to be unconventional and under the radar. They occupy unequal spaces, foster alliances with like-minded organizations and movements, and find gaps that allow them to flourish. One can construe their
activities as malleable, flexible, and innovative, primarily due to these
conditions that force them to fashion an alternative habitus. But their
activities, it must be said, are not simply based on an overnight project or
a resurgence with the recent successes of the BJP but a long-term strategy and presence that makes them intransient, even if the BJP and their
electoral presence dissipates into the background. They will continue unabated, shaping hearts and minds over the *longue durée*. Who are these
foot soldiers ready to weather the storm come what may? What are their
stories and motivations in serving for their cause and the nation? This is
where this book began.

I have focused attention on the workers of the Sangh, the individual
commitments that made them conscripts or that brought them to the
region, and the institutional ideologies that pervade their activities, as
they shape, modify, and change them subtly along the way. The purpose
is not to treat these Hindutva ideas as normative or monolithic; nor am I
interested in pursuing these ideas solely outside of the people that inhabit
them. But by taking these actors seriously and highlighting their voices,
this book brings the human dimension and their conversations as "meaningful striving" (Mahmood 1996, 21), unfolding in real time. The four biographies I sketch in the introduction represent the different sources of
their inspiration and the way their activities might lead us to question
normative Hindutva posturing.

As much as this book is about Sangh activities and their mission to transform this region into their idea of "one India," it is also about my entrenchment as an ethnographer. I highlight my own role in gaining access and negotiating the difficult terrain of working with people whose views may be objectionable, unpalatable, or even outright violent. My attempt to understand their activities, dispassionately, made conversation across tables and chairs possible. Their judgment of me as an "objective researcher" certainly opened doors, but my previous work on indigenous movements and their knowledge of my involvement with non-Christian groups in the region added another layer of openness to our interactions.

Like the many scholars working on right-wing movements across the world (Hansen 2002, 2009; Harding 1991; Mouffe 1993; Pilkington 2016), I am aware how easily one might treat these forces as irrational and how quickly we might retreat to our own political biases of painting them with one broad brushstroke. Hindutva, like many right-wing ideologies, takes on different hues and demonstrates their heterodox and diffuse political natures within a spectrum of views and attitudes sometimes closely associated with their institutions but also departing from them in interesting ways. Much of what the book tries to explain is how the politics of homelands, which is so embroiled in the region, competes with a political perspective based on a singular idea of national oneness. It seems that the Sangh are gradually learning to work in the messy territorial and ethnic politics in the region. To highlight what this means, let me turn to the example of Tripura and the larger question of the Citizenship Amendment Bill (now an act) to tease out the finer points of how territoriality, electoral politics, ethnic competition, and issues surrounding migration resonate in the region.

While Tripura has a large Bengali population, many of whom arrived from East Pakistan-Bangladesh post Indian independence, the political balance is always going to be sensitive. Entering the electoral landscape of Tripura also highlighted the complicated nature of ethnic homelands. It shed light on the IPFT's position vis-à-vis the BJP, questions over the Citizenship Amendment Bill of 2016, and the majoritarian politics of Hindutva and the Bengali Hindus. One could argue that the demand of statehood, Twipraland, by the IPFT acknowledges the reality over the impossibility of Bengali deportation to Bangladesh (maintained by other indigenous parties, such as the Indigenous Nationalist Party of Twipra [INPT]) and this made the alliance with the BJP possible. It also demonstrates that the Bengali Hindu dominance of all the parties—BJP, CPI-M, and the Congress—suggests the tribal/nontribal arithmetic remains crucial not only for electoral politics but for the reenvisioning of the region within the bigger designs of Akhand Bharat. It is the Sangh who are keen to pursue this idea of Akhand Bharat where Greater Tripura—that incorporates Bangladesh—is part of their larger consciousness and design. What will happen to indigenous peoples and their movements if their voices are constantly undermined by dominant groups, whose population not only exceeds them but whose livelihoods depend precisely on land belonging to indigenous peoples?

The Citizenship Amendment Bill of 2016, which ignited protests all over the region, is one example of the contested nature of belonging. While minority religions—including Hindus, Buddhists, Jains, Parsis, Sikhs, and even Christians—escaping persecution from predominantly Muslim countries (Pakistan, Bangladesh, and Afghanistan) will be rehabilitated in India, the question remains as to what extent this will generate debate, protest, and even violence. If Muslims are the Other in the larger Hindutva imagination, what place will they have within the debate over the Citizenship Amendment Bill or the National Register of Citizens (in Assam) that explicitly excludes them, even when many of their homes are in India? Will the bill and the NRC be used as a pretext to consistently exclude Muslims from the region?

Speaking about the broader discourse of citizenship, the BJP president Amit Shah recently argued, in a speech in Assam, that the BJP and the National Democratic Alliance (NDA) will prevent Assam from becoming "another Kashmir." For the BJP, both the Citizenship Amendment Bill and the NRC, according to *The Hindu*, are understood as methods of "keeping Muslims of Bangladeshi origin out of the State historically allergic to migrants." Shah is reported as saying, "The BJP felt the Bill was necessary to prevent Assam from becoming a Muslim-majority State like Kashmir."[1]

The NRC was started in parts of Assam after the census of India in 1951 but was only published on 30 July 2018. It includes information on twenty-eight million people but excludes some four million residents of India considered ineligible for citizenship. In Assam, if people could prove their residency on or before 24 March 1971 via relevant documentation, they were included in the NRC. This meant the large number of migrants from East Pakistan moving into Assam after the partition of 1947 were eligible for citizenship. However, it excluded more recent migrants, some of whom could have lived in Assam for over three decades.

The NRC can be viewed as an extension of what Sunil Amrith (2014), a historian of global migration, argues is "the disavowal of migration" in the context of modern citizenship in South and Southeast Asia. It was meant to accommodate and pacify the indigenous population and to bring normalcy to a political order still reeling under the postcolonial ramifications of partition that fixed the boundaries of the Indian nation-state. The promise of the NRC was to distinguish citizens from noncitizens, calling into question the rights of those excluded from the register and proving especially divisive in Assam.

The compromise of the Assam Accord of 1985 (Hazarika 1999) agreed that foreign migrants registered between 1961 and midnight on 24 March 1971, the date of the start of the Bangladesh War of Independence, would be accepted as citizens. The NRC, which began as an initiative in tracking population mobility, is now central to the effort to identify those illegally settled in Assam post-1971 and to, therefore, deny them citizenship. Unlike the appeal to religious indices for deciding who is included and excluded, which seems to be the BJP's approach, the NRC is largely an exercise unencumbered by religion. Women, indigenous peoples, Hindus and Muslims, and those with no easy access to documents have been excluded in the data published by the NRC in July 2018. However, Amit Shah and the BJP machine seem to press this issue further by suggesting the NRC will be extended to all of India. What started as an issue over the demographic balance in Assam over questions of immigration (not Hindu/Muslim) has slowly given way to the polarization of identities by the BJP on the basis of religion.

During the public discussions around the NRC and the citizenship bill in Northeast India in 2018, I received various WhatsApp messages from Sangh activists supporting the bill but who were unsure about

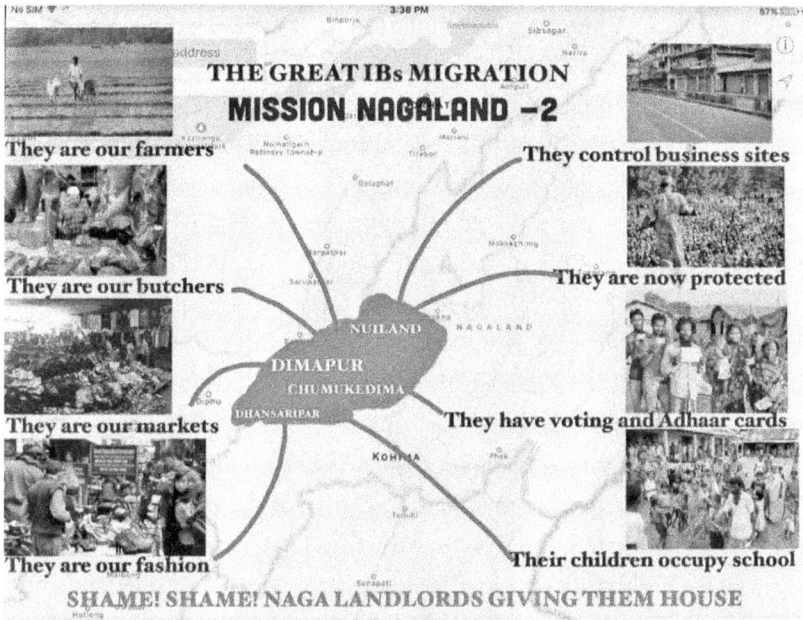

THE GREAT IBs MIGRATION
MISSION NAGALAND -2

They are our farmers

They control business sites

They are our butchers

They are now protected

NUILAND   NAGALAND

DIMAPUR
CHUMUKEDIMA
DHANSARIPAR

KOHIMA

They are our markets

They have voting and Adhaar cards

They are our fashion

Their children occupy school

SHAME! SHAME! NAGA LANDLORDS GIVING THEM HOUSE

Figure E.1. "The Great Illegal Bangladeshi Migration." Circulated by an RSS pracharak in Nagaland via WhatsApp. Courtesy of the author.

the NRC, since Hindus were also struggling to produce their papers as evidence of their residence in Assam. One message accompanied by a diagram, which was being circulated on social media, was particularly striking. It was forwarded by an RSS pracharak in Dimapur and contained what it called "The 10 Commandments to deal with IBs [Illegal Bangladeshi Immigrants]." These do nots range from "do not rent your house to IBs" to "do not give them land to cultivate" and "do not employ IBs." Accompanying this message is a diagram showing the "Great IBs Migration" (see fig. E.1) and reprimanding Naga landlords for giving them shelter. These obvious anxieties are couched in the polarizing discourse of "us versus them," clearly targeting the Muslim population.

Similarly, in an election rally on 12 April 2019 in West Bengal, Shah lashed out at illegal Muslims from Bangladesh. Referring to such illegal immigrants as "termites in the soil of Bengal," Shah said: "A Bharatiya Janata Party government will pick up infiltrators one by one and throw them into the Bay of Bengal."[2] The push for the NRC and the Citizenship Amendment Bill of 2016 demonstrates the BJP's tactic. While the NRC may exclude those of minority religions, the bill, passed on 8 January 2019, includes them. This means out of the four million excluded in the draft NRC of July 2018, those with minority religion status will gain automatic entry as legal migrants as a result of the bill. Only the Muslims will remain illegal migrants and disqualified from citizenship. While this effectively shuts out the Muslims, it allows Hindus to gain entry through this bill, which, in a state like Tripura, for example, where an estimated 70 percent are Bengali Hindus from Bangladesh/East Pakistan, will have ramifications beyond the electoral landscape discussed in Chapter 7. Not only does this raise questions about the future of indigenous peoples' movements when issues surrounding land, identity, and resources occupy many around the world, but the fact that the region is an ultimate borderland—with Bhutan, China, Bangladesh, and Myanmar—highlights pressing issues regarding ethnic homelands and shared histories, set against the global challenge of human migration.

Indeed, these challenges confront many nations around the world. Issues surrounding immigration, identity, and the political discourse around nationalisms have become widespread. Not only are physical symbols, such as walls, mounted to keep certain populations at bay, but sensitive debates regarding the movement of people from war-torn countries bring to focus the emotional and physical trauma of human lives, which, when beamed across media frequently, makes us almost immune to their plight. The collective responsibilities of communities and nation-states to deal with these tragic situations, against the growing tide of xenophobia and Far Right movements, are making these debates entrenched into one that is increasingly pitched as us versus them, threatening the very fabric upon which collaboration and cooperation were built. This book highlights some of these arguments and issues.

In this global context, what can we learn from a region in India that has been marginalized for so long? It is not only an example of a right-wing organization investing in a region resistant to its ideology and changing and adapting to make alliances with its audience. But it also enables us to reflect on how indigeneity and indigenous movements are appealed to and utilized to make this broader goal of uniting India while, at the same time, reinforcing its division from others. However, this book began with the idea that Hindutva is attempting to promote a singular identity by deconstructing, remaking, and reassembling the very nature of Hindutva. In this way, the question remains: Will the Sangh ability to be malleable and changing, in such a contested space, enable the region's inclusion within Hindutva? Or does this process of becoming, being made, produce a parallel process in the indigenous resistance?

NOTES

CHAPTER 1

1. "Abducted RSS Men Killed in Tripura," *Times of India*, 29 July 2001.

2. Christophe Jaffrelot, "This Land, This Nation," *Indian Express*, 12 January 2016. Myanmar/Burma are used interchangeably, depending on the sources and context, throughout this book.

3. Sikkim, recognized as one of the northeastern states, has been omitted from my analysis, but some issues may resonate.

4. These processions also happened in Shillong, a Christian-majority city in Meghalaya, demonstrating their newfound confidence. Albert Thyrniang, "Shillong RSS Linked to Nazism and Fascism!," *Shillong Times*, 29 January 2016.

5. "Overview," My Home India, accessed 15 January 2020, https://www.myhomeindia.org/overview/.

6. Neha Dixit, "Operation #BetiUthao," *Outlook Magazine*, 8 August 2016.

7. These Gyan Sangams are now a national phenomenon. Express News Service, "Research Reality Check at RSS Workshop for V-Cs, Teachers," *Indian Express*, 27 March 2017.

8. The NRC is an attempt to determine who is a genuine citizen of Assam (and India) based on the 1951 census. After the 1971 Indo-Pakistan War and the formation of Bangladesh, there occurred mass migration into Assam. Indian citizenship is now being ascertained on the basis of the NRC compiled in 1951 and electoral rolls up to 1971. In the absence of electoral rolls, other documents (such as land and tenancy records) up to midnight 24 March 1971 can also be submitted to prove one's residence. The 1971 cutoff date (25 March to be exact, when the Indo-Pakistan War began) was an attempt by the then Rajiv Gandhi Congress government, along with the All Assam Students Union (ASSU) and the All Assam Gana Sangram Parishad (AAGS)—known as the Assam Accord—to end the agitation in the state (1979–85) concerning the issue of "illegal migrants" that entered Assam during the political instability of the Indo-Pakistan War. This is addressed in more detail in Chapter 7, but see also Aviral Virk, "What Is the NRC & What Happens if You're Not on the List," *The Quint*, 1 August 2018; Sanjoy Barbora, Joydeep Biswas, Bidyut Sagar Boruah, Debarshi Das, Sanjib Deblaskar, Anshuman Gogoi, Gaurav Rajkhowa, and Ankur Tamuli Phukan, "Why Hindutva Inspired Citizenship (Amendment) Bill, 2016 Needs to be Opposed," *Raiot*, 7 May 2018.

CHAPTER 2

1. Tongam Rina, "Only the BJP Needs Convincing That Arunachal Is Indeed a Part of India," *The Wire*, 2 April 2018.

2. Taba Ajum and Karyir Riba, "A Twist in the Myth: Rukmini's Vague Arunachal Connection," *Arunachal Times*, 28 March 2018.

3. Rina, "Only the BJP."

4. Jyoti Malhotra, "Krishna-Rukmini Bind Gujarat with North-East," *Indian Express*, 28 March 2018.

5. Malhotra, "Krishna-Rukmini."

6. Narendra Joshi's book entitled *Ashwattha*, published by the VK in 2000, has been a crucial primary written source for this chapter. An RSS activist working for the VK gave me this book. He said that most of what the Sangh say about the Northeast is preserved in writing in this book. Indeed, many of the oral interviews and Sangh local publications also closely corroborate many of the points made in this book. It suggests that the author has intimate knowledge of these texts and views. I could not ascertain Joshi's precise identity; he could have worked extensively in Arunachal Pradesh and Assam, places where the VK are strong in number and the two places that feature prominently in this book. The sources Joshi uses are idiosyncratic and hard to trace. Although he provides a bibliography at the end, matching these to the quotes has been difficult, as well as time-consuming. Therefore, I often let Joshi's text speak for itself, and where needed, I provide additional context based on how I have been able to track and make sense of the references.

7. A. Z. Phizo, "Phizo's Plebiscite Speech," accessed 15 January 2020, http://www .neuenhofer.de/guenter/nagaland/phizo.html.

8. Press Trust of India, "Gujarat's Madhavpur Mela to Showcase Cultural Integration with Northeast," *Indian Express*, 24 March 2018.

9. Press Trust of India, "Gujarat's Madhavpur Mela."

10. The speeches in this section are taken from the Mela and translated from Hindi to English by Aheli Moitra: "Madhavpur Ghed Festival 2018- LIVE," posted by Doordarshan Girnar, YouTube video, accessed 15 January 2020, https://www.youtube.com/watch?v =YlKgqFVJEXU.

11. Biren Singh was criticized heavily by the people of his state for making claims that Manipur did not exist as a geopolitical entity: Sangeeta Barooah Pisharoty, "NE Dispatch: The Distortion of Manipur's History and Assam's Debate on Citizenship," *The Wire*, 31 March 2018.

12. Phizo, "Phizo's Plebiscite Speech."

13. Razzeko Dele, "Krishna-Rukmini, Idu Mishmi-Bishmak Nagar Phenomenon: An Insider's View," *Dawnlit Post*, n.d., accessed April 8, 2020, https://thedawnlitpost.com /krishna-rukmini-idu-mishmi-bishmak-nagar-phenomenon-an-insiders-view/.

14. This refers to the myth of Shakti Peeth, where various body parts related to the goddess Sati fell in South Asia and the trans-Himalayan region, as a mourning Shiva carried her. In the Northeast there are three sites—Kamakhya in Assam (genitals), Tripura Sundari in Tripura (right leg), and Jayanti in Meghalaya (left thigh). The sacred geography through the distribution of Sita's body is another example of the region's mythological association with Indic culture.

15. The inability to name and traverse the landscape is also telling. Mizoram is a place of failed relations; it largely remains unmapped through this Indic register, due to its unknowability and masked by its Christianity (see Chapter 4).

16. *Merriam-Webster*, s.v. "time immemorial," accessed 15 January 2020, https://www.merriam-webster.com/dictionary/time%20immemorial.

CHAPTER 3

1. International Labour Organisation, "C169—Indigenous and Tribal Peoples Convention, 1989 (No. 169)," accessed 15 January 2020, https://www.ilo.org/dyn/normlex/en/f?p=NORMLEXPUB:12100:0::NO::P12100_ILO_CODE:C169.

2. In 1995, the Supreme Court of India deliberated on whether Hinduism/Hindutva is a way of life. In the judgment, it acknowledged the indeterminate nature of these terms—*Hindu/Hinduism/Hindutva*—and declared that "it is difficult to appreciate how the term '*Hindutva*' or '*Hinduism*' *per se* can be assumed to mean and be equated with narrow fundamentalist Hindu religious bigotry. . . . These terms are indicative more of a way of life of the people" (Jacobsohn 2003: 200–202; see also Saxena 2018). In response to this statement, the *Organiser*, a major English-language publication of the RSS, noted in its editorial, "The Supreme Court has put its seal of judicial imprimatur on the Sangh ideology of Hindutva by stating that it is a way of life or state of mind and that it is not to be equated with religious fundamentalism" (*Organiser*, 24 December 1995; quoted in Jacobsohn 2003, 203).

3. According to the Constitution of India, STs are broadly to be given "protective arrangements" to eliminate inequities and promote equality, "affirmative action" (or reservation) in jobs, education to accelerate the integration of STs into mainstream society, and "development," whereby STs are provided resources and benefits to bridge the socioeconomic gap with other communities (see Sengupta and Corbridge 2010).

4. Although the Sangh and the indigenous elite sometimes use the idea of "way of life" as equivalent to "religion as faith" as opposed to "religion as ideology" (Bharucha 1993), the former is rather broad and vague and is also used to make certain "truth claims" that are beyond rational explanation (Bharucha 1993). Using the classification "religion," another inaccurate, complex, but nevertheless popular term, allows me to conflate the two—faith and ideology—as a helpful heuristic device to show the contestation over the nature of syndicating practices into religions, such as indigenous and Hinduism. It also speaks to broader ideological influences at play both in a national and transnational context.

5. International Labour Organisation, "C169."

6. I have been unable to trace the exact words that Kamei uses in his article on the draft declaration, but the language appears similar to the various drafts since 1984 and the revision that was finally adopted in September 2007. For a full account of this, see Charters and Stavenhagen 2009.

7. For example, article 12 (1): "Indigenous peoples have the right to manifest, practise, develop and teach their spiritual and religious traditions, customs and ceremonies; the right to maintain, protect, and have access in privacy to their religious and cultural sites; the right to the use and control of their ceremonial objects; and the right to the repatriation of their human remains." United Nations, *United Nations Declaration on the Rights of Indigenous Peoples*, 13 September 2007, http://www.un.org/esa/socdev/unpfii/documents/DRIPS_en.pdf.

8. The JFCPF is primarily an intellectual forum comprising representatives from each of the non-Christian indigenous religions.

9. In the next three paragraphs I draw on Jamatia's document (Jamatia 2011, 15–19).

10. These reform activities have strong parallels with the Indian reform movements in the eighteenth and nineteenth centuries through such figures as Rammohan Roy, Dayananda Saraswati, Swami Vivekananda, and Mohandas K. Gandhi, who were partly influenced by the orientalist projection of Indian "spirituality" that led to the development of an anticolonial Hindu nationalism (P. Chatterjee 1993; King 1999).

11. "The Role of RSS in Religious Conversion in Arunachal," *Eastern Mirror*, 12 May 2014.

12. However, Redfield's continuum thesis is drawn from Srinivas's work on Sanskritization (see also Sinha 1958). Srinivas argued that "Sanskritic Hinduism," based on Brahmanical orthodoxy, provided Indian society with social mobility without cultural disruption. Sanskritization is when lower castes take on the Sanskritic model of the higher castes, thus ensuring social mobility, while also providing flexibility to traditional social systems (Srinivas 1952). Sanskritic Hinduism provided India with a common and enduring basis for its indigenous civilization (Sackley 2012, 584).

13. Jawaharlal Nehru University (website), "Rethinking Religious Pluralism and the Relationship between Religions," n.d., accessed 15 January 2020, https://www.jnu.ac.in /content/rethinking-religious-pluralism-and-relationship-between-religions.

14. *The Wire* Staff, "Objecting to Papers on Adivasi Religion, Government Body Cans Philosophy Meet," *The Wire*, 7 April 2018.

15. *The Wire* Staff, "Objecting to Papers."

16. *The Wire* Staff, "Objecting to Papers."

17. The relationship between the problematic classifications, caste and tribe, is worth noting here primarily due to the mobility between the two, by which some tribes have historically been absorbed as castes. While Hinduism was traditionally represented as caste-centric, based on hierarchy and ritual purity (Dumont 1981), others have complicated this picture, especially in the case of the modern era, by describing caste as increasingly a "horizontal array of disconnected ethnic groups" (Fuller 1992, 22). In the Northeast of India, the Hindu right have told me that the tribes could easily be integrated into the Kshatriya (warrior) caste. But such mobility has been challenged by sociologists like Virginius Xaxa, who questions the idea of "the Hindu method of tribal absorption," which denies tribes their distinctiveness in language, culture, tradition and social organization (2005, 1364).

18. "International Center for Cultural Studies—ICCS," accessed 4 May 2020, https:// www.facebook.com/pg/iccsglobal/about/?ref=page_internal.

19. "Exploring Divinity Through the Feminine in Ancient Cultures", ICCS, accessed 4 May 2020, https://mailchi.mp/85a6ccf8a40a/iccs-us-newsletter-465959?e=082d92ab26.

20. "Exploring Divinity Through the Feminine in Ancient Cultures".

21. David Hill, "Indigenous Peoples Are the Best Guardians of World's Biodiversity," *The Guardian*, 9 August 2017, https://www.theguardian.com/environment/andes-to -the-amazon/2017/aug/09/indigenous-peoples-are-the-best-guardians-of-the-worlds -biodiversity.

22. "A Spiritual Relationship with the Land," taken from the UNESCO teaching material entitled *Living by Indigenous Knowledge*, accessed 20 January 2020, http://www .unesco.org/education/tlsf/mods/theme_c/mod11.html.

23. This commonality is also reiterated by the United Kingdom Pagan Federation, particularly in an interview done by Michael York of the main leader, Prudence Jones. "Europe's Ancient Nature Worshippers, the Pagans, Call for a Hindu Alliance," Hinduism Today, accessed 4 May 2020, https://www.hinduismtoday.com/modules/smartsection /item.php?itemid=795.

24. "Europe's Ancient Nature Worshippers."

25. "Secretary-General's Remarks at the Opening of the World Conference on Indigenous Peoples," United Nations Secretary-General, 22 September 2014, un.org/sg/en /content/sg/statement/2014-09-22/secretary-generals-remarks-opening-world-conference -indigenous.

26. "A Spiritual Relationship with the Land."

CHAPTER 4

1. I draw on comments made by the NSCN-IM in the local Naga newspaper, the *Morung Express*. "3 August Framework Agreement Restored Lost Sovereignty," *Morung Express*, 2 June 2017.

2. There are many Christian denominations ranging from the Roman Catholics to such Protestant sects as the Baptists, Revivalists, and Presbyterians. My focus in Nagaland is on the Baptists and the Revivalists, partly because they are by far the biggest groups.

3. For a political history of the movement, see Chasie 2005; Franke 2008; Nibedon 1978. For Christianity's role, see Longkumer 2018a; Nuh 1986; Thomas 2016. For nationalism as experience and human rights abuses, see Iralu 2000. For territorial issues, see Wouters 2018a. And for democracy, see Kikon 2005.

4. These archives are kept by different people, some in their homes, some in personal libraries. For example, the most extensive collection of documents on the Naga struggle is maintained by Rev. Nuh, called the *Naga Archives and Research Centre* in Dimapur. Others have been compiled into a published volume (Heimi 2007).

5. The SAK are from the Sumi tribe, while the members of the Shisa Hoho, a national prayer center, are from the Chakhesang tribe.

6. The SAK last published one in 2016.

7. "Good Governance Day on December 25 Irks Naga Church Body," *Times of India*, 5 December 2016.

8. Utpal Parashar, "Meghalaya BJP Leader Quits over Beef Party; Another May Be Asked to Resign," *Hindustan Times*, 14 June 2017.

9. Parashar, "Meghalaya BJP Leader Quits."

10. NEFA went on to become the Indian state of Arunachal Pradesh in 1972, and the southern region, Tuensang, merged with the Naga Hills District in 1957 and together went on to become the state of Nagaland in 1963.

11. The blowing of the trumpet is reminiscent of Joshua's victory in the Battle of Jericho. The Israelites marched around the walls of Jericho for six days; on the seventh day, the trumpet was blown, and the walls came down (Joshua 6:1–27).

CHAPTER 5

1. Press Trust of India, "Hindu Outfit Plans to 'Finish' Islam, Christianity by 2021," *Indian Express*, 19 June 2014.

2. There is much blurring of boundaries between the different Hindu organizations in the Northeast of India who increasingly use common resources and ideas. I use the moniker Sangh throughout to refer to the overall Hindutva ideology and shared ideals of these groups, and where necessary, I use JVS to contextualize their work in Nagaland.

3. The Sangh's treatment of Christianity is surprisingly uniform. They do not, for example, distinguish between the different denominations; nor are they concerned specifically about the numerous positions and theological differences that mark these groups.

4. Stephen Knapp, "My Northeast India Mission of 2003–4," accessed 6 May 2020, http://www.stephen-knapp.com/my_northeast_india_mission.htm.

5. Knapp, "My Northeast India Mission of 2003–4."

6. Knapp, "My Northeast India Mission of 2003–4."

7. The work of the VHP is interesting in this regard. While it denigrates Western forms of secular attainment as "foreign exports" in India, in the United States, it openly espouses liberalization and globalization as key components of progress due to its many Indian constituents ascribing to those values. This ambiguity is telling in how they present themselves: in India they are a nationalist movement; in diaspora they are a global religious movement (van der Veer 2002; see also Rajagopal 1997).

8. Knapp, "My Northeast India Mission of 2003–4."

9. Narratives of loss and nostalgia are not new, and one can see this in much of the early anthropological literature and accounts of native culture more broadly and more specifically in the region as well (Boym 2001; Stirn and van Ham 2003).

10. While Vivekananda Kendra and the Ramakrishna Mission offer a more spiritually oriented service organization as compared with the overt political form of Hinduism of the RSS (Beckerlegge 2003; Kanungo 2012), in the Northeast they are nevertheless affiliated with the Sangh and cooperate on numerous issues, particularly when it comes to sharing such resources as education and publications and hosting events and festivals for janjatis.

11. The Naga Club was formed in 1918 by a group of mission-school-educated Nagas, who were mainly teachers, government officials, village elders, and pastors—products of the colonial and missionary schools. They would later go on to form the Naga National Council (NNC).

CHAPTER 6

1. On Ambedkar, see Ashish Tripathi, "Politics, Netaji Bose and the 'Ramzade' Version of Hindutva," *Times of India*, 2 October 2015; Divya Trivedi, "Ambedkar's Legacy: Idolatry vs Ideology," *Frontline*, 31 January 2015.

2. In classical Indic terms, *murtis* refer to icons, which are defined as "anything which has definite shape and limits, a form, body, figure, an embodiment, incarnation, manifestation. Thus, *murti* is more than a likeness, it is the deity itself taken 'form'" (Eck 1998a, 38). Icons also relate to image (Eck 1998a, 32), which is "any likeness, figure, motif, or form that appears in some medium or other" (Mitchell 2006, 1). In popular Hindu traditions, the materiality of the image is infused with *prāṇa* (life) by the priest or even the ordinary

worshipper. The multivalence of images is normal (Waghorne, Cutler, and Narayana 1985), and therefore, there need not always be a clash—just different interpretations, albeit some more often endorsed by "great traditions" and others by "little traditions" (and of course there is mutual appropriation [Marriott 1955]). So the fluidity of signs is important, where the default mode of Hindu traditions is diversity. Diverse people entail diverse forms of the divine, in addition to the continuum and overlaps between human and divine.

3. Jagdamba Mall's book *Freedom Fighter Rani Gaidinliu* was published by the Heritage Foundation, Guwahati, 2014, and was translated from Hindi into English by Avikasit Keshaw. Due to this translation, the exact page numbers are difficult to reference, but Mall has divided the text into points, which I have maintained for those interested in comparing the Hindi text with the English translation.

4. Bhuban cave is in the Cachar District of Assam and was a place that Gaidinliu and Jadonang met to receive instructions from the god Bhuban in the late 1920s–1930s. Jadonang was another Naga leader who was hanged by the British in 1931, charged with threatening to massacre the British and bring an end to the Raj in order to establish a Naga raj in Manipur (see Longkumer 2017a).

5. Reid 1949, Mss. EUR. E.278/19, British Library, London.

6. *Pothang* derives from *pot* (baggage) and *thang* (to carry). Under the law, every village had to provide service to the visiting king of Manipur, members of his family, and state officials when they toured the village or the region, along with free food and accommodation. This went unopposed until a new law came to pass in 1910 that exempted some while putting the rest of the population under archaic feudal obligations (Singh 2002, 119–22).

7. MS95022 Higgins Collection, School of Oriental and African Studies (SOAS), 15, 11–18.

8. Folio 534–44, L/P&S/13/1002, British Library, London.

9. Folio 483–84, L/P&S/13/1002, British Library, London.

10. Folio 412, 414–17; 394, British Library, London.

11. Folio 412, 414–17; 394, British Library, London.

12. A ritual tying of a thread popular in South Asia to signify protection is exchanged usually among siblings—sisters to brothers—but can also be exchanged with benefactors and leaders. The annual rite is called Raksha Bandhan and usually occurs in August.

13. Darshan is a common Hindu practice of exchanging vision with a deity or a holy person. To be able to do this is seen as highly auspicious (see Eck 1998a; Fuller 1992).

14. The Kalyan Ashram have produced a documentary on Rani Gaidinliu, which was screened during her birth centenary celebration in India in 2015.

15. "Nagaland Government Clarifies on Rani Gaidinliu Museum," *Northeast Today*, 25 September 2015.

16. "Nagaland Government Clarifies."

17. Samudra Gupta Kashyap, "Some Nagas Are Against Memorial to Rani Gaidinliu in Kohima. Why?," *Indian Express*, 29 September 2015.

18. "Gaidinliu an Alien to Nagas; Former CM Answerable, Says APO," *Morung Express*, 3 September 2015; Kashyap, "Some Nagas Are Against Memorial to Rani Gaidinliu in Kohima. Why?"

19. A copy was given to me by the general secretary of the NBCC as I could not find the copy of the published letter.

20. "Gaidinliu an Alien to Nagas; Former CM Answerable, Says APO."

21. "The Driving Force of Rani Gaidinliu Celebration," *Morung Express*, 27 August 2015.

22. "The Driving Force of Rani Gaidinliu Celebration."

23. TT Bureau, "Sowing Saffron, Reaping Lotus," *The Telegraph*, 22 May 2016.

24. TT Bureau, "Sowing Saffron, Reaping Lotus."

25. Zeliangrong People's Association, "Rejoinder to the Misgivings on Rani Gaidinliu," *Morung Express*, 1 September 2015.

26. Zeliangrong People's Association, "Rejoinder."

27. The issue of Gaidinliu as Rongmei and from the state of Manipur relates to the recognition of the Rongmei tribe as one of the indigenous tribes of Nagaland, as they are already recognized as one of the tribes in the state of Manipur. The Nagaland Tribes Council, for example, is against this, while the chief minister, T. R. Zeliang, has supported this move. However, in April 2017, it was suggested that the government of Nagaland withdraw recognition of the Rongmei tribe. "Nagaland Govt Withdraws Recognition of Rongmei Tribe," *Morung Express*, 3 June 2017.

28. In Nagaland, for example, proposals for a 33 percent reservation of seats for women in the state assembly ignited debate in 2016–17. Headed by the pan-Naga body the Naga Hoho, they called for a boycott on the 33 percent reservation of seats for women in the Urban Local Bodies (ULB) elections, saying that it clashed with Naga Customary Law—based on tribal notions tied to land, resources, and traditions—as protected under article 371 (A) of the Constitution of India. On the other side, the Naga Mothers' Association (NMA), argued that the reservation "only aims to translate to full fruition the idea of gender equity under the Naga Customary Law. The Constitution of India does not infringe upon the social practices of the Nagas." Samudra Gupta Kashyap, "Opposed to 33% Reservation for Women, Naga Bodies Call for Boycott of Civic Polls," *Indian Express*, 5 January 2017. See also Dolly Kikon, "Nagaland and the Fight for the Women's Quota," *Open Democracy*, 17 March 2017.

29. This is based on an unpublished Zeme manuscript, which was given to me by Ramkhui in 2006. The two texts (Hindi and Zeme) largely cohere, though there are subtle differences in the way it is written—the Hindi text is for an obvious Hindutva audience.

30. Ipsita Chakravarty, "What BJP Posters of Bharat Mata in Tripura Tribal Gear Say About Its North East Strategy," *Scroll*, 2 December 2017.

31. Priyanka Deb Barman, "BJP Plans a Tribal Makeover for Bharat Mata Ahead of Tripura Polls," *Hindustan Times*, 30 November 2017.

32. Mohammad Ali, "Deoband Fatwa Says No to Worship of 'Bharat Mata,'" *The Hindu*, 8 September 2016.

33. The governor of Nagaland, P. B. Acharya; the chief minister of Nagaland, T. R. Zeliang; the chief minister of Manipur, O. Ibobi Singh; and Union Ministers Rajnath Singh, Arun Jaitley, Mahesh Sharma, and Jitendra Singh were present.

34. Modi's speech is available in Hindi here: "PM Inaugurates Birth Centenary Celebrations of Rani Gaidinliu," Narendra Modi, accessed 7 May 2020, http://www.narendramodi.in/pm-inaugurates-birth-centenary-celebrations-of-rani-gaidinliu-282577. The speech was translated into English with the help of Avikasit Keshaw.

CHAPTER 7

1. I use Tripura to refer to the Indian state, though various ethnonationalist groups use the term *Twipra*. I used them according to context.

2. All names are pseudonyms except for well-known public figures like Bijoy Hrangkhwal, whose views are already well known and expressed widely in the media. All the people I interviewed—tribal and Bengali—had Bengali names; therefore, I maintain that system of naming.

3. Dipankar De Sarkar, "Why Tripura Election Is Epochmaking," *Live Mint*, 9 March 2018.

4. In its website, it says that the Indian Foundation "seeks to articulate Indian nationalistic perspective on issues. India Foundation's vision is to be a premier think tank that can help understand the Indian civilizational influence on our contemporary society." India Foundation, "About Us," accessed 8 May 2020, https://indiafoundation.in/about-us/.

5. Staff Reporter, "How India's BJP Used Data Analytics to Swing Voters," *PR Week*, 17 September 2014.

6. A similar sentiment was also expressed in Meghalaya. Despite winning only two seats, the BJP overshadowed the National People's Party (NPP), who have twenty seats (equal to the Congress). A senior journalist I spoke to even remarked that the NPP is often known as the "baby of the BJP, the B-team of the BJP." She continued, "You should see the photographs of when the government was sworn in; everything was saffron."

7. Richard Kamei, "The BJP's Rise to Power in Manipur Is a Result of the State's Complex Political Landscape, Not Hindutva Politics," *The Caravan*, 16 March 2017.

8. Kamei, "BJP's Rise to Power."

9. The tribes of Tripura consist primarily of Debbarma, Jamatia, Reang (Bru), Mogs, Uchai, Noatia, Kalai, Halam, Rupini, Murasing, Tripura, Roaza, Hrangkhawl, Kaipeng, Garo, Chakma, and Kuki. The Tripuri name is primarily centered on the Kokborok language, and the main speakers are the Debbarma, Tripura, Murasing, Jamatia, Noatia, Reang (Bru), Koloi, Uchui, and Rupini.

10. Both these events have been studied extensively. While I refer to these events briefly and strategically, and in light of the elections in 2018, for a more detailed analyses of these events and their aftermath, see Bal 2007; Chatterji 2007; Cons 2016; Samaddar 1999; Sur 2014; van Schendel 2005.

11. The raja (king) of Tippera, Rajdhur Manikya, had large estates known as Chakla Roshnabad, which are spread over Sylhet, Tippera, and Noakhali (now the greater Comilla region of Bangladesh) (Sen 2018, 55).

12. Bijoy Kumar Hrangkhawl, "Speech of Shri B.K. Hrangkhawl, MLA, President of the Indigenous Nationalist Party of Twipra at the 20th meeting of the Working Group of Indigenous Population (WGIP)—2002 Held at Geneva, from 22nd July to 26th July, 2002," accessed 8 May 2020, http://cendoc.docip.org/collect/cendocdo/index/assoc/HASH38af/0e351c64.dir/476_AS.pdf.

13. Jayanta Bhattacharya, *Ramification of Conflicts in Tripura and Mizoram*, n.d., accessed 25 January 2020, http://www.mcrg.ac.in/Core/Northeast_Ramification_Tripura_Mizoram.pdf

14. This is a special provision under the Constitution of India in the administration of tribal-dominated areas that has created "autonomous districts and autonomous regions." This is article 244 of the Constitution of Indian for the administration of tribal-dominated areas in four states in the Northeast—Assam, Meghalaya, Tripura, and Mizoram. The Constitution of India, "Sixth Schedule [Articles 244(2) and 275(1)]," accessed 8 May 2020, https://www.mea.gov.in/Images/pdf1/S6.pdf.

15. The emergence of these tribal groups happened largely as a result of the migration of Bengalis into tribal land, occupying them. The Sengkrak (meaning "clenched fist") emerged in the 1960s to fight against the influx of Bengalis entering Tripura and taking over tribal lands, during the Bengali-dominated Congress party. The Tripura Tribal Youth League (Tripura Upjati Juba Samiti [TUJS]) was established in June 10, 1967. They demanded the adoption of Kokborok as the official language of Tripura and the restoration of land occupied by migrants. The Tripura National Volunteers (TNV) was established on December 21, 1978, to promote Tripura independence from India, and they were actively fighting the government until 1988. The National Liberation Front of Tripura (NLFT) was established in opposition to the government on March 12, 1989. Former members of the Tripura National Volunteers (TNV) led by Ranjit Debbarma established the All Tripura Tiger Force (ATTF) on July 11, 1990. Aside from the ATTF, most of the organizations were anti-Left, blaming the Communists for exacerbating the occupation of tribal lands by Bengalis (see Bhaumik 2007, 15; 2009, 106–9).

16. Press Trust of India, "IPFT Will Not Raise Demand for Separate State: BJP Leader," *Indian Express*, 22 January 2018.

17. Personal communication, 7 January 2019.

18. Government of India, *Report on Fifth Annual Employment—Unemployment Survey (2015–16)*, vol. 1, accessed 8 May 2020, http://labourbureaunew.gov.in/UserContent/EUS _5th_1.pdf.

19. Anandaroop Sen,. "How the Left Lost the Tribal Plot in Tripura," *The Wire*, 7 March 2018, https://thewire.in/government/how-the-left-lost-the-tribal-plot-in-tripura.

20. M. S. Nileena, "The BJP Makes Forays into Tripura, Where Demands for a Separate Tribal State Have Reemerged," *The Caravan*, 23 August 2017.

21. T. Arvind and A. S. Nazir Ahamed, "2016 West Bengal Assembly Election Results: As It Happened," *The Hindu*, 12 September 2016.

22. Special Correspondent,. "Proposal for Alliance with CPI-M Can Be Discussed: Mamata." *The Hindu*, 21 April 2016.

23. Press Trust of India, "Muslims Are also Hindus: Mohan Bhagwat in Tripura," *The Quint*, 18 December 2017.

24. Sangeeta Barooah Pisharoty,. "Meet Sunil Deodhar, the Man Who Changed the BJP's Fate in Tripura," *The Wire*, 15 February 2018.

25. As I finalize the manuscript the Citizenship Amendment Bill (CAB) has become the Citizenship Amendment Act (CAA), passed in parliament on 11 December 2019. I have thus been unable to include much of the discussions around the CAA and protests all over the country. However, much of the discussion around CAB also applies to the CAA.

26. For the original Citizenship Amendment Bill 2016 document, see the Citizenship (Amendment) Bill, 2016, accessed 8 May 2020, http://www.prsindia.org/uploads/media /Citizenship/Citizenship%20(A)%20bill,%202016.pdf.

27. Debasree Purkayastha,. "What is the Citizenship (Amendment) Bill, 2016?," *The Hindu*, 26 May 2018.

28. Special Correspondent, "'Citizenship Amendment Bill Communally Motivated': Activists," *The Hindu*, 1 November 2016.

29. In Assam, alongside this bill, which has been debated in the state assembly with opposition on numerous fronts, there is also the issue of the National Register of Citizens (NRC) in Assam.

30. Sanjoy Barbora, Joydeep Biswas, Bidyut Sagar Boruah, Debarshi Das, Sanjib Deblaskar, Sonai, Anshuman Gogoi, Gaurav Rajkhowa, and Ankur Tamuli Phukan, "Why Hindutva Inspired Citizenship Amendment Bill 2016 Needs to Be Opposed," *Raiot Collective*, 7 May 2018, http://raiot.in/why-hindutva-inspired-citizenship-amendment-bill -2016-needs-to-be-opposed/.

31. Barbora et al, "Why Hindutva Inspired Citizenship Amendment Bill 2016 Needs to Be Opposed."

32. Daulat Rahman, "Himanta Support for Citizenship Bill," *The Telegraph*, 9 September 2016.

33. Press Trust of India, "BJP Asks Tripura Party Unit to Woo Chakma, Bru Voters in Five Mizoram Assembly Constituencies," *Firstpost*, 8 November 2018. The Mizo National Front won the elections and formed the government, but they have rejected forming an alliance with the BJP due to their Hindutva ideology, strongly resisted in a Christian-dominated state. See Prasanta Mazumdar, "Mizoram's Ruling MNF Shuts Alliance Door on BJP," *New Indian Express*, 5 June 2019.

EPILOGUE

1. Special Correspondent, "Amit Shah Swears by Citizenship Bill," *The Hindu*, 17 February 2019.

2. Devjyot Ghoshal,. "Amit Shah Vows to Throw Illegal Immigrants into Bay of Bengal," *Reuters*, 12 April 2019.

REFERENCES

Afshar, Haleh. 1987. *Women, State, and Ideology*. London: Macmillan.

Amin, Shahid. 1984. "Gandhi as Mahatma: Gorakhpur District, Eastern UP, 1921–2." In *Subaltern Studies III*, edited by Ranajit Guha, 1–61. Delhi: Oxford University Press.

Amrith, Sunil S. 2014. "Currents of Global Migration." *Development and Change* 45:1134–54.

Anderson, Benedict. 1999. "The Goodness of Nations." In *Nation and Religion: Perspectives on Europe and Asia*, edited by Peter van der Veer and Hartmut Lehmann, 197–203. Princeton, NJ: Princeton University Press.

Anderson, Edward. 2015. "'Neo-Hindutva': The Asia House M. F. Husain Campaign and the Mainstreaming of Hindu Nationalist Rhetoric in Britain." *Contemporary South Asia* 23 (1): 45–66.

Anderson, Edward, and Arkotong Longkumer, eds. 2019. *Neo-Hindutva: Evolving Forms, Spaces, and Expressions of Hindu Nationalism*. Oxford: Routledge.

Appadurai, Arjun. 2013. *The Future as Cultural Fact: Essays on the Global Condition*. London: Verso.

———. 2004. "The Capacity to Aspire: Culture and the Terms of Recognition." In *Culture and Public Action*, edited by Vijayendra Rao and Michael Walton, 59–84. Stanford: Stanford University Press.

———. 2000. "Grassroots Globalization and the Research Imagination." *Public Culture* 12:1–19.

Asad, Talal. 1993. *The Genealogies of Religion*. Baltimore: Johns Hopkins University Press.

Austin, Christopher. 2018. "Rukmiṇī." In *Hinduism and Tribal Religions. Encyclopedia of Indian Religions*, edited by Pankaj Jain, Rita Sherma, and Madhu Khanna. Dordrecht, Netherlands: Springer. https://doi.org/10.1007/978-94-024-1036-5_555-1.

Baago, Kaj. 1966a. "The Post-Colonial Crisis of Missions." *Indian Missiological Review* 55 (219): 322–32.

———. 1966b. "The Post-Colonial Crisis of Missions." *Indian Missiological Review* 55 (221): 99–103.

Babu, Ramesh. 2017. "Borai Bathou—the Eternal Faith of the Bodos." *Heritage Explorer* 16 (11): 16–18.

Bakhle, Janaki. 2010. "Country Frist? Vinayak Damodar Savarkar (1883–1966) and the Writing of Essentials of Hindutva." *Public Culture* 22 (1): 149–86.

Bakhtin, Mikhail. 1981. *The Dialogic Imagination: Four Essays*. Edited by Michael Holquist and translated by Caryl Emerson and Michael Holquist. Austin: University of Texas Press.

Bal, Ellen. 2007. *They Ask if We Eat Frogs: Garo Ethnicity in Bangladesh*. Singapore: ISEAS.

Banerjee, Sikata. 2006. "Armed Masculinity, Hindu Nationalism and Female Political Participation in India." *International Feminist Journal of Politics* 8 (1): 62–83.

Barbora, Sanjay. 2019. "The Crisis of Citizenship in Assam." *The India Forum: A Journal-Magazine on Contemporary Issues*, March 8.

———. 2015. "Uneasy Homecomings: Political Entanglements in Contemporary Assam." *South Asia: Journal of South Asian Studies* 38 (2): 290–303.

Barkataki-Ruscheweyh, Meenaxi. 2017. *Dancing to the State: Ethnic Compulsions of the Tangsa in Assam*. New Delhi: Oxford University Press.

Barthes, Roland. 1993. *Mythologies*. Selected and translated from the French by Annette Lavers. London: Vintage.

Baruah, Sanjib. 2013. "The Mongolian Fringe." *Himal Southasian* 26 (1): 82–86

———. 2007. *Durable Disorder: Understanding the Politics of Northeast India*. New Delhi: Oxford University Press.

———. 2004. "Series Editor's Note." In Bodhisattva Kar, *What Is in a Name? Politics of Spatial Imagination in Colonial Assam*. Guwahati: Centre for Northeast India, South and Southeast Asia Studies, Omeo Kumar Das Institute for Social Change and Development.

———. 1999. *India Against Itself: Assam and the Politics of Nationality*. New Delhi: Oxford University Press.

Basso, Keith. 1996. *Wisdom Sits in Places: Landscape and Language Among the Western Apache*. Albuquerque: University of New Mexico Press.

Basu, Tapan, Pradip Datta, Sumit Sarkar, Tanika Sarkar, and Sambudda Sen. 1993. *Khaki Shorts and Saffron Flags*. New Delhi: Orient Longman.

Baum, Robert. 2015. *West Africa's Women of God: Alinesitoué and the Diola Prophetic Tradition*. Bloomington: Indiana University Press.

Baviskar, Amita. 2007. "Indian Indigeneities: Adivasi Engagements with Hindu Nationalism in India." In *Indigenous Experience Today*, edited by Marisol de la Cadena and Orin Starn, 275–304. Oxford: Berg.

Bayly, Susan. 2004. "Imagining 'Greater India': French and Indian Visions of Colonialism in the Indic Mode." *Modern Asian Studies* 38 (3): 703–44.

Beckerlegge, Gwilym. 2003. "Saffron and Seva: The Rashtriya Swayamsevak Sangh's Appropriation of Swami Vivekananda." In *Hinduism in Public and Private: Reform, Hindutva, Gender, Sampraday*, edited by Anthony Copley, 31–65. New Delhi: Oxford University Press.

Bénéï, Veronica. 2008. *Schooling Passions: Nation, History, and Language in Contemporary Western India*. Stanford, CA: Stanford University Press.

Benjamin, Walter. 2002. *The Arcades Project*. Translated by Howard Eiland and Kevin McLaughlin prepared on the basis of the German volume edited by Rolf Tiedemann. Cambridge, MA: Harvard University Press.

———. 1999. *Illuminations*. Edited and with an introduction by Hannah Arendt. Translated by Harry Zorn. London: Pimlico.

Berti, Daniela, Nicholas Jaoul, and Pralay Kanungo, eds. 2011. *Cultural Entrenchment of Hindutva: Local Mediations and Forms of Convergence*. Delhi: Routledge.

Béteille, Andre. 2012. *Democracy and Its Institutions*. New Delhi: Oxford University Press.

———. 1998. "The Idea of Indigenous People." *Current Anthropology* 39 (2): 187–91.

Bharatiya Janata Party. 2005. *Evolution of BJP*. Party documents, vol. 8. New Delhi: Bharatiya Janata Party.

———. 1992. *National Executive Resolution*, April 30, Gandhi Nagar, Gujarat.

Bharucha, Rustom. 1993. *The Question of Faith*. New Delhi: Orient Longman.

Bhatt, Chetan. 2001. *Hindu Nationalism: Origins, Ideologies and Modern Myths*. Oxford: Berg.

Bhattacharjee, Malini. 2016. "Tracing the Emergence and Consolidation of Hindutva in Assam." *Economic and Political Weekly* 51 (16): 80–87.

Bhattacharya, Neeladri. 1993. "Myth, History and the Politics of Ramjanmabhumi." In *Anatomy of a Confrontation: Ayodhya and the Rise of Communal Politics in India*, edited by Sarvepalli Gopal, 122–40. London: Zed Books.

Bhaumik, Subir. 2016. *The Agartala Doctrine: A Proactive Northeast in Indian Foreign Policy*. New Delhi: Oxford University Press.

———. 2009. *Troubled Periphery: The Crisis of India's North East*. New Delhi: Sage.

———. 2007. "Insurgencies in India's Northeast: Conflict, Co-option and Change." *East-West Center Washington Working Papers* 10:1–46.

———. 2002. "Disaster in Tripura." In *Porous Borders, Divided Selves: A Symposium on Partitions in the East*. India Seminar no. 510. Accessed 20 January 2020. http://www.india-seminar.com/2002/510/510%20subir%20bhaumik.htm.

Bhide, Mananeeya Nivedita. 2010. "One as Beautiful Many." *Quest* 4 (1): 54–74.

———. 2004. "Prologue." In *Traditional Customs and Rituals of Northeast India, Vol. 2*, edited by P. C. Sarma, vii–xxxiii. Guwahati, India: Vivekananda Kendra Institute of Culture.

———. 2002. "Prologue." In *Traditional Customs and Rituals of Northeast India, Vol. 1*, edited by P. C. Sarma, xiv–xxxvi. Guwahati, India: Vivekananda Kendra Institute of Culture.

Bialecki, John. 2014. "Does God Exist in Methodological Atheism? On Tanya Lurhmann's *When God Talks Back* and Bruno Latour." *Anthropology of Consciousness* 25 (1): 32–52.

Biehl, Joao, and Peter Locke. 2017. "Introduction: Ethnographic Sensorium." In *Unfinished: The Anthropology of Becoming*, edited by Joao Biehl and Peter Locke, 1–38. Durham, NC: Duke University Press.

Bird-David, Nurit. 1999. "'Animism' Revisited: Personhood, Environment, and Relational Epistemology." *Current Anthropology* 40 (S1): S67–S91.

BJP—see Bharatiya Janata Party.

Blom, Ida, Karen Hagemann, and Catherine Hall, eds. 2000. *Gendered Nation: Nationalism and Gendered Order in the Nineteenth Century*. New York: New York University Press.

Bourdieu, Pierre, and Marie-Claire Bourdieu. 2004. "The Peasant and Photography." *Ethnography* 5 (4): 601–16.

Bower, Ursula Graham. 1952. *Naga Path*. London: Readers Union/John Murray.

Boym, Svetlana. 2001. *The Future of Nostalgia*. New York: Basic Books.

Brosius, Peter J. 2001. "Local Knowledges, Global Claims: On the Significance of Indigenous Ecologies in Sarawak, East Malaysia." In *Indigenous Traditions and Ecology: The Interbeing of Cosmology and Community*, edited by John A. Grim, 125–58. Cambridge: Harvard University Press.

Brown, Judith. 2003. "Who Is an Indian? Dilemmas of National Identity at the End of the British Raj in India." *Missions, Nationalism and the End of Empire*, edited by Brian Stanley, 111–31. Grand Rapids, MI: Wm. B. Eerdmans.

Buragohain, Romesh, ed. 1994. *The Lost Trails: A Study on the Tai Peoples of North-East India*. Assam, India: Ban-Ok Pup-Lik Mioung-Tai.

Cancilini, Néstor García. 1995. *Hybrid Cultures: Strategies for Entering and Leaving Modernity*. Translated by Christopher L. Chiappari and Silvia L. López. Minneapolis: University of Minnesota Press.

Carrier, James G. 2003. "Introduction." In *Occidentalism: Images of the West: Images of the West*, edited by James G. Carrier, 1–32. Oxford: Clarendon.

Carter, Paul. 1987. *The Road to Botany Bay: An Essay in Spatial History*. London: Faber & Faber.

Carter, Paul, and David Malouf. 1989. "Spatial History." *Textual Practice* 3 (2): 173–83.

Cashman, Richard I. 1975. *The Myth of the Lokamanya: Tilak and Mass Politics in Maharashtra*. Berkeley: University of California Press.

Castree, Noel. 2004. "Differential Geographies: Place, Indigenous Rights and 'Local' Resources." *Political Geography* 23:133–67.

Chakrabarty, Dipesh. 2001. "Clothing the Political Man: A Reading of the Use of Khadi/White in Indian Public Life." *Postcolonial Studies* 4 (1): 27–38.

———. 2000. *Provincializing Europe: Postcolonial Thought and Historical Difference*. Princeton, NJ: Princeton University Press.

———. 1992. "Postcoloniality and the Artifice of History: Who Speaks for 'Indian' Pasts." *Representations* 37:1–26.

Chandra, Lokesh. 1970. *India's Contribution to World Thought and Culture*. Madras: Vivekananda Rock Memorial Committee.

Charters, Claire, and Rodolfo Stavenhagen, eds. 2009. *Making the Declaration Work: The United Nations Declaration on the Rights of Indigenous Peoples*. Copenhagen: IWGIA.

Chasie, Charles. 2005. *The Naga Imbroglio: A Personal Perspective*. Kohima, India: City Press.

Chatterjee, Indrani. 2013. *Forgotten Friends: Monks, Marriages and Memories of Northeast India*. New Delhi: Oxford University Press.

Chatterjee, Partha. 1993. *The Nation and Its Fragments*. Princeton, NJ: Princeton University Press.

Chatterji, Angana P., Thomas Blom Hansen, and Christophe Jaffrelot, eds. 2019. *Majoritarian State: How Hindu Nationalism Is Changing India*. London: Hurst.

Chatterji, Joya. 2007. *The Spoils of Partition: Bengal and India, 1947–1967*. Cambridge: Cambridge University Press.

Chatterji, Suniti Kumar. 1970. *The Place of Assam in the History and Civilisation of India*. Guwahati, India: University of Gauhati.

Chhibber, Pradeep K., and Susan L. Ostermann. 2014. "The BJP's Fragile Mandate: Modi and Vote Mobilizers in the 2014 General Elections." *Studies in Indian Politics* 2 (2): 1–15.

Chidester, David. 1996. *Savage Systems: Colonialism and Comparative Religion in Southern Africa*. Charlottesville: University Press of Virginia.

Clark, Mary. 1907. *A Corner in India*. Philadelphia: American Baptist Publications Society.

Clifford, James. 2001. "Indigenous Articulations." *Contemporary Pacific* 13 (2): 468–90.

———. 1988. *The Predicament of Culture: Twentieth-Century Ethnography, Literature, and Art*. Cambridge, MA: Harvard University Press.

Cody, Francis. 2011. "Publics and Politics." *Annual Review of Anthropology* 40:37–52.

Coffey, John. 2013. *Exodus and Liberation: Deliverance Politics from John Calvin to Martin Luther King Jr.* Oxford: Oxford University Press.

Cohen, Richard S. 2002. "Why Study Indian Buddhism?" In *The Invention of Religion*, edited by Derek Peterson and Darren Walhof, 19–36. Rutgers, NJ: Rutgers University Press.

Cohn, Bernard. 1987. *An Anthropologist Among the Historians and Other Essays*. Delhi: Oxford University Press.

Coleman, Tracy. 2003. "The Abduction of Rukmiṇī: A Translation of *Bhāgavata Purāṇa* 10.52.18–10.54.60." *Journal of Vaishnava Studies* 12 (1): 25–56.

Comaroff, John L., and Jean Comaroff. 2009. *Ethnicity, Inc.* Chicago: University of Chicago Press.

Cone, James. 1969. *Black Theology and Black Power*. New York: Seabury.

Cons, Jason. 2016. *Sensitive Space: Fragmented Territory at the India Bangladesh Border*. Seattle: University of Washington Press.

Copeman, Jacob. 2013. "The Art of Bleeding: Memory, Martyrdom, and Portraits in Blood." *Journal of the Royal Anthropological Institute* 19 (1): S149–S171.

———. 2012. "The Mimetic Guru: Tracing the Real in Sikh–Dera Sacha Sauda Relations." In *The Guru in South Asia: New Interdisciplinary Perspectives*, edited by Jacob Copeman and Aya Ikagame, 156–80. Oxford: Routledge.

———. 2009. "Gathering Points: Blood Donation and the Scenography of 'National Integration' in India." *Body and Society* 15 (2): 71–99.

Copeman, Jacob, and Aya Ikegame. 2012. "The Multifarious Guru: An Introduction." In *The Guru in South Asia: New Interdisciplinary Perspectives*, edited by Jacob Copeman and Aya Ikagame, 1–45. Oxford: Routledge.

Cox, James L. 2007. *From Primitive to Indigenous: The Academic Study of Indigenous Religions*. Aldershot, UK: Ashgate.

Croatto, Jos Severino. 1981. *Exodus: A Hermeneutic of Freedom*. Maryknoll, NY: Orbis Books.

Csordas, Thomas. 1997. "Prophecy and the Performance of Metaphor." *American Anthropologist* 99 (2): 321–32.

Dalmia, Vasudha. 1997. *The Nationalization of Hindu Traditions: Bharatendu Harishchandra and Nineteenth-Century Banaras*. New Delhi: Oxford University Press.

Davis, Richard H. 1997. *The Lives of Images*. Princeton, NJ: Princeton University Press.

Debbarma, R. K. 2017. "Celebrating a New 'New Year' in Tripura: Space, Place and Identity Politics." In *Northeast India: A place of Relations*, edited by Yasmin Saikia and Amit R. Baishya, 201–24. New Delhi: Cambridge University Press.

———. 2013. "Heroes and Histories: The Making of Rival Geographies of Tripura." *NMML Occasional Paper, History and Society*, n.s., 34:1–35.

de Castro, Eduardo Viveiros. 1998. "Cosmological Deixis and Amerindian Perspectivism." *The Journal of the Royal Anthropological Institute* 4 (3): 469–88.

de Certeau, Michel. 1988. *The Writing of History*. Translated by Tom Conley. New York: Columbia University Press.

———. 1984. *The Practice of Everyday Life*. Translated by Steven Rendall. Berkeley: University of California Press.

Deka, Harekrishna. 2005. "The Assamese Mind: Contours of a Landscape." *India International Centre Quarterly* 32 (2/3): 189–202.

de la Cadena, Marisol. 2017. "An Interview with Marisol de la Cadena." By Yoko Taguchi. NatureCulture. Accessed 8 May 2020. https://www.natcult.net/interviews/an-interview-with-marisol-de-la-cadena/.

Deleuze, Gilles, and Felix Guattari. 2013. *A Thousand Plateaus: Capitalism and Schizophrenia*. Translated and forward by Brian Massumi. London: Bloomsbury.

———. 2000. *Anti-Oedipus: Capitalism and Schizophrenia*. Translated from the French by Robert Hurley, Mark Seem, and Helen R. Lane. Minneapolis: University of Minnesota Press.

Descola, Philippe. 2013. *Beyond Nature and Culture*. Chicago: University of Chicago Press.

Dev, S. C. 1988. *Nagaland: The Untold Story*. Calcutta: Mrs Gouri Dev, Regent Estate.

Dimitrova, Diana. 2007. "The Development of Sanatana Dharma in the Twentieth Century: A Radhasoami Guru's Perspective." *International Journal of Hindu Studies* 11 (1): 89–98.

Doniger, Wendy, and Martha Nussbaum, eds. 2015. *Pluralism and Democracy in India: Debating the Hindu Right*. New York: Oxford University Press.

Downs, Frederick. 2010. "Miles Bronson—a Tale of Two Valleys." *American Baptist Quarterly* 29 (1–2): 46–62.

———. 1992. *North East India in the Nineteenth and Twentieth Centuries, Vol. 5, Part 5, History of Christianity in India*. Bangalore: Church History Association of India.

———. 1980. "Christianity as a Tribal Response to Change in Northeast India." *Missiology: An International Review* 8 (4): 407–16.

Dumont, Louis. 1981. *Homo Hierarchicus: The Caste System and Its Implications*. Chicago: University of Chicago Press.

———. 1971. "Religion, Politics, and Society in the Individualistic Universe." *Proceedings of the Royal Anthropological Institute for 1970*: 31–41.

Dutta, Akhil Ranjan. 2017. "BJP's Electoral Victory in Assam, 2016: Co-opting the Khilonjiyas." *Social Change* 47 (1): 108–24.

Eck, Diana. 1998a. *Darsan: Seeing the Divine Image in India*. New York: Columbia University Press.

———. 1998b. "The Imagined Landscape: Patterns in the Construction of Hindu Sacred Geography." *Contributions to Indian Sociology* 32 (2): 165–88.

Elst, Koenraad. 2015. *Return of the Swastika: Hate and Hysteria versus Hindu Sanity*. Budapest: Arktos Media.

Empson, Rebecca ed. 2006a. "Introduction." In *Time, Causality and Prophecy in the Mongolian Cultural Religion: Visions of the Future*, edited by Rebecca Empson, 1–20. Folkestone: Global Oriental.

———. 2006b. *Time, Causality and Prophecy in the Mongolian Cultural Religion: Visions of the Future*. Folkestone, UK: Global Oriental.

———. 2005/2006. "Reproducing People and Prophecy." *Cambridge Anthropology: A Journal of the Department of Social Anthropology* 25 (3): 52–60.

Ferguson, James, and Akhil Gupta. 2002. "Spatializing States: Toward an Ethnography of Neoliberal Governmentality." *American Ethnologist* 29 (4): 981–1002.

Fisk, Anna. 2017. "Appropriating, Romanticizing and Reimagining: Pagan Engagements with Indigenous Animism." In *Cosmopolitanism, Nationalism, and Modern Paganism*, edited by Kathryn Rountree, 21–42. London: Palgrave Macmillan.

Foucault, Michel. 1995. *Discipline and Punish: The Birth of the Prison*. Translated from the French by Alan Sheridan. New York: Vintage Books.

———. 1982. "The Subject and Power." *Critical Inquiry* 8 (4): 777–795.

———. 1972. *Archaeology of Knowledge*. Translated by A. M. Sheridan. New York: Pantheon.

Franke, Marcus. 2008. *War and Nationalism in South Asia: The Indian State and the Nagas*. London: Routledge.

Froerer, Peggy. 2007. *Religious Division and Social Conflict: The Emergence of Hindu Nationalism in Rural India*. New Delhi: Social Science.

Fuller, Chris J. 1992. *The Camphor Flame: Popular Hinduism and Society in India*. Princeton, NJ: Princeton University Press.

Gallagher, Anne-Marie. 2009. "Weaving a Tangled Web? Pagan Ethics and Issues of History, 'Race' and Ethnicity in Pagan Identity." In *Handbook of Contemporary Paganism*, edited by M. Pizza and J. R. Lewis, 577–90. Leiden, Netherlands: Brill.

Gellner, David. 2009. "The Awkward Social Science? Anthropology on Schools, Elections, and Revolution in Nepal." *Journal of the Anthropological Society of Oxford* 1 (2): 115–40.

———. 2004. "Hinduism: None, One or Many?" *Social Anthropology* 12 (3): 367–71.

Ghassem-Fachandi, Parvis. 2012. *Pogrom in Gujarat: Hindu Nationalism and Anti- Muslim Violence in India*. Princeton, NJ: Princeton University Press.

Ghosh, Bishnupriya. 2011. *Global Icons: Apertures to the Popular*. Durham, NC: Duke University Press.

Ghurye, Govid Sadashiv. 1980. *The Scheduled Tribes*. Bombay: Prakashan.

Gillan, Michael. 2007. "Assessing the 'National' Expansion of Hindu Nationalism: The BJP in Southern and Eastern India, 1996–2001." In *Hindu Nationalism and Governance*, edited by John McGuire and Ian Copeland, 30–56. New Delhi: Oxford University Press.

———. 2002. "Refugees or Infiltrators? The Bharatiya Janata Party and 'Illegal' Migration from Bangladesh." *Asian Studies Review* 26 (1): 73–95.

Gilmartin, David. 2012. "Towards a Global History of Voting: Sovereignty, the Diffusion of Ideas, and the Enchanted Individual." *Religions* 3:407–23.

Glaude, Eddie, Jr. 2000. *Exodus! Religion, Race, and Nation in Early Nineteenth-Century Black America*. Chicago: University of Chicago Press.

Gold, Daniel. 2015. *Provincial Hinduism: Religion and Community in Gwalior City*. New York: Oxford University Press.

Golwalkar, Madhav Sadashiv. 2000. *Bunch of Thoughts*. Bangalore: Sahitya Sindhu Prakashana.

Goody, Esther. 1978. "Towards a Theory of Questions." In *Questions and Politeness: Strategies in Social Interaction*, edited by Esther Goody, 17–43. Cambridge: Cambridge University Press.

Gopal, Sarvepalli, ed. 1993. *Anatomy of a Confrontation: Ayodhya and the Rise of Communal Politics in India*. London: Zed Books.

———. 1979. *Jawaharlal Nehru: A Biography*. Vol. 2. Cambridge: Harvard University Press.

Gorringe, Hugo. 2017. *Panthers in Parliament: Dalits, Caste, and Political Power in South India*. Delhi: Oxford University Press.

Goswami, Praphulladatta. 1967. "Hindu and Tribal Folklore in Assam." *Asian Folklore Studies* 26 (1): 19–27.

Gould, William. 2004. *Hindu Nationalism and the Language of Politics in Late Colonial India*. Cambridge: Cambridge University Press.

Gregory, Derek. 1994. *Geographical Imaginations*. Cambridge, MA: Blackwell.

Guha, Sumit. 2003. "The Politics of Identity and Enumeration in India c. 1600–1990." *Comparative Studies in Society and History* 45 (1): 148–67.

Gupta, Charu. 2001. "The Icon of Mother in Late Colonial North India: 'Bharat Mata', 'Matri Bhasha' and 'Gau Mata.'" *Economic and Political Weekly* 36 (45): 4291–99.

Gutierrez, Gustavo. 1973. *A Theology of Liberation: History, Politics and Salvation*. Maryknoll, NY: Orbis Books.

Haberman, David L. 2013. *People Trees: Worship of Trees in Northern India*. New York: Oxford University Press.

Hallowell, Irving. 1960. *Ojibwa Ontology, Behavior, and World View*. New York: Columbia University Press.

Hamilton, Walter. 1820. *A Geographical, Statistical, and Historical Description of Hindostan, and the Adjacent Countries*. Vol 1. London: John Murray.

Handler, Richard. 1988. *Nationalism and the Politics of Culture in Quebec*. Madison: University of Wisconsin Press.

Hansen, Thomas Blom. 2009. *Cool Passion: The Political Theology of Conviction*. Amsterdam: Vossiuspers UvA.

———. 2002. *Wages of Violence: Naming and Identity in Postcolonial Bombay*. Princeton, NJ: Princeton University Press.

———. 1999. *The Saffron Wave: Democracy and Hindu Nationalism in Modern India*. Princeton, NJ: Princeton University Press.

Hansen, Thomas Blom, and Christophe Jaffrelot, eds. 2001. "Introduction: The Rise to Power of the BJP." In *The BJP and the Compulsions of Politics in India*, edited by Thomas Blom Hansen and Christophe Jaffrelot, 1–21. New Delhi: Oxford University Press.

Harding, Susan. 1991. "Representing Fundamentalism: The Problem of the Repugnant Cultural Other." *Social Research* 58 (2): 373–93.

Harvey, Graham. 2005. *Animism: Respecting the Living World*. New York: Columbia University Press.

———, ed. 2000. *Indigenous Religions: A Companion*. New York: Cassell.

Harvey, Graham, and Charles D. Thompson Jr. 2005. "Introduction." In *Indigenous Diasporas and Dislocations*, edited by Graham Harvey and Charles D. Thompson Jr., 1–14. Aldershot, UK: Ashgate.

Hasan, Mushirul. 1994. "Minority Identity and Its Discontents: Ayodhya and Its Aftermath." *South Asia Bulletin: Comparative Studies of South Asia, Africa, and the Middle East* 14:24–40.

Hawley, J. S. 1991. "Naming Hinduism." *Wilson Quarterly* 15:3, 20–34.

Hawley, Stratton. 1996. "Prologue: The Goddess in India." In *Devi: Goddesses of India*, edited by John Stratton Hawley and Donna Marie Wulff, 1–28. Berkeley: University of California Press.

Hazarika, Sanjoy. 1995. *Strangers of the Mist: Tales of War and Peace from India's Northeast*. New Delhi: Penguin.

Heimi, Shapwon. 2007. *God's Hand upon Nagas and Nagaland*. Published by the author.

Herzfeld, Michael. 1997. *Cultural Intimacy: Social Poetics in the Nation-State*. New York: Routledge.

Hills, Carol, and Daniel C. Silverman. 1993. "Nationalism and Feminism in Late Colonial India: The Rani of Jhansi Regiment, 1943–1945." *Modern Asian Studies* 27 (4): 741–60.

Holmberg, David. 2008. "All Politics is Local." In *Views from the Field: Anthropological Perspectives on the Constituent Assembly Elections*, Baha Occasional Papers 2, edited by D. Holmberg, J. Pettigrew, and M. S. Tamang, 9–22. Lalitpur, Nepal: Social Science Baha.

ICCS—see International Center for Cultural Studies.

Ingold, Tim. 2011. "Against Space: Place, Movement, Knowledge." In *Boundless Worlds: An Anthropological Approach to Movement*, edited by Peter Wynn Kirby, 29–44. New York: Berghahn Books.

———. 2006. "Rethinking the Animate, Re-animating Thought." *Ethnos: Journal of Anthropology* 71 (1): 9–20.

———. 2000. *The Perception of the Environment: Essays on Livelihood, Dwelling and Skill*. London: Routledge.

International Center for Cultural Studies. n.d. "Promotional Material." Nagpur, India: ICCS.

Iralu, Kaka. 2000. *Nagaland and India: The Blood and the Tears*. Kohima, India: Kaka Iralu.

Ivakhiv, Adrian. 2005. "Nature and Ethnicity in East European Paganism: An Environmental Ethic of the Religious Right?" *Pomegranate* 7 (2): 194–225.

Jackson, Michael. 2002. *The Politics of Storytelling: Violence, Transgression, and Intersubjectivity*. Copenhagen: Museum Tusculanum.

Jackson, Rosemary. 1981. *Fantasy: The Literature of Subversion*. London: Methuen.

Jacobsohn, Gary J. 2003. *The Wheel of Law: India's Secularism in Comparative Constitutional Context*. Princeton, NJ: Princeton University Press.

Jaffrelot, Christophe. 2017. "India's Democracy at 70: Toward a Hindu State?" *Journal of Democracy* 28 (3): 52–63.

———. 2015. "The Modi-centric BJP 2014 Election Campaign: New Techniques and Old Tactics." *Contemporary South Asia* 23 (2): 151–66.

———, ed. 2007. *Hindu Nationalism: A Reader*. Princeton, NJ: Princeton University Press.

———. 2005. "The BJP at the Centre. A Central or a Centrist Party?" In *The Sangh Parivar: A Reader*, edited by Christophe Jaffrelot, 268–317. New Delhi: Oxford University Press.

———. 1998. *The Hindu Nationalist Movement in India*. New York: University of Columbia Press.

———. 1996. *The Hindu Nationalist Movement and Indian Politics: 1925 to the 1990s*. London: Hurst.

Jain, Kajri. 2007. *Gods in the Bazaar: The Economies of Indian Calendar Art*. Durham, NC: Duke University Press.

Jamatia, B. B. 2011. *Religious Philosophy of the Janajatis of Northeast Bharat*. Guwahati, India: Heritage Foundation.

Jaoul, Nicolas. 2006. "Learning the Use of Symbolic Means: Dalits, Ambedkar Statues and the State in Uttar Pradesh." *Contributions to Indian Sociology* 40 (2): 175–207.

Jeremiah, Anderson. 2012. *Community and Worldview Among Paraiyars of South India: "Lived" Religion*. London: Continuum.

Johnson, Greg, and Siv Ellen Kraft. 2017. "Introduction." In *The Brill Handbook of Indigenous Religion(s)*, edited by Greg Johnson and Siv Ellen Kraft, 1–24. Leiden, Netherlands: Brill.

Johnstone, James. (1896) 2006. *My Experiences in Manipur and the Naga Hills*. London: Elibron Classic Series.

Joshi, Narendra Madhav. 2000. *Ashwattha*. Chennai: Vivekananda Kendra Prakashan Trust.

Kamei, Gangmumei. 2006. *Essays on Primordial Religion*. New Delhi: Akansha.

———. 2004. *A History of the Zeliangrong Nagas: From Makhel to Rani Gaidinliu*. New Delhi: Spectrum.

———. 2002. "Speech of Prof. Gangmumei Kamei During All India Conference of the Akhil Bharatiya Vanvasi Kalyan Ashram at Varanasi. 27–29 September 2002." *Heritage Explorer* 1 (8–9): 4, 10.

Kanungo, Pralay. 2012. "Fusing the Ideals of the Math with the Ideology of the Sangh? Vivekananda Kendra, Ecumenical Hinduism and Hindu Nationalism." In *Public Hinduisms*, edited by John Zavos, Pralay Kanungo, Deepa Reddy, Maya Warrier, and Raymond Brady Williams, 119–40. New Delhi: Sage.

———. 2011. "Casting Community, Culture and Faith: Hindutva's Entrenchment in Arunachal Pradesh." In *Cultural Entrenchment of Hindutva: Local Mediations and Forms of Convergence*, edited by Daniela Berti, Nicolas Jaoul, and Pralay Kanungo, 91–117. New Delhi: Routledge.

Kapila, Kriti. 2008. "The Measure of a Tribe: The Cultural Politics of Constitutional Reclassification in North India." *Journal of the Royal Anthropological Institute* 14 (1): 117–34.

Kar, Bodhisattva. 2004. *What Is in a Name? Politics of Spatial Imagination in Colonial Assam*. Guwahati, India: Centre for Northeast India, South and Southeast Asia Studies, Omeo Kumar Das Institute for Social Change and Development.

Karlsson, Bengt G. 2011. *Unruly Hills: A Political Ecology of India's Northeast*. Oxford: Berghahn Books.

———. 2006. "Anthropology and the 'Indigenous Slot': Claims to and Debates About Indigenous Peoples' Status in India." In *Indigeneity in India*, edited by Bengt G. Karlsson and Tanka Subba, 52–74. London: Kegan Paul.

———. 2001. "Indigenous Politics: Community Formation and Indigenous Peoples' Struggle for Self-determination in North-East India." *Identities: Global Studies in Culture and Power* 8 (1): 7–45.

Karlsson, Bengt G., and Tanka Subba, eds. 2006. *Indigeneity in India*. London: Kegan Paul.

Kaur, Raminder. 2005. *Performative Politics and the Cultures of Hinduism: Public Uses of Religion in Western India*. London: Anthem.

Keane, Webb. 2007. *Christian Moderns: Freedom and Fetish in the Mission Encounter*. Berkeley: University of California Press.

Khare, R. S. 1976. *The Hindu Hearth and Home*. Delhi: Vikas.

Khilnani, Sunil. 2016. *The Idea of India*. Gurgaon, India: Penguin Books.

Khimun, Latsam. 2017. "Genius of Indigenous." *Heritage Explorer* 16 (11): 14.

———, ed. 2012. *Socio-cultural and Spiritual Traditions of Northeast Bharat*. Guwahati, India: Heritage Foundation.

Kikon, Dolly. 2019. *Living with Oil and Coal: Resource Politics and Militarization in Northeast India*. Seattle: University of Washington Press.

———. 2005. "Engaging Naga Nationalism: Can Democracy Function in Militarised Societies?" *Economic and Political Weekly* 40 (26): 2833–37.

Kim, Sebastian. 2005. *In Search of Identity: Debates on Religious Conversion in India*. Delhi: Oxford University Press.

King, Richard. 1999. *Orientalism and Religion*. London: Routledge.

Kingsbury, Benedict. 1998. "'Indigenous Peoples' in International Law: A Constructivist Approach to the Asian Controversy." *American Journal of International Law* 29 (3): 414–57.

Kopf, David. 1992. "*Imagining India* by Ronald Inden." *Journal of the American Oriental Society* 112 (4): 674–77.

Kovacs, Anja. 2004. "You Don't Understand, We Are at War! Refashioning Durga in the Service of Hindu Nationalism." *Contemporary South Asia* 13 (4): 373–88.

Kraft, Siv Ellen. 2017. "U.N. Discourses on Indigenous Religion." In *The Brill Handbook of Indigenous Religion(s)*, edited by Greg Johnson and Siv Ellen Kraft, 80–91. Leiden, Netherlands: Brill.

Kravel-Tovi, Michal, and Yoram Bilu. 2008. "The Work of the Present: Constructing Messianic Temporality in the Wake of Failed Prophecy Among Chabad Hasidim." *American Ethnologist* 35 (1): 64–80.

Kumar, B. B. 2015. *Social and Cultural Continuum in India with Special Focus on the Northeast*. Guwahati, India: Vivekananda Kendra Institute of Culture.

Kuper, Adam. 2003. "The Return of the Native." *Current Anthropology* 44 (3): 389–402.

Latour, Bruno. 2004. "Whose Cosmos: Which Cosmopolitics? Comments on the Peace Terms of Ulrich Beck." *Common Knowledge* 10 (3): 450–62.

———. 2002. "What is Iconoclash? Or Is There a World Beyond the Image Wars?" In *Iconoclash: Beyond the Image Wars in Science, Religion, and Art*, edited by Bruno Latour and Peter Weibel, 16–38. Cambridge, MA: MIT Press.

Latour, Bruno, and Peter Weibel, eds. 2002. *Iconoclash: Beyond the Image Wars in Science, Religion, and Art*. Cambridge, MA: MIT Press.

Leavitt, John. 1999. "Prophecy." *Linguistic Anthropology* 9 (1–2): 201–14.

Lefebvre, Henri. 1991. *The Production of Space*. Translated by Donald Nicholson-Smith. Oxford: Wiley-Blackwell.

Lepselter, Susan. 2016. *The Resonance of Unseen Things: Poetics, Power, Captivity, and UFOs in the American Uncanny*. Ann Arbor: University of Michigan Press.

Li, Tania. 2000. "Articulating Indigenous Identity in Indonesia: Resource Politics and the Tribal Slot." *Comparative Studies in Society and History* 42 (1): 149–179.

Lintner, Bertil. 2012. *Great Game East: India, China and the Struggle for Asia's Most Volatile Frontier*. New Delhi: Harper Collins.

———. 1990. *Land of Jade: A Journey Through Insurgent Burma*. Edinburgh: Kiscadale.

Lipner, Julius. 2006. "The Rise of 'Hinduism'; or, How to Invent a World Religion with Only Moderate Success." *Hindu Studies* 10:91–104.

Longkumer, Arkotong. 2019. "'Along Kingdom's Highway': The Proliferation of Christianity, Education, and Print Amongst the Nagas in Northeast India, 1872–1955." *Contemporary South Asia* 27 (2): 160–78.

———. 2018a. "Bible, Guns and Land: Sovereignty and Nationalism Amongst the Nagas of India." *Nations and Nationalism* 24 (4): 1097–116

———. 2018b. "'10/40 Window: Missionaries as 'Spiritual Migrants' and the Religious Experience in Asia." In *Asian Migrants and Religious Experience: Transnational Religious Mobility*, edited by Brenda Yeoh and Bernardo Brown, 153–76. Amsterdam: University of Amsterdam Press.

———. 2017a. "Freedom and Frustrated Hope: Assessing the Jadonang Movement, 1917–1932." In *Northeast India: A Place of Relations*, edited by Yasmin Saikia and Amit R. Baishya, 181–200. Delhi: Cambridge University Press.

———. 2017b. "Is Hinduism the World's Largest Indigenous Religion?" In *The Brill Handbook of Indigenous Religion(s)*, edited by Siv Ellen Kraft and Greg Johnson, 263–78. Leiden, Netherlands: Brill.

———. 2017c. "Moral Geographies: The Problem of Sovereignty and Indigeneity Amongst the Nagas." In *Rethinking Social Exclusion in India: Castes, Communities and the State*, edited by Minoru Mio and Abhijit Dasgupta, 147–67. Oxford: Routledge.

———. 2016a. "'Lines That Speak': The Gaidinliu Notebooks as Language, Prophecy, and Textuality." *HAU: Journal of Ethnographic Theory* 6 (2): 123–47.

———. 2016b. "Rice Beer, Purification, and the Debate over Religion and Culture in Northeast India." *South Asia: Journal of South Asian Studies* 39 (2): 444–61.

————. 2015a. "'As Our Ancestors Once Lived': Representation, Performance, and Constructing a National Culture Amongst the Nagas of India." *Himalaya* 53 (1): 51–64.

————. 2015b. "Inserting Hindutva in Nagaland." *Hindu Centre for Politics and Public Policy*. February 20. Chennai.

————. 2010. *Reform, Identity and Narratives of Belonging: The Heraka Movement of Northeast India*. London: Continuum.

Longkumer, Arkotong, and Michael Heneise. 2019. "The Highlander: An Introduction to Highland Asia." *The Highlander: Journal of Highland Asia* 1 (1): 1–18.

Lotha, Abraham. 2009. *Articulating Naga Nationalism*. PhD diss., City University of New York.

Lorenzen, David. 1999. "Who Invented Hinduism?" *Society for Comparative Study of Society and History* 41:4, 630–59.

Ludden, David. 2003. "Presidential Address: Maps in the Mind and the Mobility of Asia." *Journal of Asian Studies* 62 (4): 1057–78.

————, ed. 1996. *Contesting the Nation: Religion, Community, and the Politics of Democracy in India*. Philadelphia: University of Pennsylvania Press.

Luhrmann, Tanya. 2012. *When God Talks Back: Understanding the American Evangelical Relationship with God*. New York: Knopf.

Luithui, Luingam, and Nandita Haksar. 1984. *Nagaland File: A Question of Human Rights*. Delhi: Lancer International.

Madianou, Mirca, and Daniel Miller. 2012. "Polymedia: Towards a New Theory of Digital Media in Interpersonal Communication." *International Journal of Cultural Studies* 16 (2): 169–87.

Mahmood, Cynthia Keppley. 1996. *Fighting for Faith and Nation Dialogues with Sikh Militants*. Philadelphia: University of Pennsylvania Press.

Malkki, Liisa. 1992. "National Geographic: The Rooting of Peoples and the Territorialization of National Identity Among Scholars and Refugees." *Cultural Anthropology* 7 (1): 24–44.

Mall, Jagdamba. 2014. *Freedom Fighter Rani Gaidinliu* (in Hindi). Guwahati, India: Heritage Foundation.

Marriott, McKim. 1955. "Little Communities in an Indigenous Civilization." In *Village India*, edited by McKim Marriott, 171–222. Chicago: University of Chicago Press.

Marshall, Ruth. 2010. "The Sovereignty of Miracles: Pentecostal Political Theology in Nigeria." *Constellations* 17 (2): 197–223.

Masuzawa, Tomoko. 2005. *The Invention of World Religions: Or, How European Universalism Was Preserved in the Language of Pluralism*. Chicago: University of Chicago Press.

Maxwell, Neville. 1973. *Indian and the Nagas*. London: Minority Rights Group.

May, Andrew J. 2016. "'To Lay Down the Frontier of an Empire': Circumscribing Identity in Northeast India." *Studies in History* 32 (1): 5–20.

McDuie-Ra, Duncan. 2016. *Borderland City in New India: Frontier to Gateway, Asian Borderlands*. Amsterdam: Amsterdam University Press.

————. 2012. *Northeast Migrants in Delhi: Race, Refuge and Retail*. Amsterdam: Amsterdam University Press.

McGuire, John, and Ian Copland, eds. 2007. *Hindu Nationalism and Governance*. New Delhi: Oxford University Press.

McKean, Lise. 1996a. "Bharat Mata: Mother India and Her Militant, Matriots." In *Devi: Goddesses of India*, edited by John Stratton Hawley and Donna Marie Wulff, 228–50. Berkeley: University of California Press.

———. 1996b. *Divine Enterprise: Gurus and the Hindu Nationalist Movement*. London: University of Chicago Press.

Mehta, Deepak. 2015. "Naming the Deity, Naming the City: Rama and Ayodhya." *SAMAJ: South Asia Multidisciplinary Academic Journal* 15:1–20.

Michaud, Jean. 2010. "Editorial: Zomia and Beyond." *Journal of Global History* 5:187–214.

Michelutti, Lucia. 2007 "The Vernacularisation of Democracy: Popular Politics and Political Participation in North India." *Journal of the Royal Anthropological Institute*, n.s., 13:639–56.

Misra, Sanghamitra. 2011. *Becoming a Borderland: The Politics of Space and Identity in Colonial Northeastern India*. New Delhi: Routledge.

Misra, Udayon. 2000. *The Periphery Strikes Back: Challenges to the Nation-State in Assam and Nagaland*. Shimla, India: Indian Institute of Advanced Study.

———. 1999. "Identity Transformation and the Assamese Community: Illusion and the Reality." In *Dynamics of Identity and Intergroup Relations in North East India*, edited by K. S. Aggarwal, 98–116. Shimla, India: Indian Institute of Advanced Study.

Mitchell, Thomas W. J. 2006. *What Do Pictures Want? The Lives and Loves of Images*. Chicago: University of Chicago Press.

———. 2002. *Landscape and Power*. Chicago: University of Chicago Press.

Miyazaki, Hirokazu. 2004. *The Method of Hope: Anthropology, Philosophy, and Fijian Knowledge*. Stanford, CA: Stanford University Press.

Mody, Perveez. 2008. *The Intimate State: Love-Marriage and the Law in Delhi*. London: Routledge.

Mosse, David. 1994. "The Politics of Religious Synthesis: Roman Catholicism and Hindu Village Society in Tamil Nadu, India." In *Syncretism/Anti-Syncretism: The Politics of Religious Synthesis*, edited by Charles Stewart and Rosalind Shaw, 85–107. London: Routledge.

Mouffe, Chantal. 1993. *The Return of the Political*. London: Verso.

Mukherjee, D. P., P. Gupta, and N. K. Das. 1982. "The Zeliangrong or Haomei Movement: An Historical Study." In *Tribal Movements in India Vol. 1*, edited by K. S. Singh, 67–96. Delhi: Manohar.

Naga National Council. 2004. *A. Z. Phizo Birth Centenary 1904–2004*. Nagaland, India: Naga National Council.

Nagel, Jaone. 1998. "Masculinity and Nationalism: Gender and Sexuality in the Making of Nations." *Ethnic and Racial Studies* 21 (2): 243–69.

Nanda, Meera. 2009. "Hindu Triumphalism and the Clash of Civilisations." *Economic and Political Weekly* 44 (28): 106–14.

———. 2004. "Dharmic Ecology and the New Pagan Movement: The Dangers of Religious Environmentalism in India." Eighteenth European Conference on Modern South Asian Studies, Lund University, Sweden, July.

Newbigin, Lesslie. 1972. "Baptism, the Church and Koinonia." *Religion and Society* 19 (1): 69–70.

Newme, Ramkui. 1990. *Rani Maa Gaidinliu* (in Hindi). New Delhi: Suruchi Prakashan.

Nibedon, Nirmal. 1978. *Nagaland: The Night of the Guerrillas.* New Delhi: Lancers.

Niezen, Ronald. 2011. "Indigenous Religion and Human Rights." In *Religion and Human Rights: An Introduction,* edited by John Witte and M. Christian Green, 119–34. Oxford: Oxford University Press.

———. 2003. *The Origins of Indigenism: Human Rights and the Politics of Identity.* Berkeley: University of California Press.

NNC—see Naga National Council.

Nora, Pierre. 1989. "Between Memory and History: Les Lieux de Mémoire." In "Memory and Counter-Memory," special issue, *Representations* 26:7–24.

Nuh, V. K. 1986. *Nagaland Church and Politics.* Kohima, India: Vision.

Overholt, Thomas W. 1989. *Channels of Prophecy: The Social Dynamics of Prophetic Activity.* Minneapolis: Fortress.

Pachuau, Joy, and Willem van Schendel. 2015. *The Camera as Witness: A Social History of Mizoram, Northeast India.* New Delhi: Cambridge University Press.

———. 2014. *Being Mizo: Identity and Belonging in Northeast India.* New Delhi: Oxford University Press.

Palmer, Helen, and Vicky Hunter. 2018. "Worlding." *New Materialism.* 16 March 2018. https://newmaterialism.eu/almanac/w/worlding.html.

Palshikar, Suhas. 2015. "The BJP and Hindu Nationalism: Centrist Politics and Majoritarian Impulses." *South Asia: Journal of South Asian Studies* 38 (4): 719–35.

Pandey, Gyanendra. 2012. "Un-archived Histories: The 'Mad' and the 'Trifling.'" *Economic and Political Weekly* 47 (1): 37–41.

Panikkar, Raymond. 1964. *The Unknown Christ of Hinduism.* London: Darton, Longman & Todd.

Pasternak, Shiri. 2017. *Grounded Authority: The Algonquins of Barriere Lake Against the State.* Minneapolis: University of Minnesota Press.

Pauwels, Heidi. 2007. "Stealing a Willing Bride: Women's Agency in the Myth of Rukmiṇi's Elopement." *Journal of the Royal Asiatic Society* 17 (4): 407–41.

Peirce, Charles Sanders. 1996. *Charles S. Peirce: Selected Writings.* Edited by Philip Weiner. New York: New York University Press.

Permanent Forum on Indigenous Issues. 2010. "Study of the Need to Recognise and Respect the Rights of Mother Earth." United Nations, ninth session, New York, 19–30 April. http://www.un.org/esa/socdev/unpfii/documents/E.C.19.2010.4%20EN.pdf.

Phanjoubam, Pradip. 2018. "How BJP Won Without Winning in Nagaland." *Economic and Political Weekly* 53 (12). https://www.epw.in/engage/article/bjp-won-without-winning -nagaland.

Phukan, Girin. 1996. *Regionalism in North East India.* New Delhi: Spectrum.

Pietz, William. 1985. "The Problem of the Fetish I." *Res* 9 (13): 23–45.

Piliavsky, Anastasia. 2014. "Introduction." In *Patronage as Politics in South Asia,* edited by Anastasia Piliavsky, 1–35. Cambridge: Cambridge University Press.

Pilkington, Hilary. 2016. *Loud and Proud: Passion and Politics in the English Defence League.* Manchester: University of Manchester Press.

Pinney, Christopher. 2004. *Photos of the Gods: The Printed Image and Political Struggle in India.* New York: Reaktion.

———. 2001. "Piercing the Skin of the Idol." In *Beyond Aesthetics: Art and the Technologies of Enchantment*, edited by Christopher Pinney and Nicholas Thomas, 158–80. London: Berg.

———. 1997. *Camera Indica: The Social Life of Indian Photographs.* London: Reaktion Books.

Pintchman, Tracy. 1994. *The Rise of the Goddess in the Hindu Tradition.* Albany: State University of New York Press.

Pollock, Sheldon. 1998. "The Cosmopolitan Vernacular." *Journal of Asian Studies* 57 (1): 6–37.

Povinelli, Elizabeth A. 1995. "Do Rocks Listen? The Cultural Politics of Apprehending Australian Aboriginal Labor." *American Anthropologist* 97 (3): 505–18.

Probst, Peter. 2012. "Iconoclash in the Age of Heritage." *African Arts* 45 (3): 10–13.

Rajagopal, Arvind. 2001. *Politics After Television: Hindu Nationalism and the Reshaping of the Public in India.* Cambridge: Cambridge University Press.

———. 1997. "Transnational Networks and Hindu Nationalism." *Bulletin of Concerned Asian Scholars* 29:49–50.

Ramachandran, Sujata. 1999. "Of Boundaries and Border Crossings: Undocumented Bangladeshi 'Infiltrators' and the Hegemony of Hindu Nationalism in India." *Interventions: International Journal of Postcolonial Studies* 1 (2): 235–53.

Ramaswamy, Sumathi. 2004. *The Lost Land of Lemuria.* Berkeley: University of California Press.

———. 2001. "Maps and Mother Goddesses in Modern India." *Imago Mundi* 53:97–114.

Redfield, Robert. 1941. *The Folk Culture of Yucatan.* Chicago: University of Chicago Press.

Research Institute of World's Ancient Traditions Cultures and Heritage. n.d. "Promotional Material." Roing, India: RIWATCH.

Rival, Laura, ed. 1998. *The Social Life of Trees: Anthropological Perspectives on Tree Symbolism.* Oxford: Berg.

RIWATCH—see Research Institute of World's Ancient Traditions Cultures and Heritage

Roberts, Nathaniel. 2016. *To Be Cared For: The Power of Conversion and Foreignness of Belonging in an Indian Slum.* Berkeley: University of California Press.

Robinson, Rowena. 1998. *Conversion, Continuity and Change: Lived Christianity in Southern Goa.* New Delhi: Sage.

Rosaldo, Renato. 1989. *Culture and Truth: The Remaking of Social Analysis.* Boston: Beacon.

Rountree, Kathryn. 2012. "Neo-Paganism, Animism, and Kinship with Nature." *Journal of Contemporary Religion* 27 (2): 305–20.

Roy Burman, B. K. 1992. "Indigenous and Tribal Peoples." *Mainstream*, 5 September.

Sackley, Nicole. 2012. "Cosmopolitanism and the Uses of Tradition: Robert Redfield and Alternative Visions of Modernization during the Cold War." *Modern Intellectual History* 9 (3): 565–95.

Said, Edward. 1986. "Michael Walzer's Exodus and Revolution: A Canaanite Reading." *Grant Street* 5:246–59.

Saikia, Yasmin. 2004. *Fragmented Memories: Struggling to Be Tai-Ahom in India*. Durham, NC: Duke University Press.

Saikia, Yasmin, and Amit R. Baishya. 2017. *Northeast India: A Place of Relations*. New Delhi: Cambridge University Press.

Sale, Kirkpatrick. 1990. "How Paradise Was Lost: What Columbus Discovered." *The Nation* 251 (13): 444–46.

Samaddar, Ranabir. 1999. *The Marginal Nation: Transborder Migration from Bangladesh to West Bengal*. New Delhi: Sage.

Samvad. 2012. "Newsletter." *Samvad* (Delhi): 1–8.

Sandys, E. F. (1915) 1997. *History of Tripura*. Agartala, India: Tripura State Tribal Cultural Research Institute and Museum, Government of Tripura.

Sarkar, Sumit. 1996. "Indian Nationalism and the Politics of Hindutva." In *Contesting the Nation: Religion, Community, and the Politics of Democracy in India*, edited by David Ludden, 270–93. Philadelphia: University of Pennsylvania Press.

Sarkar, Tanika. 2012. "Hindutva's Hinduism." In *Public Hinduisms*, edited by John Zavos, Pralay Kanungo, Deepa S. Reddy, Maya Warrier, and Raymond Brady Williams, 264–82. New Delhi: Sage.

———. 2001. *Hindu Wife, Hindu Nation: Community, Religion, and Cultural Nationalism*. London: Hurst.

———. 1995. "Heroic Women, Mother Goddesses: Family and Organisation in Hindutva Politics." In *Women and the Hindu Right*, edited by Tanika Sarkar and Urvashi Butalia, 181–215. New Delhi: Kali for Women.

Sarkar, Tanika, and Urvashi Butalia, eds. 1995. *Women and the Hindu Right: A Collection of Essays*. Delhi: Kali for Women.

Savarkar, Vinayak Damodar. 1969. *Hindutva: Who Is Hindu?* Delhi: Hindi Sahitya Sadan.

Saxena, Saumya. 2018. "'Court'ing Hindu Nationalism: Law and the Rise of Modern Hindutva." *Contemporary South Asia* 26 (4): 378–99.

Scheid, Claire. 2015. "Talom Rukbo and the Donyipolo Yelam Kebang: Restructuring Adi Religious Practices in Arunachal Pradesh." *Internationales Asienforum* 46 (1–2): 127–48.

Scott, James C. 2009. *The Art of Not Being Governed: An Anarchist History of Upland Southeast Asia*. New Haven, CT: Yale University Press.

———. 1998. *Seeing Like the State: How Certain Schemes to Improve the Human Condition Have Failed*. New Haven, CT: Yale University Press.

———. 1990. *Domination and the Arts of Resistance: Hidden Transcripts*. New Haven, CT: Yale University Press.

Searle-Chatterjee, Mary. 2000. "'World Religions' and 'Ethnic Groups': Do These Paradigms Lend Themselves to the Cause of Hindu Nationalism?" *Ethnic and Racial Studies* 23 (3): 497–515.

Sen, Anandaroop. 2018. "Sutured Landscapes: Making of an Imperial Frontier in Tripura (1848–1854)." In *Geographies of Difference: Explorations in Northeast Indian Studies*, edited by Mélanie Vandenhelsken, Meenaxi Barkataki-Ruscheweyh, and Bengt G. Karlsson, 53–71. New Delhi: Routledge.

Sen, Atreyee. 2015. "The Hindu Goddess in Indian Politics." *Political Theology Today*, 29 May. https://politicaltheology.com/the-hindu-goddess-in-indian-politics-atreyee-sen/.

———. 2009. "Inventing 'Women's History': Female Valor, Martial Queens, and Right-Wing Story-Tellers in the Bombay Slums." *Focaal—European Journal of Anthropology* 54:33–48.

Sengupta, Chandan, and Stuart Corbridge. 2010. *Democracy, Development and Decentralisation in India: Continuing Debate.* New Delhi: Routledge.

Sethi, Rajat, and Shubhrastha. 2017. *The Last Battle of Saraighat: The Story of the BJP's Rise in the North-East.* New Delhi: Viking.

Sharma, Jyotirmaya. 2011. *Hindutva: Exploring the Idea of Hindu Nationalism.* New Delhi: Penguin Books.

Sharpe, Eric. 1977. *Faith Meets Faith: Some Christian Attitudes to Hinduism in the Nineteenth and Twentieth Centuries.* London: SCM Press.

Shepoumaramth. 1995. *The Shepoumaramth in the Naga National Movements.* Shepoumaramth, India: GPRN.

Shnirelman, Victor A. 2017. "Obsessed with Culture: The Cultural Impetus of Russian Neo-pagans." In *Cosmopolitanism, Nationalism, and Modern Paganism*, edited by Kathryn Rountree, 87–108. London: Palgrave Macmillan.

Singer, Martin. 1972. *When a Great Tradition Modernises.* Chicago: University of Chicago Press.

Singh, Joykumar N. 2002. *Colonialism to Democracy: A History of Manipur 1819–1972.* Guwahati, India: Spectrum.

Sinha, Surajit. 1958. "Tribal Cultures of India as a Dimension of Little Tradition in the Study of Indian Civilization." *Journal of American Folklore* 71 (4): 504–18.

Skaria, Ajay. 2000. *Hybrid Histories: Forests, Frontiers, and Wildness in Western India.* Delhi: Oxford University Press.

Souvenir. 1999. *Silver Jubilee: Zeliangrong Heraka Association North-East India 1974–1999.* Publisher unknown.

Spencer, Jonathan. 2007. *Anthropology, Politics, and the State Democracy and Violence in South Asia.* Cambridge: Cambridge University Press.

———. 1997. "Post-Colonialism and the Political Imagination." *Journal of the Royal Anthropological Institute* 3 (1): 1–19.

Srinivas, M. N. 1952. *Religion and Society Among the Coorgs of South India.* New Delhi: Oxford University Press.

Stengers, Isabelle. 2005. "The Cosmopolitical Proposal." In *Making Things Public*, edited by Bruno Latour and Peter Weibel, 994–1003. Cambridge, MA: MIT Press.

Stirn, Aglaja, and Peter van Ham. 2003. *The Hidden World of the Naga: Living Traditions in Northeast India and Burma.* Munich: Prestel.

Strathern, Marilyn. 1995. *The Relation: Issues in Complexity and Scale.* Cambridge: Prickly Pear.

Sur, Malini. 2014. "Divided Bodies: Crossing the India-Bangladesh Border." *Economic and Political Weekly* 49 (13): 31–35.

Swarup, Ram. 1994. "'Liberal' Christianity." In *Catholic Ashrams: Sannyasins or Swindlers?*, edited by Sita Ram Goel, 182–98. New Delhi: Voice of India.

Tafjord, Bjørn Ola. 2017. "Towards a Typology of Academic Uses of 'Indigenous Religion(s)', or Eight (or Nine) Language Games That Scholars Play with This Phrase." In *The Brill Handbook of Indigenous Religion(s)*, edited by Greg Johnson and Siv Ellen Kraft, 25–51. Leiden, Netherlands: Brill.

Tagg, John. 1988. *The Burden of Representation: Essays on Photographies and Histories.* London: Basingstoke.

Tagore, Dessan. 1986. *Israel in India.* Published by the author.

Tarlo, Emma. 1996. *Clothing Matters: Dress and Identity in India.* Chicago: University of Chicago Press.

Thapar, Romila. 1989. "Imagined Religious Communities? Ancient History and the Modern Search for a Hindu Identity." *Modern Asian Studies* 23 (2): 209–31.

———. 1985. "Syndicated Moksha?" *Seminar: The Hindus and Their Isms* 313 (September): 14–22.

Therwath, Ingrid. 2012. "Cyber-Hindutva: Hindu Nationalism, the Diaspora and the Web." *Social Science Information* 51 (4): 551–77.

Thomas, John. 2016. *Evangelising the Nation: Religion and the Formation of Naga Political Identity.* New Delhi: Routledge.

Thomas, M. M. 1972. "Baptism, the Church and Koinonia." *Religion and Society* 19 (1): 69–70.

Tsing, Anna. 2005. *Friction: An Ethnography of Global Connections.* Princeton, NJ: Princeton University Press.

Turner, Victor. 1974. *Dramas, Fields, and Metaphors: Symbolic Action in Human Society.* Ithaca, NY: Cornell University Press.

Tylor, Edward B. 1871. *Primitive Culture.* Vol. 1. London: John Murray.

Uberoi, Patricia. 1994. *Family, Kinship and Marriage in India.* New Delhi: Oxford University Press.

Udupa, Sahana. 2018. "Enterprise Hindutva and Social Media in Urban India." *Contemporary South Asia* 26 (4): 453–67.

Upadhyay, Brahmabandhab. 1991. "Are We Hindus?" In *The Writings of Brahmabandhab Upadhyay I*, edited by Julius Lipner and George Gispert-Sauch, 24–25. Bangalore: United Theological College.

Urban, Hugh B. 2009. "Hinduism in Assam and the Northeast States." In *Encyclopedia of Hinduism*, edited by Knut Jacobsen, 13–23. Leiden, Netherlands: Brill.

Vandana, Mataji, ed. 1993. *Christian Ashrams: A Movement with a Future?* Delhi: ISPCK.

Van der Veer, Peter. 2002. "Transnational Religion: Hindu and Muslim Movements." *Global Networks* 2 (2): 95–109.

———. 2001. *Imperial Encounters: Religion, Nation, and Empire.* Princeton, NJ: Princeton University Press.

———. 1994. *Religious Nationalism: Hindus and Muslims in India.* Berkeley: University of California Press.

Van Schendel, Willem. 2018. "Afterword: Contested, Vertical, Fragmenting: De-partitioning 'Northeast India' Studies." In *Geographies of Difference: Explorations in Northeast Indian Studies*, edited by Mélanie Vandenhelsken, Meenaxi Barkataki-Ruscheweyh, and Bengt G. Karlsson, 272–88. New Delhi: Routledge.

———. 2016. "A War Within a War: Mizo Rebels and the Bangladesh Liberation Struggle." *Modern Asian Studies* 50 (1): 75–117.

———. 2005. *The Bengal Borderland: Beyond State and Nation in South Asia.* London: Anthem.

———. 2002. "Geographies of Knowing, Geographies of Ignorance: Jumping Scale in Southeast Asia." *Environment and Planning D: Society and Space* 20:647–68.

Varshney, Ashutosh. 1993. "Contested Meanings: India's National Identity, Hindu Nationalism, and the Politics of Anxiety." *Daedalus* 122 (3): 227–61.

Viswanathan, Gauri. 1998. *Outside the Fold: Conversion, Modernity and Belief.* Princeton, NJ: Princeton University Press.

Waghorne, Joanne Punzo, Vasudha Narayanan, and Norman Cutler. 1985. *Gods of Flesh/Gods of Stone: The Embodiment of Divinity in India.* New York: Columbia University Press.

Wagner, Roy. 1981. *The Invention of Culture.* Chicago: University of Chicago Press.

Walzer, Michael. 1984. *Exodus and Revolution.* New York: Basic Books.

Winichakul, Thongchai. 1994. *Siam Mapped: A History of the Geo-body of a Nation.* Honolulu: University of Hawaii Press.

Wouters, Jelle. 2018a. *In the Shadows of Naga Insurgency: Tribes, State and Violence in Northeast India.* New Delhi: Oxford University Press.

———. 2018b. "Introduction: Exploring Democracy in Nagaland." In *Democracy in Nagaland: Tribes, Traditions and Tensions*, edited by Jelle Wouters and Zhoto Tunyi, 1–42. Kohima, India: Highlander Books.

Wouters, Jelle, and Tanka Subba. 2013. "The 'Indian Face', India's Northeast, and 'the Idea of India.'" *Asian Anthropology* 12 (2): 126–40.

Xaxa, Virginius. 2005. "Politics of Language, Religion and Identity: Tribes in India." *Economic and Political Weekly* 40 (13): 1363–70.

———. 1999. "Tribes as Indigenous People in India." *Economic and Political Weekly* 18 (12): 3589–95.

Yonuo, Asoso. 1982. *Nagas Struggle Against the British Rule Under Jadonang and Rani Gaidinliu 1925–1947.* Kohima, India: Leno.

Zavos, John. 2008. "'Stamp It Out!' Disciplining the Image of Hinduism in a Multicultural Milieu." *Contemporary South Asia* 16 (3): 323–38.

———. 2001. "Defending Hindu Tradition: Sanatana Dharma as a Symbol of Orthodoxy in Colonial India." *Religion* 31 (2): 109–23.

———. 2000. *The Emergence of Hindu Nationalism in India.* Oxford: Oxford University Press.

Zeliang, N. C. 2005. "Westernisation Threat to Naga Culture." *Organiser* 10 (April): 37–38.

Zeliang, Tasile. 2012. *Glimpses from the Life of Rani Gaidinliu.* Guwahati, India: Heritage Foundation.

Zou, David. 2016. "Environment, Social Identity and Individual Freedom in the Current Historiography of Northeast India." *Studies in History* 32 (1): 117–29.

Zou, David, and Satish M. Kumar. 2011. "Mapping a Colonial Borderland: Objectifying the Geo-Body of India's Northeast." *Journal of Asian Studies* 70 (1): 141–70.

Zournazi, Mary. 2002. *Hope: New Philosophies for Change*. Annandale, Australia: Pluto.

The authorized representative in the EU for product safety and compliance is:
Mare Nostrum Group
B.V Doelen 72
4831 GR Breda
The Netherlands

www.ingramcontent.com/pod-product-compliance
Lightning Source LLC
Chambersburg PA
CBHW031727280326
41926CB00098B/622